Best Rose Guide

A Comprehensive Selection

Best Rose Guide

A Comprehensive Selection

Roger Phillips & Martyn Rix

FIREFLY BOOKS

A FIREFLY BOOK

Published by Firefly Books Ltd. 2004
Copyright © 2004 Roger Phillips and Martyn Rix

First printing

Publisher Cataloging-in-Publication Data (U.S.)
(Library of Congress Standards)
Phillips, Roger.
Best rose guide : a comprehensive selection /
Roger Phillips and Martyn Rix. —1st ed.
[288] p. : col. ill., photos.; cm.
Includes bibliographical references and index.
Summary: Over 850 roses are described and illustrated. Entries are arranged by group with information on the original wild species and the history of the cultivated roses. Further sections include cultivation and companion planting.
ISBN 1-55297-844-3
1. Roses. 2. Rose culture. 3. Rose—Varieties. I. Rix, Martyn.
II. Title.
635.9/33734 21   SB411.P55 2004

National Library of Canada Cataloguing in Publication Data
Phillips, Roger, 1932-
   Best rose guide: a comprehensive selection / Roger Phillips, Martyn Rix.

Includes bibliographical references and index.
ISBN 1-55297-844-3

   1. Roses—Varieties. 2. Rose culture. I. Rix, Martyn
II. Title.
SB411.P44   635.9'33734   C2003-906526-X

Published in the United States in 2004 by:
Firefly Books (U.S.) Inc.
P.O. Box 1338, Ellicott Station
Buffalo, New York 14205

Published in Canada in 2004 by:
Firefly Books Ltd.
66 Leek Crescent
Richmond Hill, Ontario, L4B 1H1

Printed in Singapore

COVER DESIGN: Jacqueline Hope Raynor
DESIGNER: Jill Bryan
ASSISTANT DESIGNER: Debby Curry
EDITOR: Candida Frith-Macdonald
EDITORIAL MANAGEMENT: Charis Cotter
NORTH AMERICAN TEXT EDITING: Judith Adam
CONSULTANT: Bill Grant
PRODUCTION: Jacqueline Hope Raynor
FRONT COVER PHOTOGRAPH: 'Gold Medal'
   © S. Nielsen/DRK PHOTO
OTHER COVER PHOTOGRAPHS: Roger Phillips & Martyn Rix
FRONT FLAP PHOTOGRAPH: 'Hermosa China'
SPINE PHOTOGRAPH: 'Mme Isaac Péreire'
BACK COVER PHOTOGRAPHS (left to right): 'Spice So Nice', 'Francis Dubreuil', 'Crazy Quilt'

Contents

Visual Key

Roses are divided into groups according to their history and parentage. The groups have their different characteristics, and a typical example of each group is illustrated in the following pages.

Centifolia Roses

The large, rounded, double, pink blooms of these roses are found in 17th-century Dutch flower paintings. The original Centifolia rose, *R. × centifolia*, is thought to have originated in Dutch gardens in the late 16th century, and has produced many 'sports' or mutations. *(See page 58.)*

'Gloire de Guilan'
Damask

Rosa fedtschenkoana
Wild Rose

Wild roses

There is a huge array of wild roses, all bearing simple flowers with five petals and a mass of stamens, followed by fleshy hips. Within this basic pattern there is a large range of sizes, colors, and scents. *(See page 12.)*

Damasks

Damask roses have been grown for thousands of years for distillation of attar of roses, and are still cultivated for this purpose today. This ancient group bear numerous flowers with an intense scent. Summer Damasks flower only in midsummer, but autumn Damasks flower both in summer and again in autumn. *(See page 42.)*

'Fantin Latour'
Centifolia

Moss Roses

Moss roses are easily recognized by the dense, mossy covering, either bright green or brownish in colour, on the flower stalks and backs of the sepals. There was a craze for these roses in the middle of the 19th century, and they were often depicted in decorations on pottery and china. *(See page 66.)*

'Bizarre Triomphant'
Gallica

Gallica Roses

Gallicas are among the oldest cultivated roses. They are suckering plants with dark green leaves, and form thickets of low, thin, bristly stems if grown on their own roots. The red, pink, or purple flowers are produced in early summer. Their scent is sweet and heavy, and they have traditionally been used for flavoring and medicine. *(See page 32.)*

Rosa × alba 'Semiplena'
Alba

Alba Roses

The earliest Alba roses, such as 'Alba Semi-plena', are likely to have been grown by the Romans and are probably among the most ancient of all cultivated plants. Alba roses are large shrubs with tall, arching stems, grayish-green leaves, and white or pale pink flowers with excellent scent, produced in great quantity over a short period. They are tough roses, and plants have been known to survive many years of neglect in abandoned gardens. *(See page 50.)*

Rosa × centifolia
'Muscosa'
Moss

'Comte de Chambord'
Portland

Portland Roses

Portland roses are a small group, which was significant in the late 18th century as being similar to Gallicas, but repeat flowering in autumn. Crossed with Chinas, they formed the important Hybrid Perpetuals. Portland roses have leafy stems and bright red or pink, short-petalled flowers, and are very hardy, tough plants. *(See page 76.)*

'Mutabilis'
China

China Roses

In the late 18th century the perpetual-flowering trait was introduced into European garden roses through roses brought from China. Chinas have smooth leaves, few thorns, and flowers with thick petals and little scent. *(See page 80.)*

Tea Roses

Among the roses brought from China in the early 19th century was 'Hume's Blush Tea-scented China', a dwarf, repeat-flowering Tea rose. It was crossed with the once-flowering climber 'Parks' Yellow Tea-scented China', and from them came this important group. Teas have smooth leaves, few thorns and flowers of pink, creamy yellow, and apricot shades; some of them are dwarf, others climbing. They have since been eclipsed in popularity by the hardier, showier Hybrid Teas, but make beautiful, graceful plants in a warm climate. *(See page 90.)*

'Rêve d'Or'
Noisette

Noisette Roses

Noisettes combine the good scent and late flowering of the cultivated musk rose *R. moschata* with the larger flowers of the Teas and Chinas. 'Blush Noisette' has masses of small double, pale pink flowers; later varieties were raised with fewer, larger flowers. Despite their French name, the ancestral Noisette, 'Champneys Pink Cluster', originated in North America. *(See page 102.)*

'Général Schablikine'
Tea Rose

'Cupid' hips
Tea Rose

Bourbon Roses

Bourbon roses date from the early 19th century and are named after the Île de Bourbon, now called Réunion, near Mauritius in the Indian Ocean. They usually have well-scented and rather rounded flowers in small sprays in autumn as well as in spring, combining the traits of their presumed parents: the scent of *R. damascena* var. *semperflorens* and the perpetual flowering of the China rose 'Parson's Pink China'. *(See page 110.)*

'Mme Isaac Péreire'
Bourbon

Hybrid Perpetuals

These roses, popular in the late 19th century, combine repeat flowering, large flowers, excellent scent, and strong colors, with many reds and purples, rare in the Teas that were popular at the same time. The Hybrid Perpetuals are hardier than the Teas, but are coarser and leafier plants. They are susceptible to powdery mildew, but useful in some climates with extremely hot summers. *(See page 120.)*

'Phyllis Bide'
Rambler

'Ferdinand Pichard'
Hybrid Perpetual

Climbing Roses

Most cultivated roses are descended from climbing roses. Hybrid Tea roses, valued as low bushes, have sometimes mutated to produce climbing forms, while other Climbing roses have been raised from crosses of large-flowered climbers, similar in habit to their climbing Tea rose ancestors, or even from crosses of shrubs. *(See page 130.)*

'Altissimo'
Climber

Ramblers

Most Ramblers are distinguished from large-flowered Climbers by their masses of small flowers, which make a superb show. They are usually produced in one flush on long, often flexuous branches. Ramblers are mostly crosses of white-flowered wild climbers and other cultivated roses *(See page 144.)*

'Warwickshire'
Groundcover

Groundcover Roses

Groundcover roses are a relatively recent development, bred to be low growing with arching, spreading stems, continuous flowering, and ideally with dense enough leaf cover to suppress weeds once they are established. They need minimal maintenance, and many may be cut back hard with a saw or mower every few years. *(See page 162.)*

Hybrid Musk Roses

This small group includes some of the very best of all roses for garden use. The flowers are produced in large, loose bunches or sprays and are small or medium-sized, usually white, cream, pink, or buff, mostly with excellent scent and repeating through the season. *(See page 168.)*

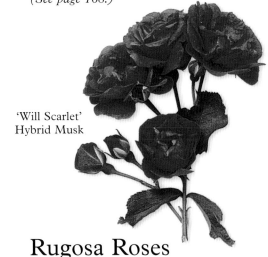

'Will Scarlet'
Hybrid Musk

Rugosa Roses

Rose breeders have fairly recently begun to use the exceptionally hardy and tough *R. rugosa*, which grows well in poor, sandy soils, to breed healthy, cold-tolerant roses. Their rugose (that is, rough with impressed veins) leaves are salt tolerant and also very disease resistant, seldom suffering from blackspot or mildew. The flowers are principally in white and shades of pink, with few yellows and deeper reds; many of the single-flowered cultivars produce the large, showy hips so characteristic of the species. *(See page 180.)*

'Fru Dagmar Hastrup'
Rugosa

Shrub Roses

Shrub roses, with their unusual parentage of wild roses crossed with modern cultivars, do not fit into any of the other recognized groups. Most form large and robust shrubs, their characteristics varying according to the wild roses that were used in their breeding. *(See page 188.)*

Polyantha Roses

Polyanthas had a brief period of popularity in the first half of the 20th century, before they were surpassed by their offspring, the Floribundas. Polyanthas are repeat-flowering dwarf plants bearing many small flowers, some like miniature Hybrid Teas. *(See page 222.)*

'The Fairy'
Polyantha

'Nevada'
Shrub

'Kirsten Poulsen'
Floribunda

English Roses

David Austin's English roses have been bred to combine the shapes, scents, and subtle colors of the old roses with the repeat flowering and disease resistance of the modern roses. They have started a new trend, and other breeders are now producing their own roses along similar lines *(See page 248.)*

'Scepter'd Isle'
English Rose

Hybrid Tea Roses

This is the most popular of all the rose groups, combining healthy growth with, large, scented flowers in all colors but a pure blue. The distinctive flowers combine the tall bud and delicate flowers of the Teas with the larger, flatter, coarser blooms of the Hybrid Perpetuals. *(See page 198.)*

Floribundas

Floribundas were bred for their masses of smaller flowers, which combine with their freedom of flowering to give color throughout the season. They are one of the dominant rose groups of the 20th century. *(See page 226.)*

'Red Devil'
Hybrid Tea

'Golden Angel'
Miniature

Miniature Roses

Miniature roses are an ancient group, distinguished by the small size of all their parts, but they only became important in the mid-20th century, when breeder Ralph Moore's work with them led to a surge in their popularity. Other breeders have seen the potential of these dwarfs as flowering pot plants. *(See page 262.)*

Introduction

FROM THE EARLIEST civilizations, roses have occupied a unique place in man's appreciation and love of flowers. References to roses have been found in Assyrian tablets and Homer wrote that Hector's body was anointed with rose-scented oil. In the 6th century BC the Ionian poet Anacreon praised the rose as perfume of the gods, joy of men, and flower of Venus. By Roman times roses were grown on a large scale near the city, and imported from Egypt in winter. They were used on family occasions and in huge quantities for the extravagant and decadent feasts of the *nouveaux riches*.

More recently a love of roses was encouraged by the French Empress Josephine, the wife of Napoleon, who collected every variety she could in her garden at Malmaison near Paris, making roses highly fashionable in 19th century France. From this French craze for roses came most of the old roses we grow today, as well as the ancestors of modern varieties. These old roses, which are often called Heritage Roses in America, Old Garden Roses in England, or *Roses Anciennes* in France, are genuine antiques and still popular. Some were taken to North America and planted in gardens or cemeteries, for instance in Bermuda and the Gold Rush country in California, where they survived a century or more of neglect. Enthusiasts now seek out these "found" roses, grow them and try to determine their original names.

Modern roses officially begin with 'La France,' raised in 1867 by Jean-Baptiste Guillot from a cross of a Tea and a Hybrid Perpetual. This was the first of a new class, the enduringly popular Hybrid Tea. Modern roses also encompass Floribundas, Shrub roses derived from wild species, and more recent developments such as Groundcovers, Miniatures, and "modern old" roses, such as English Roses.

Nearly all of these garden roses, old and modern, have been bred from just seven wild species. There are 150 or more wild species, although only around 50 are commonly cultivated. We have looked at the origin of each group of cultivated roses and the wild species from which they originated. The roses are grouped here according to their supposed relationships: "supposed" because many are ancient garden plants from China, Persia, or Turkey, and their likely ancestry has been deduced from their structure, their chromosomes, and the possible wild ancestors available in the area where they are believed to have originated. Modern DNA analysis is starting to unravel some of the outstanding questions about rose parentage, but this is complicated and expensive, and there is still a great deal more to be done.

Rather than produce another bulky encyclopedia with every possible rose included, whatever its merits, we have made a selection of those that have appealed to us in some way. While availability, scent, and health have been criteria in our choices, these are above all the roses that we love or have found memorable or striking for one reason or another, including some that are completely new. We hope to guide the reader through the morass of over 12,500 names offered by nurseries around the world. We have tried to make this a personal book, using the ideas we have had over the past five decades of growing and studying roses, first as ordinary gardeners in England, later as writers of rose books and on our travels to see roses around the world.

Over 850 roses are described and illustrated in this book: while these are as accurate as possible, roses naturally respond to their environment, and flower shades do vary with climate. On our website, www.rogersroses.com we have text and pictures of over 4,000 roses of all types, and are continually adding new ones, the great advantage a website has over any book. Rose lovers can join our web rose club and make full use of the site, meeting online other rose enthusiasts from all over the world. Some of the best and most interesting rose nurseries in many countries offer discounts to our members, and there is also the opportunity to exchange seeds, cuttings, or budwood with other members.

Rosa sherardii, a wild dog rose *(above)*
Rosa gallica 'Officinalis', an ancient medicinal rose *(right)*

Wild Roses

Rosa chinensis
var. *spontanea*
from Pingwu,
northeastern Sichuan

WILD ROSES MAKE beautiful garden plants. All have simple, five-petaled flowers with a mass of stamens in the centre, followed by fleshy hips, but within this basic pattern there is a large range of size, color, and scent. The plants may be giant climbers, stiff tall shrubs, or small shrubs that form thickets by suckering. There is no consensus among botanists as to the number of wild roses in the world: 150 is a conservative estimate, but many more have been named, because some groups, particularly dog roses, have complicated breeding systems that produce large numbers of similar but still distinguishable species. Even species with normal reproduction show much variation between individuals from different areas, in the same way that the human species varies from race to race.

Roses were widely grown by ancient civilizations: around the Mediterranean, particularly by the Romans, in central Asia by the Persians, and in China, but only when the Chinese and Eurasian roses came together through trade in the late 18th century did rose breeding begin on a large scale in western Europe. Only a few wild rose species have contributed to the thousands of roses that have been bred over the past two centuries, and the following seven species are ancestors of nearly all the huge range of cultivated varieties: *R. chinensis* and *R. gigantea* (*opposite*), *R. multiflora* (*see p.17*), *R. moschata* (*see p.18*), *R. fedtschenkoana* (*see p.22*), *R. gallica* (*see p.27*), and *R. foetida* (*see p.30*). One or two other species have been used more frequently in recent years: *R. rugosa* (*see p.23*), for example, is valuable for its hardiness and disease resistance.

Wild roses are generally grouped into sections by leaf type, hip, and the arrangement of the styles. This makes it easier to recognize the numerous wild species, which are covered geographically and by section on the following pages.

Rosa gigantea growing in a ditch near the Burma Road west of Kunming in southwestern China

These roses comprise the small section Indicae: they are fairly tender, have large flowers and hips, and are found from eastern India through Myanmar (formerly Burma) to western China.

Rosa gigantea (also called *R. macrocarpa*)   A large, arching shrub or huge climber with stems clambering 100 ft (30 m) into trees, bearing leaves with five to seven long-pointed, limp-looking leaflets. The white or yellowish flowers are up to 6 in (15 cm) across, and the hips very large, usually ripening yellow. Found wild from Yunnan in southwestern China westward across Myanmar (formerly Burma) to Manipur in India, in cool-temperate forest, ravines in mountain scrub, and hedges, flowering from March to May. In Yunnan it is not common, and varies, often being rather small and pure white (as shown here), possibly by hybridization with *R. longicuspis*, growing in the same area. Plant hunter Frank Kingdon Ward described those in Manipur as exceptionally large, and yellow in bud. Roger and I found another variety with a pale pink, single flower 5 in (12 cm) across in a village by the road from Dali to Lijiang. Cultivated double forms, such as 'Lijiang Road Climber', are often planted in hedges and village gardens.

   Garden notes   The main ancestor of the Tea Roses and through them the modern Hybrid Teas and other groups. Best in warm climates, such as California and southern France, but may be grown outside on a warm wall in southern England. Hardy perhaps to 14°F (-10°C), in Zone 8, varying with origin.

'Cooper's Burmese' (also called 'Cooperi', *R. gigantea* 'Cooperi')   A rampant hybrid of *R. gigantea* and probably *R. laevigata* (*see p.15*), raised at Glasnevin in Ireland from seeds collected by plant hunter Roland Cooper around 1926 in Myanmar, then Burma. It differs from *R. gigantea* in its very shiny, shorter-pointed leaflets and bristly stalks, and from *R. laevigata* in its red stems, looser leaves with five leaflets, and floppier petals. The flowers, 5 in (12 cm) across, are scented.

   Garden notes   This grows to 30 ft (10 m) or more and flowers more freely than *R. gigantea*. It is also slightly hardier; it will be damaged, but not killed, at 14°F (-10°C), even on a warm wall, and is best in Zone 8 or 9.

Rosa chinensis var. ***spontanea*** (also called *R. chinensis*, 'Henry's Crimson China')   This is the wild China rose, closely related to *R. gigantea* and an ancestor of most modern groups through Chinese cultivated roses (*see p.81*). It is usually a large, arching, evergreen shrub to 10 ft (3 m), but can climb to 18 ft (5.5 m) if growing up through trees. It has very sharp, recurved thorns, and leaves with five to seven stiff leaflets, shining dark green above and smooth beneath. The solitary flowers, on short shoots on the previous year's wood, are around 2 in (5 cm) across, with a delicate scent. The petals are usually red, but some populations vary from creamy-white with a pink edge to blackish-crimson, or pink with a darker eye . The hips are smooth, not very large, and ripen orange. It is native of western China from southwestern Sichuan to southern Gansu and western Hubei, growing in warm- and cool-temperate areas in open, grassy places, mountain scrub, and by rivers,flowering in April and May, at the same time as *R. banksiae* (*see p.14*).

   Garden notes   Easily grown, but needs warmth to flower well. It should do well outside in southern North America and in Australia; in England it needs a greenhouse or very warm wall. Hardy to 5°F (-15°C) in Zone 7.

'Cooper's Burmese'

The roses on this spread are all native of the warmer parts of China. *Rosa banksiae* and *R. cymosa* are both in the section Banksianae, and have unusually small flowers. The others are each the only member of their section: they have large flowers and are quite individual in their other characteristics.

Rosa banksiae var. ***normalis*** This is the wild, single type of *R. banksiae*, and seen in gardens much less often than the white- or yellow-flowered double forms. The small flowers are in rounded clusters of one or several, and are around ¾ in (2 cm) across. Their scent is delicate, like violets. Evergreen in mild winters, it has usually five leaflets, which are lance-shaped, thin-textured, dark green above, shiny beneath. It is native of central and western China, where it is common in hedges, growing into trees, or hanging down steep rocky hillsides in warm- to cool-temperate areas. It usually flowers in March to June according to altitude, well before any of the white roses of the Synstylae section (*see pp.16–19*).

Garden notes Although the wild *R. banksiae* is seldom cultivated, there is also a single white cultivated form with the larger, softer leaf type of the yellow double and very few thorns, which may be a sport of the double white. Hardy to 5°F (-15°C), in Zone 7, for short periods.

Rosa bracteata A dense, thorny climber introduced to the West in 1793 by Lord Macartney's embassy to the Emperor in China, where it grows mainly in the southeast and Taiwan and reaches 20 ft (6 m). The leaves have five to eleven shining, rounded, evergreen leaflets, to 2 in (5 cm) long. Solitary white flowers to 4 in (10 cm) across appear over a long season from midsummer to autumn, their stalks hidden by soft, hairy bracts. Graham Thomas describes the scent as "rich … of lemons."

Garden notes This is a good rose for a warm climate, but does not do well in cool areas, though it survives and flowers on a warm wall at the Royal Botanic Gardens, Kew, near London. It has seldom been used for breeding, but is a parent of the lovely yellow-flowered climber 'Mermaid' (*see p.133*). Hardy to 10°F (-12°C), Zone 8, for short periods.

Rosa cymosa (also called *R. microcarpa*, *R. sorbiflora*) This rose bears distinctive flat clusters of very small flowers and miniature hips. Usually it is a climber with smooth or hairy stems to 15 ft (5 m) and rather few, hooked thorns. The young shoots and leaves are bright red, the leaves with usually seven

Rosa banksiae var. *normalis* cascades over a roadside hedge between Dali and Lijiang

Rosa banksiae var. *normalis*

Rosa bracteata

Rosa laevigata

Rosa leavigata in the Villa Val Rahmeh Exotic Botanic Garden, in Menton-Garavan, France

narrowly lance-shaped or elliptic leaflets, rounded at the base and with a slender, curved point, short-stalked, with small, fine and curved teeth, shining green beneath. The numerous flowers are small and in rounded or flat-topped, branching clusters, creamy-white, ½ in (1–1.5 cm) across, the sepals sometimes pinnate with spiny lobes. The stamens are almost as long as the petals and the softly hairy styles protrude slightly. The round hips are dull or scarlet-red, with many small seeds, and around ¼ in (5 mm) across.

Native of China, *R. cymosa* is widespread from the coast in Fujian to western Sichuan at fairly low altitudes, growing in warm areas in scrub and gorges, and in bamboo plantations.

Garden notes This rose is unique in its wide heads of small flowers. We have seen it in several places in western Sichuan, growing in hedges and hanging down roadside cliffs, flowering in late May and early June, long after *R. banksiae* has gone over in the same areas. The red young growth is a conspicuous feature in gardens. We introduced seed (C.D. & R. 2511) in 1995 from Min shan, near Ya-an, where we had seen plants in flower in hedges between the tea gardens when filming 'Quest for the Rose'. The clone 'Rebecca Rushforth', from seed from Mount Omei, was named for the wife of its collector Keith Rushforth. Hardy to 5°F (-15°C), in Zone 7.

Rosa laevigata Laevigatae (also called Cherokee Rose)
A climbing rose with evergreen leaves and large, white flowers that grows wild in rocky places, where I have seen it grazed to form a compact bush. The stems can reach 30 ft (10 m) or more, with hooked thorns and bristles. The three evergreen leaflets are lance-shaped on the long shoots but ovate or nearly round on flowering shoots, short-stalked, with fine, curved teeth, smooth and shining above and beneath. The white flowers are solitary, on bristly stalks, up to 4 in (10 cm) across, and well scented. The large, bristly hips are orange-red, with persistent, bristly sepals.

Native of much of central China westward to Sichuan, and of Taiwan at low altitudes, flowering in spring, it is naturalized in the southern states of North America, where it was introduced in the early 17th century. The 18th-century French botanist Michaux, who first described it in *Flora Boreali Americana* (1803), believed it to be a native American plant.

Garden notes This beautiful, white-flowered rose is not very hardy, being killed to the ground in cold winters in southern England, and flowering only after hot summers. It grows and flowers well in North America from Georgia southward, and in southern Europe and other countries bordering the Mediterranean. Hardy to 10°F (-12°C), Zone 8 for short periods only.

Rosa cymosa

'Kiftsgate', the commonly cultivated clone of *R. filipes*

Rosa longicuspis from the pass southwest of Lijiang, China

The roses on the next four pages all have pyramidal clusters of small, white flowers. They are in section Synstylae, recognized easily by their styles, fused into a small, column-like structure. They are also known as Musk Roses, due to their musk-like scent, which carries well. They are mostly climbers, sometimes very large, with backward-pointing, hooked thorns toward the ends of the shoots and on the leaf stalks to help them climb.

Rosa brunonii (also called *R. moschata nepalensis*, Himalayan Musk Rose)   A climbing rose to 50 ft (15 m) or more, with hooked thorns, especially near the shoot tips. Sometimes partly evergreen, the leaves have usually seven leaflets, ¾–2½ in (2–6 cm) long, pale green, ovate to elliptic, very short-stalked, coarsely toothed with large and small teeth, finely hairy above, especially on the veins, and with glands beneath. The flowers are in large, loose, flat-topped clusters, creamy-white, well scented, and 1¼–2½ in (3–6 cm) across. The short sepals sometimes have two or three pairs of lobes, and the stalks have glands. The hips are up to ½ in (1 cm) long, softly hairy when young, with stalked glands, reddish, inversely egg-shaped, with the sepals soon falling; the styles protrude, united into a column ⅜–½ in (8–10 mm) long.

It is found from Afghanistan and Kashmir eastward to Bhutan, Myanmar (formerly Burma), and southwestern China, north as far as Sichuan, climbing on trees and scrambling over shrubs by rivers, flowering in April to July according to altitude.

Garden notes Named for the botanist Robert Brown in 1820, and introduced to cultivation in Europe in 1822, *R. brunonii* is a fine sight when in flower, the display lasting about two weeks in midsummer, and it is also conspicuous when covered in red hips. Hardy to -10°F (-23°C), Zone 6.

Rosa filipes A particularly rampant climbing rose, to 20 ft (6 m) and more, with hooked thorns and purplish young shoots. The deciduous leaves have five to seven leaflets, narrowly ovate to lance-shaped, with long points, smooth and hairless above, usually smooth and with a slight grayish bloom beneath, very short-stalked, with small, sharp teeth. The small, white flowers open cup-shaped, up to 1 in (2.5 cm) across, in very large, loose, flat-topped clusters, 45 cm (18 in) or more across, on slender stalks ¾–1¼ in (2–3 cm) long, with short-stalked glands; bracts soon falling. Their sweet, heavy scent is carried on the air. Sepals about ½ in (1 cm) long, sometimes lobed. The round hips, ⅜–½ in (8–12 mm) across, have hairy styles protruding from them and scattered, stalked glands.

Found wild in northwestern Sichuan and Gansu in China, this grows in hedges and thickets in cold-temperate areas, flowering in June and July.

Garden notes 'Kiftsgate' is the clone of *R. filipes* usually cultivated; beyond the fact that it came from E.A. Bunyard's nursery, its origin is not known. The original plant at Kiftsgate Court, Gloucestershire grows mightily into a large beech tree. This is perhaps the most rampant of all roses, producing clouds of small flowers with a wonderful scent; it needs a large tree to cover, if it is to develop to its full potential, or it can hide an ugly building. Hardy to -20°F (-29°C), Zone 5.

Rosa longicuspis (also called *R. yunnanensis*)   A robust evergreen climber to 20 ft (6 m) or more, it has dark green, shining leaves with three to seven narrowly ovate to elliptic leaflets 2–4 in (5–10 cm) long, shining red stems, and neat white flowers that turn pink as they age. The flowers are around 2 in (5 cm) across, up to 15 in a sometimes rounded head. Their petals are silky on the back. The flower stalks and the dark red hips are often glandular and hairy.

Native from Assam in India eastward to Yunnan and Sichuan in China, this grows in sub-tropical and warm-temperate areas, in hedges, scrub, and among rocks, flowering in May and June.

Rosa soulieana

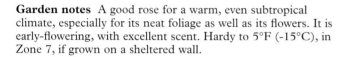

Rosa brunonii

Rosa multiflora

Garden notes A good rose for a warm, even subtropical climate, especially for its neat foliage as well as its flowers. It is early-flowering, with excellent scent. Hardy to 5°F (-15°C), in Zone 7, if grown on a sheltered wall.

Rosa multiflora This small-flowered rose is easily recognized by its rather long, pointed heads of small flowers, and by the deeply divided, feathery stipules, like narrow wings, at the base of the leaf stalks. Stems reach to 20 ft (6 m), with long shoots often climbing into hedges and low trees, and bear deciduous leaves with usually seven leaflets. The flowers are white or pink, ¾–1 in (2–2.5 cm) across, with the styles joined and emerging from the ovary like a small column, and the hips small and red.

This rose is native of China and Japan, and naturalized in much of eastern North America, where it is becoming a pest. Double forms were cultivated by the Chinese, as was a dwarf that flowered throughout the season on short shoots, instead of forming long, arching stems (*see R. multiflora* 'Nana', *p. 223*). This became the parent of the Floribunda roses, and probably also of the Hybrid Teas through 'Parson's Pink China' (*see p. 82*).

Garden notes This is hardier and lower-growing than some larger-flowered roses, and attractive in a hedge, though too wild and small-flowered for gardens. Hardy to -20°F (-29°C), Zone 5.

Rosa soulieana An upright shrub or climber to 12 ft (4 m) with blue-gray, deciduous leaves and small, creamy white flowers all along the stems, which have numerous hooked thorns. There are usually seven leaflets, rounded, hairless, and usually less than 1 in (2.5 cm) long. Flowers are up to 1½ in (4 cm) across, in clusters to 6 in (15 cm) across, with glands on the stalks. The orange hips are around ½ in (1 cm) long. Native of China, in western Sichuan, mainly in the Min river valley, on rocky limestone hillsides, where it flowers in July.

Garden notes This is an attractive rose for a sunny position in a dry area; it can be grown on a large tripod, or planted to climb through a low tree or hedge. It is one of the neatest of this group, and very free flowering, growing very well in central London. The Shrub rose 'Wickwar' is a lovely hybrid with *R. soulieana* as one parent. Hardy to -10°F (-23°C), Zone 6.

Rosa soulieana from the Min valley, Sichuan

Rosa abyssinica rarely seen, here in the Parc de la Tête d'Or in Lyon, France

Rosa sempervirens

Rosa wichurana

Rosa moschata

Rosa setigera

Most of these Musk Roses (*see introductory note, p.16*) are white-flowered, evergreen, and from warm climates, mainly Asia and the Arabian Peninsula. The exception is *R. setigera*, which often has pink flowers and grows in North America.

Rosa abyssinica (also called *R. moschata* var. *abyssinica*) This is the only rose found wild in sub-Saharan Africa, growing in Ethiopia, Somalia, and across the Red Sea in Saudi Arabia and Yemen. It is also remarkable for its long flowering period and its strong scent, combining the usual rose scent with that of cloves. The stems, to 12 ft (4 m), with many short, recurved thorns, form a straggly shrub or sometimes climb. The evergreen leaves have usually seven bright green leaflets, ovate to oblong, with very fine, shallow, sharp teeth, ½–1 in (1–2.5 cm) long. The flowers are 1¼–1½ in (3–4 cm) across, white, solitary or in groups of two or three on short shoots; their long-pointed sepals have few, narrow lobes. Styles protrude to around ¼ in (6 mm). The egg-shaped hips are ½ in (1.5 cm) long, usually smooth, and red or reddish-black.

Garden notes This rose has proved both heat- and drought-tolerant in gardens in Pretoria, South Africa, and seldom suffers from greenfly or blackspot. Its long flowering period is also a favorable trait, and it would be useful in breeding drought-tolerant shrubs. It may be a parent of the ancient Holy Rose, *R. × richardii*, sometimes called *R. sancta* or 'St. John's Rose', which grows around monasteries in Ethiopia and has been found by archaeologists in Egyptian funeral garlands from about A.D.170. Probably hardy to 12°F (-11°C), in Zone 8.

Rosa moschata (also called Musk Rose) An ancient and historic rose with a wonderful scent. Despite intensive research, its native distribution is still uncertain. It is a low climber with stems to 15 ft (5 m) and very few, rather straight thorns. The light green leaves have five to seven leaflets, to 2 in (5 cm) long, ovate, sometimes softly hairy on the veins beneath, the central stalk without thorns. Flowers are creamy-white, around 2 in (5 cm) across, in loose clusters on slender stalks to 1¼ in (3 cm) or longer, with fine hairs and glands. The sepals, around ¾ in (2 cm) long, have long, slender points and a few small side lobes. The hips are small and oval, with the styles protruding.

Garden notes A graceful and interesting climber for a warm wall, or fence in a hot climate, with flowers formed at the ends of long, arching shoots. These appear in late summer and autumn, and the plant is often in full flower into September.

This rose is interesting as one of the parents of the Damask roses. It is itself an ancient cultivated plant, which was perhaps grown by the Moghuls and distributed through their empire, where it still survives in old gardens. It arrived in England from Italy in the mid-16th century, and has been cultivated since then, first for medicine, as a purgative, and later for ornament; the strong scent is carried on the air. In recent times the Musk Rose nearly died out in cultivation in England, but was found by rosarian Graham Thomas in the garden of E.A. Bowles, at Myddelton House, just north of London; as Graham Thomas describes, Bowles records that he received it from Canon Ellacombe at Bitton, near Bath, the founder of Bath Botanical Gardens. Hardy to perhaps -10°F (-23°C), Zone 6.

Rosa phoenicia A climber with tight heads of large flowers and very coarsely toothed leaves. It has stems to 20 ft (6 m), with numerous, slightly curved thorns. The leaves are deciduous, with usually five bluish-green, obovate or oval leaflets, ¾–1¾ in (2–4.5 cm) long, with broad, blunt teeth, sparsely hairy above, densely short-haired beneath. The flowers are 1¼–2 in (3–5 cm) across, in a dense cluster or solitary on short shoots, white, and well scented, with the outer sepals pinnatifid, ½–¾ in (1–2 cm) long. The styles protrude to around ¼ in (6 mm). The hips are ½ in (1 cm) long, usually smooth, and red.

Native of northeastern Greece, Cyprus, and European Turkey southeastward to Lebanon, growing in hedges in moist places by streams and ditches at low altitudes. It is commonly found in damp areas along the coastal plain and on low hills in southern and western Turkey, where it flowers in late May and early June.

Garden notes A valuable rose for warm, moist climates, such as Florida and the Gulf coast, because it is one of the few that tolerate wet ground. It was formerly thought to be one of the parents of the Damasks, but recent DNA studies have shown that it was not involved. Hardy to -10°F (-23°C), Zone 6.

Rosa sempervirens This is a climber in warm areas with shining green leaves and white flowers. The stems reach 20 ft (6 m) or more, sometimes forming a dense, spreading shrub. They bear few, recurved thorns, and evergreen leaves with usually five dark green, ovate to ovate-lance-shaped leaflets, 1¼–3¼ in (3–8 cm) long, with fine, sharp teeth. Well-scented white flowers, 1¼–2 in (3–5 cm) across, are produced in clusters of three to twelve or singly on short shoots, with unlobed sepals, ⅜–½ in (9–15 mm) long, with glands. Hairy styles protrude around ¼ in (6 mm). The hips are round, ½ in (1–1.5 cm) long, usually smooth, red.

Native of Portugal and of the Mediterranean area from North Africa and Spain to western Turkey at low altitudes, flowering in April and May.

Garden notes This is a suitable species for Mediterranean climates such as California, and is happy scrambling through dry scrub. A creeping coastal form from Nice in the south of France has been used in creating groundcover roses suited to dry climates, such as the Meidiland Groundcover roses Hardy to 0°F (-18°C), Zone 7.

Rosa setigera (also called Prairie Rose) A climber or large, arching shrub with few, very coarse leaflets and pink or white flowers, this rose grows wild in North America from southern Ontario to Nebraska and southward to Florida and Texas on prairies and in thickets. The stems, to 15 ft (5 m) or more, are thornless or with few recurved thorns, and deciduous leaves with usually three dark green, ovate to ovate-lance-shaped leaflets, 1¼–3½ in (3–9 cm) long, sometimes hairy on the midrib, with fine, sharp teeth and impressed veins. Unscented white or pink flowers around 2½ in (6 cm) across are borne in clusters of three to twelve, on softly hairy stalks with stalked glands. The sepals are ⅜–½ in (9–15 mm) long, with glands, and the styles protrude around ¼ in (6 mm). The hips are round, red, around 3¼ in (8 cm) long, and usually with glands.

Garden notes This is valuable for its hardiness, and in the best forms for the bright pink flowers produced from June to August. It is also a parent of hybrids such as 'American Pillar' (*see p.157*) and possibly also the attractive, late-flowering 'Baltimore Belle' (*see p.154*). Hardy to -30°F (-34°C), Zone 4.

Rosa wichurana (also called *R. wichuraiana*, 'Memorial Rose') This rose is found in Japan in Honshu, Shikoku, and Kyushu, and in Korea, Taiwan, and eastern China. It grows among rocks and on dunes by the sea, the young shoots often creeping along the sand, and in scrub in the lowlands, flowering usually in July and August.

The green stems trail to 20 ft (6 m), with numerous, slightly curved thorns, and bear shining, dark green leaves, mostly evergreen, rather stiff, paler beneath. There are five to nine leaflets, usually seven, all much the same size, ovate-lance-shaped to obovate, ½–1¼ in (1–3 cm) long. The flowers, borne in branched, narrow, elongated, pyramidal clusters, are white, or pink-tinged in forma *rosiflora*, well scented, and small, around 1¼ in (3 cm) across, with sepals around ½ in (1 cm) long, soon falling. The hips are small, with scattered stalked glands, and the styles protruding in a thick, hairy column.

Garden notes This is often called 'Memorial Rose' in North America, because it is used in graveyards as groundcover or to trail over a bank. It is named for German botanist Max Ernst Wichura, and is an important parent of many ramblers, such as 'Dorothy Perkins' (*see p.158*), whose small leaves, long shoots, and late flowering differ from the ramblers descended from *R. multiflora* (*see p.17*). Hardy to -20°F (-29°C), Zone 5.

Rosa phoenicia in a pomegranate tree near Antalya, Turkey

WILD ROSES

These roses, in section Cinnamomae, are from western China, growing among forests of *Deutzia*, *Rhododendron*, *Sorbus*, and other familiar garden shrubs in the mountains bordering Tibet. They have tall, arching shoots and the largest and most spectacular hips of all roses, but little scent.

Rosa davidii (also called 'Père David's Rose')   An arching shrub with clusters of pale pink flowers and large hips. The shoots grow to 10 ft (3 m) and have straight or slightly curved prickles, but no bristles. The leaves have seven to eleven leaflets, which are softly hairy beneath. Pale pink flowers are born in loose, flat-topped clusters of four to twelve, the stalks with glands. Their sepals are long and slender, to 1 in (2.5 cm), and flattened at the tip. The styles protrude a little. The large hips, around ¾ in (2 cm) long, are flask-shaped and red; var. *elongata* has larger leaflets, fewer flowers, which may be deep pink, and more elongated fruit. Native of western China, in western Sichuan, growing in mountain scrub and flowering in July.

   Garden notes   Both *R. davidii* and the very similar *R. setipoda* are most spectacular when laden with fruit in early autumn. They should be grown as free-standing shrubs and allowed to develop to their full size. Hardy to -20°F (-29°C), Zone 5.

Rosa davidii

Rosa giraldii   A bushy shrub to 8 ft (2.5 m) tall with few prickles, often in pairs. The seven to nine leaflets are oval or elliptic, and sometimes hairy on both sides. Flowers are solitary or in clusters of up to five, deep pink, their stalks often hidden by large bracts. The hips are round and red. Native of northwestern China, from Shaanxi southward to northern Sichuan and northwestern Hubei, flowering in summer.

   Garden notes   Attractive both in flower and in fruit. Hardy to -30°F (-34°C), Zone 4.

Rosa moyesii   A large, arching shrub, to 20 ft (6 m) tall, usually with few thorns. The seven to thirteen widely spaced, rounded leaflets are up to 1½ in (4 cm) long. Flowers are solitary or in groups of two to four, usually pink, more rarely red, with bristly or smooth stalks and hips. The large, red hips usually have green sepals. It is native of western China, in western Sichuan and Yunnan in mountain scrub, flowering in June and July.

   Garden notes   One of the best shrubs for its hips, but some clones fruit much more freely than others. 'Geranium' has good red flowers and large hips on a stiff bush to 8 ft (2.5 m), lower than other clones. 'Sealing Wax' has pink flowers but good hips. 'Hillieri', possibly a hybrid, has wonderful dark crimson flowers but few hips. Hardy to -20°F (-29°C), Zone 5.

Rosa davidii at the Hillier Arboretum, southern England

Rosa moyesii

Rosa giraldii

Rosa setipoda

Rosa moyesii hips

Rosa setipoda A large shrub to 10 ft (3 m) tall and wide, with arching branches covered with bristles and prickles. The leaves have seven to nine ovate, well-spaced, and scented leaflets. There are up to 20 or more flowers in a cluster, pale pink, sometimes with a white center. The flower stalks and young hips are purplish, with numerous gland-tipped bristles, and the hips turn red when ripe. It is native of western China, in northwestern Hubei and eastern Sichuan, in mountain scrub, flowering in June.

Garden notes The best forms of this species have large, very pale flowers and make substantial shrubs. They need deep, rich, and moist soil. Hardy to -20°F (-29°C), Zone 5.

Rosa multibracteata A bushy shrub to 10 ft (3 m) tall, with very prickly stems, and slender pairs of thorns all along the thin shoots. The five to nine leaflets are obovate to round, less than ½ in (1.5 cm) long, sometimes hairy on the midrib beneath. Flowers are in clusters, bright pink, around 1½ in (3.5 cm) across with protruding styles; the stalks are short, with glands and rounded bracts. The small, red, flask-shaped hips have long, persistent sepals. It is native of northwestern China, mostly in northern Sichuan, growing on stony slopes in dry river gorges and flowering in June to August.

Garden notes An attractive shrub with bright flowers and hips, suitable for a dry bank or poor, alkaline soil. Interesting as one of the parents of the very distinctive Shrub rose 'Cerise Bouquet' (*see p.196*). Hardy to -20°F (-29°C), Zone 5.

Rosa multibracteata

Rosa glauca hips of the cultivated form

Rosa glauca flowers of a wild form

These roses are hardy, northern species in the Cinnamomae, mostly with deep pink, not pale pink flowers, usually with little scent, followed by large, bristly hips. They are found in woods and rocky mountains all around the Arctic Circle, relics of a time when North America, Asia, and Europe were joined. Many other plants are found around the Arctic, and sometimes extend south along the Rockies, the Alps, and the mountains of Japan.

Rosa acicularis (also called Prickly Rose)   A shrub to 3 ft (1 m), the main stems densely covered with weak, needle-like, flattened prickles in pairs, the side branches sometimes smooth. The leaves have three to seven rather broad leaflets, usually softly hairy beneath, with wide stipules. Flowers are solitary, deep pink, and to 2 in (5 cm) across, and hips are flask-shaped. This is the northernmost of all roses, native of northern North America from New York to Alaska, in the Rockies to Wyoming, and of northeastern Asia, growing on rocky hillsides.

Var. *nipponensis*, found in the mountains of Japan, usually has seven to nine narrower leaflets, ½–1¼ in (1–3 cm) long, and bristly fruit stalks with glands. Wild plants are often very dwarf with large flowers, whereas those in cultivation under that name are taller with arching branches and clusters of flowers on red twigs: equally attractive, but not exactly the same.

Garden notes   The plant usually cultivated, var. *nipponensis*, is an attractive rose for a bank or informal shrubbery, showy when in flower and fruit, but natural enough for a wild area. Hardy to -40°F (-40°C), Zone 3.

Rosa fedtschenkoana   A suckering shrub to 6 ft (2 m), usually less. The stems are thorny, with bristles and prickles, the leaves grayish, with usually seven leaflets. White flowers are followed by bristly, orange-red hips. Native of central Asia, in the rocky foothills of the Ala-tau, Tien Shan, and Pamir-Alai mountains eastward to northwestern China, flowering from June to September.

It is named for the Russian botanist Olga Fedtschenko. The Fedtschenkos were a remarkable family: Alexei was born in Irkutsk on Lake Baikal, and made a three year collecting expedition with his wife Olga. After he was killed climbing in the Alps, she brought up their infant son Boris to be a botanist, and together they pioneered the botanical exploration of central Asia and the Pamirs.

Garden notes   Attractive for its grayish leaves, long flowering season, and good hips, this rose is also significant as a probable parent of the Damask roses. Hardy to -30°F (-34°C), Zone 4.

Rosa glauca (also called *R. rubrifolia*, *R. ferruginea*)   A rose well known for its grayish or purplish leaves with five to seven leaflets. Stems to 7 ft (2.2 m), bristly but with few thorns, suckering when grown on its own roots. The flowers are rather small, around 1½ in (3.5 cm) across, with narrow petals, and usually bright pink. Hips bright red, with a few glands. Native of the mountains of southern Europe, growing on grassy slopes and the margins of woods, flowering in June and July.

Garden notes   This shrub forms a gray accent in borders and is very useful for its foliage, which can be cut for flower arrangements. It is tough and easy to grow, and can be cut to the ground if the plants get old and woody. Will survive down to -13°F (-25°C), in Zone 5.

Rosa majalis (also called *R. cinnamomea*)   A tall, suckering shrub rose with reddish-brown bark and stems to 5 ft (1.5 m), with pairs of slightly curved or straight thorns at the nodes.

Rosa acicularis var. *nipponensis*
cultivated form

Rosa majalis

with glands, and fringed with fine hairs. The flowers are usually solitary, on short shoots, purplish-pink or white, around 3 in (7 cm) across, well-scented, and produced over a long period; their stalks are thick, hairy, and bristly. The hips are like a flattened sphere in shape, with a few stalked glands and erect and persistent sepals.

Native of eastern Siberia, northern China, Korea, and Japan, growing in sandy places near the sea. It is naturalized in much of northeastern North America, northern Europe, and especially on sand dunes in England and Scotland, where the underground suckering shoots help to stabilize the sand, and the plant may flower at only 18 in (45 cm) tall.

Garden notes *Rosa rugosa* is said to have been cultivated in China since A.D.1100. There are several garden varieties; all are healthy, with a long flowering period, and modern breeders such as David Austin are now using *R. rugosa* to introduce hardiness and disease resistance into Shrub roses. Will survive down to -13°F (-25°C), in Zone 5.

The five to seven leaflets are narrowly elliptical to obovate, ½–1¼ in (1.5–4.5 cm) long, bluish-green above, smooth, hairless, and pale blue-green beneath, with broad, thin, smooth stipules. Flowers are solitary, on short, smooth shoots, deep purplish-pink, and up to 2 in (5 cm) across, with unlobed, slender sepals. The smooth, red hips are short and almost round, and have persistent sepals. Found on scrubby slopes and among rocks in northern and central Europe from France, Switzerland, and Germany, mainly in the mountains, eastward to Siberia, flowering from May to July.

Garden notes This rose forms open thickets, often in partial shade of open woods. The double-flowered form, which was the first to be described, is sometimes found naturalized in Scotland. *Rosa pendulina*, a dwarf alpine species, has similar flowers, longer hips, and usually bristly stalks. Hardy to -30°F (-34°C), Zone 4.

Rosa rugosa A medium-sized shrub with upright stems to 6 ft (2 m), but usually around 5 ft (1.5 m), densely covered with bristles, prickles, and straight thorns. The five to nine broadly elliptical, overlapping, short-stalked leaflets are rough with impressed veins and shining on the upper surface, pale grayish and hairy beneath. The stipules are large, green, and more than ¼ in (5 mm) wide,

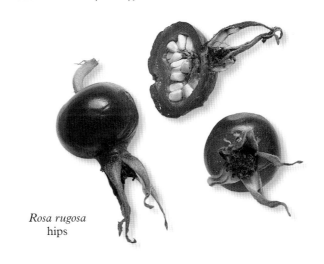

Rosa rugosa hips

Rosa fedtschenkoana

Rosa rugosa on dunes by the Sea of Okhotsk in northern Japan

Rosa nitida hips and autumn color

Rosa nitida

Rosa californica

Rosa palustris

American wild roses are less diverse than Asiatic ones, but include some excellent garden plants that will tolerate extreme cold. Apart from minor differences in leaf, thorn type, and hip, the differing ecological preferences of these American species aid identification. Some grow in wet places, others on rocky hills or by streams in hot areas. *Rosa californica* and *R. woodsii* are in Cinnamomae (*see also pp. 20–21*), the rest in Carolinae; these two sections are similar, and are sometimes joined.

Rosa californica   An upright shrub to 10 ft (3 m) tall, forming dense thickets, with stout, flattened, and curved thorns. Sprays of pale pink flowers with little scent are followed by red, flask-shaped hips; the flower stalks and young hips are finely hairy. Native from south Oregon to Baja California, usually in canyons and by streams, flowering from May to August.
   Garden notes   The plant often grown as *R. californica* 'Plena' is now considered a form of *R. nutkana*, a similar rose with more northerly distribution, as far north as Alaska. The wild *R. californica* is suitable for natural plantings. Hardy to around -13°F (-25°C), in Zone 5.

Rosa nitida (also called Shining Rose)   A low-growing rose found wild from Newfoundland south as far as Connecticut. The stems are usually less than 2 ft (60 cm), though up to 3 ft (1 m) in gardens, and densely covered with slender bristles; the seven to nine narrow leaflets are shining on the upper surface. The flowers are bright pinkish-purple, 2 in (5 cm) across, and usually solitary, and have a sweet scent. The hips are bright red, covered with bristles and glands, with persistent, unlobed sepals. *Rosa nitida* grows in bogs and wet thickets on acid soils.
   Garden notes   This is a beautiful rose for wet soil, at the edge of a lake or pond, or in a bog; it can be underplanted with an early flowering perennial, such as *Caltha*, that will have finished before the rose leaves develop. The autumn color is particularly fine, even in climates where colors are usually not as intense as in its native area. Hardy to -40°F (-40°C), Zone 3.

Rosa palustris (also called Swamp Rose)   This tall shrub has stems around 6 ft (2 m), and usually seven narrow leaflets, hairy on the veins beneath, with hooked prickles in pairs at the bases. The flowers are often several together, pink, sometimes with a deeper center, around 2 in (5 cm) across, and scented like lily-of-the-valley in the evening. The round hips have a few scattered glands. Native of North America from Nova Scotia

Rosa woodsii var. *ultramontana*

Rosa woodsii var. *fendleri*

and Quebec to Wisconsin, Minnesota, and south to Florida, in swamps and by lakes, flowering from June to August.

Garden notes Though growing wild in wet ground, this rose is happy in ordinary good garden soil, and grows well in The Royal Botanic Gardens, Kew, near London. It is valuable for its late flowering, and the best forms have a red glow in the center. Hardy to -30°F (-34°C), Zone 4.

Rosa virginiana This rose can make a leafy shrub to 6 ft (2 m), but is often shorter; it has hooked thorns in pairs at the leaf bases, and a few scattered between. There are seven to nine leaflets, and large stipules on the upper leaves. The flowers are pale pink, with long, slender sepals, and solitary or in groups; there is little scent. The hips and their stalks have gland-tipped bristles. Native of North America from Newfoundland to Ontario and southward to Virginia and Alabama, growing in dry, rocky places, flowering from May to July.

Garden notes *Rosa virginiana* is usually cultivated in one of its double-flowered forms, var. *plena*, 'D'Orsay Rose', or

'Rose d'Amour'. The species is the most common wild rose in eastern North America, suitable for wild plantings where the soil is rather dry. Hardy to -40°F (-40°C), Zone 3.

Rosa woodsii (also called Mountain Rose, Woods' Rose) A low shrub to 3 ft (1 m), with rather few, slender, straight spines, mostly at the base of the leaves, which have five to seven narrowly ovate leaflets. The flowers are pink, rarely white, to 2 in (5 cm) across, solitary or in small groups, with rounded bracts and little scent. The hips are round, with unlobed sepals. Native of North America, from Saskatchewan and British Columbia south to Kansas and Utah: var. *fendleri*, with glands on the stipules and petioles, extends south to Arizona and northern Mexico, growing in prairies, while var. *ultramontana* grows down the west coast from British Columbia to California, forming suckering thickets with the flowers often in sprays.

Garden notes These wild roses are more showy in hip than in flower, and are suitable for wild-looking areas of a garden or park. Hardy to -40°F (-40°C), Zone 3.

Rosa virginiana

Rosa canina

Rosa rubiginosa

Rosa gallica var. *pumila*

Shown here are the dog rose and the related downy rose and eglantine, all common across Europe. Because of their complex breeding system these roses, section Caninae, are very varied: numerous very similar roses have been given different names, and even these hybridize readily, adding to the confusion.

Rosa canina (also called Dog Rose)   The common wild rose in most of Europe and across temperate Asia, this is naturalized in North America from Nova Scotia southward; white-centered, pale pink flowers and strong, hooked thorns distinguish it from most wild American species. Most dog roses are strong shrubs to 10 ft (3 m), or scramble into trees. The seven leaflets are usually smooth beneath. Flowers are solitary or in groups of up to six, pale pink or white, with mostly lobed sepals; hips are smooth, bright red, the sepals usually falling as the hip ripens.

Garden notes These large bushes are lovely for a few weeks in midsummer, and suitable for rough hedges; other more showy species are usually preferred in gardens. Hardy to -30°F (-34°C), Zone 4.

Rosa rubiginosa (also called *R. eglanteria*, Eglantine, or Sweetbriar)   The eglantine has long been famous for its aromatic leaves, which smell of fresh apples, especially after rain. Eglantines are recognized by the many glands on the leaves, fruit stalks, and hips, in addition to numerous hooked thorns of all sizes. In England it is most common on alkaline or limestone soils. There are several closely related species, found throughout Europe and eastward to central Asia. *Rosa rubiginosa* itself is also naturalized in eastern North America. Dwarf species such as *R. pulverulenta* (also called *R. glutinosa*) and *R. serafinii* are especially prickly, with sticky, aromatic leaves and hips; found on dry mountains in southern Europe, they will survive in cold mountain areas.

Garden notes The eglantine is often used for recreating medieval or Shakespearian gardens. Though its stems are very thorny, it should be planted near a path, to surprise you with its scent as you walk past. Hardy to -30°F (-34°C), Zone 4.

Rosa sherardii (also called Downy Dog Rose) The downy dog roses, such as *R. sherardii*, *R. mollis*, and *R. villosa*, form a distinct group in the Caninae, often with deep pink or white flowers and grayish-green leaves, velvety-hairy beneath. The hips are often almost round, with scattered glands, sometimes ripening crimson or almost purplish. While *R. canina* often climbs, the downy roses are usually upright shrubs around 8 ft (2.5 m) tall. Most of the species are found throughout Europe, particularly in the north and east to central Asia.

Garden notes These are attractive shrubs for a wild-looking part of the garden, or for a mixed hedge; both flowers and hips are attractive in an understated way. 'Wolley-Dod', also called *R. villosa* 'Duplex', is a semidouble form or hybrid of *R. villosa*, named after Colonel A.H. Wolley-Dod, who studied British dog roses. Hardy to -30°F (-34°C), Zone 4.

Rosa roxburghii
hip

Rosa roxburghii f. *normalis* overlooking the lower Min river near Omei Shan in Sichuan

The wild *R. gallica* from Europe and *R. roxburghii* from China are both isolated and widely separate from other roses, but form hybrids with them.

Rosa gallica   This is the wild *R. gallica*, familiar in gardens; as a garden plant it is described under Gallicas (*see p.33*). The dwarf shown here, var. *pumila*, has suckering stems to 8–12 in (20–30 cm), oval to rounded leaflets, and single flowers with sparse glands on the stalks and calyx. It is reported wild in Spain and Italy, and the form from Sigale in the Alpes Maritimes belongs to this variety; this has flowers around 2½ in (6 cm) across, sometimes deep red veined with purple, sometimes pale pink. It is illustrated by Redouté as *R. pumila* or 'Rosier d'Amour', the Rose of Love. It is said to be frequent in Germany where it is called Rosier d'Autriche, but should not be confused with Austrian Briar, which is *R. foetida* (*see p.30*).

The roses of section Gallicanae are native to Europe and eastward to the Caucasus, Turkey, and northern Iraq. The section is an isolated one, but the most important ancestor of most groups of ancient and modern European garden roses.

Garden notes   The various wild forms of *R. gallica* are all attractive, suckering, low-growing shrubs, with good scent. Hardy to around -30°F (-34°C), Zone 4, perhaps colder.

Rosa roxburghii f. normalis (also called Single Chestnut Rose)   This unusual Chinese rose is easily recognized by its numerous small leaflets and its hips, which are covered with green spines and topped by large, leafy sepals. The flowers are large and in various shades of pink in the wild form, or very double in an ancient cultivated Chinese form. It is found wild mainly in Sichuan and Yunnan. Eventually it makes a small, rugged tree with attractive reddish-brown, peeling bark. The twigs have very few thorns; the leaves have nine to nineteen leaflets. It belongs to section Microphyllae, which includes also the very similar Japanese species *R. hirtula*.

Garden notes   In western China this is common on banks between rice fields, where it receives ample water in summer. It needs a warm position, and takes some years to flower when grown from seed. Surviving in Zone 8, it is damaged by temperatures below 14°F (-10°C) for any length of time.

Rosa sherardii from a hedge in southwestern England

Rosa × hibernica

Rosa stellata var. *mirifica* at Kasteel Hex, Belgium

Rosa pimpinellifolia growing wild in the Alpes Maritimes, France

The roses in section Pimpinellifoliae have small leaflets and are useful for poor, sandy soils. The flowers may be white, pink, or yellow: yellow-flowered species are on the following pages.

Rosa × hibernica (also called 'Hibernica', Irish Rose)
A hybrid of *R. pimpinellifolia* with *R. canina* pollen. It suckers freely and may have arching stems with curved thorns and prickles. The five to nine leaflets have sharp teeth, and sometimes glands on the tips and on the stipules. Flowers may be pink. This and other similar hybrids with dog roses have been recorded a few times, particularly in Northern Ireland.
   Garden notes A rare, unusual small shrub for a wild, sunny area. Hardy to -30°F (-34°C), Zone 4.

Rosa pimpinellifolia (also called *R. spinosissima*, Scotch Rose, Burnet Rose)   A low-growing species, with small flowers, often suckering in sandy soils; easily recognized by its creamy-white flowers, small, rounded leaflets, and blackish, shining hips. Stems rarely over 3 ft (1 m), covered with thin, straight prickles and bristles. The seven to eleven leaflets are ¼–½ in (5–15 mm) long. Flowers to 2 in (5 cm) across, sometimes pale yellow, white, or pale pink. The wild form is common on coastal dunes, more rare on dry hills inland, in many parts of England and western Europe from Iceland to Russia. 'Grandiflora', probably from Siberia, has larger flowers and stems to 6 ft (2 m) tall.
   Garden notes Old garden varieties of the Scotch rose include pinks, whites, and yellows, singles and doubles. All will grow and flower on poor, shallow soils, so often persist on roadsides and in abandoned gardens. They are early flowering, producing flowers for about a month, with a scattering of later flowers in wet summers. Hardy to -30°F (-34°C), Zone 4.

Rosa sericea subsp. ***sericea***   A spreading shrub with very varied leaves and nodding white or cream flowers in late spring. The arching shoots, densely covered with hairs, bristles, and prickles, can reach 10 ft (3 m); strong new shoots spring up from the base. The deciduous leaves have seven to eleven often narrow, hairy leaflets. Solitary flowers 1–2½ in (2.5–6 cm) across with usually five, sometimes four, sepals and petals are followed by round to pear-shaped hips of dark purplish-crimson, scarlet, orange, or yellow, on narrow stalks. Native of the Himalayas from northwestern India and northern Bhutan to western China, growing in hedges, on the edges of forests and streams and in scrub, flowering in May.

Rosa minutifolia

Rosa sericea subsp. *omiensis* f. *pteracantha*

Rosa sericea subsp. *omeiensis* hips

Subsp. **omeiensis** differs in having less hairy leaves, with 11 to 19 leaflets and often with a red central stalk and stipules, and usually pure white flowers, always with four sepals and petals. The fruit tapers into a fleshy stalk, and is variously colored and sometimes bicolored; it may be ripe as early as July. It is found mainly in China, in Yunnan, Sichuan, and Hubei, but extends west to Nepal. The form commonly grown is f. **pteracantha**, the wingthorn rose, with large, flattened, red thorns, which can be nearly 1½ in (4 cm) wide at the base.

The subspecies do not seem to be well separated in western China: many plants from there have fruit with narrow stalks. However, the extremes are very different, western Himalayan plants being generally hairier, with longer, narrower leaflets.

Garden notes As general garden plants, the ordinary forms are good for their delicate tracery of foliage, the whole shrub looking like a giant fern set with wide, white bells along the branches. The best forms of *pteracantha* have very striking stems, especially when the plants are growing strongly and have had good soil and plenty of water in the growing season; the translucent thorns are wonderful with the sun shining through them. Wide, red thorns are found in other species too, notably in the yellow-flowered *R. xanthina* f. *hugonis* (*see p.31*) in western China. Hardy to 0°F (-18°C), Zone 7.

Rosa stellata and *R. minutifolia* are both generally put in the subgenus Hesperhodos or the section Minutifoliae. They are true desert shrubs, both from southwestern North America, tolerant of summer heat and drought.

Rosa minutifolia This is a desert rose with very small leaves and pink or white flowers, native of Baja California, growing on dry hills. It makes a low, bushy shrub to 20 in (50 cm), the stems bearing slender, brown prickles. The leaves have five to seven finely hairy leaflets ⅛–½ in (3–10 mm) long, and flowers are up to 1 in (2.5 cm) across.

Garden notes This must be the most drought- and heat-tolerant of all roses, but it is much less showy than *R. stellata*. In dry areas, it is possibly hardy to 0°F (-18°C), Zone 7.

Rosa stellata var. **mirifica** (also called The Gooseberry Rose, Sacramento Rose) A low, spreading bush with small leaves and remarkably large, bright pink flowers. The stems, to around 3 ft (1 m), have straight prickles and soft, star-shaped hairs and glands in var. *stellata*, glands only in var. *mirifica*.

The three, sometimes five, leaflets are usually less than ½ in (1 cm) long. Flowers are solitary, to 2½ in (6 cm) across, and bright purplish-pink. Native of western Texas, southern New Mexico, and northern Arizona, especially around the Grand Canyon, growing in dry, rocky places at around 6500 ft (2000 m), flowering from June to September.

Garden notes One of the very best species for dry, cold areas; it also grows and flowers well in Europe. Should do well with full sun in a hot position. Hardy to -20°F (-29°C), Zone 5.

Rosa sericea subsp. *sericea*

Rosa foetida 'Persiana'

Rosa foetida 'Bicolor'

Rosa hemisphaerica from central Turkey

These rose species all have bright yellow flowers and little scent, and all except *R. persica* belong to section Pimpinellifoliae. Although *R. persica* is considered very different to other species, because of its simple leaves, it will hybridize with other yellow roses growing nearby. All these species are wild in dry parts of the Middle East, central Asia, and northwestern China.

Rosa ecae A thorny shrub with very small leaves and masses of small, intense yellow flowers with rather narrow petals in late spring. Stems to 8 ft (2.5 m) in gardens, usually less in the wild, with straight, flattened thorns. The leaves have seven to nine leaflets to ¼ in (5 mm) long, with glands, usually obovate. Flowers are ¾–1¼ in (2–3 cm) across, the petals usually not overlapping, and hips ¼ in (5–7 mm) long and reddish-brown.

Native of central Asia from Afghanistan to the Pamir-Alai and the Tien Shan ranges, eastward to Shaanxi in northern China, growing on rocky mountains at up to 9800 ft (3000 m), and also common on the southern foothills of the Ferghana valley in Uzbekistan. Flowers from April to June according to altitude.

Garden notes An interesting species for a dry, cold garden. The name is derived from E.C.A., the initials of the wife of Surgeon-Major Aitchison, who discovered this species while accompanying the Afghan Delimitation Commission in 1880. Hardy to -20°F (-29°C), Zone 5.

Rosa foetida (also called Austrian Briar) *Rosa foetida* is a bright yellow rose with dark green leaves; several forms are cultivated. The flowers of **'Bicolor'** or 'Austrian Copper' are yellow outside, but bright orange inside. This is an old Turkish variety, recorded in the 12th century, and brought first to Vienna from Constantinople, hence its association with Austria. **'Persiana'** or 'Persian Yellow' is another ancient Eastern garden rose, brought to England from Persia in 1837. This brought the strong yellows into modern roses, and at the same time the numerous spines and susceptibility to blackspot

Rosa persica

Rosa ecae

'Canary Bird'

often associated with the older yellow roses. *Rosa foetida* is found apparently wild from Turkey eastward to Pakistan, and in central Asia; however, it is possible that it is not a true wild species but a seedling or hybrid of *R. kokanica*, a wild species from central Asia.

Garden notes All varieties of *R. foetida* grow best in dry, warm areas, such as inland California, the drier western United States, Australia, and southern Europe. In damper areas the plants suffer from blackspot, which can defoliate the plants by midsummer; they recover but do less well than in dry-summer climates. Hardy to -30°F (-34°C), Zone 4.

Rosa hemisphaerica (also called *R. sulphurea*, Sulphur Rose) The name *hemisphaerica* was originally given to the double form of this rose, a hemisphere of yellow; this was one of the early introductions to Europe from Turkey in the 16th century, and is often shown in 17th-century Dutch flower paintings. The single form is sometimes called *R. rapinii*. It is a bushy shrub to 5 ft (1.5 m), with many strong, curved prickles. The leaves have five to seven gray-green leaflets, paler and finely hairy beneath, and toothed stipules. The flowers are rather pale yellow and 1½–2 in (4–5 cm) across, and the hips orange-red.

Native of Turkey, Iran, Armenia, and Turkmenistan, growing on dry hills at up to 5900 ft (1800 m), flowering in May. I have seen this rose flowering among the rock churches and cave dwellings of Cappadocia in central Anatolia, Turkey.

Garden notes This is a good yellow rose for a warm, sunny climate, being less harsh in color and less susceptible to blackspot than *R. foetida*. It is also hardy, probably to -20°F (-29°C), Zone 5.

Rosa persica (also called *R. berberidifolia, Hulthemia persica*) A dwarf spiny shrub, creeping and suckering in desert soils, unique among roses in its simple leaves and red-centered flowers, characteristics that have led some to put it in its own subgenus, that of Hulthemia. Whitish stems, to 20 in (50 cm), bear numerous straight and recurved thorns. The leaves, which are not divided into leaflets, are green or grayish, sometimes softly hairy, to ½ in (15 mm) long. The solitary flowers, to 1 in (2.5 cm) across, have purple anthers, adding to the effect of the red center; they are followed by bristly, blackish hips.

Native of Iran, Afghanistan, central Asia, northwestern China, and western Siberia, this rose is found growing in deserts and cornfields and on grassy hills, flowering from April to June.

Garden notes This species has a reputation of being very sparing with its flowers. Plants from hot parts of Iran grew poorly and failed to flower for me in southern England even under glass, while plants from the cooler, moister hills near Tashkent in Uzbekistan grew and flowered well in a frame at Wisley. This species should do well in hot, dry areas such as the Rockies and higher parts of California and Texas. Several hybrids between *R. persica* and other species have retained the intersting red center of the flower.

Rosa xanthina* f. *spontanea *Rosa xanthina* is a Chinese garden plant with double flowers introduced in the early 19th century. It is still commonly grown around Beijing, for example along the road from the airport to the city. The wild form was collected in Shanxi by the plant hunter Frank Meyer, and has also been reported in Korea and in gardens in Beijing. The flowers are bright yellow, the leaves grass-green, with usually nine rounded leaflets. **'Canary Bird'** appears to be a very good clone of *R. xanthina*, or perhaps a hybrid of f. *spontanea* and f. *hugonis*, a native of northwestern China that is also sometimes called *R. hugonis*. It is common in dry valleys in northern Sichuan, and further north into Gansu. I have seen it in the Min valley in Sichuan with wide, red thorns like those of *R. sericea* subsp. *omiensis* f. *pteracantha* (*see p. 29*).

Garden notes This rose, and particularly the clone 'Canary Bird', are among the best yellow roses for English or New England gardens, and the first to flower. 'Golden Chersonese' and 'Helen Knight' are similar, but have smaller, deeper yellow flowers, and are hybrids with *R. ecae*. Very hardy, to -30°F (-34°C), Zone 4.

Rosa xanthina f. *spontanea*

Gallica Roses

Rosa gallica
'Officinalis'

GALLICAS ARE RECOGNIZED by their low, thin, bristly stems, dark green leaves, and red, pink, or purple flowers produced in early summer. When they are grown on their own roots, Gallicas sucker prolifically, forming spreading thickets. Their scent is sweet and heavy, and they have traditionally been used for flavoring jam and for medicine.

The large, semi-double 'Officinalis' is probably one of the oldest cultivated roses. It was almost certainly grown by the Romans, and is probably the red rose that can be seen on one of the surviving murals in Pompeii, in southern Italy. The painting, which is preserved in the house of the Vettii, shows a nightingale singing on a post and includes daisies growing beneath. The artist even shows the partly folded leaflets of the rose, paler underneath.

'Officinalis' is said to have been brought from Damascus, Syria to France in the 13th century by Thibault IV Le Chansonnier on his return from the Crusades. It became known as the Red Damask or Red Rose of Provins, much cultivated in France in medieval times for its perfume and medicinal properties. There are good representations of it in early Renaissance painting, notably in the great Portinari altarpiece in Ghent Cathedral, Belgium, painted in Italy around 1430.

Many of the older Gallicas have deep purple flowers, but they were developed to their highest expression in early 19th-century France, where the craze for roses was encouraged by the interest of Napoleon's Empress Joséphine, who had her own collection at Malmaison, on the outskirts of Paris. Double, spotted, striped, and picotee Gallicas were bred, and others in subtle pinks, mauves, and grays.

One of their main characteristics is the way they open reddish, with purple and often paler tones developing as the flower ages. The famous flower painter P.J. Redouté, originally commissioned by Joséphine herself, published his great work *Les Roses* in 1830, including many of the early Gallicas and other old roses that are still grown today.

When bought as grafted plants, Gallicas require the same treatment as other roses, and are best planted in winter or early spring as bare-root plants. Cut back the roots of roses to 8 in (20 cm) or even 6 in (15 cm) long. They sprout vigorously from the cut ends, and are best kept short and straight, not coiled around in the planting hole.

When planting from suckers, put five stems in the planting hole to make a better bush in the first year or two, and shorten the stems to 6 in (15 cm). The decorative period of these once-flowering roses can be extended by planting a delicate clematis or an annual climber, such as a sweet pea (*Lathyrus odorata*), to scramble over them; *Clematis × durandii* is a good choice to continue the purple theme.

Gallicas grown on their own roots will grow and sucker freely in rich, heavy soil, but they do not thrive in poor, light soils. Their thin, often floppy shoots need supporting. Grafted plants bought from a nursery would probably do better in poor conditions, and would not form suckers.

Gallicas do not need pruning every year, but if they are tidied and their supports checked will form a graceful cascade. To keep plants dwarf, all shoots can be cut back to about 3 ft (1 m) every winter. Most are hardy to -30°F (-34°C), a few perhaps even hardier, and best in Zones 4 to 8.

GALLICA ROSES

'Complicata'

Garden notes This makes a most attractive spreading shrub, with large flowers freely produced on flopping stems. It is very hardy and easy to grow; this and its striped sport 'Versicolor' are often planted as informal hedges. Hardy to -30°F (-34°C), Zone 4, or possibly even lower; although satisfactory in southern California, it is better with a cold winter.

***Rosa gallica* 'Versicolor'** (also called 'Versicolor', *R. gallica* 'Variegata', Rosa Mundi, *R. praenestina variegata*) A strong-growing shrub with stems to 5 ft (1.5m), easily grown and very free-flowering over a long period in midsummer. The flowers are red with variable pink or white streaks or patches, the scent sweet and rich, but not very strong. This is an ancient mutation of 'Officinalis' and often reverts to it. It is illustrated well in a early work by the 15th-century Italian painter Botticelli, of the Virgin adoring the Christ Child. It is also illustrated in the German *Hortus Eystettensis* of 1613 under the name *R. praenestina variegata*.

Garden notes This makes a most attractive spreading shrub. It is similar to its parent 'Officinalis', but the effect of the flowers en masse is softer. Very hardy, to -30°F (-34°C), Zone 4, and worth trying in even colder areas.

'Complicata' The origin of this rose is something of a mystery, but it seems to be a hybrid between *R. gallica* and a wild dog rose, *R. complicata* from the Jura mountains of central Europe, first recorded in the garden at Roseraie de l'Haÿ-les-Roses in France around 1902. It forms a large shrub to around 7 ft (2.2 m) or a climber to 10 ft (3 m) if trained into a tree or on a wall. The flowers are large, around 4 in (10 cm) across, single, and pink with a paler center. They have a delicate scent, derived from *R. gallica*.

Garden notes This rose can create a wonderful effect, like a superb dog rose, with large, pale-centered flowers in early to midsummer only, and is most appropriate climbing into a small apple tree or forming a large hedgerow, if trained along a fence. Little pruning is needed. Hardy to -30°F (-34°C), Zone 4.

Rosa gallica (also called The French Rose, Provins Rose) The wild Gallica rose (*see also p.27*) forms a suckering, low shrub up to 2½ ft (75 cm) high, forming large patches of thin stems with prickles and glandular bristles. It has three to seven leaflets, around 2 in (5 cm) long, 1 in (2.5 cm) across, rounded at the apex, double toothed, bluish-green and smooth above, paler beneath. The flowers are single, solitary or with up to four in a group, scented, pale to deep pink or red, and the hips round to egg-shaped, sometimes with bristly glands around the base.

It grows wild in southern and central Europe, from eastern France and Belgium eastward to Turkey and the Caucasus. It is reported to be naturalized in Spain and Portugal, and also in North America. It grows in places with heavy, slightly alkaline soil, often in areas that are very wet in spring.

Garden notes In its various wild forms this makes a most attractive low shrub, with single flowers and stiff, leathery leaves. Very hardy, to -30°F (-34°C), Zone 4, possibly lower.

***Rosa gallica* 'Officinalis'** (also called The Apothecary's Rose, The Provins Rose, Red Damask, The Red Rose of Lancaster) A spreading shrub with thin, green twigs to 5 ft (1.5 m) with large, semi-double, red flowers, fading to purplish, which are produced only in midsummer but over several weeks. The leaves are green, with finely serrated teeth and a rough upper surface, usually bent down somewhat from the midrib. This is the usual form of the Gallica leaf and can be used to recognize the group. The flowers have some twisted inner petals and numerous yellow stamens, and a typical sweet rose scent.

A hedge of *Rosa gallica* 'Versicolor' at Hidcote Manor in Gloucestershire

Rosa gallica wild type

'Surpasse Tout'

'Rose des Maures'

'Bizarre Triomphant'

'Bizarre Triomphant' (also called 'Charles de Mills' 'Charles Wills') The origin of this rose is disputed; it was mentioned in 1790 under the name 'Bizarre Triomphant', which is earlier than 'Charles de Mills' though almost certainly the same rose. 'Nestor' is very similar, but has paler flowers. This rose has one of the most superb flowers of all roses, to 3 in (9 cm) across, flat, and very densely double, with a swirling mass of petals and a green button eye; sadly the scent is slight. The stems generally reach 5 ft (1.5 m) and arch under the weight of the flowers; they have few thorns.

Garden notes This is a good rose for a bank or border, and will grow in grass, but the huge, hanging flowers can be seen to advantage if it is trained on a trellis. I have it growing through some *Cistus* bushes, which support the canes with their stiff twigs. Hardy to -30°F (-34°C), Zone 4.

'Cardinal de Richelieu' This hybrid between a Gallica and a China was raised by Louis Parmentier in Belgium before 1847. The stems reach 5 ft (1.5 m) in good conditions, with few thorns. The flowers open reddish-purple, fading through dark purplish shades with a paler center to the petals and often with a green eye, and the petals reflexing to form a sphere. This darkening of the flowers as they age is a characteristic of the China roses, as are the wide, thin leaflets. The scent is poor. Richelieu was minister of state to Louis XIII of France in the 17th century.

Garden notes This is one of the best of the old roses for its dark colored flowers. It needs particularly good feeding to give its best. Hardy to -30°F (-34°C), Zone 4.

'La Belle Sultane' (also called 'Cumberland', 'Maheka', 'Rose de Serail', 'Sultane', 'Violacea') An old rose of uncertain origin, but widely grown under various names. The stems can reach 5 ft (1.5 m); the leaflets are rounded. The flowers are single, but with two rows of five or six petals, in color opening deep red, becoming purplish; there is surprisingly little scent.

Who was La Belle Sultane? Tradition holds that she was Aimée Dubucq de Rivery, Empress Joséphine's cousin and like her born on the Caribbean island of Martinique. Returning from her schooling in France at the age of 18, her ship was blown by a storm close to the Barbary coast of North Africa and captured by corsairs, who were always on the look out for white slaves. Her beauty brought her to the harem of the Bey of Algiers, who, wishing to please the Sultan of Turkey, sent her to Constantinople (now Istanbul) in 1783. Here she became Naksidil, mother of Mahmut II, who succeeded in 1808. Certainly around this time there was greatly increased French influence at the Turkish court.

'Bizarre Triomphant'

GALLICA ROSES

The rose is said to have been introduced to France from Holland by Du Pont in 1811. The photograph here was taken in the garden of Kasteel Hex in Belgium, which has a fine collection of roses.

Garden notes Hardy to -20°F (-29°C), Zone 5.

'Rose des Maures' (also called 'Sissinghurst Castle') A low shrub forming a thicket of canes around 3 ft (1 m) tall, this has deep red flowers that turn dark purple as they age, double but showing good stamens in the center, and with a very strong and rich scent. When the English poet and novelist Vita Sackville-West and her diplomat husband moved into the ruined Tudor castle at Sissinghurst in southeastern England in 1947, she found that this rose had persisted through centuries of neglect in the garden; a large bed of it survives there still. The French rose historian François Joyaux cruelly suggests that this is not an ancient rose but 'Rose des Maures', probably of early 19th-century Dutch origin, an appropriate name since the colors are just those of a black mulberry as it ripens from deep red to almost black.

Garden notes A tough old rose, useful for historic plantings and for cold areas. Hardy to -30°F (-34°C), Zone 4.

'Surpasse Tout' (also called 'Cérisette la Jolie') A strong-growing Gallica, raised in Holland before 1823. The stems usually reach 4 ft (1.2 m), and arch slightly; the leaves are handsome, with five leaflets folded up from the midrib. The flowers are in groups of two or three, very densely double, with the innermost petals curled inwards; their color is rich cerise-pink, fading to lilac, and their scent is excellent.

Garden notes This is a typical Gallica, healthy and strong-growing, suitable in a mixed border of blues and pinks. Hardy to -20°F (-29°C), Zone 5.

'Cardinal de Richelieu'

'Tuscany' (also called 'Old Tuscan', 'Old Velvet Rose') A very old variety, even darker than 'Rose des Maures' and with more petals, though still showing some stamens when fully open. Stems to 4 ft (1.2 m). Flowers in groups of up to five, with a few white streaks on the central petals. Scent very strong and rich. 'Tuscany Superb' is a larger-flowered seedling of 'Tuscany' raised by Thomas Rivers in England shortly before 1837.

Garden notes Fine ancient roses for collectors and those who love dark colors. Hardy to -30°F (-34°C), Zone 4.

'La Belle Sultane'   'Tuscany'

'Cramoisi Picoté'

'Duc de Guiche'

'Alain Blanchard'   A shrub to 5 ft (1.5 m), with arching stems and numerous thorns and leaflets. The flowers, in groups of two or three, are medium-sized, cupped, and semi-double with well-developed stamens. They open red, becoming purple mottled with crimson, and have little scent. Raised by Vibert of Angers, France in 1839. Alain Blanchard was a French hero, prominent in the English seige of Rouen in 1418.

   Garden notes   A well-colored flower, interesting in its mottled petals; there is also a striped mutation. Hardy to -30°F (-34°C), Zone 4.

'Cramoisi Picoté'   A Gallica raised by Vibert in France in 1834. The flowers are crimson with a paler edge, often with a green eye. They are rather small but very double, the outer petals reflexed when fully open, and sometimes have a strong scent. This should not be confused with the China rose 'Cramoisi Supérieur' (*see p. 84*).

   Garden notes   An upright plant, growing to nearly 6 ft (2 m) tall, and very striking with its small sprays of bicolored flowers, this is suitable for the middle of a border. Hardy to -20°F (-29°C), Zone 5.

'Duc de Guiche' (also called 'Sénat Romain')   A rose of uncertain origin, before 1810; it was described as 'Sénat Romain' by Prévost of Rouen, France in 1824. The stems grow to 5 ft (1.6 m), arching over; the leaflets are rather broad.

Large, well-scented flowers open crimson and cup-shaped, becoming flat and fully double, often quartered, veined with purple in hot weather and fading to purplish-pink, showing a green eye.

Garden notes This has proved particularly hardy, to -30°F (-34°C), Zone 4.

'James Mason' A modern Gallica hybrid, introduced by Peter Beales in England in 1982; the parentage is the Shrub 'Scharlachglut' and 'Tuscany Superb' (*see under* 'Tuscany', *p.35*). The stems have the extra height of 'Scharlachglut', growing to 6 ft (2 m), with curved thorns. The flowers are large, almost single with two rows of velvety petals and numerous stamens, and bright blood-red in color. The scent is good.

Garden notes Named for the actor James Mason, famous for his roles in films such as 'North By Northwest' and 'A Star is Born'. A good strong and colorful rose, close to a true Gallica. Hardy to -20°F (-29°C), Zone 5.

'Lord Scarman' A very modern Gallica, this is a seedling of *R. gallica* 'Officinalis' (*see p.33*) raised in 1996 by John Scarman and named for his father, a renowned English High Court Judge. The stems are upright, to 4 ft (1.2 m), the flowers loosely semi-double, rather cup-shaped, deep reddish-pink, the petals paler on the back.

Garden notes This is shorter than most Gallicas, like a more refined 'Officinalis'. Hardy to -20°F (-29°C), Zone 5.

'Robert le Diable' A lax shrub with stems to around 4 ft (1.2 m), and loosely double flowers. Its origin is uncertain, and it was first recorded in 1837. The flowers are cerise, mixed with purples and grays as they fade, with a good scent. Robert the Devil was Duke of Normandy in France around 1025 and father of William the Conqueror, and 'Robert le Diable' was the title of an opera by Meyerbeer, first performed in 1831.

Garden notes A charming and unusual variety, with more modest flowers than most Gallicas, and with a subtle combination of colors. Hardy to -20°F (-29°C), Zone 5.

'Alain Blanchard'

'James Mason'

'Robert le Diable'

'Lord Scarman'

'Camaïeu'

'Aimable Amie' A lax shrub with arching stems around 5 ft (1.5 m) long, with prickles and bristles and elliptic, deep green leaflets. The flowers are in groups of two or three, with a dense swirl of petals and often quartered in the center, medium-sized, deep pink in the middle, becoming gradually paler towards the edge, with average scent. It is likely that this rose was raised in Holland in the early years of the 19th century, but it was first recorded in France in 1843.

Garden notes This is a classic pink Gallica, suitable for a mixed border with perennials, where the very splendid flowers can be seen close up. It is also a very hardy variety, good in cold climates such as Sweden and Canada. Hardy to -30°F (-34°C), Zone 4.

'Camaïeu' (also called 'Camaieux') A shrub growing to 5 ft (1.5 m), bearing red to purplish flowers, striped and mottled with white, which are cupped and fully double, with some scent. Introduced by Gendron, an amateur breeder in Angers, France, in 1826.

Garden notes This is a good shrub with well-marked flowers. A plain-colored variety, without the white markings, is sold by Vintage Gardens in California. Hardy to -20°F (-29°C), Zone 5.

'Georges Vibert' The rather small flowers open deep pink with barely visible stripes; when they fade to pale pink the deeper stripes are very striking, and the petals reflex almost to a sphere; the green styles are usually conspicuous in the center of the flower. The fresh buds and older flowers shown in the photograph show the way they change. The scent is excellent.

The stems are upright, to 5 ft (1.5 m), with rather small leaves. It was introduced in France by Robert 1853.

Garden notes This rose is striking and worth growing for its very marked color change. Hardy to -20°F (-29°C), Zone 5.

'Président de Sèze' (also called 'Mme Hébert') Many of the best characteristics of the Old Roses are combined in this rose. The fully double flowers, in groups of two or three, have a swirl of crimson petals in the center and often a hint of a green eye; the edges are pale, almost white. The exact color varies with temperature and includes shades of pink, violet, magenta, and almost gray. The leaves and strong, sweet scent are typical of a Gallica. It was raised in Rouen, France by an amateur breeder, Mme Hébert, in 1828. 'Jenny Duval' is often thought to be the same rose; it is similar, but the flowers of the true 'Jenny Duval' show more stamens and are less pale on the edges.

Garden notes This is one of the loveliest of all Gallica roses, in its graceful arching habit, with stems around 4 ft (1.2 m), and crimson flowers fading to palest pink on the edges. Place it at the front of a bed, where the details of the flowers can be appreciated. Very hardy, to -30°F (-34°C), Zone 4.

'Tour de Malakoff' A Gallica hybrid, probably with a China or perhaps a Bourbon, with stems to 7 ft (2.2 m). The very large, double flowers have a crimson center and a paler edge, fading to grayish-mauve, and good scent. American grower and lecturer Suzanne Verrier explains that there were two roses with a similar name, a Gallica raised by Robert in France, and a Centifolia raised by Soupert et Notting in Luxembourg in 1856.

Garden notes This rose needs supporting and is suitable for training on a pillar. Hardy to -20°F (-29°C), Zone 5.

'Tricolore de Flandre' A strongly striped variety that does not fade, first recorded in the catalog of Van Houtte in Ghent, Belgium in 1846. Large, almost spherical flowers of very pale pink, heavily marked with red, become purple, with a green eye. Scent is average. A dense but floppy plant, to 3 ft (1 m).

Garden notes One of the brightest of the old striped roses. Hardy to -20°F (-29°C), Zone 5.

'Président de Sèze'

'Aimable Amie'

'Georges Vibert'

'Président de Sèze' at Mottisfont Abbey, southern England

'Tour de Malakoff'

'Tricolore de Flandre'

'Agathe Incarnata'

'Bellard'

'Rose de Schelfhout'

'Agathe Incarnata' (also called 'Agathe Carnée')
Of unknown origin, but first recorded in 1811 and illustrated by Redouté in 1824. It has arching, very thorny stems, to 4 ft (1.2 m) or sometimes more, and grayish-green leaves with elliptic, downy leaflets. The clear, pale pink flowers are fully double, quartered, and flat, with a small button eye, and the sepals unusually long and divided. The scent is very good. This is probably a hybrid, possibly between a Gallica and a Damask; some authorities, such as Old Rose researcher Brent Dickerson, consider that 'Agathe Incarnata' is the same as 'Blush Belgique' (also called 'Empress Joséphine') in the *R. × francofurtana* group.

Garden notes An excellent, free-flowering small rose with flowers evenly pink all over. Hardy to -20°F (-29°C), Zone 5.

'Bellard' (also called 'Bellart') This is an old variety which appears in Van Houtte's catalog in Ghent, Belgium in 1842. The stems are upright, to 5 ft (1.5 m), with numerous thorns and prickles. The flowers are in groups of two to six, rather small and flat, double and quartered with a button eye, but showing some stamens when fully open. They are translucent white with a pink heart and with pink on the margin, and their scent is good.

Garden notes This is one of the few white Gallicas which is not obviously a hybrid. Hardy to -20°F (-29°C), Zone 5.

'Belle Isis' A low-growing variety to 4 ft (1.2 m), often with rather floppy stems but upright flowers in pairs or threes. The flowers are small, fully double, cupped and filled with petals, pale pink with deeper color in the center. The strong scent is said to be like myrrh. Raised by Parmentier in Belgium in 1845.

Garden notes This is a good garden rose, and notable as one of the parents of David Austin's pink roses, particularly his first great rose, 'Constance Spry' (*see p.136*), which also has the scent of myrrh. Hardy to -20°F (-29°C), Zone 5.

'Duchesse d'Angoulême' (also called 'Reine de Prusse', Wax Rose) A lovely rose, pale for a Gallica. The beautiful, nodding flowers have thin, almost translucent petals of the most delicate blush pink, with a deeper blush in the heart. The scent is delicious. It forms a low bush to 4 ft (1.2 m), with arching branches and unusually smooth, pale green leaves. Introduced by Vibert in 1821, this is generally thought to be a Gallica hybrid, but DNA studies indicate that it is close to a Portland or even Hybrid Perpetual; the smooth leaves also indicate the presence of *R. chinensis* (*see p.13*) in its ancestry.

Garden notes The flowers are heavy for the floppy stems and the plant needs careful support, but it is well worth the extra trouble. Hardy to -10°F (-23°C), Zone 6.

'Belle Isis'

GALLICA ROSES

'Duchesse d'Angoulême' at Mottisfont Abbey, southern England

'Theresa Scarman'

'Duchesse de Montebello' An upright, leafy bush with almost thornless stems to 6 ft (2 m) or more; the leaflets are broad. Clusters of small flowers open flat or reflex. The petals are often quartered, with a pale yellow eye. Its parentage is uncertain, and it has been considered a cross with a China, Centifolia, Alba, or Damask. The historian of Gallica roses, François Joyaux, records that this rose was introduced in France by Laffay in 1824–25, while he was working for M Ternaux at Auteuil, near Paris, and that the Duchesse de Montebello was the wife of Maréchal Lannes, a soldier who became a general after the battle of Montebello in 1800 and was made Duc de Montebello by Napoleon.

  Garden notes Definitely on the tall side for a Gallica, suitable at the back of a border or on a low wall or pillar. Hardy to -20°F (-29°C), Zone 5.

'Rose de Schelfhout' A low-growing variety to 4 ft (1.2 m) with arching stems and bright green leaves with elliptic leaflets. The flowers are small or medium-sized, fully double, cupped and often neatly quartered, filled with petals, and pale flesh-pink with deeper color in the center. The scent is medium to strong. Raised by Louis Parmentier in Belgium before 1847.

  Garden notes This is a rarely seen but beautiful rose, which deserves to be more widely grown. Hardy to -20°F (-29°C), Zone 5.

'Theresa Scarman' A new and unusual Gallica, found as a chance seedling by John Scarman in England and introduced in 1996. The stems are up to 4 ft (1.2 m), the leaves bright green and healthy. The flowers are pale pink, double, and quartered, with good scent.

  Garden notes A low-growing variety, which would possibly make a substitute for an Alba in small gardens. Hardy to -20°F (-29°C), Zone 5.

'Duchesse de Montebello'

41

Damask Roses

Rosa × *damascena*
'Versicolor'

DAMASK ROSES ARE an ancient group, valued for their numerous flowers and intense scent, and grown for thousands of years for distillation of attar of roses. The geneticist C.C. Hurst, who studied the origins of old roses in the 1930s, considered that *R.* × *damascena* var. *semperflorens* was used in the cult of Venus in Samos in the 10th century B.C. and is the twice-flowering rose of Paestum mentioned by Virgil in the *Georgics*; others have been less sure.

Roses were important in Roman rites connected with the family, and were used in large quantities by the *nouveaux riches*, particularly at banquets. Damasks and Gallicas were probably the roses used.

Today the main centers of production of attar of roses are around Kazanlık or Kazanlăk in Bulgaria, and near Isparta in central Anatolia, Turkey. The Isparta rose fields were developed when the Turkish population of Bulgaria moved there in 1920. The rose used is the Damask 'Trigintipetala', sometimes called 'Professeur Émile Perrot', and very close if not identical to a mid-pink *R.* × *damascena* 'Versicolor'.

In the Turkish rose fields we found one or two mutations of the white from the mid-pink. Further details of Turkish production of attar of roses can be found in issue 23 of *Cornucopia*, an English-language magazine "for connoisseurs of Turkey."

There are two groups of Damasks: summer Damasks, which flower only in midsummer, and autumn Damasks, which flower in summer and again in autumn. Until recently, the two types were reckoned to have different parentage, but DNA studies published in Japan in 2000 by Iwata, Ohno, and Kato suggest that both groups have the same parentage. While the details are still uncertain, these studies indicate that the original seed parent seems to have been *R. moschata* (*see p.18*) crossed with the central-Asian species *R. fedtschenkoana* (*see p.22*), while the pollen parent is *R. gallica* (*see p.33*). C.C. Hurst considered that the most likely parent of the summer Damasks was *R. phoenicia* (*see p.19*), not *R. moschata*, but Iwata and Kato have ruled out *R. phoenicia* as a likely parent.

Rosa* × *damascena* var. *semperflorens (also called 'Autumn Damask', 'Quatre Saisons', *Rosa* × *damascena* 'Bifera') An ancient variety, thought to be mentioned by Herodotus in the 5th century B.C., growing in the garden of King Midas. Forms a sprawling shrub to 4 ft (1.2 m) with bristly stalks and ovate leaflets with slightly impressed veins. The flowers are mid-pink, loosely and untidily double, with long, narrow sepals, produced mainly in early summer, but some in autumn as well. This rose has sported to produce 'Quatre Saisons Blanche Mousseuse' (*see p. 67*), which often reverts. The Portland 'Rose de Puteaux' is also very similar.

Garden notes Like all Damasks, this rose is best in a dry climate. It is hardy to -20°F (-29°C), Zone 5.

***Rosa* × *damascena* 'Versicolor'** (also called *Rosa* × *damascena* var. *versicolor*, 'York and Lancaster') An ancient Damask, recorded in 1551, the year of William Turner's *A New Herball*, the first herbal in English, and referred to in Shakespeare's 'Henry VI'. It forms a rather lanky shrub to 6 ft (2 m), with thorny stems and narrowly ovate, dark green leaflets. Loose clusters of buds with long, narrow sepals open to flowers of unstable color, very pale or mid-pink, and often irregularly containing both colors (hence the name 'York and Lancaster', York for the white rose, Lancaster for the red). It has sometimes been confused with *R. gallica* 'Versicolor', the Rosa Mundi (*see p. 33*), but that is an altogether bolder plant with larger flowers of pale pink striped with pinkish-red.

Garden notes An interesting antique, but much less showy than *R. gallica* 'Versicolor'. Breeder Jack Harkness damns this rose as "a poor, uninteresting thing", but rosarian Graham Thomas praises it when well-grown and says it needs good, rich feeding; a dry climate would also reduce blackspot, to which it is prone. Hardy to -20°F (-29°C), Zone 5, possibly lower.

'Trigintipetala' (also called 'Kazanlik', 'Professeur Émile Perrot', 'Rose à Parfum de Grasse', 'Summer Damask') An ancient summer Damask of unknown origin. It makes an upright or arching shrub, eventually to 6 ft (2 m) tall, with thorny stems. The buds are in loose heads with long, narrow sepals with narrow side lobes. The flowers are loosely double, with a slightly muddled center, sometimes showing stamens, pale pink, medium-sized, and very well-scented.

There is considerable doubt as to the exact nature of this rose, and whether one clone or several very similar clones are grown in gardens. The rose grown for perfume in Bulgaria

'Trigintipetala' growing for attar of roses perfume near Isparta in Turkey

Rosa × *damascena* var. *semperflorens*

around Kazanlık, or Kazanlăk, is 'Trigintipetala' or something very similar. The same rose is now grown for perfume around Isparta, by Turks who left Bulgaria in the early 20th century. In his 1978 *Manual of Broad-leaved Trees and Shrubs*, Krüssman reports that several closely related clones are grown in Bulgaria. There is also the question of whether 'Trigintipetala' is the rose from which *R.* × *damascena* 'Versicolor' is a variegated sport: I have seen white-flowered sports in the rose fields in Turkey.

Modern usage, as in the *RHS Plant Finder*, seems to consider that 'Professeur Émile Perrot' is the correct name for the clone cultivated in Britain, though this name dates only from 1930. The most practical solution for rosarians would seem to be to call all the roses of this group 'Trigintipetala', while recognizing that this may be not one but several very similar clones.

Garden notes This is a very tough rose, best in dry climates with some frost in winter, where it makes a large, free-flowering shrub with well-scented flowers. It is not so satisfactory in climates with cool, wet summers. It is hardy to -20°F (-29°C), Zone 5, or possibly lower.

'Blush Damask'

'Hebe's Lip'

'Leda'

'Armide'   Raised by Vibert of Angers and introduced in 1817. This is probably a China-Damask cross, as indicated by the bluish-green leaves, but it is sometimes classed as an Alba. It forms an upright shrub to 4 ft (1.2m). The buds are pink, in small clusters, with short, pinnate sepals, and the flowers open white, fully double with a ring of tightly curled inner petals around a button eye. Its scent is excellent, and flowers are produced in both summer and autumn. Armide was a sorceress in Tasso's 16th-century epic poem 'Jerusalem Delivered', and the title of Glück's major opera of 1777.

   Garden notes   This rose is valuable for its autumn flowers, but surprisingly rare in gardens. Hardy to -13°F (-25°C), in Zone 5.

'Blush Damask' (also called 'Blush Gallica')   A rather small-flowered rose of unrecorded origin, known since 1759. The parentage is probably the Damask crossed with a Scotch rose, *R. pimpinellifolia* (*see p.28*), and it resembles the Scotch rose in its twiggy, prickly shoots, tendency to sucker, and rather small leaflets. The stems, which have both straight and curved thorns, can reach 6 ft (2 m) tall; the flowers are well scented, fully double with rather untidy slightly darker centers, of a lilac pink with pale edges, and have a tendency to nod. It flowers only in early summer.

'Armide'

Garden notes   An attractive semi-miniature, with neat flowers in small sprays. Gertrude Jekyll recommended it for growing in dry places, even partially under trees. Hardy to -13°F (-25°C), in Zone 5.

'Hebe's Lip' (also called 'Rubrotincta', 'Margined Hip', 'Reine Blanche')   A Damask of unknown origin, possibly a hybrid with a sweetbriar, *R. rubiginosa* (*see p.26*). It makes a short bush around 5½ ft (1.6 m) tall, with very thorny stalks and bright green leaves. The buds are in bunches, red with short sepals, opening to almost single, cupped flowers, the petals creamy-white margined with red, and quite large when fully open. The flowers are followed by a good crop of hips. The other Damask with red-tipped flowers is 'Leda' which has fully double, very flat flowers.

   This rose was listed by Lee in 1846 and is said to have been reintroduced by William Paul of Waltham Cross, in 1912. However, it is mentioned by Gertrude Jekyll in *Roses for English Gardens* in 1902 as "newly found" but really an old garden rose, and William Paul himself mentions it in the Country Life *Century Book of Gardening* in 1900.

   The Vineyard nursery of Lee and Kennedy was one of the most famous London nurseries through the late 18th and early 19th centuries. It was founded around 1745 in Hammersmith, which was then a village west of London, by James Lee and Lewis Kennedy. Lee corresponded with Linnaeus and subscribed to many plant-collecting expeditions; Redouté visited the nursery when he visited London in 1786–87. James Lee died in 1795, and was suceeded by his son John, who supplied large numbers of rare plants for the French Empress Joséphine's garden at Malmaison, even when Britain and France were at war. By 1846, the nursery had become J.&C. Lee and continued until 1877.

   Garden notes   The prettiest and most charming flowers with an unusual scent, on a tall, somewhat leggy plant. Hardy to -13°F (-25°C), in Zone 5.

'Leda' (also called 'The Painted Damask')   A Damask of unknown origin, first recorded in 1827. It forms a low bush around 3 ft (1 m) tall, with very thorny stems with recurved red thorns, typical of a Damask, and dark green leaves with rather rounded leaflets. The bunches of deep crimson buds have narrow, much-divided sepals with rather leafy tips. They open to white flowers with red edges to the outer petals, which

DAMASK ROSES

'Mme Zöetmans'

reflex when the flower is fully open; the inner petals are often quartered with a small button eye. The scent is good, and a few flowers are often produced in autumn as well.

    Garden notes A low, leafy bush with white flowers from red buds, valuable for the front of a border or a low planting: 'Pink Leda' (*p. 47*) is a sport. Hardy to -13°F (-25°C), in Zone 5.

'Mme Hardy' (also called 'Félicité Hardy') A Damask, probably crossed with an Alba, raised by M Jules-Alexandre Hardy, head gardener of the Jardin de Luxembourg in Paris in 1832, and named for his wife. It is stronger growing than most Damasks, forming long, arching, thorny branches to 6 ft (2 m) or more, which can be pegged down or trained on a low fence. The leaves are a good deep green. The buds are palest pink, in clusters, with short but much-divided sepals. The flowers are perfect: pure white, fully double, quartered, with a green button eye, and an excellent scent. Sometimes this has been considered a Centifolia, and may be found illustrated as *R. centifolia alba*; preliminary DNA studies do link it with the Centifolias, to which it would belong if it is a Damask-Alba cross. M Hardy, as well as being an amateur rose breeder, published both a journal and a list of plants in the Jardin de Luxembourg.

    Garden notes This is one of the most reliable and easy to grow of the old roses, praised by many English rose specialists from William Paul and Dean Hole to Graham Thomas: I can confirm it, having grown it in southeastern England. The branches flower along their length if trained on a fence or supported on a framework. Hardy to -13°F (-25°C), in Zone 5.

'Mme Zöetmans' (also called 'Mme Soetmann') A Damask raised by Marest in France in 1830. The stems are rather floppy, to 4½ ft (1.3 m), and the leaves bright, fresh green. Buds of palest pink, with short, pinnate sepals, open to fairly small, white flowers with a pale pink flush in the center, rather cupped and later reflexed, with a button eye. The scent is good.

    Garden notes A low-growing rose, smaller than 'Duchesse de Montebello' (*see p. 41*), with lax stems, which need support. Greg Lowery of Vintage Gardens in California links this to the Gallicas, because of its habit. Hardy to -13°F (-25°C), in Zone 5.

'Mme Hardy'

DAMASK ROSES

'Marie Louise'

'Celsiana' A Damask or Alba-Damask hybrid of unknown origin, first recorded in 1750 and probably originating in the Netherlands. It forms a tall shrub to 6 ft (2 m), with numerous short thorns and glandular bristles; the leaves are grayish-green. The buds are in upright clusters, touched with red, and the sepals are short but deeply divided, with narrow points. The flowers open deep pink, soon becoming paler and fading to almost white when fully open; they are beautiful, quite large and semidouble, with delicate, translucent, crinkly petals. The scent is very good and typical for a Damask.

Redouté painted this rose, as *Rosa Damascena* Celsiana, showing clearly the pink opening flowers and a fully-blown white one, and the bush with flowers apparently of two colors is mentioned in Thory's accompanying text. Jacques-Martin Cels was a Paris nurseryman who grew many other rare plants in addition to roses, and Redouté illustrated two volumes of new and rare plants from Cels' garden in 1800 and 1803.

Garden notes One of the largest and most beautiful of the Damasks, this is a good candidate for the centerpiece of a bed of ancient roses. Hardy to -22°F (-30°C), just into Zone 4.

'Celsiana' photographed at Mottisfont Abbey in southern England

'Omar Khayyám'

'Pink Leda'

'Gloire de Guilan' A Damask, introduced by English society gardener Nancy Lindsay in 1949 from Iran, where she found it being used for attar of roses. It makes a floppy bush to 4½ ft (1.3 m) or more tall and wide, with broad, mid-green leaflets. The buds are touched with red, the flowers relatively large, neatly double, sometimes quartered and slightly cupped, clear mid-pink with deeper shadows. Guilan, now called Gilan, is a district on the Caspian coast of Iran.

Garden notes The bush needs support, because the stems are rather thin, but the flowers are neat and the leaves a good fresh green. Hardy to -13°F (-25°C), in Zone 5.

'Marie Louise' A Damask or Gallica hybrid, grown at Malmaison, Paris in 1813. The stems reach 4½ ft (1.3 m), with Gallica-like leaves and relatively small leaflets. The buds are rather pale pink, with short and nearly simple sepals, and the flowers are mauve-pink, fading to almost white, with a small green eye and a powerful scent. They are huge and open flat, some say blowsy. As Jack Harkness puts it, they are "unkindly named after Napoleon's next wife", whom he married in 1810 after divorcing Joséphine in 1809: Joséphine kept Malmaison, but was sent away from Paris to live in the Château de Navarre in Normandy until her death in 1814. This rose has similarities with the 'Agathe' group of Gallicas, and Joyaux gives 'Agathe Marie Louise' as a synonym of 'Agathe Incarnata' (*see p. 40*).

Garden notes The stems arch over under the weight of the flowers and need support. Hardy to -13°F (-25°C), in Zone 5.

'Omar Khayyám' A Damask rose raised from seed collected in Iran. It forms a rather stiff, upright shrub to 6 ft (2 m), with very thorny stems, narrow leaflets, and sprays of deep pink buds with long, thin, narrow sepals. The flowers are medium-sized, fully double but rather untidy in outline, with an excellent scent.

Edward Fitzgerald's translation of the 12th-century quatrains 'The Rubáiyát of Omar Khayyám' must be the most famous Persian poetry outside Persia (now Iran), full of allusions to love, wine, roses, and the sadness of the passing years:

> "Alas, that spring should vanish with the rose
> That youth's sweet-scented manuscript should close!
> The nightingale that in the branches sang,
> Ah, whence, and whither flown again, who knows!

William Simpson, an artist on the *Illustrated London News*, visited Naishapur (now called Neyshabur) in northeastern Iran in 1884, and collected seed from a rose growing on the grave of Khayyám, who was the Astronomer Royal as well as a poet. The seeds were grown on at the Royal Botanic Gardens, Kew, London, where one flowered in 1894. A plant from Kew was put on Edward Fitzgerald's grave in the churchyard at Boulge, in Suffolk: from here it was rescued by Frank Knight of Notcutt's nursery in 1947, and propagated by them.

Garden notes It must be admitted that the story is rather prettier than the rose itself, which has small and poorly-shaped flowers. Hardy to -13°F (-25°C), in Zone 5.

'Pink Leda' This is a pink sport of 'Leda' (*see p. 44*), with the same habit and foliage but with flowers of a pink ground color edged with crimson. Rosarian Graham Thomas reports that this form was more common in mainland Europe than in Britain: indeed it seems to have been unavailable in Britain for some years, though it is available in the United States, Canada, and Australia.

Garden notes This is a good pink rose, but without the unique coloring of 'Leda'. Hardy to -13°F (-25°C), in Zone 5.

'Gloire de Guilan'

DAMASK ROSES

'Rose de Rescht'

'Ispahan' (also called 'Isfahan', 'Parfum d'Ispahan', 'Pompon des Princes') A Damask of unknown origin, known since 1832. A tall shrub to 6 ft (2 m), opening early and continuing well into the summer. The leaves are unusually shiny. The buds are in clusters, with short sepals; the flowers are mid-pink, fully double and quartered with a green button eye, and the outer petals finally becoming reflexed. Some authorities say that this is loosely or semidouble, so there may be different varieties under this name. The scent is excellent. There seems to be no evidence that the rose originated in the Iranian city of Isfahan.

   Garden notes This is free-flowering and with a longer flowering season than most summer Damasks. Reported to be very resistant to blackspot, mildew, and rust. Hardy to -13°F (-25°C), in Zone 5.

'La Ville de Bruxelles' A Damask raised in France by Vibert in 1849, making a rounded, leafy bush to 4½ ft (1.6 m) across, with thorny twigs. The leaves are fresh green, with the terminal leaflet tapering to a narrow point; the buds are in small bunches, with quite short sepals, which are well-divided and have a narrow point. The flowers are large, bright pink, fully double, opening flat and quartered, with an excellent scent.

   Garden notes One of the best of all old roses. The Gallica-like, flat flowers fade a little around the edges when fully open, making a perfect circle. Hardy to -13°F (-25°C), in Zone 5.

'Oeillet Parfait'

'Ispahan'

'St Nicholas'

'West Green'

DAMASK ROSES

'Oeillet Parfait'   There has long been confusion over this rose. The historian of the Gallicas François Joyaux explains that the first 'Oeillet Parfait', dating from before 1830, was a striped Gallica. The later one, raised by Foulard in France in 1841, was a Damask and had medium-sized, pink flowers striped with lilac and purple. A striped rose of this name that could answer either description survives at the Rosarium Sangerhausen in Germany, where it is classed as a Gallica. Its flowers are rather small and pale.

However, in *The Old Garden Roses* Graham Thomas describes a warm, rich pink rose, fading slightly paler. The rose shown here is from Mottisfont Abbey in southern England, and agrees with Graham Thomas' description: it does not have striped flowers, but fully double, flat flowers of a plain, rich pink. It leaflets are unusually wide for a Damask. 'Tour d'Auvergne' is a possible synonym of this unstriped variety.

Garden notes   A good, low-growing Damask. Hardy to -13°F (-25°C), in Zone 5.

'Rose de Rescht'   A Portland Damask, introduced from Iran by English society gardener Nancy Lindsay in 1940 and sent out from 1950 onward. It forms an upright, leafy shrub to 6 ft (2 m), with slightly bluish leaves and rich pink, very double flowers, the center petals often incurved to form a tight rosette. I cannot resist repeating Miss Lindsay's own description of this rose from her catalog: "N.L. 849. Happened on it in an old Persian garden in ancient Rescht, tribute of the tea caravans plodding Persia-wards from China over the central Asian steppes; it is a sturdy, yard-high bush of glazed lizard-green, perpetually emblazoned with full camellia flowers of pigeon's blood ruby, irised with royal purple, haloed with dragon sepals like the painted blooms on oriental faience."

Garden notes   The flowers sit close on top of the leaves, and appear at intervals through the summer, connecting this with the Portland roses; it is good and healthy, but lacks the subtlety of some of the older varieties. Hardy to -13°F (-25°C), in Zone 5.

'St Nicholas'   A Damask, or possibly Damask-Gallica cross, which appeared in 1950 in the garden created by the Hon. Robert James at St Nicholas in Richmond, Yorkshire, famous for its rose collection. It forms an upright bush to 4½ ft (1.3 m) tall, the stems covered with small, red thorns. The buds are in bunches, red, with rather long sepals with small side lobes. The flowers are semidouble, opening deep pink with a paler center and fading to silvery, with well-developed stamens in the center. The well-developed hips are conspicuous in autumn.

Garden notes   The semidouble flowers in clusters make this an excellent garden shrub. Hardy to -13°F (-25°C), in Zone 5.

'West Green'   A Damask of unknown origin, grown in the collection at Mottisfont Abbey, southern England. Stems to 5½ ft (1.6 m) tall, with only very small thorns on the stalks. The buds are red and pale pink, with rather long sepals. The flowers are large, quite loosely double, bluish-pink and nodding on rather weak stems. It possibly came from the garden at West Green House, near Hartley Wintney, Hampshire, now the property of the National Trust.

Garden notes   A healthy bush, with nodding flowers and lush, bright green foliage. Hardy to -13°F (-25°C), in Zone 5.

'La Ville de Bruxelles'

Alba Roses

'Alba Semi-plena'

ALBA ROSES ARE recognized by their tall, arching stems, grayish-green leaves, and white or pale pink flowers, which are produced in great quantity over a short period. Their scent is excellent, and they were probably first cultivated for their perfume as much as for their ornamental value. Even today, they are first-class roses for the garden, forming large and exceptionally hardy shrubs that are unrivaled in an informal garden setting, as might be expected from a rose that has a wild rose as one parent.

The earliest Albas, such as 'Alba Semi-plena', are probably among the most ancient of all cultivated plants to survive, and 'Alba Semi-plena' is likely to have been grown by the Romans for both scent and ornament; even today, plantations are still found in Bulgaria for the production of attar of roses. The scientist and philosopher Albertus Magnus described a double white rose that forms a large shrub in the 13th century.

In medieval painting throughout Europe, roses, especially white roses, were particularly associated with the Virgin Mary. In the English royal conflicts from 1455, which came to be called the Wars of the Roses, the white rose was the badge of York and the red rose the badge of Lancaster; after his victory at the Battle of Bosworth in 1485, Henry VII took as his symbol the Tudor rose, made up of a small red rose superimposed upon a white one, beginning the reigns of the Tudors, which lasted until the death of Queen Elizabeth I.

The parentage of *R. × alba* is still in some doubt. C.C. Hurst, a pioneer in the field of chromosomes who studied roses between 1920 and 1940, considered that Albas were crosses between a dog rose, *R. canina* (*see p.26*), and a Damask.

Graham & Primavesi's BSBI handbook *Roses of Great Britain and Ireland* (1993) gives the parentage as *R. arvensis* and *R. gallica* (*see p.33*). Both these parentages could result in the same number of chromosomes; the latter would make the plant a fertile hybrid that should come true from seed. A general survey of the DNA of cultivated roses shows the Albas well separated from other groups, and suggests that the *R. canina* parentage is more likely; the general habit of the larger types is also consistent with this theory.

Albas are tough shrubs, often surviving in abandoned gardens long after the nearby house or cottage has collapsed; they do well in grass and will flower in more shade than other rose groups. The long, arching shoots that they send up in summer should be encouraged, because they will produce next year's flowers. When the new shoots are well developed, in late summer, the old shoots that have flowered may be cut away or tidied up; however, some varieties, such as 'Semi-plena', give a fine crop of hips which can be left to ripen, and then any pruning can be left till winter. As with all roses, a good top-dressing of manure or compost will give stronger growth, but Albas will thrive in poorer soils than most roses.

Albas flower only in midsummer, but will make perfect hosts for late-flowering climbers such as *Clematis viticella* and its hybrids. The stronger-growing species of clematis, such as *C. orientalis*, will need cutting to the ground after flowering, so that they do not totally smother the rose. More restrained climbers with annual stems, such as *Aconitum*, *Codonopsis*, or *Dicentra* will do no harm to even the most delicate Alba rose.

'Alba Maxima' (also called 'Great Double White', 'Maxima', Cheshire rose, Jacobite rose, White rose of York)   A large shrub with arching branches to 6 ft (2 m) or more long when allowed to reach its full extent. It has grayish-green leaves with usually seven broad leaflets. The double flowers are white with a hint of yellowish-pink in the center when first open, and well-scented. The center has small, irregular petals and some stamens showing when fully open, when the flowers are 3–4 in (7–10 cm) across. It is similar in leaf and habit to 'Alba Semi-plena', and has been known to revert to it. Flowering is prolific, but lasts only a few weeks, less in hot weather.

Garden notes   This rose, like many Albas, is among the best roses for a cool position. Albas also do well in the heat of southern California, although the flowers are short-lived in hot weather, so the whole flowering season can be over in a week or two. Hardy to -40°F (-40°C), Zone 3, and probably lower.

'Alba Semi-plena'   A shrub with arching branches to 9ft (2.75 m) or more long, producing strong new stems from the base. The leaves are grayish-green, with broad leaflets. The pure white flowers are semi-double, with well-developed stamens, and around 3 in (7 cm) across. They have excellent scent, and are produced in midsummer only. Hips are usually formed.

'Alba Semi-plena' is an ancient rose, almost certainly grown by the Romans, and probably by earlier civilizations. A single white rose is recorded as a sport on 'Alba Semi-plena', and was illustrated in *Hortus Eystettensis*, published in Germany in 1613, with single and double flowers shown on the same branch.

Garden notes   In a garden setting both 'Alba Semi-plena' and the similar but fully double 'Alba Maxima' are suitable for the back of a large border of mixed shrubs, in a tall hedge, or on the edge of woodland. They are appropriate near the edge of a garden where an informal shrub is needed, or planted in a small group to stand alone in rough grass or in an old orchard.

This is one of the hardiest roses, surviving where other roses would not thrive. Both this rose and 'Alba Maxima' are good in cooler climates, such as Scotland, but they also thrive in regions with hot summers, such as Bulgaria, where they are grown along with Damasks for attar of roses. Generally reckoned to survive to -40°F (-40°C), Zone 3.

'Alba Suaveolens'   This sweet-scented rose is usually considered to be the same as 'Alba Semi-plena', and has been grown for perfume in Bulgaria. However, when Roger and I visited the rose fields near Isparta in Turkey, we did not see Alba roses being grown there. Our illustration of 'Alba Suaveolens', grown by my brother Richard Rix in southeastern England, is a plant obtained from Jensen's Rosarium Glücksburg in Germany and shows flowers with more petals than 'Alba Semi-plena' but fewer than 'Alba Maxima'. American rose-grower and lecturer Gerry Krueger records that 'Alba Semi-plena' has anthers on the inner petals, while 'Alba Suaveolens' does not.

Garden notes   Similar to 'Alba Semi-plena' in the garden. Hardy to -30°F (-34°C), Zone 4, maybe lower.

'Alba Semi-plena'

'Alba Maxima'

'Alba Suaveolens'

'Jeanne d'Arc'

'Königin von Dänemark'

'Alba Foliacea' An old variety, illustrated by Redouté in 1824, with pink buds opening to white, semi-double flowers. The plant is tall, with arching canes similar to 'Alba Semi-plena' (*see p.51*). The special feature of this plant is very leafy sepals; the form grown at the present time does not seem to be as leafy as Redouté's, and may be a similar but independent mutation of 'Alba Semi-plena'. There is a similar Centifolia with leafy sepals, painted by Redouté as *R. × centifolia foliacea.*

Garden notes A curiosity, grown for its strange buds, but in general aspect the same as 'Alba Semi-plena'. Hardy to -30°F (-34°C), Zone 4, and probably lower.

'Celeste' (also called 'Celestial', *Rosa damascena* 'Aurora') Known from Holland since the end of the 18th century, this was illustrated by Redouté under the name *Rosa damascena* 'Aurora'. An upright shrub to 6 ft (2 m), but usually less. The leaves are pale blue-green, with seven broad, finely toothed leaflets and wide stipules. The flowers, in small clusters, open from slender buds, neat and semi-double with the outer petals reflexing as the flower opens, around 3¼ in (8 cm) across; both bud and flowers are a pale bluish-pink. The scent is very good.

Garden notes This is easily grown and flowers well in poor conditions, though at the same time being worthy of good treatment. It is one of the most beautiful of old roses for its strikingly blue-green leaves and perfect half-opened flowers of a rich, pale pink. It is also very healthy. I have photographed 'Celeste' in a garden in England where it was planted against the farm fence separating the garden from a wheatfield; its informal habit perfectly suited this position. Hardy to -30°F (-34°C), Zone 4, and probably lower.

'Great Maiden's Blush' (also called 'Cuisse de Nymphe', 'Incarnata', 'La Séduisante' 'Maiden's Blush', 'Virginale') A large rose whose arching branches can reach 6 ft (2 m) tall; the whole shrub can reach 8 ft (2.5 m) or more across, suckering when grown on its own roots. The leaves are a beautiful, bluish gray-green, often puckered, with red on the upper side at the base of the stalk. The flowers are around 3 in (7 cm) across, in small sprays arching downward, and yellowish-pink in bud, opening pale pink and fading to white. The center is muddled, showing some stamens, and the scent very sweet. The sepals are pinnate.

'Great Maiden's Blush' is ancient rose, known since the 15th century. Forms with a slightly deeper pink blush than usual are called 'Cuisse de Nymphe Émue' (*émue* meaning touched or affected); it is uncertain whether this is a distinct clone or whether the deeper color is caused by soil or temperature. According to the list of the roses at the German Rosarium Sangerhausen, 'Cuisse d'émue Nymphe' was introduced by planthunter Dumont de Courset in 1802.

Garden notes This is the classic, large Alba, suitable as a wide shrub standing on its own, or planted at the back of a border; it would even make a fine, large, and informal hedge, clipped lightly in late summer. Hardy to -40°F (-40°C), Zone 3, and probably lower.

'Jeanne d'Arc' (also called *Rosa anglica minor*, Small Double White) An Alba raised in France by Vibert in 1818. It is like a small-flowered version of 'Alba Maxima' (*see p.51*), with broad, dark blue-green leaflets and arching stems to 5 ft (1.5 m) tall, and suckering if grown on its own roots. The half-open buds

'Alba Foliacea'

are very pale flesh pink, the open flowers white, with a good scent, around 2½ in (6 cm) across. My mother found this rose in an old garden in Kent, in southeastern England, and we grew it for some years before discovering its name.

There are two other roses named 'Jeanne d'Arc': a Noisette, introduced in Paris by Verdier in 1848, and a white Polyantha, a sport of 'Mme Norbert Levevasseur', introduced by Levavasseur in Orléans, France, in 1909.

Garden notes This is an easy, tough, and long-lived rose; though the leaves are often infected by rust in late summer, it never fails to flower well the following spring. Hardy to -30°F (-34°C), Zone 4, and probably lower.

'Königin von Dänemark' (also called 'Queen of Denmark', 'Naissance de Vénus') An Alba or Alba hybrid with a Damask, raised by Booth in 1816. Arching stems up to 6 ft (2 m), but usually closer to 5 ft (1.5 m), are rather floppy and covered with numerous fine thorns. The leaves are bluish-green, but darker than most Albas. The flowers are pale pink, deeper pink in the center, fully double, and sometimes with a quartered center and button eye, with a sweet, Damask-type scent. 'Königin von Dänemark' is one of the shorter and most richly colored Albas; the flush in the center is particularly beautiful,

described by rosarian Graham Thomas as "vivid carmine." There is a controversy surrounding the origin of this rose, described by Graham Thomas in the 1983 edition of *The Old Shrub Roses*. John Booth, of the north German nursery James Booth & Söhne of Flottbeck, said that the rose flowered first there in 1816, as a seedling of 'Great Maiden's Blush'. Booth obtained permission from the King of Denmark to name it after the Queen (Danish territory then extended south into present-day Germany). In 1828 Professor Lehmann, Director of the botanic gardens in Hamburg, claimed that the rose was the same as 'Belle Courtisanne', a cross between *R. × centifolia* (*see p.59*) and 'Great Maiden's Blush' and that this was offered for sale in a French catalog in 1806, was generally known in France, and had been illustrated by Redouté. Booth apparently wrote to all the well-known rose breeders and to Redouté, all of whom answered that they did not know 'Belle Courtisanne'. Booth futher claimed that he sold plants of it for three guineas each (roughly equivalent to eight months' wages for a live-in maid at the time) to Lee & Kennedy of Hammersmith, who entered it in their catalog of 1830 as 'Queen of Denmark'.

Garden notes One of the best garden roses, with tightly double flowers, although the stems flop to the ground unless supported. Hardy to -30°F (-34°C), Zone 4, probably lower.

'Great Maiden's Blush'

'Celeste'

'Amélia'

'Blanche de Belgique'

'Chloris'

'Amélia' (also called 'Amelié')   An Alba or Alba-Damask hybrid, raised in Paris, France by Vibert in 1823. It is low-growing for an Alba, the stems reaching no more than 5 ft (1.5 m) and generally less. The bluish-green leaves have very broad leaflets; the twigs bear numerous small, red thorns. The flowers are semi-double, around 3 in (7 cm) across, of quite a rich pink, opening flat with a mixture of small petals and stamens in the center; the sepals are distinctly pinnate or bipinnate. This rose is noted for its scent, which David Austin likens to a tea rose. 'Amélia' has many of the characteristics of a Damask, and is sometimes considered to be a synonym of 'Celsiana' (*see p.46*), which has less pinnate sepals and more cupped flowers with more regular petals.

Garden notes   This is a smaller Alba, suitable for a mixed planting of old roses and perennials. May survive down to -30°F (-34°C), Zone 4.

'Belle Amour'   An Alba or an Alba-Damask hybrid of unknown origin, found by English society gardener Nancy Lindsay at a convent in Elboeuf, Normandy in 1940. The stems are arching and spreading, to 5 ft (1.5 m); the twigs bear few, long prickles. The dark green leaves are sharp-pointed, with a smooth texture. The neat, semi-double flowers, in loose sprays, are rich pink with shades of salmon; the sepals have very few lobes. Hips are freely produced. Its scent is of myrrh, or a hint of anise, which caused rosarian Graham Thomas to speculate that 'Belle Amour' might be a hybrid of the Shrub or Climbing rose 'Ayrshire Splendens', which has similar coloring and scent.

Garden notes   This rose is easy to grow and reputed to be good in poor soils. Hardy to -30°F (-34°C), Zone 4.

'Blanche de Belgique' (also called 'Blanche Superbe') Raised in Paris, France by Vibert in 1817, this is a medium-sized, bushy shrub to 5 ft (1.5 m), with gray-green leaves. The flowers are in nodding clusters, white, around 3¼ in (8 cm)

across, fully double with a tight central rosette of small petals, which block the center of the flower. The scent is very good, compared by some to hyacinths.

Garden notes   This variety is reported to be good in partial shade. Hardy to -30°F (-34°C), Zone 4, and probably lower.

'Chloris' (also called 'Rosée du Matin')   An Alba hybrid, known since 1820, and probably raised by Descemet in St Denis, France in 1800. Its stems are rather upright, to 6 ft (2 m), with dark green, leathery leaves and very few if any thorns. The flowers are pale pink; the buds and opening flowers have a deeper center, with the outer petals reflexing when fully open; the middle of the flower is sometimes quartered, with a button eye. Good scent.

The great 19th-century rosarian Gravereaux, in his account of *Les roses de l'impératrice Joséphine* classed 'Chloris' with the Gallicas.

'Belle Amour'

ALBA ROSES

'Félicité Parmentier' at The Garden of the Rose in St Albans, southern England

In her 1995 study *Rosa gallica*, American grower and lecturer Suzanne Verrier considered that there were in fact two roses named 'Chloris', one a Gallica, the other an Alba, while the French historian and amateur grower François Joyaux held in *La Rose de France* in 1998 that there is only one 'Chloris', and that it is an Alba or an Alba hybrid. In a study of rose DNA by Maurice Jay, 'Chloris' came out among the Gallicas. The synonym 'Rosée du Matin', dew of morning, is suitably poetic. In Greek mythology, Chloris was the wife of Zephyrus, the west wind, and became Flora in Latin.

Garden notes Unusually stiff and upright for an Alba, so suitable for a restricted space or sheltered corner. Richard Rix reports that 'Chloris' is particularly healthy, in fact "totally disease-free." Hardy to -30°F (-34°C), Zone 4.

'Félicité Parmentier' An Alba-Damask hybrid, of uncertain origin, known since 1834. It makes a bushy, rather upright shrub to 5 ft (1.5 m), with rough, grayish-green leaves with impressed veins and dark thorns. The flowers are around 3 in (7 cm) across, usually upright, in dense sprays. They are yellowish in bud, opening cupped and flesh-pink, and fading to white when fully open; at this stage the outer petals are reflexed, and the innermost tightly rolled in around a button eye. In spite of being crowded together, the flowers are not spoiled by rain.

Garden notes One of the shorter Alba-type roses, 'Félicité Parmentier' is free-flowering with an excellent scent; the flowers are paler in hot weather, and the plant is said to tolerate some shade. Hardy to -30°F (-34°C), Zone 4, and probably lower.

'Mme Legras de St Germain' An old Alba or Alba hybrid, possibly with a Noisette, of French origin, known since 1848, when it was described in the first edition of rosarian William Paul's *The Rose Garden*. A tall-growing shrub with stems to 6 ft (2 m); if supported, they can reach 15 ft (5 m). It has pale bluish-green leaves, and twigs with few thorns. The flowers are fully double, opening flat, and white with a yellowish flush in the center; excellent scent.

Garden notes The buds sometimes ball in wet weather, but otherwise this is a good rose. Hardy to -30°F (-34°C), Zone 4.

'Crimson Blush'

'Summer Blush'

'Royal Blush'

'Tender Blush'

'Lemon Blush'

'Princesse Lamballe'

'Mme Plantier' on the stump of an apple tree in the orchard at Sissinghurst Castle, southeastern England

'Crimson Blush' A new Alba hybrid with a red *kordesii* rose, raised by Sievers in Germany and introduced in 1988. The stems reach 5 ft (1.5 m). Large, red flowers are produced in quantity, but only in early summer.

Garden notes Hardy to -30°F (-34°C), Zone 4.

'Lemon Blush' A new Alba hybrid with a red *kordesii* rose, introduced in 1988 by Sievers in Germany. The stems reach 5 ft (1.5 m). The flowers are pale yellow fading to cream, and fully double with an old-fashioned shape. Produced prolifically, but only in early summer, they have a sweet scent.

Garden notes Hardy to -30°F (-34°C), Zone 4.

'Mme Plantier' An old Alba hybrid, probably with a Noisette or perhaps with *Rosa moschata* (*see p.18*), raised by Plantier in Lyons, France in 1835. When supported, the stems can reach 12 ft (4 m); otherwise the plant can be grown as a spreading shrub around 5 ft (1.5 m) across. The leaflets are bluish-green and rather rounded. The flowers have reddish buds and open creamy-white with a yellowish center, before becoming white, often with a green button eye; the sepals are feathery. The scent is sweet and heavy, carried on the air like a Musk rose.

Garden notes 'Mme Plantier' is ideal for planting up a small tree or support; it is not so powerful that it can pull down the tree, like some species climbers. A lovely example was grown up an apple tree at Sissinghurst in Kent by Vita Sackville West; the combination of bright pink buds and white flowers is especially charming. Alba collector Richard Rix reports that 'Madame Plantier' is good on a north wall in southern England, and rosarian Clair Martin that it grows well in California, often surviving in old graveyards or by abandoned homesteads. Hardy to -15°F (-26°C), in Zone 5.

'Princesse Lamballe' An Alba or possibly Alba hybrid, known since around 1850. The stems grow to 5 ft (1.5 m), and the flowers are double and pure white. It is sometimes called 'Princesse de Lamballe'.

Garden notes Healthy plants flower prolifically. This is a rare variety, available in the United States from Mary's Plant Farm, Ohio, or in Europe from Jensen's Rosarium Glücksburg in Germany. Hardy to -30°F (-34°C), Zone 4.

'Royal Blush' A new Alba hybrid with a red *kordesii* rose, introduced in 1988 by Sievers in Germany, with robust stems, to 5 ft (1.5 m), and grayish leaves. The blush-pink flowers are fully double, often quartered, and borne over several weeks in early summer. The scent is good.

Garden notes Hardy to -30°F (-34°C), Zone 4.

'Summer Blush' A new Alba hybrid with a red *kordesii* rose, introduced in 1988 by Sievers in Germany. It has strong-growing, arching stems, to 5 ft (1.5 m). The flowers are bright red, fully double, and almost Gallica-like, produced only in early summer, with a strong, sweet scent.

Garden notes Hardy to -30°F (-34°C), Zone 4.

'Tender Blush' A new Alba hybrid with a *kordesii* rose, introduced in 1988 by Sievers in Germany. The stems reach 5 ft (1.5 m). The flowers are light pink touched with creamy orange, loosely double, and borne only in early summer.

Garden notes Hardy to -30°F (-34°C), Zone 4.

Centifolia Roses

'Cristata'

THE ORIGINAL CENTIFOLIA ROSE,
R. × *centifolia,* is often called 'The Old
Cabbage Rose', or 'Provence Rose':
this is not to be confused with the Rose of
Provins, R. *gallica* (*see p.33*). *Rosa* × *centifolia* is
thought to have originated in Dutch gardens
between the late 16th and the early 18th centuries,
and to be a hybrid between a Damask and an Alba.
Preliminary DNA studies suggest there is a close
relationship to the Damasks, but not to the Albas.

This rose was mentioned in 1581 by the botanist
Lobelius, also called Matthias de l'Obel, but the
date often given for it is 1596. This is the date of
Gerard's Herball, in which it is called "R. damascena
flore multiplici, the Great Holland rose, commonly
called the Province rose." In the 1597 edition it
appears as "R. Hollandica sive Batava, the Great
Holland Rose or Great Province". The association
with the Netherlands is confirmed by its frequent
and conspicuous occurrence in the foreground of
great Dutch flower paintings of the 17th century.

Some Centifolias are hybrids: because the original
R. × *centifolia* is sterile, these were created making
use of a single-flowered sport, which was first
recorded in 1796 but is now so rare that I have
never seen it. However, a particular feature of the
Centifolias is the readiness with which they mutate,
with a different rose appearing as a branch on the
main bush. Many of the varieties are known to have
arisen in this way, and also to have reverted to the
basic R. × *centifolia,* and the pure Centifolia roses
are mutations, or sports, as they are often called.

Many of the Moss roses, which are shown in a
separate section in this book, are also sports of
R. × *centifolia;* the original mossy sport, which
produced the old moss rose R. × *centifolia*
'Muscosa' (*see p.67*), was first recorded in 1696;
other old Moss roses are sports of Damasks.

A third group of Centifolia sports are the dwarfs,
which are similar to the large Centifolias, but
smaller in all their parts; they have also sported a
miniature moss, the 'Moss de Meaux'.

CENTIFOLIA ROSES

Rosa × centifolia (also called 'The Old Cabbage Rose', 'Centifolia', 'Provence Rose', 'Rose des Peintres')   An old rose, recorded in *Gerard's Herball* in 1596, and illustrated in *Hortus Eystettensis* in 1613. Stems to 5½ ft (1.6 m), variably thorny. The dark green leaves have sharp, coarse teeth. Loose clusters of pink buds touched with rosy red, the sepals with side lobes and a long tip, open to pale pink flowers. When half open these are nodding, cup-shaped, and more deeply colored in the center; later the outer petals recurve, the inner ones remaining upright. The flowering season is in summer only, and the scent is excellent.

Garden notes   A lovely, upright shrub with rather lush, dark leaves, and beautiful, pale flowers, suitable for the center of a rose border, or as a handsome free-standing shrub, especially if three are planted together. Hardy to -13°F (-25°C), in Zone 5.

'Bullata' (also called 'À Feuilles de Laitue', 'Lettuce Rose', *Rosa × centifolia* 'Bullata')   A sport of *R. × centifolia*, recorded in 1801 according to geneticist C.C. Hurst, and illustrated by Redouté in 1817. The particular feature of this variety is the leaves, which appear swollen between the veins. The flowers are the usual ones found on *R. × centifolia*.

Garden notes   Similar to *R. × centifolia* but for the large, puckered leaves. Hardy to -13°F (-25°C), in Zone 5.

'Cristata' (also called 'Chapeau de Napoléon', 'Crested Moss', *Rosa × centifolia* 'Cristata')   A sport of *R. × centifolia*, said to have been found in 1820 growing on a convent wall at Fribourg in Switzerland. The flowers and leaves are typical of *R. × centifolia*, but the sepals have stiff and repeatedly branching edges pushed together into three ridges, resembling a cockaded hat. It is not a true Moss, despite the synonym 'Crested Moss'.

Garden notes   Similar to *R. × centifolia*, but for the buds. Hardy to -13°F (-25°C), in Zone 5.

'Unique Blanche' (also called *Rosa × centifolia* 'Mutabilis', *Rosa provincialis alba*, 'Rose Unique', 'Unica Alba', 'Vièrge de Cléry', 'White Provence')   A sport of *R. × centifolia*, with stems to 4 ft (1.2 m) and dark green leaves with coarse, blunt teeth. The buds are greenish, tipped with crimson, and the flower stalks are distinctly reddish. The flowers themselves are pure white, with an inrolled rosette in the center and touches of crimson on the edges and sometimes in the center.

This rose is recorded by the botanical artist Henry Andrews in 1775 as *R. provincialis alba*, from a hedge near the premises

Rosa × centifolia

of a Dutch merchant at Needham in Suffolk; a "white province rose" is also mentioned in Tradescant's garden list of 1656. Other slightly different versions of the story of how this rose came to be commonly grown in England are mentioned by the geneticist C.C. Hurst in Graham Thomas' *The Old Shrub Roses*, but all agree that it was introduced from Suffolk by Daniel Grimwood Junior, who had a nursery with his father at Little Chelsea, near London. White Centifolia-like roses are also mentioned by Graham Thomas as being shown in works by Jan van Huysum and other 17th-century Dutch flower painters.

Garden notes   The shrub is shorter than most Centifolias; the white flowers are produced over a long period, "some six weeks longer than most Centifolias" according to Graham Thomas. Hardy to -13°F (-25°C), in Zone 5.

'Unique Blanche'

'Bullata'

CENTIFOLIA ROSES

'Village Maid'

'Le Rire Niais'

'Juno' A Centifolia-like rose raised in France by Laffay, who introduced one rose by this name in 1832, and then another in 1847, which was a pale pink China-Gallica hybrid. The flowers are like *R. × centifolia* (*see p.59*), but the leaves are smooth and show the influence of a China or Tea rose, and the rose shown here may be the China-Gallica hybrid. The plant is low, to 3½ ft (1.3 m), and the leaves are bright green, with quite small teeth. The flowers are often single or in pairs, of a lovely pale pink, beginning cup-shaped, the outer petals reflexing, and the whole flower finally opening rather flat. Whichever 'Juno' this is, it is a beautiful, delicately colored rose with a good scent.

Garden notes This is a lovely, low-growing rose; the flowering stems need support, preferably from a framework that is hidden at flowering time by the arching shoots. Hardy to -13°F (-25°C), in Zone 5.

'Le Rire Niais' (also called 'À l'Odeur de Punaise') A Centifolia raised by Dupont before 1810. Stems to 3 ft (1 m). The flowers are double, pink, and medium-sized. The

synonym 'À l'Odeur de Punaise' can be translated as the scent of a bug or, more attractively, of dogwood.

Garden notes An undistinguished rose with an unusual scent. It is available mainly in France. Hardy to -13°F (-25°C), in Zone 5.

'Prolifera de Redouté' A sport of *R. × centifolia* (*see p.59*) recorded in 1801, and painted by Redouté in 1824. It is a normal *R. × centifolia*, except that the flowers tend to proliferate in the center, producing another flower on top of the previous one. The flowers are a particularly full double, the outer petals becoming reflexed when the flower is fully open. Redouté also illustrates *R. × centifolia foliacea*, with the sepals enlarged and becoming leaflike, which is still listed by a few nurseries across North America, Europe, and Australia as 'Centifolia Foliacea'.

Garden notes Similar to *R. × centifolia*, but for the proliferating flowers. Hardy to -13°F (-25°C), in Zone 5.

'Reine des Centfeuilles' A Centifolia, first recorded in Belgium in 1824. Stems to 5 ft (1.5 m), bearing large, densely double, mid-pink flowers with a delicate scent.

Garden notes The growth habit is sometimes untidy, but the plant makes up for it by being very free-flowering. Hardy to -13°F (-25°C), in Zone 5.

'Village Maid' (also called 'Belles des Jardins', 'Cottage Maid', *Rosa × centifolia* 'Variegata') A striped sport of *R. × centifolia* (*see p.59*) introduced by the French breeder Vibert in 1845. This makes a bush to 6 ft (2 m) tall, with the usual rather puckered leaves of *R. × centifolia*. The flowers are white streaked with pale pink, and of delicate texture, easily spoiled by rain. They have been known to revert to normal pink *R. × centifolia*. It shares the synonym 'Village Maid' with the Gallica 'La Rubanée', which had pink flowers striped with white and violet and was recorded in 1832 in the catalog of the Paris garden owner Cels; French rosarian François Joyaux considers that this variety is extinct. 'Cottage Maid' is also a synonym of another striped Gallica, 'Perle des Panachées'.

Garden notes A very pale example of a striped rose, with the habit of *R. × centifolia* but more delicate flowers. Hardy to -13°F (-25°C), in Zone 5.

'Reine des Centfeuilles'

'Juno' at Hidcote Manor, southwestern England

'Prolifera de Redouté'

'Petite de Hollande'

'Petite de Hollande' (also called 'Pompon des Dames')
A small Centifolia, known since the late 18th century. It makes
a spreading shrub to 4½ ft (1.3 m), with typical Centifolia
leaves that are smaller than usual, and perfect double pink
flowers around 2½ in (6 cm) across.

    Garden notes This is a very pretty dwarf; the sprays of
flowers weigh down the branches, so it needs a little discreet
support. Hardy to -13°F (-25°C), in Zone 5.

'Petite Lisette' (also called 'Petite Liselette') A Damask-
Centifolia cross or perhaps a Damask, raised by Vibert of
Angers in 1817. Stems to 4½ ft (1.3 m), with numerous small,
recurved thorns. The leaflets are dark green with grayish down.
Sprays of red buds, with much-divided sepals
about as long as the petals, open to rather
small, mid- to pale pink, fully double and
quartered flowers with a good scent.

    Garden notes This is not as dwarf as
'Rose de Meaux', but makes a fairly bushy
plant, with neat leaves and flowers. Hardy
to -13°F (-25°C), in Zone 5.

'Petite Orléanaise' (also called 'Petite de
Orléanaise') A Centifolia or Gallica, first
mentioned by Paris nurseryman Verdier in
his 1843 catalog. Stems to 5 ft (1.5 m).
The light-green leaves have fine teeth,
slightly smoother than usual for a Gallica,
and the sepals have side lobes. Rather small,
fully double flowers, in clusters of two to six,
open flat with a rosette of small petals curled
around a button eye. They are deep pink, fading
at the edges, and the scent is very good.

    Garden notes An attractive, strong bush with small flowers.
French rosarian Joyaux damns it with faint praise as a "pleasant,
unassuming little rose." Hardy to -13°F (-25°C), in Zone 5.

'Rose de Meaux' (also called 'De Meaux', *Rosa pomponia*)
A miniature sport of *R. × centifolia* (*see p.59*), first recorded in
1637 according to Ellen Willmott's *Genus Rosa*. The plant has
many upright stems to 3 ft (90 cm) and small, pink flowers just
1¼ in (3 cm) across, early in the rose season. They are pale
pink, at first cup-shaped, later opening flat. The mossy sport of
this rose, called 'Mossy de Meaux' or 'Moss de Meaux', was

'Rose de Meaux'

'Petite Lisette'

'Rose de Meaux'

recorded in 1801. 'Parvifolia', also called 'Burgundian Rose', is a similar dwarf; it is often erroneously called *R. × centifolia* 'Parvifolia', but is a mutation of *R. gallica*, not of *R. × centifolia*.

Garden notes This is a real miniature, forming a thicket of upright stems. It should be grown at the front of a border or in other places where it can be seen up close. Hardy to -13°F (-25°C), in Zone 5.

'Spong' First recorded in Henry Andrews' *Roses* in 1805, this is a sport of 'Rose de Meaux' and has been known to revert to it. It makes a low shrub to 4½ ft (1.3 m), with rather stiff stems, very rounded and blunt-toothed leaflets, and rounded, loosely double flowers. 'Spong' is said to be the name of a nurseryman who raised large numbers of this rose.

Garden notes Mainly grown for historical interest, though the cupped flowers are very pretty. They have the untidy and unattractive habit of staying on the plant after they have turned brown, so the plant needs a little care after flowering. Hardy to -13°F (-25°C), in Zone 5.

'Spong'

'Petite Orléanaise'

'Blanchfleur' at Mottisfont Abbey, southern England, where roses and herbaceous plants are grown together

'Blanchfleur' A Centifolia hybrid, sometimes classed as a Damask, raised in France by Vibert in 1835. It forms a spreading bush to 6 ft (2 m) tall, with spiny, thorny stems and leaves of a rather pale green. Clusters of buds are pale pink with red touches, the sepals with a long point and side lobes. The flowers are palest pink on opening, becoming white with a pale pink center, fully double, neat and quartered with a small button eye, and very sweetly scented.

  Garden notes A neat and most attractive flower on a tall and spiny bush; the long shoots can be either reduced in length or tied down onto a low fence to flower along their length. Hardy to -13°F (-25°C), in Zone 5.

'Blue Boy' A seedling of the old Moss rose 'Louis Gimard' crossed with 'Independence' (a scarlet Floribunda), and introduced by Kordes in Germany in 1958. Stems upright, around 5 ft (1.5 m). The flowers are produced only in summer and are deep reddish-purple, with a tall bud but opening very double with a muddled center, and have an excellent scent.

  Garden notes A most interesting cross, valued for its dusky purple flowers. Rarely cultivated, but available from Vintage Gardens in California. Hardy to -13°F (-25°C), in Zone 5.

'Fantin-Latour' This favorite dates from around 1900; surprisingly, in view of its popularity, its origin is still unknown. It appears to be a hybrid between a Gallica and a Hybrid Tea, or it may be a Bourbon, but has the general look of *R. × centifolia* (*see p. 59*).

'Fantin Latour'

Stems grow to 6 ft (2 m), with large, dark green leaves that have smooth, overlapping leaflets. The buds are pink with red touches, the sepals narrow and mostly undivided. The flowers are large, around 3¼ in (8 cm) across. They open flat and fully double, with a mass of pale pink petals incurved around a small eye, and deeper pink flushes at the base of the petals. Finally the outer petals are reflexed. The scent is excellent.

The 19th-century French painter Henri Fantin-Latour is best known for his many still life paintings of flowers, and especially of roses.

Garden notes A large and blowsy rose, which forms a large, spreading bush or can be trained on a pillar. Flowering is only at midsummer, but it is still one of the best of the old shrub roses. Hardy to -13°F (-25°C), in Zone 5.

'Paul Ricault' A Centifolia hybrid, probably with a China, raised in Gentilly, France by Portemer in 1845, and sometimes classed as a Hybrid Perpetual. It forms an upright bush to 6 ft (2 m); the leaves are smooth, with small fine teeth. The sepals have few small, narrow side lobes. The flowers are very double, opening flat and quartered with a small button eye, deeper pink than *R. × centifolia* (*see p.59*), or even rich cerise on opening, fading to pale purplish-pink around the edges, with very good scent. Flowers are produced mainly in early summer.

Garden notes A loose shrub with large, nodding flowers, good for the center of a bed of old roses. Hardy to -13°F (-25°C), in Zone 5.

'The Bishop' (also called 'Évêque', 'La Rose Évêque', 'L'Évêque', 'Le Rosier Évêque', 'Manteau d'Évêque', 'Pourpre Belle Violette', 'Rosier Évêque') Although often classed as a Centifolia, this has much in common with the Gallicas, particularly in the purplish-gray color; it is first recorded in 1790, in the catalog of the Parisian nurseryman François. The stems grow to 6 ft (1.8 m), but are rather arching; the leaves are bright green. The flowers are fully double, in shades of magenta, gray, and purple, with a light scent.

Garden notes According to Graham Thomas "in the evening and after a hot day, this rose more nearly approaches blue than any other." It is a must for those who love dusky colors. Hardy to -13°F (-25°C), in Zone 5.

'Paul Ricault' at Mottisfont Abbey, southern England

'Blue Boy'

'The Bishop'

Moss Roses

'Quatre Saisons
Blanche Mousseuse'

MOSS ROSES WERE POPULAR in the 19th century, and were often used in decoration on pottery and china. In habit and flower colors they are like other Old Roses, but they are easily recognized by the dense, mossy covering on the flower stalks and backs of the sepals. This "moss" is formed by a large increase in the number of bristles and stiff hairs on the flower stalks, each tipped with a sticky and aromatic droplet of resinous liquid. The moss may be either bright green or brownish, which suggests that the mossy mutation has occurred at least twice; it is green and soft in Mosses mutated from Centifolias, and stiffer and brownish in those mutated from Damasks.

Most different varieties were introduced in France: they have been called "mousseux," but recent usage is changing to "mousseuse." One of the main raisers was Phillipe-Victor Verdier, whose nursery was at Ivry, near Paris, though his main efforts were directed toward Hybrid Perpetuals. Mosses were mostly once-flowering, so Verdier's aim was to raise Mosses that flowered in autumn as well as spring;

by using Autumn Damasks and Portlands, and possibly China roses as well, the nursery succeeded in producing reliable repeat-flowering Mosses. 'Baron de Wassenaer' (*see p. 72*), introduced in 1854, was one of Verdier's most successful Mosses.

Since the mid-19th century, the craze for Mosses has declined, but new ones have been introduced from time to time, such as 'Goethe' (*see p. 72*) in 1911, and 'Golden Moss' (*see p. 69*) in 1932. Even today Moss roses appear occasionally, and very pretty miniature Mosses are being introduced by Ralph S. Moore in California. One of these is the creeping 'Red Moss Rambler'.

Mosses need much the same treatment as their Damask or Centifolia parents; they need little pruning other than cutting off the dead flowering shoots and encouraging the new summer shoots. In the taller varieties these can be pegged down in autumn to make a low shrub, trained on a fence or a pillar, or even cut back by a third or more to keep them more compact. As with all Old Roses, feed well and prune after flowering.

Rosa × *centifolia* **'Muscosa'** (also called 'Centifolia Muscosa', 'Common Moss', Old Moss Rose) This is the original mossy mutant of *R.* × *centifolia* (*see p.59*), and it was first reported in the late 17th century growing in Carcassonne, France. It did not reach northern Europe until the early 18th century; Philip Miller of the Chelsea Physic Garden, London recorded that he saw it first in 1727 in a garden near Leyden in Holland, and brought it back to London from there.

The flowers and leaves are similar to the common *R.* × *centifolia*, but the flower stalks and sepals are covered in dense, soft, aromatic moss. The stems can reach 6 ft (1.8m). Flowering is in midsummer, but lasts for several weeks in a cool climate; scent is excellent, heavy and sweet.

Garden notes The stems can be trained on a fence or low support, or shortened by a third or more in late autumn. As good as ordinary *R.* × *centifolia*, but with the added bonus of the charming mossy buds. Hardy to -13°F (-25°C), in Zone 5.

'Centifolia Muscosa Alba' (also called 'Shailer's White Moss', 'White Bath') This white sport of *R.* × *centifolia* 'Muscosa' was first noted in 1788. It makes a loose bush to 5 ft (1.5m), with the same shape of flowers as its parent, usually all white with a pink flush on opening, though sometimes one flower appears that partially or wholly reverts to pink. They often show a green button eye. The scent is excellent.

Garden notes A companion for the original pink. Hardy to -13°F (-25°C), in Zone 5.

'Quatre Saisons Blanche Mousseuse' (also called 'Perpetual White Moss', 'Quatre Saisons Blanc Mousseux', *Rosa* 'Bifera Alba Muscosa') A white, mossy mutant of *R.* × *damascena* var. *semperflorens* (*see p.43*), which is sometimes also called

'Quatre Saisons', this first appeared in 1835, and its origin is confirmed by the regularity with which it reverts. It makes an upright bush to 5 ft (1.6m), with medium-sized, white flowers from very mossy flower stalks and buds with long, narrow sepals. The leaves are pale green with fine teeth. The flowers are well scented and are produced mainly in summer, with extra flowers into autumn. Good scent.

Garden notes The flowers are poorly formed in comparison with some other Moss roses, but it makes up for this with freedom of flowering in summer and a bonus in autumn. Hardy to -20°F (-29°C), Zone 5.

'Oeillet Panaché' (also called 'Striped Moss') A Damask Moss raised by Du Pont in Marseilles in 1880. The leaflets are rather narrow, on a small shrub to just under 3 ft (1 m). It has medium-sized, pale pink flowers streaked with deep pink; the scent is average.

'Oeillet Panaché'

Garden notes A useful rose for a large pot or tub, because of its short stature. Hardy to -20°F (-29°C), Zone 5.

Rosa × *centifolia* 'Muscosa' at Kasteel Hex, Belgium

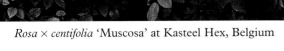

'Centifolia Muscosa Alba'

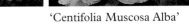

'Golden Moss'

'Contesse de Murinais'

'Duchesse d'Abrantes'

'Blanche Moreau' A Damask Moss with sweetly scented white flowers with a pale flesh-pink flush and good scent. The leaves are dark green. The strong stems, to 7 ft (2 m), have purplish, rather sparse moss. Introduced by Moreau-Robert of Angers, France in 1880. Most of the flowers are in summer, but a few are produced later in the year; this repeat flowering comes from the parent, 'Quatre Saisons Blanche Mousseuse' (*see p.67*), which was crossed with 'Comtesse de Murinais'.

Garden notes The tall stems need reducing to keep the plant tidy. Hardy to -20°F (-29°C), Zone 5.

'Comtesse de Murinais'
A tall shrub with upright stems to around 8 ft (3.5 m), and dark green leaves rather prone to mildew. The flowers are medium-sized, opening very pale pink before becoming white, produced mostly in summer with a few in autumn; both flowers and moss are well-scented. Riased by Vibert of Angers in 1843.

Garden notes This rose is tall enough to train on a pillar or as a low climber. Hardy to -20°F (-29°C), Zone 5.

'Duchesse d'Abrantes' A rather lax shrub to 5 ft (1.5 m) with bright pink, fully double flowers in summer only. Raised by Robert of Angers in 1851.

Garden notes A very rare but attractive rose, this is close to *R. × centifolia* 'Muscosa' (*see p.67*), but with brighter pink flowers. Hardy to -20°F (-29°C), Zone 5.

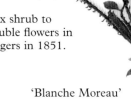

'Blanche Moreau'

MOSS ROSES

'Golden Moss' (also called 'Yellow Moss')   A tall, upright shrub with strong upright stems to 10 ft (3 m). The pinkish-orange buds open to rich, warm golden flowers with silky petals and excellent scent. Raised by Pedro Dot in Spain and introduced in 1932: the parentage is 'Frau Karl Druschki' (*see p. 122*) crossed with a seedling of the Hybrid Tea 'Souvenir de Claudius Pernet' and 'Blanche Moreau'.

    Garden notes   Rosarian Graham Thomas records that this is rather shy-flowering in England, but does better in warmer parts of North America, around the Mediterranean, and in the southern hemisphere. It is once-flowering, but worth growing for its unusual coloring. Hardy to -20°F (-29°C), Zone 5.

'Mme Louis Lévêque'   A Moss raised by Lévêque of Ivry, France in 1898. It makes a stiff, upright, bushy plant to 4 ft (1.2 m) with lush, bright green leaves. The sweetly scented flowers are pale pink and cupped, of Bourbon or Hybrid Perpetual rather than Damask shape, with the outer petals reflexing. They are produced mainly in summer; some late ones usually appear in autumn.

    Garden notes   A good garden shrub, with sprays of large flowers. The stems have little moss, and the flowers are similar to those of 'Mrs John Laing' (*see p. 125*). A Tea and a Hybrid Perpetual also with the name 'Mme Louis Lévêque' were introduced at around the same time; they are now lost. It appears that the plant shown here is sometimes grown as 'Gloire des Mousseuses'. Hardy to -20°F (-29°C), Zone 5.

'Marie de Blois'   A Moss raised by Robert in France in 1832. The stems, to 5 ft (1.5 m), are arching, with red thorns and dense red moss. The flowers are in clusters, of medium size, loosely double, and brilliant pink with paler highlights.

    Garden notes   This rose makes a charming, dense shrub with excellent scent, both from the flowers and the moss. It is often reported to flower from summer into autumn, though other accounts say it is once-flowering only. Hardy to -20°F (-29°C), Zone 5.

'Marie de Blois'

'Mme Louis Lévêque'

'Mme Louis Lévêque' at Mottisfont Abbey, southern England

'Soupert et Notting' at Mottisfont Abbey, southern England

'Mousseaux du Japon'

'Comtesse Doria' A Damask Moss, raised by Portemer fils in France in 1854. The flowers are double, purplish-pink with brighter highlights, with a good scent, produced in summer only.

   Garden notes A tall-growing variety, this is rare in gardens, but can be found at Rosarium Sangerhausen in Germany. Hardy to -20°F (-29°C), Zone 5.

'Eugénie Guinoisseau' A repeat-flowering Moss raised by Bertrand Guinoisseau in Angers, France in 1864. The clusters of flowers open deep pink, becoming maroon-purple shaded with lavender; both the flowers and the moss are well scented. Gregg Lowery of Vintage Gardens in California suggests that this is the true name for the repeat-flowering rose often grown as 'Mme de la Rôche-Lambert'.

   Garden notes A reliable repeat-flowerer, of no great height, perhaps to 5 ft (1.5 m). Guinoisseau also raised the famous deep crimson Hybrid Perpetual 'Empereur du Maroc' (*see p.121*) in 1858. Hardy to -20°F (-29°C), Zone 5.

'Little Gem' A miniature Damask Moss with deep pink flowers of good shape on a small bush up to 3 ft (1 m) high. An English variety raised by William Paul in 1880. Good scent.

   Garden notes The flowers are held in stiffly upright clusters; the moss is long and rather whiskery, but the plant is otherwise charming. Once-flowering only. Hardy to -20°F (-29°C), Zone 5.

'Mousseux du Japon' (also called 'Japonica', 'Moussu du Japon', 'Muscosa Japonica') A pleasant rose of unknown origin, which may have been raised in Japan, but was reintroduced in Europe in the 20th century. The stems grow to around 3 ft (1 m). The flowers are rich purplish-pink, surrounded by green moss.

   Garden notes A little-known rose, suitable for a choice position. Almost the whole plant is covered with green moss. Hardy to -20°F (-29°C), Zone 5.

'Soupert et Notting' An almost perpetual-flowering Damask Moss with a Bourbon-like flower. A short plant to 4 ft (1.2 m), with buds and flower stalks densely covered in green moss. The flowers are a good pink with a deeper center and well scented. This was raised by Pernet père in Lyon, France in 1874, and named for Soupert et Notting, a nursery in Luxembourg.

   Garden notes One of the best of all the Moss roses, with small sprays of neat flowers. Hardy to -20°F (-29°C), Zone 5.

'René d'Anjou' A Moss with pale purplish-pink flowers, raised by Robert in Angers in 1853. The leaflets are rather narrow, and the flower stalks thin, with brownish moss. Flowers are produced mainly in summer with a second flush in autumn. Gregg Lowery of Vintage Gardens, California reports that the older, once-flowering 'Gracilis', raised by Prévost before 1829, is often grown under the name 'René d'Anjou'; it is also very close to 'A Longues Pédoncules', but that has broader leaflets and pale, clear pink flowers.

   Garden notes This rose makes a tallish shrub, with stems to 5 ft (1.5 m), and loose sprays of flowers arching over, especially in wet weather. Hardy to -20°F (-29°C), Zone 5.

'Little Gem'

'Comtesse Doria' photographed at the Rosarium Sangerhausen in Germany

'Eugénie Guinoiseau'

'René d'Anjou'

'Louis Gimard'

'Baron de Wassenaer' A lovely rose with cupped flowers of rich pink with a good scent, produced in large clusters over a long period. The flower shape suggests that one parent may have been a Bourbon. It was raised by Victor Verdier in Paris, France in 1854, a time when Bourbons were very popular. The moss is brownish; the leaves have broad leaflets. Good scent.

Garden notes The bushes are upright, to 4 ft (1.2 m), gracefully arching under the weight of flowers. The color is unusual and most attractive in an old-fashioned way. Hardy to -20°F (-29°C), Zone 5.

'Gloire d'Orient' A Moss rose with deep purplish-red flowers, medium-sized, with a good scent, introduced by Jean Béluze of Lyon in 1856. The stems reach around 5 ft (1.5 m).

Garden notes A rare variety, photographed at Rosarium Sangerhausen in Germany. Hardy to -20°F (-29°C), Zone 5.

'Goethe' A relatively modern Moss, raised by Peter Lambert in Trier, Germany in 1911. The stems reach 7 ft (2 m) or more, and the flowers, produced only in summer, are carried in upright sprays. They are quite small, almost single, and crimson with a white center and white streaks on some of the petals, making this one of the most wild-looking of the Mosses.

Garden notes The new stems are striking, with masses of red thorns in addition to the moss. In naming this rose Peter Lambert must have had in mind Goethe's 'Heidenröslein' of the boy who picks a beautiful wild rose despite its thorns. Hardy to -20°F (-29°C), Zone 5.

'Laneii' (also called 'Lane's Moss') One of the older Moss roses, introduced by Laffay in Bellevue-Meudon, France in 1845. This is one of the repeat-flowering Mosses, with mauve-pink, fully double flowers held upright on a stiff stalk.

Garden notes A tall-growing shrub, with brownish, sticky moss, and flowers of muted color suitable for subdued color schemes. Hardy to -20°F (-29°C), Zone 5.

'Louis Gimard' A Damask Moss, probably a China cross, raised by Pernet père in Lyon in 1877. It makes a low bush around 5 ft (1.5 m) tall, with dark green leaves. The flowers are well scented, purplish-pink with a crimson center on opening, with good scent. The moss is also well scented.

Garden notes The stems arch down under the weight of the large flowers. Hardy to -20°F (-29°C), Zone 5.

'Laneii'

'Gloire d'Orient'

'Goethe'

'Baron de Wassenaer' at Mottisfont Abbey, southern England

'William Lobb' at Hidcote Manor, Gloucestershire

'Black Boy' This modern Moss was raised by Kordes in Sparrieshoop, Germany in 1958 by crossing the dark red Floribunda 'World's Fair' with 'Nuits de Young'. The buds are not very mossy; the flowers are large, fully double, with an excellent scent, and very dark crimson.

Garden notes A strong-growing, upright shrub with light-green, leathery leaves. Flowers in midsummer only. Hardy to -20°F (-29°C), Zone 5.

'Capitaine John Ingram' (also called 'Captain John Ingram') A dark-flowered Damask Moss, raised by Laffay in Bellevue-Meudon, France in 1854. the flowers are close to 'Nuits de Young', but they have neater, reflexing petals of slightly richer color, opening crimson, becoming purple, and with a good scent. It makes a shrub to 4 ft (1.2 m) high, and the leaflets are broad with impressed veins. The moss on the stalks and flower buds is rather thin.

Garden notes These almost black Moss roses tend to have rather small flowers, but look very impressive contrasting with pinks and reds. Hardy to -20°F (-29°C), Zone 5.

'Crimson Globe' A modern Moss rose of unrecorded parentage, which was introduced by William Paul of Waltham Cross, England in 1890. It has strong-growing stems that reach to perhaps 5 ft (1.5 m). The flowers are deep crimson, large and remaining globular after opening, with excellent scent, but only flowering in summer.

Garden notes This rose does not thrive in wet, cool summers, such as it often gets in England, but does well in

warmer and drier climates, such as North America. This example was photographed in the United States by Bill Grant at Lowe's Roses of Nashua, New Hampshire. Hardy to -20°F (-29°C), Zone 5.

'Henri Martin' (also called 'Red Moss') A Damask Moss raised by Laffay in Bellevue-Meudon, France in 1863. The stems reach 7 ft (2.2 m). The flowers are semidouble, a good crimson on opening, becoming purplish and showing stamens as they fade. The scent is sweet, typical of Old Roses. The flower stalks are unusually long and slender, and well covered in long, thin moss.

Garden notes The tall stems of this rose are best with some support, and it is said to

'Capitaine John Ingram'

do well on a north wall in hotter areas; this position will also improve the intensity of color of the flowers. Hardy to -20°F (-29°C), Zone 5.

'Nuits de Young' (also called 'Black Moss', 'Old Black') A Damask Moss with very dark purple flowers raised by Laffay in Bellevue-Meudon, France 1845. The plant is upright, to 5 ft (1.5 m), and the leaves are small and dark. The medium-sized flowers are among the darkest of all Old Roses, as dark as the ancient Gallicas, and showing some stamens when fully open. Their scent is good.

Garden notes With its rather small flowers, this has the aspect of a mossy Gallica, and like the Gallicas it suckers freely when grown on its own roots. Hardy to -20°F (-29°C), Zone 5.

'William Lobb' (also called 'Duchesse d'Istrie', 'Old Velvet Moss') A tall shrub, throwing up long canes to over 8 ft (2.5 m). The medium-sized flowers are formed in clusters and are purplish crimson on opening, fading to purple and then almost gray. Raised by Laffay of Bellevue-Meudon, France in 1855. Although this is a Bourbon cross, it flowers only once. Good scent.

Garden notes This rose often survives in old gardens and is very tough and long-lived. Like 'Comtesse de Murinais' (*see p.68*), it is suitable for the back of a border or for training up a pole or on a fence, because the long, stiff summer shoots will fall over in an unattractive way if left unsupported. Hardy to -20°F (-29°C), Zone 5.

'Black Boy'

'Henri Martin'

'Nuits de Young'

'William Lobb'

'Crimson Globe'

Portland Roses

'Rose du Roi'

PORTLAND ROSES TAKE their name from Margaret Cavendish Bentinck, second Duchess of Portland: in 1805 the botanical artist Andrews noted in his *Roses* that they were named "in compliment to the late Duchess." She grew them in her botanic garden at Bulstrode in Gloucestershire, and the name was in use from about 1775, although the original Portland rose, 'Portlandica', with red, semidouble flowers, said to have come from Italy, was first recorded as a Portland rose in 1782.

One theory about the parentage of 'Portlandica' was that it came from the Autumn Damask, *R. × damascena* var. *semperflorens* (*see p.43*), crossed with *R. gallica* 'Officinalis' (*see p.33*), and this has been supported recently by DNA studies. Later theories included *R. chinensis* var. *semperflorens* or 'Slater's Crimson China' (*see p.83*) in the parentage, but these are now thought less likely.

After 1835, however, the Portlands were eclipsed by their progeny, the Hybrid Perpetuals, or the Hybrides Remontants as they are more accurately termed in France, which have the parentage of Portland roses crossed with China hybrid or Bourbon roses. Some of the roses shown here are listed by others as Hybrid Perpetuals, but here we have kept the ones with Gallica-like flowers with the Portlands. These later Portlands have fully double, pink and cerise flowers, and they are taller growing, but they remain a small group, closely allied to the Autumn Damask, and sometimes called Damask Perpetuals.

The small number of true Portlands introduced may have been due not to a lack of popularity, but to the difficulty in breeding the repeat-flowering Damask; it has been reported that of the many thousands of seeds of 'Rose du Roi' that were sown by the celebrated amateur breeder M. Desprez, all produced once-flowering roses.

Portlands can be recognized by their short flower stalks and large upper leaves: the flowers appear to sit tightly down on the leaves. All are very hardy, surviving down to -20°F (-29°C) and thriving in tough climates such as Texas, where cold and intense heat can weaken more delicate groups.

'Mogador'

'Portlandica' at Mottisfont Abbey in southern England

'Indigo' A fine flower of the bluest purple, especially after it has been open for a day or two, is characteristic of this rose. It was raised by Laffay in France before 1854. The flowers appear in autumn as well as in summer, and the scent is excellent. The stems are upright, to 4 ft (1.2 m).

Garden notes This distinct rose is very rare, but is in two great European rose collections, at Sangerhausen in Germany and at Mottisfont in England, as well as a number of specialist nurseries in North America, Europe, and Australia. Hardy to -20°F (-29°C), Zone 5.

'Mogador' (also called 'Roi des Poupres', 'Rose du Roi à Fleur Pourpre') A sport of 'Rose du Roi', introduced by Victor Varangot in Melun, France in 1844. The large, cupped flowers are bright crimson shaded with purple. Upright stems to 4 ft (1.2 m) bear numerous small, red thorns and bristles; the leaves are light green. Its parent, 'Rose du Roi', was valued in the early 19th century as the best repeat-flowering red.

Garden notes The general effect of the plant is close to 'Rose du Roi', but the flowers are much more double and of a darker red. Hardy to -20°F (-29°C), Zone 5.

'Portlandica' (also called 'Duchess of Portland', 'Portland Rose', *Rosa paestana*, *Rosa × portlandica*) Rather short stems, to 3 ft (1 m), with few thorns and Damask-like leaves form a suckering thicket. The numerous bright red, semidouble flowers are produced both in summer and again in autumn. The repeat-flowering and the brighter red hue distinguish this from *R. gallica* 'Officinalis' (*see p.33*); it is not surprising that they are so similar, since this rose is around three-quarters Gallica.

Garden notes Because of its suckering habit, this rose needs a space in which it will not become a nuisance if grown on its own roots, and it is not really special enough for a choice spot; on a rough bank or hillside it will make a fine splash of red. Hardy to -20°F (-29°C), Zone 5.

'Rose du Roi' (also called 'Lee's Crimson Perpetual', 'Rose Lelieur') This classic rose, parent of so many later hybrids and most modern rose groups, was raised in 1819, possibly by a M. Écoffay, gardener to M. Souchet, a florist in Sèvres, France. The stems reach around 3 ft (1 m), and bear numerous small thorns and red bristles. The flowers are fully double, bright red shot with purple, and around 2½ in (6 cm) across, with good scent.

Garden notes A low grower, similar to 'Portlandica', but with a finer flower and a good repeater; it is only let down by its harsh coloring, which is now out of favor having been superseded by duskier crimsons or brighter reds. Hardy to -20°F (-29°C), Zone 5.

'Indigo'

'Comte de Chambord'

'Yolande d'Aragon'

'Comte de Chambord' (also called 'Mme Boll', 'Mme Knorr') One of the best of the pink-flowered old roses, raised by Robert and Moreau in Angers around 1860. Upright stems reach 4 ft (1.2 m); the leaves have unusually few leaflets, three to five, which are smooth and rich green. The bright pink flowers, with hints of lilac, are large and open flat, on a thick stalk with short bristles, which tapers into the ovary. The scent is excellent, and good flowers are produced well into autumn.

Garden notes The great rosarian Graham Thomas calls this "a first class plant"; strange then that it received little praise when it was introduced. Rose historian Brent Dickerson accounts for this by saying that the true 'Comte de Chambord' was not outstanding, and the rose now called by this name is another, originally called 'Mme Boll', also raised in Angers and named for a New York rosarian. 'Mme Boll' was greatly praised in its day, and had the unusual trait of three or five leaflets, so it is highly likely that the names have become confused and the rose shown here should be called 'Mme Boll'; it is often classed as a Hybrid Perpetual. 'Mme Knorr' is also sometimes quoted as the correct name for the rose grown as 'Comte de Chambord', but according to several early accounts this had markedly two-tone flowers. Hardy to -20°F (-29°C), Zone 5.

'Jacques Cartier' (also called 'Marchesa Boccella') Usually known as 'Jacques Cartier', this rose should probably be called 'Marquise de Boccella'. It was raised by M. Desprez in Yébles, France in 1840. The stems are up to 5 ft (1.5 m) and the leaves are bright green, with five to seven long-pointed leaflets. The flowers are perfectly double, quartered with a button eye, pale pink, often with leafy sepals, and have an excellent scent.

Garden notes The second flowering is often as late as October in England, but the rose is an excellent one for a small garden, since its habit is neat and upright. As with 'Comte de Chambord', this is often found listed with the Hybrid Perpetuals. Hardy to -20°F (-29°C), Zone 5.

'Rembrandt' photographed at the Rosarium Sangerhausen in Germany

'Marbrée'

'Comte de Chambord' in the walled garden at Mottisfont Abbey, southern England

'Marbrée'   A Portland raised by Robert and Moreau in Angers, France in 1858. Stems to 4 ft (1.2 m). The flowers are bright pink, marbled with white, and have little scent.
   Garden notes   This is essentially a striped 'Portlandica' *(see p. 77)*. Hardy to -20°F (-29°C), Zone 5.

'Rembrandt'   A Portland or Portland-China hybrid, raised by Moreau-Robert in Angers in 1883. The flowers are large and mauve-pink shaded with carmine, sometimes with a few white streaks: these white streaks are a very clear characteristic of the red Chinas.
   Garden notes   A strong-growing shrub, flowering over a long season from summer to autumn. This is often found listed under Hybrid Perpetuals. Hardy to -20°F (-29°C), Zone 5.

'Yolande d'Aragon' (also called 'Iolande', 'Jolanda d'Aragon') A Portland raised by Vibert in Angers, France in 1843. The stems are upright, to 5 ft (1.5 m), and the leaves light green. The flowers are often in sprays, fully double, deep pink in the center fading towards the edges, with excellent scent.
   Garden notes   This is good for its late flowering, as well as for its large flowers, which are globular with a flat top. It is often found listed under Hybrid Perpetuals, and the name is also open to doubt. Hardy to -20°F (-29°C), Zone 5.

'Jacques Cartier'

79

China Roses

'Sanguinea'

IN THE LATE 18TH CENTURY the China rose brought the gene for more-or-less continual production of flower buds into European garden roses. Perpetual-flowering garden roses had been grown in China for many years before they came to Europe. It is not known exactly where or when this mutation arose: the earliest example is the rather slender evidence of a painting on silk, dating from around A.D. 965, but there are very few references to roses in Chinese horticultural literature until the 18th century.

The date of first introduction to Europe is equally uncertain. Roses in 16th-century Italian paintings have been identified as Chinas. Among 32 roses in his garden at Lambeth, London in 1656, John Tradescant listed *R. mensalis*, the monthly rose; it is also mentioned by John Evelyn in his *Elysium Britannicum*, written between 1650 and 1706, as coming from Italy. A specimen is found in the herbarium of Gronovius, named in 1733, but the dates given in the entries here, when living plants were brought by ship from Canton, are those generally accepted in rose literature, and these were the first China roses used for breeding on any scale. The early China roses were soon improved upon by breeders in France, and it is mainly because of their great toughness and reliable perpetual flowering that the older ones shown here have survived at all. In time these China hybrids led to the massive development of the Teas and Hybrid Teas in the 20th century.

The wild China rose is a once-flowering climber with solitary flowers: the roses on this spread are those closest to it in appearance. The cultivated Chinas as defined at present are repeat-flowering, dwarf roses with their flowers in small clusters, and are probably hybrids with a dwarf, repeat-flowering mutation of *R. multiflora* var. *cathayensis*. Genetic studies have shown the cultivated Chinas and the Noisettes to fall into the same group, described as ill-defined, and showing transitions to the Teas, Bourbons, Hybrid Perpetuals, and Polyanthas. This explains why the Chinas are so varied: in the complex world of Old Roses, the traditional catagories cannot be defined exactly.

Early chromosome counts showed that some, such as 'Parson's Pink China' (*see p.82*) and most of the other pink ones, were fertile diploids, and that others, mostly the red ones, were sterile triploids; later counts gave rather different results, with the earliest red varieties all diploid, and the Bourbon-like 'Hermosa' (*see p.82*) a triploid. Some of the original varieties became extinct in Europe, but in the 1950s were found to have survived in the warm climate and relative isolation of Bermuda, and brought back from there to general cultivation.

Chinas need only a little pruning and the tidying away of dead wood and old flowering stems, but thrive on rich feeding, with ample warmth and water in summer. The climbing varieties need extra feeding and watering to make good-size plants.

'Matteo's Silk Butterflies'

'Matteo's Silk Butterflies' (also called LETsilk)   A China hybrid, raised by Kleine Lettunich, California in 1992. Height to 5 ft (1.5 m), and as much across. Large, branched sprays of delicate, single flowers with a sweet scent open cream and turn pink; flowering continues into winter in mild climates. It is close to the species, being a seedling of 'Mutabilis', possibly with 'Francis E. Lester' (a seedling of 'Kathleen') as the other parent, which makes it a Hybrid Musk. The scent is not strong.

Garden notes   This is a particularly free-flowering rose: due to the large number of flowers compared with its leaf area, it needs good feeding and plenty of water to appear at its best. It is wonderful in California, less free-growing in the cooler climate of northern Europe. Hardy to 5°F (-15°C), in Zone 7.

'Mutabilis' (also called *Rosa chinensis* var. *mutabilis*, 'Tipo Ideale')   One of the most charming old China roses, bearing masses of single flowers in loose, branched, red-twigged heads throughout warm weather until the first serious frost. The flowers open pale apricot, becoming pink. Of unknown origin, but probably an old Chinese garden rose, and seen recently in China by Japanese botanist Mikinori Ogisu. It has little scent.

Though the name 'Mutabilis' dates from 1934, according to Graham Thomas this was first recorded in Italy in 1894 when Prince Giberto Borromeo took a specimen to an exposition in Geneva, and it was seen by Henri Correvon; it was growing in the Borromeo garden on Isola Madre in Lago di Maggiore,

where it formed a hedge around 6 ft (2 m) high. It is said to have come to Italy from the island of Réunion.

Garden notes   A robust bush to 6 ft (2 m) or more if grown on a warm wall where it can form strong, woody shoots. One of the prettiest single roses for a warm climate such as California. Hardy to 5°F (-15°C), in Zone 7.

Rosa chinensis var. *spontanea* (also called *Rosa chinensis*, 'Henry's Crimson China') This climber, once-flowering in the wild, is a very variable species, with flowers that may be red, pink, or creamy white. Another form is shown with the description of this species in its native habitat in the Wild Roses section (*see p.13*).

Garden notes   A fine garden shrub for warm climates such as California, probably also from Virginia southwards in areas with warm spring weather, since cold, wet springs damage the flower buds. Hardy to 5°F (-15°C), in Zone 7.

'Mutabilis'

'Sanguinea' (also called 'Bengal Crimson', 'Miss Lowe', 'Rose de Bengale')   A single-flowered China of unknown origin, with flowers with firm petals, around 3½ in (9 cm) across, deep red, or pink in cold weather. Leaves smooth and bluish-green. Smaller-flowered forms are often called 'Miss Lowe's Variety'.

Garden notes   The same plant can be either a dwarf shrub to 2 ft (60 cm) tall, or, with support or on a warm wall, a large shrub 10 ft (3 m) or more high and wide. In warm climates it is truly continuous flowering. Hardy to 5°F (-15°C), in Zone 7.

'Single Pink China'   This may be a single sport of 'Parson's Pink China' (*see p.82*), but is also an old Chinese variety, still to be found in gardens there. It was mentioned in Vibert's catalog of 1820, so was one of the early introductions. Little scent.

Garden notes   I have seen this in Chengdu, China, forming a bush around 6 ft (1.8 m) tall. In cool gardens in Europe it is usually much smaller, to 2 ft (60 cm). Ample water, fertilizer, and warmth are needed to form a good plant. Hardy to 5°F (-15°C), in Zone 7.

Rosa chinensis var. *spontanea*
from Leibo, southern
Sichuan

'Single Pink China'

'Bengale d'Automne'

'Camélia Rose'

'Multipetala'

'Bengale d'Automne' (also called 'Rosier des Indes') Repeat-flowering, bearing clusters of nodding, mid- to deep pink, fully double, medium-sized flowers with little scent. This is similar to, but deeper pink than 'Hermosa'. Introduced by Laffay in France in 1825, but possibly an import from China via India; Laffay was a prolific raiser of Chinas, and in 1829 Desportes listed no less than 253 named varieties of so-called "Bengales", meaning Chinas, Teas, and their hybrids.

Garden notes A lax shrub with stems around 4 ft (1.2 m), the flowers tend to nod under their weight especially in wet weather. Hardy to 5°F (-15°C), in Zone 7.

'Camélia Rose' (also called 'Camellia Rose') A China with possibly some Noisette influence, raised by Prévost of Rouen in around 1830. It is a strong-growing plant to 5 ft (1.5 m). The flowers are double, pink suffused with purple, and produced continually through the summer. The good scent indicates Noisette parentage.

Garden notes Though quite rare in cultivation, this pretty rose is grown by several nurseries across North America, Europe, and Australia. Hardy to 5°F (-15°C), in Zone 7.

'Hermosa' (also called 'Mélanie Lemaire', 'Armosa') A China-Bourbon hybrid, like an improved version of 'Parson's Pink China'. The flowers are cupped, plain lilac-pink, fully double, with firm petals, with a delicate scent. The stems have few thorns, and the smooth leaflets are bluish beneath. Raised by Marcheseau in France in 1834, probably from 'Parson's Pink China' crossed with 'Mme Desprez', a pink Bourbon.

Garden notes A good rose that flowers particularly well in autumn, even in wet seasons when other roses fail. In the bush form the stems reach 5 ft (1.5 m); a climbing sport, 'Setina', was introduced in 1879. Hardy to 5°F (-15°C), in Zone 7.

'Multipetala' An old China rose, grown at Kasteel Hex in southern Belgium since the 18th century. It was sent to the Prince Bishop of Liège, Charles de Velbrück, by La Compagnie des Indes, and is one of a large collection of old roses grown at this chateau. Flowers double, nodding, pale pink, somewhat similar to 'Parson's Pink China', with little scent.

Garden notes A shrub to around 5 ft (1.5m), flowering continuously from summer to early winter. Hardy to 5°F (-15°C), in Zone 7.

'Parson's Pink China' (also called R. × odorata 'Pallida', 'Old Blush', 'Common China', 'Old China', 'Monthly Rose') This, one of the original China roses, was definitely brought to Europe from Canton by the explorer Peter Osbeck in 1751, but may have already been growing in southern Europe. Some authors attribute it to Captain Ekeberg around 1763, or to James Kerr, chief surgeon to the East India Company from 1774. It was introduced into commerce from the garden of Mr Parsons of Rickmansworth near London in 1793, and from him derived its common English name.

'Hermosa'

'Parson's Pink China' in a village garden in Sichuan, western China

'Slater's Crimson China'

Around five to ten mid-pink flowers, which darken as they age, are produced in a branching head. They are loosely double, and just over 2 in (6 cm) across. The shrub form grows to 4 ft (1.2 m); there is a climbing form, which can reach 8 ft (2.5 m). It is an old Chinese garden rose with little scent, and may have some *R. multiflora* var. *cathayensis* in its ancestry.

Garden notes This is a hardy, free-flowering shrub, easy to root from cuttings. We have seen it growing in village gardens in western China as well as by old farms in Devon. 'Parson's Pink China' is still a good garden rose in a mild climate: long-lived, flowering throughout the summer and autumn, and growing well in humid summers. Hardy to 5°F (-15°C), in Zone 7.

'Slater's Crimson China' (also called 'Belfield', 'Bengale de Chine Semperflorens'. 'Monthly Rose', 'Old Crimson China', *Rosa chinensis* 'Semperflorens', *Rosa × odorata* 'Semperflorens') Usually a dwarf shrub, around 1 ft (30 cm) tall, with deep red flowers flecked with white, on slender, nodding stalks. An early introduction to Europe from Chinese gardens, reported in 1790. It was considered lost in Europe until reintroduced in

1956 from Belfield in Bermuda. It was the parent of most of the early deep red roses, to which it gave the rather weak flower stalks, and often the presence of a white streak or two on the inner petals. Little scent.

Garden notes This rose is still grown in western China: though long-lived in gardens, it is never very strong, needing good cultivation, warmth, and rich soil to grow into a decent bush. Hardy to 5°F (-15°C), in Zone 7.

'Parson's Pink China'

'Carnation Rose'

'Carnation Rose' (also called 'Carnation')   A found China rose from Bermuda. Flowers upright, medium pink with a paler reverse and pale, slightly crinkled edges, and little scent.
  Garden notes This is one of the ancient roses that became extinct in Europe, but survived in warmer Bermuda. It makes a small shrub to 5 ft (1.5m). Hardy to 5°F (-15°C), in Zone 7.

'Cramoisi Supérieur' (also called 'Agrippina', 'Lady Brisbane', 'Queen of Scarlet')   A China rose raised in 1832 by M. Coquereau at La Maître-École near Angers, and introduced into trade by Vibert; it is reported to be a seedling of 'Slater's Crimson China' (*see p.83*). The flowers are deep crimson-red, fully double with the outer petals reflexed, showing a few stamens when fully open, flowering over a long period, with little scent. The leaflets have coarse, uneven teeth. There is a climbing sport, known as 'James Sprunt' in America.
  Garden notes This makes a low shrub with stems growing to 3 ft (1 m), and has a long flowering period. The cupped,

richly colored flowers were considered a great improvement on those of its parent. Hardy to 5°F (-15°C), in Zone 7.

'Fabvier' (also called 'Colonel Fabvier', 'Général Fabvier')
A China raised by Laffay in 1832, with loose clusters of flowers around 2½ in (6 cm) across, crimson-scarlet with the odd white streak, semidouble and showing golden stamens when fully open. There is little scent. The leaves are dark green.
  Garden notes Slender but upright stems reach around 3 ft (1 m). The flowers are reported to be more tolerant of wet weather than those of other red Chinas. Hardy to 5°F (-15°C), in Zone 7.

'Fellemberg' (also called 'Fellenberg')   A China, sometimes listed as a Noisette, raised by Fellemberg in 1835. A tall plant, to 10 ft (3 m), it is free-flowering from summer to late autumn, with rather small flowers in sprays of up to 50, loosely double and cupped, bright crimson to deep pink, with white streaks. Probably a cross of 'Slater's Crimson China' (*see p.83*) and repeat-flowering *R. multiflora* (*see p.17*), this may have been an introduction from China.
  Garden notes Roses of this type are commonly seen growing through hedges and other shrubs in old Chinese gardens, for example on Mount Omei. It is particularly good in warm climates; the autumn flowers are often finer than those produced in the summer. Hardy to 5°F (-15°C), in Zone 7.

'Fellemberg'

'Cramoisi Supérieur' in Georgetown Cemetery, California Gold Country

'Fabvier'

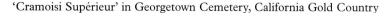

'Fellemberg' at Mottisfont Abbey in southern England

'Gloire des Rosomanes' (also called 'Ragged Robin', 'Red Robin')   A China-Bourbon hybrid with thorny stems up to 15 ft (5 m) in a warm climate. The flowers are semidouble with numerous stamens, deep crimson, with the petals white at the base and with the occasional white streak, sweetly-scented, and repeat-flowering well into autumn. The leaflets have long, curved teeth. Raised by M. Plantier of La Guillotière, Lyon, and introduced by Vibert in 1825.

Garden notes This rose was used as a rootstock in the past, and is now often found apparently wild, for instance in California, usually on the site of a deserted cottage or cemetary. As a garden plant it is tough and especially suitable for poor soils. Hardy to 5°F (-15°C), in Zone 7.

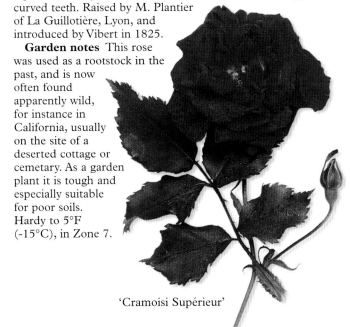

'Cramoisi Supérieur'

'Gloire des Rosomanes'

'Le Vésuve', a large example at Mottisfont Abbey, southern England

'Comtesse du Caÿla'   A China hybrid raised by Guillot in Lyon, France in 1902. The flowers are well scented, produced regularly throughout the season, semidouble, and generally coppery-orange with varying amounts of red, depending on the temperature. The parentage is a seedling of the Teas 'Rival de Paestum' and 'Mme Falcot', crossed with 'Mme Falcot'.

   Garden notes   A small plant, usually less than 3 ft (1 m), making it suitable for a choice spot in the front of a border.

'Sophie's Perpetual'

This is one of the most modern China hybrids, which have much in common, with small Teas, particularly in their range of coloring. Hardy to 5°F (-15°C), in Zone 7.

'Duke of York'   Raised by William Paul of Waltham Cross, England in 1894, and usually classed as a China hybrid. The flowers are pinkish-apricot, becoming redder as they age; their scent is good and it repeat-flowers well. There is some doubt as to whether this is true to name, since a Tea rose is also sold under this name. An early description by William Paul describes this rose as "remarkable for its bicolour peculiarity, the centres of the flowers being often flamed with carmine, and the outsides and edges almost white. Generally however the colour is rich carmine shaded with white." The leaves are dark and shining.

   Garden notes   A short plant, around 3 ft (1 m) and upright, Paul also described this as "a good grower, suitable for pots". Hardy to 5°F (-15°C), in Zone 7.

'Irene Watts'   A modern hybrid, raised by Guillot in Lyon, France in 1895, with well-shaped, fully double flowers throughout the season, well into autumn. The color varies from salmon to pale pink or white tinted with pink. The leaves are often purplish. It is a seedling of Mme Laurette Messimy, itself a Tea seedling that is usually classed as a China.

   Garden notes   A low plant, rarely reaching more than 2 ft (60 cm), and so ideal for the front of a border or other choice

'Irene Watts'

'Comtesse du Caÿla'

'Duke of York'

position, like 'Comtesse du Caÿla'. Pink 'Gruß an Aachen' (*see p. 227*) has been known to be sold under this name in the United States. Hardy to 5°F (-15°C), in Zone 7.

'Le Vésuve' (also called 'Lemesle') A lovely rose with similarities to 'Mutabilis' (*see p. 81*) and the Tea roses, raised by Laffay of Bellevue-Meudon, France in 1825 and sometimes listed with Teas. Shapely red buds open into rich pink flowers, sometimes with hints of lilac. The outer petals remain red, or the whole flower becomes rich crimson and nods gracefully, in shape like a loose Hybrid Tea. A climbing form was introduced by Guillot in 1904, but sadly it is lost.

   Garden notes I have found this an excellent rose, flowering continuously until the winter in mild climates, hardy, and free from disease. It makes a stiff, twiggy bush to 5 ft (1.5 m) tall, but often less, with red twigs, the older stems clad in strong, sharp thorns. Plant three or five together to form a really fine bush and give it good treatment. Hardy to 5°F (-15°C), in Zone 7.

'Sophie's Perpetual' A China hybrid, sometimes listed as a Bourbon, striking for its pale center and deep red outer petals. The flowers are double, cupped, in small sprays, and well scented; the stems have few thorns. This rose must have been planted before 1928, but was named around 1960 by Humphrey Brooke, a connoisseur of old roses, for his wife's grandmother Sophie, Countess Beckendorf, wife of the last Czarist ambassador to London, who started the garden at Lime Kiln, Essex.

   Garden notes A striking bicolor, growing to 8 ft (2.4 m) in a warm position. Its origin is unknown, but similar roses are found in western China; at a temple near Lijiang there is one that shows a similar color change. Some claim that it is the same as 'Bengale Centfeuilles', raised by Noisette, or 'Dresden China', raised by Paul. Hardy to 5°F (-15°C), in Zone 7.

'Pompon de Paris' against a wall with *Ceanothus* 'Puget Blue'

'Bébé Fleuri' A China hybrid raised in 1906 by Dubreuil in Lyon, France. The flowers are small, in clusters of three to five, pink or red, sometimes with white stripes, and lightly scented.

Garden notes A low-growing shrub to around 2 ft (60 cm). Hardy to 5°F (-15°C), in Zone 7. This rare rose was preserved at Sangerhausen, in former East Germany. The restrictions of the two world wars, followed by the isolation of communism, led to the careful preservation of the existing roses, new ones from the West being almost impossible to obtain.

'Darius' A China-Gallica hybrid, raised in 1827 by Laffay of Bellevue-Meudon, France. It has stems to 6 ft (2 m). The lilac, often streaked flowers are medium-sized, fully double and flat like a Gallica, with a good scent, and not repeat flowering; the calyx tube is said to be often swollen on one side at the base.

Garden notes A rarity, or perhaps a misnaming, preserved in the collection at Sangerhausen like 'Bébé Fleuri', and the nurseries of Walter Branchi in Orvieto, Italy, and Pépinières Loubert, in France. Hardy to 5°F (-15°C), in Zone 7.

'Perle d'Or' (also called 'Yellow Cécile Brunner') A dwarf China or Poly-pom, raised by Veuve Rambaux in Lyon in 1875 and introduced by her son-in law Dubreuil in 1883. A low shrub with vigorous, branching shoots of numerous small, pale apricot-yellow flowers like perfect miniature Tea roses, opening flat with a crowded center. This is like a yellow version of the more common, pink-flowered 'Cécile Brunner' (*see p.223*). The parentage is 'Polyantha Alba Plena' and the Tea 'Mme Falcot'. A climbing sport of 'Perle d'Or' is recorded, but no indication of when or where it arose. It is very rare, but available in France.

Garden notes This is a lovely rose: though usually classed as a China, it is nearer to the Noisettes and is often listed, with its half-sister seedling 'Cécile Brunner' among the Polyanthas. Hardy to 5°F (-15°C), in Zone 7.

'Pompon de Paris' A miniature China, now generally seen in its climbing form. The early flowering habit, small, evergreen leaves, and solitary pink flowers are close to *R. chinensis* (*see p.81*). It is known since 1839 and was formerly sold in Paris as a dwarf pot plant. The climbing form reaches about 6 ft (2 m).

Garden notes Pretty with a *Deutzia* or *Ceanothus* flowering at the same time, or the later-flowering *Solanum jasminoides*. The climbing form flowers only in spring and is best grown through another shrub. Hardy to 5°F (-15°C), in Zone 7.

'Bébé Fleuri'

'Darius'

'Roulettii'

'Perle d'Or' photographed in California in the garden of Miriam Wilkins, founder of the Heritage Rose Group

'Rouletii'   A miniature China, introduced by Henri Correvon in 1922. The story of its introduction is that it was found growing in a pot on a window in Switzerland, and brought to M. Correvon in Geneva. This was not the first time a miniature China seedling appeared, since one, a single-flowered variety, is illustrated by Redouté, and before that by Mary Lawrance in 1796; this last had probably been introduced from China.

'Rouletii' is the ancestor of most modern miniatures; 'Baby Gold Star' raised in Spain by Pedro Dot was an early cross that showed the potential of these miniatures, but their breeding was not taken up on a large scale until Ralph Moore began his program in the late 1930's with another 'Rouletii' hybrid, 'Peon' *(see p.263)*, and 'Oakington Ruby', said to have been found by an old lady in the garden of Ely Cathedral in England.

Garden notes   'Rouletii' forms a small bush to 1 ft (30 cm) tall, with numerous deep pink, double flowers, and small, pointed leaves. It is very free-flowering and repeats well into autumn. Hardy to 5°F (-15°C), in Zone 7.

'Perle d'Or'

Tea Roses

'Parks's Yellow
Tea-scented China'

AMONG THE ROSES introduced from China in the early 19th century was one with large flowers of a delicate, pale pink, which came to be known as 'Hume's Blush Tea-scented China'. This was the first of the dwarf, repeat-flowering Tea roses in Europe. It was crossed with a second Chinese rose, the pale yellow, once-flowering climber 'Parks' Yellow Tea-scented China', and from them came an important group, the Teas, with flowers of pink, creamy yellow, and apricot shades, some of them dwarf, others climbing.

From the beginning of the 20th century, the Teas were superseded by their progeny, the Hybrid Teas. These were crosses with Hybrid Perpetuals, and therefore both hardier and stronger-growing plants.

However, true Teas still have a faithful following in areas where they really thrive, such as California, the southeastern United States, Italy, and Australia, because their delicate, subtle colors and scents have a refinement that later hybrids have lost.

Tea roses do best in warm climates, where winter temperatures stay above 10°F (-12°C). In colder climates the climbing forms are better, because they can be trained on a warm wall. They need very rich feeding and heat to reach their full potential, and given these conditions even the dwarf varieties can be built up into good-sized bushes that are covered with flowers. Flowering is mainly in late spring and autumn, and pruning after flowering helps the production of autumnal flowers.

'Bon Silène' A lovely old Tea rose, raised by Hardy in France in 1835. It is free-flowering and vigorous, with rather small flowers similar to a China. The color varies from bright pink with deep yellow in the center to crimson. The scent is good, sweet, and fruity.

Garden notes A most attractive rose, which is rare in Europe but available from Peter Beales, and grown frequently in California. The habit of the bush is somewhat spreading, with graceful, arching stems. Hardy to 10°F (-12°C), Zone 8.

'Devoniensis' (also called 'Magnolia Rose', 'Victoria') A Tea rose, introduced in bush form in 1838 and as a climber in 1858. Raised by George Foster of Oatlands near Devonport (now part of Plymouth), England, it is a cross between 'Parks's Yellow Tea-scented China' and 'Smith's Yellow', a Noisette. The foliage is similar to 'Parks's Yellow', but the stalks are green. The flowers also larger and flatter, nearly 4 in (10 cm) across, and paler with a hint of pink. The stems eventually reach 40 ft (12 m).

Garden notes The autumn flowers of this rose are much better than the spring ones, indeed in Devon it is often still in full flower in late October. Hardy to 10°F (-12°C), Zone 8.

'Hume's Blush Tea-scented China' (also called 'Odorata', *Rosa × odorata* 'Odorata', 'Spice') This is an ancestor of many Tea roses; some authorities now call this *R. × odorata* 'Odorata', but it we have kept it under its far more familiar English name. It is an old Chinese garden rose, an ancient hybrid between *R. gigantea* and *R. chinensis* (*see p.13*); it was brought to Europe from Canton in 1809 to the garden of Sir Abraham Hume at Wormleybury, Hertfordshire, and named in honour of his wife. Cuttings of the original plant were taken by the nurseryman John Kennedy to Malmaison in 1810, and it was illustrated by Redouté under the name "Rosa Indica fragrans" in 1817. This shows the globular, pale pink flower with few, long petals, hanging on an arching stalk with distinct crimson thorns.

By the early 20th century, the plant appeared to have become extinct in Europe, but what is possibly the same rose was rediscovered in Bermuda, where it was called 'Spice'. While looking for the wild *R. chinensis* in China, Roger and I found a very similar plant among other old roses in a small village garden near Pingwu, Sichuan.

Garden notes A graceful rose, worth cultivating for its own sake as well as for its historic interest. It is low-growing, with stems to 6 ft (2 m) at the most, bearing few thorns, and repeat flowers well. Hardy to 10°F (-12°C), Zone 8.

'Parks's Yellow Tea-scented China' (also called 'Flavescens', 'Lutescens Flavescens', *Rosa × odorata* 'Ochroleuca') An old Chinese garden rose introduced to England from Canton in 1824 by John Parks, who had been sent by the Horticultural Society to bring back garden plants from China. It is a strong grower to 10 ft (3 m) or more, with red young leaves and stems. Graceful, pale yellow flowers with a pinkish flush in the center are produced only in spring, and their scent is slight. This rose was important as a parent of the climbing Teas.

The rose shown here, reintroduced by Peter Beales, is once-flowering, with *R. gigantea* (*see p.13*) foliage and thorns, and is probably an old cultivar of that species; it agrees with Henry Bright's 1879 description of 'Parks's Yellow Tea-scented China', quoted by old-rose researcher Brent Dickerson. However, there is some doubt as to whether this is the original rose, which has also been described as repeat-flowering and deeper yellow.

Garden notes Still a good climber, covering a wall with elegant leaves and, in late spring, numerous pale yellow flowers sometimes with a pinkish flush. It is wonderful in a warm climate, but damaged by spring wind and rain in colder areas. Hardy to 14°F (-10°C), in Zone 8.

'Bon Silène'

'Devoniensis'

'Hume's Blush Tea-scented China'

'Alexander Hill Gray'

'Mme Scipion Cochet'

'Alexander Hill Gray' (also called 'Yellow Maman Cochet') A Tea raised by Alexander Dickson in Northern Ireland in 1911, of unknown parentage. The large, fully double flowers are dark yellow at the base, fading to creamy-white, with a strong Tea scent; their petals are long, giving a tall bud. The leaflets are pale green. The rose 'Soncy' from Bermuda is probably this.

Garden notes A relatively modern rose, forming an upright shrub to 6 ft (2 m) tall. Photographed at the Parc de la Tête d'Or, in Lyon, France, where there is a fine collection of old and species roses. Hardy to 10°F (-12°C), Zone 8.

'Belle Blanca' (also called 'White Belle Portugaise') A large climbing Tea, a pure white sport of 'Belle Portugaise' (*see p. 98*), of unrecorded origin. It flowers once, in spring, and has very long, pointed buds that open to semidouble flowers.

Garden notes This rose and its pink parent are among the largest and strongest-growing of all roses, suitable only for spacious gardens and for growing up cliffs or trees; it is fantastic in California. Hardy to 10°F (-12°C), Zone 8.

'Georgetown Tea' An old Tea rose of uncertain identity, found in Georgetown cemetery. It forms a spreading shrub to 5 ft (1.5 m) high and wide, with large, pale buff or peach-pink flowers on arching stems. This has been identified as 'Molly Sharman-Crawford', but that should have large, white flowers with a hint of green, held erect. Gregg Lowery of Vintage Gardens in California compares it to 'Comtesse de Labarthe' (*see p. 98*), but this should be more pink in color.

Garden notes 'Georgetown Tea' is an excellent pale Tea rose for warm areas. The cemeteries of the California Gold Country are a rich source of 19th-century European roses; their naming is a source of both fascination and careful detective work. Hardy to 10°F (-12°C), Zone 8.

'Mme Bravy' (also called 'Adèle Pradel', 'Alba Rosea', 'Danzille', 'Isidore Malton', 'Mme de Sertot', 'Mme Denis', 'Mme Maurin') A Tea rose raised by Guillot père of Lyon, France in 1845. The nodding flowers are produced in clusters: they are globular, fully double with a high center, and of the palest flesh pink with traces of red. The scent is good.

Garden notes This rose usually forms only a small shrub, to 3 ft (1 m). It is still grown in several places and is famous as a parent of 'La France' (*see p. 199*), which is often said to be the first Hybrid Tea. Hardy to 10°F (-12°C), Zone 8.

'Belle Blanca'

'Georgetown Tea'

'Georgetown Tea' photographed in the Georgetown Cemetery in California Gold Country   'Mme Bravy'

'Mme Scipion Cochet'   A Tea raised by Alexandre Bernaix in Villeurbanne in 1886, from a cross of 'Anna Olivier' and 'Comtesse de Labarthe' (*see p. 98*). Large, fully double flowers are creamy white with a crimson-pink edge and yellow center. The widely spaced leaflets are dark green, and shining on the upper surface. There is also a Hybrid Perpetual of the same name with deep pink or red flowers edged white.

Garden notes   This makes a low shrub to 3 ft (1 m), with very thorny stems. Hardy to 10°F (-12°C), Zone 8.

'Maitland White' (also called 'Puerto Rico')   A rose of uncertain identity, found in gardens in Bermuda. Blush-pink and cream flowers are produced in spring and again in autumn.

Garden notes   This forms a large shrub to 5 ft (1.5 m), and is hardy to 10°F (-12°C), Zone 8.

'Sombreuil' (also called 'Mme de Sombreuil', 'Mlle de Sombreuil')   A Tea of this name, not a climber, was raised by Robert in Angers in 1850, from a cross of a Hybrid Perpetual and 'Gigantesque'. It bore flat, white flowers, very double and quartered in the center, with excellent scent, continually into autumn. The rose now grown as 'Sombreuil' in North America is a climber to 12 ft (4 m), with dark green, shining leaves. Flat, quartered white flowers open from bright pink buds, with a scent of lemon, Tea rose, and apples. Grower Gregg Lowery suggests it may be a modern hybrid of perhaps *R. wichurana* (*see p. 19*). In the French Revolution Mlle de Sombreuil saved her father from the mob by drinking a cup of aristocrat's blood.

Garden notes   Whatever its parentage, this is a good and reliable rose for autumn flowering.
Hardy to 10°F (-12°C), Zone 8.

'Maitland White'

'Sombreuil'

TEA ROSES

'Adam'

'Adam' (also called 'President')   Raised in 1838 by M. Adam, a gardener in Rheims, France. The delicately scented, semidouble flowers, to 3¼ in (8 cm) across, are salmon with a pink flush and the occasional red streak. One of the earliest Tea roses, this is possibly a hybrid of 'Hume's Blush Tea-scented China' (*see p. 91*) and 'Rose Edouard', an early Bourbon.

  Garden notes   A tall grower, to 8 ft (2.5 m), with purple young shoots and thorns. Hardy to 10°F (-12°C), Zone 8.

'Lady Hillingdon' and 'Climbing Lady Hillingdon'   A Tea rose raised in England, the bush form by Lowe and Shawyer of Uxbridge in 1910, the climbing form by E.J. Hicks in Berkshire in 1917; neither were rose specialists. It is a cross of the Teas 'Papa Gontier' and 'Mme Hoste'. The climber reaches 15 ft (5 m), the bush 6 ft (2 m), with red-purple young shoots and

robust, healthy foliage. The loosely double flowers from a long bud are apricot-yellow without deeper shading, becoming paler on the edges as the flower opens, with little scent. Lady Hillingdon was wife of the Viceroy of India; she is perhaps most famous for having written of her husband "when I hear his steps outside my door I lie down on my bed, close my eyes, open my legs and think of England" in her journal, a comment reported in Charles Quest-Ritson's excellent *Climbing Roses of the World*.

  Garden notes   One of the hardiest climbing Teas, repeat flowering in autumn; the bush form repeat flowers even better. I have found this one of the best climbers in poor, stony soils, even better in deep, fertile loam. It grows well in cool north Devon, England, and is also reported to be excellent in Houston, Texas; a tough, adaptable lady! Hardy perhaps to 5°F (-15°C), so worth trying in Zone 7.

'Marie van Houtte'

'Lady Hillingdon'

94

'Lady Hillingdon'   'Safrano' in Berkeley Botanic Gardens, California

'Marie van Houtte' (also called 'The Gem') A Tea raised by Ducher in France in 1871, a cross of 'Mme de Tartas' and 'Mme Falcot', both Teas. The flowers are globular, large, and nodding, pale buff-yellow shaded with pink around the edges, becoming all pink or almost white according to temperature. The scent is good and sweet, and the repeat flowering excellent. The stems are red and thorny.

    Garden notes This is a very popular and distinctive variety. After a few years in a warm climate, this forms a large shrub, reaching 6 ft (2 m) high and across, or more if grown on a warm wall; in cold areas it is lower growing. Hardy to 10°F (-12°C), Zone 8.

'Perle des Jardins' A Tea raised by Antoine Levet of Lyon in 1874. A seedling of the Tea Mme Falcot, it makes a dense shrub to around 3 ft (1 m), with deep purple twigs. The flowers are globular, double and sometimes quartered when fully open, nodding, and rich yellow. Both the scent and the repeat flowering are good.

    Garden notes This is best in a greenhouse in wet climates, because the flowers ball badly if wetted by rain, failing to open properly and going mouldy round the edges. In warm climates it flowers continuously. Hardy to 10°F (-12°C), Zone 8.

'Safrano' (also called 'Aimée Plantier') A strong-growing Tea rose, raised by M. de Beauregard, an amateur rosarian from Angers, in 1839. Loosely double flowers are rich yellow with a hint of pink in the bud, opening apricot and fading to white in the heat of day, with the petals curling back. Repeat flowers well, with a good scent. The parentage is perhaps a cross of 'Parks's Yellow Tea-Scented China' (*see p. 91*) and the Tea 'Mme Falcot'. 'Safrano' was an important parent of many later Teas.

    Garden notes The flowers are particularly beautiful in bud, and this rose was much cultivated in the 19th century for buttonholes. The plant is strong growing, to 5 ft (1.5 m), and very free-flowering. Hardy to 10°F (-12°C), Zone 8.

'Perle des Jardins'

95

'Fortune's Double Yellow' on a medieval wall at Ninfa, Italy

'Baronne Henriette de Snoy' A Tea raised by Alexandre Bernaix in Lyon in 1897. The flowers are large, globular, and fully double, the outer petals curling at their tips. They are pale pink and salmon with a yellowish center, often marked with red, and have an excellent Tea scent. Stems to 4 ft (1.2 m) are reddish-purple, leaves becoming dark green. Its parentage is 'Gloire de Dijon' (*see p.107*) and the Tea 'Mme Lombard'.

Garden notes A vigorous bush, this is one of the hardiest of the Teas, thriving at Kasteel Hex in eastern Belgium, so probably surviving to 5°F (-15°C), into Zone 7.

'Fortune's Double Yellow' (also called 'Beauty of Glazenwood', 'Gold of Ophir', *Rosa × odorata* 'Pseudindica', 'San Rafael Rose') An old Chinese climbing Tea, discovered by Robert Fortune in 1845 in the garden of a rich mandarin at Ningpo (today Ningbo), south of Shanghai. The flowers are medium sized, bronzy or fawn-yellow, sometimes veined and shot through with pink and purple, and produced mainly in spring, when the plant hangs with the weight of flowers.

Garden notes A climber to 70 ft (20 m) or so when old, and very thorny when young. It grows best in Mediterranean climates: it is often found in hedges in northern California, and is shown here at Ninfa, near Rome, where the garden has been made in the ruins of a medieval town. Hardy to 14°F (-10°C), in Zone 8, but best in a warm climate.

'Isabelle Nabonnand' A Tea of unrecorded parentage raised by Gilbert Nabonnand of Golfe-Juan, France in 1873. It has flowers of white to palest buff with a pinker center, loosely double, and with a good scent.

Garden notes This rose is a good grower, generally with healthy foliage, and flowering until the first frosts of winter. Hardy to 10°F (-12°C), Zone 8.

'Maréchal Niel' A climbing Tea-Noisette, raised by Henri Pradel of Montauban, France in 1864. The flowers, nodding from almost every leaf bud, are very large, globular, and pale yellow with a good scent. The pale yellowish-green leaves are rather limp. Sometimes this rose flowers mainly in spring, with few late-summer flowers; other plants flower repeatedly, and it has been suggested that some stocks are weakened by virus.

This rose is easily grown from cuttings and will do well on its own roots. It is a seedling of 'Isabella Gray', a Noisette, making it one of the Tea-Noisettes, essentially indistinguishable from a

'Fortune's Double Yellow'

'Baronne Henriette de Snoy'

'Monsieur Paul Lédè'

'Isabelle Nabonnand'

'Souvenir de Gilbert Nabonnand'

climbing Tea. Very healthy indoors, and easily grown. Maréchal Niel was minister of war under Napoléon III.

Garden notes This was the most famous greenhouse rose of the late 19th century, and is still lovely and not too rampant for a conservatory; it flowers in early spring under glass, later in the open where the color is a more golden yellow. Not very hardy, surviving perhaps 14°F (-10°C), in Zone 8.

'Monsieur Paul Lédè' (also called 'Monsieur Lédè', 'Paul Lédè', 'Climbing Monsieur Paul Lédè')   A Tea or Hybrid Tea, raised by Pernet-Ducher of Lyon in 1902; the climbing sport from the bush form was introduced by Lowe in England in 1913. Both have large, double flowers of shrimp pink or apricot with paler edges. Repeat-flowering, with good Tea scent.

Garden notes This is said to be one of the early Pernetiana repeat-flowering yellow roses, with *R. foetida* (*see p. 30*) in its parentage; if so it is likely to suffer seriously from blackspot in wet climates. The bush form is tall, with stems to 6 ft (2 m) tall. Hardy to 10°F (-12°C), Zone 8.

'Souvenir de Gilbert Nabonnand'   A Tea rose of unrecorded parentage, raised by Paul Nabonnand in 1920. Flowers orange-yellow to bright red, copper, and pink. Gilbert Nabonnand was a prolific breeder of Tea roses at his nursery in Golfe-Juan, described by a contemporary as "a horticultural establishment of the first rank."

Garden notes Said to be a good rose for warm coastal climates. Hardy to 10°F (-12°C), Zone 8.

'Maréchal Niel'

'Maréchal Niel'

TEA ROSES

'**Belle Portugaise**' (also called 'Bela Portugesa', 'Belle of Portugal') A climbing Tea raised by Cayeux in France in 1903. The parentage is often given as a cross of *R. gigantea* (*see p.13*) with the climbing Hybrid Tea 'Reine Marie Henriette', but Cayeux recorded it as the climbing Tea 'Souvenir de Mme Léonie Viennot' and *R. gigantea*. It makes a very rampant plant, to 30 ft (10 m) or more. Flowers are in spring only, pale, translucent flesh-pink, with long buds, large and loosely double: they may be 6 in (15 cm) across.

   Garden notes This is a most beautiful rose, but of gigantic size, only suitable for growing on a high wall or over a large tree in a warm climate; these pale climbers look wonderful growing through evergreen conifers such as pines, particularly the Monterey pine *Pinus radiata*, or perhaps the Monterey cypress *Cupressus macrocarpa*. There is a white form, 'Belle Blanca' (*see p.92*). Hardy to 14°F (-10°C), in Zone 8; frost below this is likely to damage the flower buds.

'**Comtesse de Labarthe**' (also called 'Comtesse Ouwaroff',

'Belle Portugaise'

'Countess Bertha', 'Duchesse de Brabant') A Tea rose, raised by H.B. Bernède of Bordeaux in 1857. The nodding flowers are salmon or shrimp pink and well-scented, the long buds opening to a cup of large petals with a muddled center. There is a white sport of this rose, 'Mme Joseph Schwartz', and a climbing form.

   Garden notes This does very well in Bermuda, where it is generally known as 'Duchesse de Brabant'. It forms a strong shrub to 6 ft (2 m). Hardy to 10°F (-12°C), Zone 8.

'**Général Schablikine**' A Tea rose, raised in 1878 by Gilbert Nabonnand of Golfe-Juan. The flowers, on purplish stalks, are quite small, but of particularly rich coloring, the crimson buds opening to show pink petals with a deeper back. The open flowers are rather loose, with a delicate scent.

   Garden notes This excellent rose will form a large shrub in a mild winter climate, such as California or the Mediterranean, and flowers almost continuously. It does exceptionally well in Eccleston Square, London, planted by Roger to climb into a large *Ceanothus*, and is never without a flower. Hardy to 10°F (-12°C), Zone 8.

'**Jean Ducher**' (also called 'Comte de Sembui', 'Ruby Gold') A Tea raised by Veuve Ducher of Lyon in 1874. The flowers are large, orange-yellow with red and salmon pink shading in the center, or sometimes cream and buff in colder climates; petals large and neatly overlapping. Its parentage is not recorded.

   Garden notes Reported to do better in dry climates, since the flowers are spoiled by rain. Hardy to 10°F (-12°C), Zone 8.

'**Maman Cochet**' A lovely Tea raised by Scipion Cochet of Grisy-Suisnes, in France in 1892. The flowers are large and full, cupped, and sometimes quartered in the center. Their color is basically pale pink with a yellowish flush in the center, the outer petals touched with carmine and becoming crimson, especially in hot weather. Good scent and repeat flowers well.

'Comtesse de Labarthe' against a wall of gray coral in Bermuda

'Jean Ducher'

'Maman Cochet' in a Californian cemetery

'Général Schablikine' and a *Ceanothus dentatus* in Eccleston Square, London

Red twigs carry dark green, shining leaves. Its parentage is 'Marie van Houtte' (*see p. 95*) and the Tea 'Mme Lombard'. There is a lovely sport, 'White Maman Cochet', recommended by English garden designer Gertrude Jekyll in 1902 and grown in California, with creamy flowers, the outer petals reddish.

Garden notes A strong-growing but low shrub to 4 ft (1.2 m), or more in the climbing form. Both the white and the normal form are recommended for the warmer parts of North America, from Georgia and Kansas to California. Hardy to 10°F (-12°C), Zone 8.

'Rosette Delizy' A Tea raised in 1922 by Paul Nabonnand of Golfe-Juan. Rich yellow flowers, suffused with apricot and salmon pink, become deep red and even purple on the outside. Repeat-flowering, with a fruity scent. It is a cross of the Teas 'Général Galliéni' and 'Comtesse Bardi'.

Garden notes One of the larger Teas, to 6 ft (2 m) on a wall in a warm climate, but usually around 3 ft (1 m), with thick, dark green leaves, not affected by mildew. Hardy to 10°F (-12°C), Zone 8.

'Rosette Delizy' in the garden of Laura Mercer in Bermuda

'Archiduc Joseph'

'Mrs B.R. Cant'

'Archiduc Joseph'   A Tea rose, a seedling of the Tea rose 'Mme Lombard' raised by Gilbert Nabonnand of Golfe-Juan in 1892. The flowers are well scented, deep pink in bud, opening coppery red with purple shading on the outer petals. In hot, dry weather the color is paler, basically pink. The leaves are dark, grayish-green.

Garden notes   A particularly good variety for autumn flowering. The flowers are rounded, only the tips of the petals reflexing; it is sometimes confused with 'Monsieur Tillier', which has similar coloring. Hardy to 10°F (-12°C), Zone 8.

'Francis Dubreuil' (also called 'François Dubreuil') A Tea rose raised by Francis Dubreuil of Lyon in 1894. The parentage is not recorded, but its scent is excellent and Damask-like, suggesting that this is probably a Hybrid Tea, that is a Tea crossed with a Hybrid Perpetual; red Tea roses are very rare, and this was considered one of the best. The flowers are velvety, deep purplish-red, often hanging, and with a long bud opening to a loose and rather muddled flower. Dubreuil was a tailor in Lyons before taking up rose breeding; he was the father-in-law of Antoine Meilland, for whom the Hybrid Tea 'Papa Meilland' (*see p.217*) is named.

Garden notes   This rose eventually forms a spreading shrub to around 6 ft (2 m) tall and wide, with nodding flowers. Hardy to 10°F (-12°C), Zone 8.

'Mrs B.R. Cant' (also called 'Mrs Benjamin R. Cant')   A Tea rose of unrecorded parentage, raised by Cant of Colchester, England in 1901. The flowers are deep red outside, pinkish and suffused with buff in the center, and have an excellent scent, with hints of Damask. A climbing sport was introduced in 1960, but seems to have disappeared.

Garden notes   This was a famous rose in the early years of last century, praised for its big, globular flowers, which are produced with great freedom and well into autumn; now it is very rare in Europe, although it is still grown in California and Australia. A strong, spreading shrub, growing to 6 ft (2 m) in California. One of the hardiest Teas, probably surviving 5°F (-15°C), and worth trying in Zone 7.

'Mrs Reynolds Hole'   A Tea raised by Gilbert Nabonnand of Golfe-Juan in 1900. Its parentage is 'Archiduc Joseph' and the Tea 'André Schwartz'. The large, deep purplish-crimson flowers open from a long-stemmed bud, and their scent is excellent.

'Monsieur Tillier'

'Mrs Reynolds Hole'

'Francis Dubreuil'

'Souvenir de Thérèse Levet'

'Noëlla Nabonnand'

The Rev. Samuel Reynolds Hole was Dean of Rochester and first president of the Royal National Rose Society.

Garden notes A rarity, but offered by several nurseries in both Australia and Europe. Hardy to 10°F (-12°C), Zone 8.

'Monsieur Tillier' A Tea of unrecorded parentage, raised by Alexandre Bernaix of Villeurbanne in 1891. Rounded buds open to large, flat flowers with a quartered center; the petals can be entirely reflexed and imbricated, giving a camellia-like bloom. They are pinkish-orange to red, shaded purple on the edge.

Garden notes This was noted in its day as an exceptional and very free-flowering variety, and it has proved very hardy, surviving perhaps to to 5°F (-15°C), in Zone 7.

'Noëlla Nabonnand' A climbing Tea-style rose, raised by Gilbert Nabonnand in Golfe-Juan in 1900, a hybrid of the climbing Hybrid Tea 'Reine Marie-Henriette' and 'Bardou Job', a cross of a Bourbon and a Hybrid Perpetual. Wonderful, huge, semidouble flowers of deepest crimson to purple velvet from lovely long buds, with a rich, sweet scent. I was thrilled to find an old plant of this in the garden at La Mortola, northern Italy.

Garden notes A strong-growing rose with new shoots to 10 ft (3 m), flowering in winter in warm climates. To judge by its parentage it should be one of the hardiest so-called Teas, probably surviving 5°F (-15°C), and worth trying in Zone 7.

'Papillon' A climbing Tea of unrecorded parentage, raised by Nabonnand in 1878. The flowers are in sprays, loosely double with tight, small, muddled petals in the center, coppery orange, pink, or almost white according to temperature. There is also a China of this name, a dwarf shrub with deep purple-red flowers.

Garden notes Stems to 15 ft (5 m), suitable for training on a pillar or low wall. It is a reliable repeat flowerer, and best in a dry-summer climate, because the flowers are spoiled by wet weather. Hardy to 5°F (-15°C), in Zone 7.

'Souvenir de Thérèse Levet' (sometimes called 'Souvenir de Thérèse Lovet') A Tea rose raised by Antoine Levet of Lyon in 1882; a cross of 'Adam' (*see p.94*) and possibly the Tea 'Safrano à Fleurs Rouges'. Loosely double flowers are crimson to maroon or pinkish, presumably according to temperature. Good scent.

Garden notes A shrub to around 4 ft (1.2 m). A reliable repeat-flowering rose, recommended for hot climates and popular in Australia. Hardy to 10°F (-12°C), Zone 8.

'Papillon' at the Rosarium Sangerhausen Germany

Noisette Roses

'Mme Alfred Carrière'

NOISETTES COMBINE THE scent and late flowering of the cultivated musk rose *R. moschata* (*see p. 18*), with the large flowers of the Teas and Chinas. The original 'Blush Noisette' has masses of small double, pale pink flowers; later varieties were raised with larger flowers.

Noisettes originated in North America, around Charleston in South Carolina. The ancestral rose, 'Champneys' Pink Cluster' was raised in around 1802 by rice farmer John Champneys, and its supposed parents were a form of *R. moschata* pollinated with 'Parson's Pink China' (*see p. 82*). 'Champneys' Pink Cluster' is apparently still in existence; it is a climber, bearing large sprays of loosely double flowers.

Later a Charleston nurseryman, Philippe Noisette, sowed seeds of 'Champneys' Pink Cluster' and obtained a repeat-flowering rose with small, double flowers, which he took to his brother Louis in Paris in 1814. It was this repeat-flowering rose that became 'Blush Noisette', the first of a large and popular group. The French hybridists soon recognized the value of this new rose, and it was illustrated by Redouté in around 1820 as 'Rosier de Phillipe Noisette'.

The later Noisettes, which were crosses between 'Blush Noisette' and 'Parks' Yellow Tea-scented China' (*see p. 91*) and other Tea roses, have larger flowers, often with yellowish coloring. By the late 19th century they became almost indistinguishable from the climbing Teas; these later, large-flowered varieties are often called Tea-Noisettes, and we have kept the distinction here.

The Noisettes need a warm wall with careful treatment in cool climates, but are excellent in warmer areas, above 12°F (-11°C), in Zone 8 and above. Below this temperature, Noisette roses are good in the greenhouse, producing flowers in April and May with little heat, and again in autumn. They do best planted in the ground, and associate well with reticulata camellias, coming out when the camellias are past. Climbers may be trained along the roof, smaller varieties grown as standards or bushes. Very detailed instructions on growing tender roses in greenhouses and in pots may be found in rose books published around 1900, when this type of cultivation was in vogue; they emphasize the importance of feeding and watering the plants well after a brief summer rest in order to get a good autumn crop of flowers.

'Blush Noisette' at Longleat House, Wiltshire

'Blush Noisette' (also called *Rosa × noisettiana*) This, the original Noisette, was a seedling of 'Champneys' Pink Cluster'. It is a good repeat-flowering rose, with loose and sometimes hanging clusters of 20 or more small, rounded, semidouble flowers, opening palest pink from crimson buds. They are produced from summer until the winter frosts, when they are deeper pink. The scent is good, and likened to cloves.

Garden notes A tall shrub or climber, with stems usually up to 6 ft (2 m), but sometimes to 15 ft (5 m). One of the most satisfactory of the small-flowered climbers for a restricted space. Hardy to 0°F (-18°C), Zone 7.

'Champneys' Pink Cluster' (also called 'Champneyana') The parent of 'Blush Noisette', a cross between 'Parson's Pink China' (*see p.82*) and the musk rose *R. moschata* (*see p.18*), raised by John Champneys in Charleston, South Carolina

around 1802. The flowers are small, loosely double, in large clusters or sprays, and with very good scent.

Garden notes A climber to 10 ft (3 m), this repeat flowers well into autumn if pruned and fed after the first flowering. Hardy to 10°F (-12°C), Zone 8.

'Desprez à Fleurs Jaune' (also called 'Desprez', 'Jaune Desprez', 'Noisette Desprez') A cross of 'Blush Noisette' and the Tea 'Parks's Yellow Tea-sented China' (*see p.91*) raised by Desprez in France in 1830. This was the first stage in the production of the larger-flowered Noisettes. It repeat flowers well, with clusters of very double flowers of palest yellow or buff, the amount of pink depending on the temperature and light. It has a good, heavy rose scent.

Garden notes A good climber in a warm, dry climate, with stems usually to 15 ft (5 m). Good in autumn, as far north as Philadelphia. Hardy to 10°F (-12°C), Zone 8.

'Mme Alfred Carrière' This is probably the most commonly grown of the Noisettes; it has white flowers with a flush of warmth in the center, well-scented and produced in clusters from pink-flecked buds; flowers continue to be produced regularly after the first summer flush. Raised by J. Schwartz of Lyon in 1879.

Garden notes This very free-flowering rose is excellent on a dark wall or on a pergola in a warm area. Its growth is vigorous, to 25 ft (8 m), and it is one of the hardiest Noisettes, to 0°F (-18°C), Zone 7.

'Desprez à Fleurs Jaune'

'Champneys' Pink Cluster' photographed at the Huntington Botanical Gardens, California

'Aimée Vibert'

'Blanc Pur'

'Aimée Vibert' (also called 'Bouquet de la Mariée', 'Nivea', 'Repens')   A rambling Noisette raised by Vibert in France in 1828, and thought to be a cross of 'Champneys' Pink Cluster' (*see p.103*) and *R. sempervirens* 'Plena'. The climbing form, now usually grown, was introduced by Curtis in 1841. Bouquets of small, flat, double flowers open white from pink buds.

Garden notes   The long, whippy canes can reach 15 ft (5 m) in a season, well-clothed in rich green, lush leaves. Very good scent and excellent autumn flowering, even in northern England: grower Gregg Lowery says similar but less reliable roses may be sold by this name. Hardy to 10°F (-12°C), Zone 8.

'Alister Stella Gray' (also called 'Golden Rambler')   A Tea-Noisette raised by Alexander Hill Gray of Bath, England, and introduced by George Paul in 1894. The medium-sized flowers, produced in loose clusters, are pale yellow with deeper, egg-yolk shadows, becoming white, and have good scent. The parentage is 'William Allen Richardson' (*see p.109*) crossed with 'Mme Pierre Guillot', a coppery orange Tea rose.

Garden notes   In some places this reaches 15 ft (5 m), in others 50 ft (15 m). Excellent repeat-flowering in autumn, when the flowers may be in large heads, a characteristic of Noisettes. Hardy to 0°F (-18°C), Zone 7.

'Alister Stella Gray'

NOISETTE ROSES

'**Blanc Pur**' A Noisette raised by Mauget of Orléans in 1827, of unrecorded parentage. The flowers, in rather upright clusters, are large and double, white, greenish outside, with good scent. The stems reach 12 ft (4 m).

    Garden notes A rare variety, available in South Carolina and in southern Europe. The large thorns attract repeated comment. Hardy to 10°F (-12°C), Zone 8.

'**Lamarque**' (also called 'Général Lamarque', 'The Marshall') Raised by Maréchal in Angers, France in 1830 from 'Blush Noisette' (*see p.103*) crossed with 'Parks's Yellow Tea-sented China' (*see p.91*), the same parentage as 'Desprez à Fleurs Jaunes' (*see p.103*). 'Lamarque' has larger, paler flowers, close to 'Devoniensis' (*see p.91*) but with fewer petals, good repeat-flowering, and a very sweet scent. The stems have few prickles.

    Garden notes This is a good rose in warm climates, such as California or Australia, where it can grow to 18 ft (5.5 m) or more; in wetter or colder climates, such as in England or wet parts of western Canada, it is probably better grown in a greenhouse. Hardy to 10°F (-12°C), Zone 8.

'**Mme la Duchesse d'Auerstädt**' (also called 'Duchesse d'Auerstädt') A seedling of 'Rêve d'Or' (*see p.108*), this Noisette was raised in 1887 by Jean-Alexandre Bernaix of Villeurbanne, near Lyon. It has purplish young leaves and stems, and the flowers are large and golden yellow.

    Garden notes A good climber for a wall, with stems to 10 ft (3 m) tall. The flowers are mostly carried singly, and hang down: this is an advantage for a climber, as they can be seen better from the ground and are protected from rain, although like most Noisettes, this is best in dry weather. Hardy to 10°F (-12°C), Zone 8.

'Mme la Duchesse d'Auerstädt'

'Lamarque' in the Cypress Hill Cemetery, California

'Céline Forestier'

'Bouquet d'Or'

'Chromatella'

'Bouquet d'Or'   A Tea-Noisette, a seedling of 'Gloire de Dijon', raised by Jean-Claude Ducher of Lyon in 1872. The fully double flowers open flat, slightly quartered, showing some stamens when fully open, with the edges of the petals curled back. They are rich coppery yellow, sometimes pink-tinged or almost orange, and the scent is good. The leaves are reddish when young, later dark green, shiny, and thick.

Garden notes   A climber reaching 10–12 ft (3–4 m), with strong-growing canes turning brownish in the sun. Hardy to 10°F (-12°C), Zone 8.

'Céline Forestier' (also called 'Liésis', 'Lusiadas')   A Tea-Noisette raised by Victor Trouillard in Angers, France in 1860. It has a parentage similar to 'Lamarque' (*see p.105*). Very full, double flowers with a good scent open flat, quartered with a button eye, pale yellow becoming white, from buds sometimes tipped with red. The leaves are dark green, shiny, and thick.

Garden notes   A tall climber in a warm area, with stems to 15 ft (5 m), producing flowers throughout summer and autumn. It is reported to be resistant to mildew in southern France. Hardy to 10°F (-12°C), Zone 8.

'Chromatella' (also called 'Cloth of Gold')   A Tea-Noisette, a seedling of 'Lamarque' (*see p.105*), raised by Coquereau in Le Maître-École, near Angers, and introduced by Vibert in 1843. The nodding flowers on lovely red stalks are large, fully double, globular, quartered, deep golden-yellow, with a good scent.

Garden notes   Best in a warm climate such as Australia or California, where it can become huge and free-flowering; the flowers are sometimes born singly, sometimes, particularly in autumn, in clusters. Hardy to 10°F (-12°C), Zone 8, perhaps surviving below this, in the warmer parts of Zone 7.

'Claire Jacquier' (also called 'Mlle Claire Jacquier')   A very free-flowering Noisette raised in France by Alexandre Bernaix of Villeurban near Lyon in 1888. Loose bunches of flowers,

'Claire Jacquier'

pale orange-yellow fading to cream and loosely double, are produced mostly in midsummer, with a few later. The leaves are lush, glossy, and purplish beneath.

Garden notes A strong-growing climber to 30 ft (10 m), reported to have few thorns. Hardy to 10°F (-12°C), Zone 8.

'Crépuscule' A Tea-Noisette of unrecorded parentage raised by Francis Dubreuil of Lyon in 1904. The flowers are loose, semidouble, untidy, deep golden-yellow or apricot, the petals curling along their length when fully open. They are usually produced with great profusion and in small clusters, continuing well into autumn. The scent is sweet and musky.

Garden notes This grows best in a warm climate, such as Australia or California, but the richest color is produced in cool conditions. It reaches 8 ft (2.5 m). Charles Quest-Ritson quotes unstinting praise of this rose from the Anglo-American rosarian Francis E. Lester in *Climbing Roses of the World*. Hardy to 10°F (-12°C), Zone 8.

'Gloire de Dijon' (also called 'The Old Glory Rose') A Noisette, though closer in appearance to a Tea, raised by M. Jacotot, a nurseryman in Dijon, in 1850 and introduced in 1853. A climber with stems to 75 ft (22 m) on old specimens in warm climates, but usually less, around 15 ft (5 m). The flowers are a rich, creamy buff-yellow with pinkish and salmon tints, and have a strong Tea scent. The leaves are reddish when young, becoming dark green and thick-textured. It is a cross between 'Souvenir de la Malmaison' (*see p.111*) and 'Desprez à Fleurs Jaune' (*see p.103*) or a similar yellow climbing Tea.

Garden notes 'Gloire de Dijon' is commonly seen on warm cottage walls in Aberdeenshire in eastern Scotland, where it survives cold winters and cool summers. It also thrives in warm areas, where it is recommended for north-facing walls. One of the hardiest of all Noisettes, this will survive down to 0°F (-18°C), Zone 7.

'Crépuscule'

'Gloire de Dijon'

'Manettii' photographed on Alcatraz Island

'Aline Rozey'

'Aline Rozey' (also called 'Aline Rosey') A hybrid Noisette, also sometimes classed as a Hybrid Perpetual, of unrecorded parentage, raised by Schwartz in 1884. It has medium-sized flowers with imbricated petals, pale flesh-pink fading to white.

   Garden notes A strong grower and free-flowering rose, but surprisingly rare in cultivation: it is grown at the Parc de la Tête d'Or in Lyon, France. Hardy to 10°F (-12°C), Zone 8.

'Bougainville' A Noisette raised by Pierre Cochet (Père) and introduced by Vibert in 1822; the parentage is similar to 'Blush Noisette' (*see p.103*) but like 'Manettii' probably with a red China. The medium-sized flowers, in large sprays, are cupped and fully double. Their color is pink with paler and more lilac edges from a red bud; they have been decribed as

peachy-lilac-red! The 18th-century navigator Admiral Louis de Bougainville was owner of the Château de Suisnes and patron of Christophe Cochet; the familiar tropical climber *Bougainvillea* and the island of Bougainville were also named for him.

   Garden notes Grower Gregg Lowery describes the flowers as tiny, 1 in (2.5 cm) across, with quilled petals. Repeat flowers well. The canes are very thorny, the leaves dark green and wavy, with widely separated leaflets. Hardy to 10°F (-12°C), Zone 8.

'Manettii' (also called *Rosa × noisettiana manettii*) An unusual rose, raised by Signor Manetti, director of the gardens at Monza in Lombardy, and introduced to cultivation by Rivers in around 1840. Its parentage is uncertain, but possibly 'Slater's Crimson China' (*see p.83*) crossed with *R. moschata* (*see p.18*). The flowers are deep pink, around 1½ in (4 cm) across, single, and in small clusters. The scent is negligible.

   Garden notes This was recommended as an understock in warm areas, because it was so vigorous and easy from cuttings, so it may sometimes be found surviving in old gardens. Hardy to 10°F (-12°C), Zone 8.

'Rêve d'Or' (also called 'Condesa da Foz', 'Golden Chain', 'Golden Dream') One of the brightest of the Noisettes, with bunches of quite large, pinkish-yellow flowers, very double, the petals becoming quilled and buff as they age. The flower- and leaf-stalks are red, the leaflets shining green. Raised by Jean-Claude Ducher of Lyon in France in 1869, and said to be a seedling of the Noisette 'Mme Schultz'.

   Garden notes Flowers well again in autumn. Stems to 10 ft (3 m), quick-growing in warm climates, and one of the hardier Noisettes, perhaps surviving to 5°F (-15°C), in the warmer parts of Zone 7.

'Bougainville'

'Solfatare' (also called 'Augusta', 'Solfaterre')   Raised by Joseph Boyau in Angers, France in 1843. A good grower with handsome leaves and creamy white flowers with deeper yellow shadows, repeating in autumn.

  Garden notes   Stems to 10 ft (3 m). Recommended for Texas, this is one of the hardier Noisettes. Hardy to 5°F (-15°C), in Zone 7.

'William Allen Richardson'   A seedling of 'Rêve d'Or', introduced by La Veuve Ducher in Lyon, France in 1878. This is a free-flowering climber with good yellow or apricot flowers, loosely double, fading in hot weather, and repeat flowering well into autumn. The dark green leaves are red when young. William Allen Richardson, a rich American rose fancier from Lexington, Kentucky, was a good customer of Mme Ducher.

  Garden notes   Recommended for the warmer areas of the United States, this will climb to 12 ft (4 m). Hardy to 10°F (-12°C), Zone 8.

'Rêve d'Or' in Eccleston Square, London

'Rêve d'Or'

'Solfatare'

'William Allen Richardson'

Bourbon Roses

'Reine des Île-Bourbons'

BOURBON ROSES TAKE their name from the Île de Bourbon, now called Réunion, near Mauritius in the Indian Ocean. In the days before the Suez canal was opened this was an important port of call for French ships returning from the Far East. The story goes that *R. × damascena* var. *semperflorens* (*see p. 43*) and the China rose 'Parson's Pink China' (*see p. 82*) were planted in hedges on the island and their hybrid was found in a hedge and taken into gardens. From here seeds were sent to Paris by a botanist, M. Breon, where they were grown by M. Jacques, gardener to Louis Philippe, and named 'Rosier de l'Ile de Bourbon'. This first Bourbon, introduced in France in 1823, is now seldom seen, though it was a reliable autumn flowerer with a wonderful scent. Crossed with Tea and China roses, it contributed to a new group of roses, often tall, well scented, and usually flowering in autumn as well as in summer.

Early Bourbons were often climbers and only once-flowering, but later ones were shorter, medium-sized shrubs which flowered continuously through the summer, if given sufficient water, and into autumn. After a dry summer these autumn flowers are particularly welcome, and often better than those produced in the heat of midsummer.

By the late 19th century, breeders of roses had moved on from Bourbons and concentrated on Hybrid Perpetuals and Hybrid Teas; the few later Bourbons are sports from earlier ones, which were preserved by connoisseurs of Old Roses.

Bourbons are usually rated as hardier than Teas and Chinas because of their Damask genes, but are not without some drawbacks. The Bourbons are susceptible to mildew. They are best planted in a place where the roots get plenty of water, and the topgrowth is not in a draft: they are more likely to suffer mildew, and to suffer worse, if they are planted under the eaves of a house, or against a wall that faces away from prevailing rain-bearing winds. If they are planted in a cooler, wetter spot any mildew will not be so bad.

Blackspot is also a problem with Bourbon roses, and this is always worst on weak or half-hidden shoots. Keep the plants well fed, and prune out any feeble shoots produced near the base of the plant; they will not flower anyway. Remove and discard all affected leaves (do not compost them, because the spores will survive in the compost) as soon as they show symptoms of the disease. The bush will soon produce new leaves.

BOURBON ROSES

'Great Western' A Bourbon hybrid, probably a cross with a Gallica, raised by Jean Laffay of Bellevue-Meudon in 1838. The flowers, in generous clusters, are fully double, crimson to purplish with pink edges, and have excellent scent. The stems reach 6–8 ft (2–2.5 m), and the leaflets are large and broad.

    Garden notes Flowers only in midsummer, but with very special flowers. An unusual name for a French rose, it is taken from an Atlantic steamer. Hardy to -20°F (-29°C), Zone 5.

'Prince Charles' A Bourbon hybrid, raised by Alexandre Hardy in Paris, first recorded in 1842. The reddish-crimson flowers fade to lilac and have darker veins.

    Garden notes Once-flowering, but prolific when well grown, and well scented. The stems reach 5 ft (1.5 m). Hardy to -20°F (-29°C), Zone 5.

'Reine des Île-Bourbons' (also called 'Bourbon Queen', 'Queen of Bourbons', 'Reine de l'Île de Bourbon') A low climber, raised in Orléans, France by Mauget in 1834. The flowers are cup-shaped, fully double, rich purplish-pink with paler edges, and very well scented. The leaflets are unusually broad. The shoots, which are up to 10 ft (3 m) long, are best tied in horizontally along a fence.

    Garden notes This rampant rose is a survivor, often found in old gardens, clothing a fence or growing out of a hedge. It is disappointing among Bourbons in flowering once only, but makes up for that by covering itself with clusters of flowers for a long period in midsummer. This rose is confused with 'Céline', introduced by Laffay in around 1835; it is possible or even likely that the rose now sold as 'Reine des Île-Bourbons' is in fact 'Céline'. Hardy to -20°F (-29°C), Zone 5.

'Souvenir de la Malmaison' A large-flowered rose with flat flowers of palest pink, filled with small petals, with a shadow of deeper pink in the center. Raised by Jean Béluze of Lyon in 1843, by crossing 'Mme Desprez', a Bourbon, with a Tea rose.

'Prince Charles'

It has a white sport, 'Kronprinzessin Victoria', with a creamy center, and also a semidouble sport, 'Souvenir de St Anne's' (*see p.113*). There is an excellent climbing form introduced by Bennett in 1893, which I have found surviving in old gardens.

    Garden notes This is a reliably repeat-flowering and well-scented rose, but the very solid, fully double flowers are likely to ball and rot in wet weather. It was named in remembrance of the Empress Joséphine's garden near Paris. She was forced to quit Malmaison soon after Napoleon divorced her in 1809 and although she died in 1814, the garden continued to be looked after by her children until it was finally sold in 1824. Hardy to 5°F (-15°C), in Zone 7.

'Great Western'

'Souvenir de la Malmaison' at Mottisfont Abbey, southern England

'Souvenir de St Anne's at the Antique Rose Emporium, Texas

'Coquette des Blanches'

'Boule de Neige' (also called 'Snowball') A Bourbon with small sprays of white flowers, touched with crimson and pink on the outside, and forming almost perfect spheres, with excellent scent. Raised by François Lacharme of Lyon in 1867, by crossing 'Mlle Blanche Lafitte', a Bourbon, with 'Sapho', a Damask-Perpetual.

Garden notes This is a large shrub or low climber to around 6 ft (2 m); the canes are pale green, with red thorns, and the flowers nod slightly under their own weight. Hardy to -20°F (-29°C), Zone 5.

'Coquette des Blanches' A Bourbon with some similarities to a Noisette, raised by François Lacharme of Lyon in 1865. The medium-sized and fully double flowers are pure white with green shadows, and well scented. Its parentage is 'Mlle Blanche Lafitte', a white Bourbon, crossed with 'Sapho', a Damask-Perpetual; Lacharme also raised the roses 'Coquette des Alpes', which has slightly pinker flowers, and 'Boule de Neige' from the same parentage.

Garden notes A leafy, upright plant, forming a large bush. The leaves and stems are green, with few thorns. This rose flowers well in autumn. Hardy to 10°F (-12°C), Zone 8.

'Émotion' A Bourbon raised by Laurent Guillot (père) of Lyon in 1862. Numerous flowers appear in autumn as well as summer. They are white, with shades of silvery pink, and the scent is excellent. This is not to be confused with the rose 'Emotion' (without the accent) raised by deRuiter 1981, which is a Floribunda with orange-red flowers.

Garden notes The flowers are medium-sized, produced in sprays on a sturdy bush around 5 ft (1.5 m) tall and wide. Hardy to -20°F (-29°C), Zone 5.

'Boule de Neige'

'Émotion'

'Mme Pierre Oger'

'Mme Pierre Oger' This pale sport of 'Reine Victoria' (*see p.115*) was found by M. Oger in Caen in 1874 and was introduced by Verdier in Paris in 1878. It became even more popular than its parent, with the most delicate, very pale pink petals flushed with deeper pink and crimson in hot weather.

Garden notes The plant makes a rather gaunt, upright bush with stems to 5 ft (1.5 m); the leaves are pale green and susceptible to blackspot. Performance can be variable: some stocks are said to have virus, and these are likely to do less well than the virus-free ones. Hardy to -20°F (-29°C), Zone 5.

'Souvenir de St Anne's' A modern Bourbon, found as a sport of 'Souvenir de la Malmaison' (*see p.111*) in the garden of Lady Ardilaun, at St Anne's, Clontarf, near Dublin. It was preserved by Lady Moore in Rathfarnham and introduced by Graham Thomas, then at Hilling's nursery, in 1950; it was one of his favorite roses.

Garden notes Unlike the fully double flowers of 'Souvenir de la Malmaison' which are easily spoiled by rain and damp, those of 'Souvenir de St. Anne's'

are only semidouble and so more reliable in wet areas. It makes a tall bush, to 6 ft (2 m), with lovely, well-scented flowers in both summer and autumn. Hardy to -20°F (-29°C), Zone 5.

'Variegata de Bologna' The most flashy of the old striped roses, with crimson, then purple stripes on an almost white ground, but produced mainly in summer, with only the occasional autumn flower. A sport of 'Victor Emmanuel' introduced in Italy in 1909 by Bonfiglioli & Son.

Garden notes A strong grower with stems to 8 ft (2.5 m), which can be arched over to form a lower, wider shrub. Hardy to -20°F (-29°C), Zone 5.

'Variegata de Bologna'

'Honorine de Brabant'

'Duc de Crillon'

'Louise Odier'

'Mme Lauriol de Barny'

'Duc de Crillon' A Bourbon raised by Moreau-Robert of Angers, France in 1860. The flowers are large, flat, and fully double, bright red, becoming deep pink with purplish tinges. Their scent is excellent.

Garden notes This makes a strong-growing shrub with canes to 8 ft (2.5 m), and repeat flowers well. Hardy to -20°F (-29°C), Zone 5.

'Honorine de Brabant' This Bourbon of unknown origin has neat flowers that are produced well into autumn. They are not fully double, but cup-shaped on opening, and showing some stamens when fully open. They have deep pink or purplish stripes and flecks on a pale pink ground, and their scent is particularly good. The striped Hybrid Perpetual rose 'Ferdinand Pichard' (*see p.126*) is similar, but its flowers are both more heavily marked and more fully double.

Garden notes This makes a strong, leafy plant, its arching, thornless stems reaching 7 ft (2.2 m) in height, so may be used to clothe a pillar. Hardy to -20°F (-29°C), Zone 5.

'Louise Odier' (also called 'Mme de Stella') The repeat flowering of the typical Bourbon is shown in this lovely rose, with perfect, flat, fully double, richly scented flowers produced in loose bunches. Their color is bluish-pink, shaded with lilac. Raised in France by Margottin père of Bourg-la-Reine in 1851, from a seedling of the Bourbon 'Emile Courtier'.

Garden notes One of the best old roses, with strong stems, reaching 5 ft (1.5 m) and flowering into autumn. Hardy to -20°F (-29°C), Zone 5.

'Reine Victoria'

'Zéphirine Drouhin'

'Mme Lauriol de Barny' A Bourbon with flat, fully double flowers with good scent, formed in loose clusters, mainly in summer, but with a few later. They are pale, silvery pink with deeper shadows. Raised in France by Victor Trouillard of Angers in 1868.

    Garden notes Tall-growing, with stems to 7 ft (2.2 m) or more, so it can be trained on a fence or pillar. There are suggestions that it is a hybrid of the wild European musk rose, *R. arvensis*. Hardy to -20°F (-29°C), Zone 5.

'Reine Victoria' (also called 'La Reine Victoria') A Bourbon raised in Lyon by Joseph Schwartz in 1872. A lovely rose with loose clusters of delicate, cupped and incurved, deep pink flowers. The scent is good, and it is a reliable repeat flowerer. This and its pale sport, 'Mme Pierre Oger' (*see p.113*) are the epitome of late-Victorian roses.

    Garden notes A rose with upright stems to 5 ft (1.5 m) and pale green, smooth leaves, unfortunately susceptible to blackspot. Hardy to -20°F (-29°C), Zone 5.

'Zéphirine Drouhin' (also called 'Belle Dijonnaise', 'Charles Bonnet', 'Ingegnoli Prediletta', 'Mme Gustave Bonnet') One of the most common of the Bourbons and a very easily recognized rose, with almost thornless twigs on a tall shrub, and bright magenta-pink flowers. The flowers are loosely double and have a good scent. They are produced throughout summer and autumn, the plant rarely being without flowers, and are lovely for cutting. Raised in France by Bizot in 1868.

    Garden notes This is a low climber, suitable for training on a wall or used to form a large shrub. Its only snag is a certainty to suffer from mildew, which disfigures the leaves. Mildew is worst on plants which are dry at the roots, so this should be planted where the roots are reliably moist in summer. It also suffers blackspot, but neither affect its floriferous habit! Hardy to -20°F (-29°C), Zone 5.

'Zéphirine Drouhin'

115

'Queen of Bedders'

'Adam Messerich'　　　　'Souvenir de Victor Landeau'

'Héroïne de Vaucluse'

'Mme Isaac Péreire' with *Humulus lupulus* 'Aureus'

'Adam Messerich'   A Bourbon raised by Peter Lambert in Trier, Germany in 1920. It is a complex hybrid of different groups including Hybrid Teas, Chinas, and Bourbons, with bright pink to red, single or semidouble flowers with well-developed stamens.

   Garden notes   This is a strong-growing and continuous-flowering rose, with good autumn bloom, and a rich, fruity scent. Hardy to -20°F (-29°C), Zone 5.

'Héroïne de Vaucluse'   A Bourbon raised by Moreau-Robert of Angers, France in 1863. The flowers are large, fully double, in clusters, and bright purplish-pink.

   Garden notes   A good grower, but flowering only in summer. For this reason the name is in some doubt, as early mentions of 'Héroïne de Vaucluse' said that it was repeat-flowering. Hardy to -20°F (-29°C), Zone 5.

'Mme Isaac Péreire' (also called 'La Bienheureux de la Salle')   Raised in France in 1881 by Garçon of Rouen. The flowers are flat, very double, and around 5 in (13 cm) across. They open rich reddish-carmine and fade to purplish-pink, the outer petals curving under, the center often quartered, and in spring sometimes showing an unattractively large green center. The leaflets are broad, dark green, and overlapping.

   Garden notes   This is one of the largest-flowered of the old roses, and its stout stems can reach 7 ft (2.2 m), so the plant can be trained as a pillar rose or low climber. Hardy to -20°F (-29°C), Zone 5.

'Queen of Bedders'   A Bourbon raised by Standish and Noble of Bagshot, England in 1877; a seedling of 'Sir Joseph Paxton' (*see p.119*). It has fully double flowers of medium size, cherry red, with excellent scent, which are produced continuously well into autumn.

   Garden notes   When grown for bedding, this rose was pruned very heavily in spring, down to around 4 in (10 cm) tall, in the manner of a modern bedding Floribunda. Hardy to -20°F (-29°C), Zone 5.

'Souvenir de Victor Landeau'   A Bourbon raised by Moreau-Robert of Angers, France in 1890. The flowers are large, fully double, opening cupped, and bright red or deep rose-carmine with carmine highlights. Their scent is excellent.

   Garden notes   This makes a strong-growing shrub with thorny branches and dark green leaves. Hardy to -20°F (-29°C), Zone 5.

'Mme Isaac Péreire'

'Bouquet de Flore'

'Mme Charles Détraux' at Roseraie de l'Haÿ-les-Roses, south of Paris

'Mlle Joséphine Guyet'

'Sir Joseph Paxton'

'Bouquet de Flore' (also called 'Bouquet des Fleurs')
A Bourbon raised by Bizard in Angers in 1839. The flowers are large, fully double, well scented, and bright carmine-pink. This and 'Nemesis' seem to be Bizard's only surviving roses.

Garden notes A strong grower with dark green leaves, suitable for training on a pillar, and flowering through the summer. Hardy to -20°F (-29°C), Zone 5.

'Gruß an Teplitz' (also called 'Gruss an Teplitz') A Bourbon hybrid with many China characteristics, raised by Rudolph Geschwind of Karpona, Hungary and introduced by Peter Lambert of Trier, Germany in 1897. The parentage is complex; one parent was an unnamed seedling from a cross of 'Sir Joseph Paxton' with 'Fellemberg' (*see p. 84*), the other another unnamed cross between 'Gloire des Rosomanes' (*see p. 85*) and the Tea rose 'Papa Gontier'. The resulting rose is a good bright red, free-flowering, and well scented, with clusters of flowers.

Garden notes A good grower, like a delicate, red Hybrid Tea, forming a strong, spreading shrub. Hardy to -20°F (-29°C), Zone 5.

'Mme Charles Détraux' (also called 'Mme Charles Détreaux') A Bourbon, sometimes classed as a Hybrid Tea, raised in 1895 by Jacques Vigneron of Olivet, France. The flowers are large, globular, and bright red, with excellent scent, and produced into autumn.

Garden notes A strong grower, with bluish-green leaves, now rare. Hardy to -20°F (-29°C), Zone 5.

'Mlle Joséphine Guyet' (also called 'Mlle Joséphine Guyot') A Bourbon raised by Jean Touvais of Petit-Montrouge, France in 1863. The medium-sized flowers are deep velvety red.

Garden notes Grows to around 4 ft (1.2 m), and flowering from summer into autumn. Hardy to -20°F (-29°C), Zone 5.

'Gruß an Teplitz'

'Gruß an Teplitz' in Union Hill Cemetery, California

'Parkzierde'   A Hybrid Bourbon raised by Rudolph Geschwind of Karpona, Hungary and introduced by Peter Lambert of Trier, in Germany in 1909. The flowers show China characteristics in their scarlet to crimson coloring and moderate scent.

Garden notes This flowers very freely, although only for a short time. Hardy to -20°F (-29°C), Zone 5.

'Sir Joseph Paxton'
(also called 'Paxton')
A Hybrid Bourbon climber raised by Jean Laffay of Bellevue-Meudon in 1851. The dark pink flowers are quite large and fully double, opening flat and sometimes quartered. Their scent is good and they appear in clusters; some say it repeats well into autumn, others that it flowers once only; I have not grown it myself.

Garden notes The stems, which are very prickly, reach around 10 ft (3 m); it is suitable for training on a pillar or as a low climber. Hardy to -20°F (-29°C), Zone 5.

'Parkzierde'

Hybrid Perpetual Roses

'Baronne Prévost'

IN THE LATTER HALF of the 19th century, Hybrid Perpetuals were the most popular roses for gardens and exhibitions. They combine repeat flowering, large flowers, excellent scent, and strong colors, showing a preponderance of reds and purples, which were rare in the Teas that were popular at the same time. The Hybrid Perpetuals are hardier than the Teas, but they have one major disadvantage: many seem to suffer badly from powdery mildew.

Hybrid Perpetuals, or Hybrides Remontants as they are called in France, have a complex ancestry. 'Rose du Roi' (*see p. 77*), a repeat-flowering Portland hybrid with large, red flowers and excellent scent, appeared in 1819. Around 1835 it was crossed with hybrid Chinas (Gallica-China hybrids) and Bourbons (Autumn Damask-China hybrids), and the new class of Hybrid Perpetual was formed. 'La Reine' was one of the earliest.

Hybrid Perpetuals can be recognized by their very large, usually rather flat flowers and by the coarse leaves, which grow almost up to the base of the flower, so that the flowers seem to nestle among the leaves, a characteristic inherited from the Portlands. They therefore lack the open, graceful form that is associated with Teas and Chinas; this may also contribute to their susceptibility to mildew.

This trait was no handicap when they were grown for the exhibition of single flowers in competitions at flower shows, a popular pastime in the first half of the 20th century. The large flowers of the Hybrid Perpetuals appealed to many of the same gardeners who grew dahlias and chrysanthemums, also raised for showing in this period. Many of these roses were therefore bred for showing as single flowers, and the form and health of the shrub as a whole tended to be ignored. Today the same traits make them candidates for the cutting garden; while the form of the bush may not be the best, the flowers will make more impact than many in a vase.

When well grown, some Hybrid Perpetuals make large, striking garden shrubs, and are still popular in areas with difficult climates, such as some parts of Texas, that are hot in summer and too cold in winter for most Teas or even for many Hybrid Teas.

They tend to throw long, strong shoots from the base. These can be pegged down to flower along their length the following year, or shortened by half to keep a more compact bush. Summer pruning should be light; autumn flowers come from the same shoots as those that produced flowers in spring. Rich feeding and ample water in summer produce healthy plants and flowers.

'La Reine'

'Reine des Violettes' at Mottisfont Abbey, southern England

'Baronne Prévost'   A Hybrid Perpetual, raised by Desprez in Yebles, France in 1841 and introduced by Pierre Cochet of Grisy-Suisnes in 1842. The stems reach 5 ft (1.5 m) or more, with very numerous red thorns; the leaflets are broad and dark green. The flowers are very large, to 6 in (15 cm) across, bright pink with hints of purple, and fully double; they open flat, often with a tight, incurved center and with excellent scent. Repeat flowering is reliable, each group of flowers opening in succession. The parentage is not recorded.

   Garden notes   A strong-growing and free-flowering rose, one of the best and most popular of the Hybrid Perpetuals. Hardy to -17°F (-27°C), in Zone 5.

'Empereur du Maroc' (also called 'Emperor of Morocco')   This Hybrid Perpetual was raised by Guinoisseau in Angers, France in 1858. It is a seedling of 'Geant des Batailles' a Hybrid Perpetual. The flowers are not large, but are fully double and very well scented, opening deep red and velvety, becoming deep purple with age. 'Louis XIV', which is sometimes classed as a China, is similar in color but has flatter, smaller flowers on a smaller bush.

   Garden notes   Still one of the darkest-colored roses. It is a tall shrub, to 5 ft (1.5 m), or can be trained on a pillar or as a low climber. Hardy to -17°F (-27°C), in Zone 5.

'La Reine' (also called 'Reine des Français', 'Rose de la Reine')   A Hybrid Perpetual raised by Jean Laffay of Bellevue-Meudon, France in 1842. The flowers are large, around 4 in (10 cm) across, rounded and cup-shaped, with incurved petals, mid-pink shaded with lilac, but with little scent. It is possibly a seedling of 'William Jesse', a Bourbon, perhaps with 'Rose du Roi' (*see p. 77*).

   Garden notes   This was the first of the Hybrid Perpetuals and is tall, with stems to 5 ft (1.5 m), with few thorns and ample dark green leaves. Hardy to -17°F (-27°C), in Zone 5.

'Reine des Violettes' (also called 'Queen of Violets') This Hybrid Perpetual, a seedling of 'Pius IX', was introduced by Millet-Malet in 1860. The large flowers are incurved and cupped, opening cerise before fading to violet, and are very sweetly scented with good repeat flowering.

   Garden notes   A strong grower, still loved for its changing flowers. Breeder Peter Beales says that this is the very best of the Hybrid Perpetuals. Stems to 6 ft (2 m) with very few thorns. Hardy to -17°F (-27°C), in Zone 5.

'Empereur du Maroc'

'Enfant de France' A Hybrid Perpetual introduced by Lartay of Bordeaux, France in 1860. It bears very double, silvery pink flowers with an intense scent, and repeat flowers well. The stems reach 5 ft (1.5 m).

Garden notes Several different roses, including two Gallicas and an Alba, have been given this name, but recent consensus has rested on this silvery pink Hybrid Perpetual as Lartay's rose. Hardy to -17°F (-27°C), in Zone 5.

'Frau Karl Druschki' (also called 'Druschki', 'FK Druschki', 'Reine des Neiges', 'Schneedronningen', 'Schneekonigen', 'White American Beauty') This Hybrid Perpetual was raised by Peter Lambert in Trier, Germany in 1901. The parentage is the Hybrid Perpetual rose 'Merveille de Lyon' crossed with 'Mme Caroline Testout' (*see p.199*), so this is sometimes classed as a Hybrid Tea. It has large, white flowers that are touched with pink outside; they are fully double with a high, pointed bud, but with little scent. Frau Karl Druschki was the wife of the general superintendent of the famous Spaeth nurseries in Berlin. There is also a climbing sport, not much taller than the original.

Garden notes One of the few Hybrid Perpetuals that have never fallen out of favor, as well as being a prolific parent of other good roses. It makes a strong, upright bush, to 7 ft (2.2 m) or more, with thorny stems and smooth, broad leaflets, and repeat flowers well. It is also particularly hardy, even for a Hybrid Perpetual, down to -27°F (-33°C) in Zone 4.

'Georg Arends' (also called 'Fortuné Besson', 'Georg Ahrends', 'Rose Besson') A Hybrid Perpetual rose introduced by Wilhelm Hinner of Trier, Germany in 1910. It has bright green leaflets. The fully double flowers are soft pink with touches of lilac, well-scented, and repeat well.

Garden notes The parentage is 'Frau Karl Druschki' crossed with 'La France': it has been said that this rose was raised originally by a M. Bresson in France, then renamed by the German nurseryman Hinner. It is a tall grower, with stiff and upright stems to around 5 ft (1.5 m), which is suitable for training on a pillar. The flowers are of a good shape, closer to Hybrid Teas than those of the earlier varieties. Hardy to -17°F (-27°C), in Zone 5.

'Gloire Lyonnaise' A Hybrid Perpetual raised in 1884 by Jean-Baptiste Guillot (fils) in Lyon, France. The flowers are cream or white, loosely double, with excellent scent, and repeat flowering is good. The stems are upright, to around 6 ft (2 m), with large thorns and rather narrow leaflets. It is seedling from a cross between 'Baronne Adolphe de Rothschild' (*see p.124*) and 'Mme Falcot', a Tea.

Garden notes In many ways this looks more like a Tea rose than a Hybrid Perpetual, the flowers being delicate and easily damaged by the weather; its parentage is also that of a Hybrid Tea. Hardy to -17°F (-27°C), in Zone 5.

'Hold Slunci' A Hybrid Perpetual introduced by the Czechoslovakian Blatna nursery in Bohemia, in 1956. The light yellow, fully double flowers have little scent, but repeat well through the summer. Stems reach 3–5 ft (1–1.5 m).

Garden notes An unusual rose both in its color and in its likely breeder, Jan Bohm, who had a large nursery in southern Bohemia from 1919 until 1950. Hardy to -17°F (-27°C), in Zone 5. It is not often seen: this example was photographed at the Rosarium Sangerhausen in Germany.

'Mrs Cocker' A Hybrid Perpetual introduced by James Cocker in Aberdeen, Scotland in 1899. It has long-lasting large, mid-pink, double flowers with a strong scent. The stems reach around 5 ft (1.5 m). It is a cross of 'Mrs John Laing' (*see p.125*) and 'Mabel Morrison', both Hybrid Perpetuals.

Garden notes This rare rose is preserved at the Rosarium Sangerhausen in Germany; it was particularly valued in its day as an exhibition variety. Hardy to -17°F (-27°C), in Zone 5.

'Enfant de France'

'Gloire Lyonnaise'

'Frau Karl Druschki'

'Hold Slunci'

'Mrs Cocker'

'Enfant de France'

'Georg Arends'

'Champion of the World'

'Dembrowski'

'Jules Margottin'

'Mrs John Laing' at Kasteel Hex in Belgium

'Baronne Adolphe de Rothschild' (also called 'Baroness Rothschild') A Hybrid Perpetual, raised by Jean Pernet (père) of Lyon, France in 1868. The fresh pink flowers, with some scent, open rather flat, the inner petals incurved, the outer spreading, with very pale backs. It is a low grower, with stems around 4 ft (1.2 m).

Garden notes A typical Hybrid Perpetual with flattish flowers and large leaves reaching up to the flowers, repeat flowering well. Both this and the light pink 'Baronne Nathaniel de Rothschild' are sold as 'Baroness Rothschild' in many American nurseries. Hardy to -17°F (-27°C), in Zone 5.

'Champion of the World' (also called 'Mme de Graw', 'Mrs de Gaw', 'Mrs DeGraw') A Hybrid Perpetual, sometimes listed as a Bourbon, with very double, quartered flowers like an old Gallica, of variable pink and with good scent, flowering often better in autumn than in early summer. It was raised in England by Woodhouse in 1894 from 'Hermosa', (see p.82), crossed with 'Magna Charta', a purplish Hybrid Perpetual.

Garden notes This is recommended as a good, long-lived rose for most gardens. The stems are arching, to 5 ft (1.5 m), and the flowers often produced in large sprays. Hardy to -17°F (-27°C), in Zone 5.

'Dembrowski' (often called 'Dembroski', 'Dombrowski') A Hybrid Perpetual introduced by Jean-Pierre Vibert in France in 1840, sometimes listed as a Hybrid Bourbon. Stems around 4 ft (1.2 m). The flowers are deep pink with a silvery margin; they are fully double, with average scent, and are borne continuously during the season.

Garden notes Noted for its intense color and free-flowering character. Hardy to -17°F (-27°C), in Zone 5.

'Jules Margottin' A Hybrid Perpetual introduced in 1853 by Jacques-Julien Margottin (père) of Bourg-la-Reine, France. Double, carmine-rose flowers open flat and show some stamens when they are fully open. The thorny stems grow to 6 ft (2 m) in height. This is probably a seedling of 'La Reine' (*see p.121*).

Garden notes This rose has survived commercially since it was raised, and is an important parent of other varieties. It is free-flowering with a good scent, although only a few flowers are produced in autumn. Hardy to -17°F (-27°C), in Zone 5.

'Mrs John Laing' A Hybrid Perpetual raised by Henry Bennett in Wiltshire, England in 1887; it is a seedling of the Hybrid Perpetual 'Francois Michelon'. Long buds open to pale pink, cupped flowers with incurved petals, the edges later curling back. The flowers are large and well scented, in clusters of three or four. Bennett was a landowner, farmer, and cattle breeder, who turned to breeding roses and raised some early hybrids, including the earliest Hybrid Teas.

Garden notes This make a short plant, to 4 ft (1.2 m), with few small thorns and leaves that are resistant to mildew. The flowers stand up well to rain and are produced well into autumn. Hardy to -17°F (-27°C), in Zone 5.

'Paul Neyron' A Hybrid Perpetual raised by Antoine Levet of Lyon, France in 1869. This is one of the largest-flowered of all old roses, with huge, flat flowers opening cerise, becoming purplish pink, and good scent. It is a hybrid of 'Victor Verdier' (*see p.126*) with 'Anna de Diesbach', both Hybrid Perpetuals.

Garden notes This is still one of the most popular of the Hybrid Perpetuals, repeat flowering well with very large flowers on an upright but well-formed bush, with vigorous stems reaching 6 ft (2 m), scattered with small red thorns. Hardy to -17°F (-27°C), in Zone 5.

'Ulrich Brunner Fils' (also called 'Blue Mikey', 'Ulrich Brunner') A Hybrid Perpetual introduced by Antoine Levet of Lyon, France in 1882. The flowers are large, geranium-red to carmine, with purplish shading when old, and well scented.

Garden notes A strong grower, with stems to 5 ft (1.5 m). Ulrich Brunner was a rose grower in Lausanne. Hardy to -17°F (-27°C), in Zone 5.

'Paul Neyron' growing with delphiniums at the Rosarium Sangerhausen in Germany

'Ulrich Brunner Fils'

'Baronne Adolphe de Rothschild' at Mottisfont Abbey, southern England

125

'Victor Verdier' at Wilton Cottage, southern England

'Hugh Dickson' at Mottisfont Abbey, southern England

'Erinnerung an Brod' (also called 'Souvenir de Brod')
This is a *R. setigera* (*see p.19*) hybrid, usually classed with the
Hybrid Perpetuals, raised by Rudolph Geschwind in Bohemia
in 1886. It is repeat blooming, with quartered, strongly scented
flowers. They are unique in their color, opening cerise and
becoming crimson and finally purple as they age, resembling
the coloring of a Gallica, and one of the bluest of all old roses.
The parentage is *R. setigera* crossed with the Hybrid Perpetual
'Génie de Châteaubriand'.

    Garden notes A strong-growing shrub up to 8 ft (2.5 m),
and one of the parents of the "blue" Rambler 'Veilchenblau'
(*see p.161*) Geschwind used the very hardy North American
Prairie rose *R. setigera* for many of his hybrids, designed to
survive the hard winters of Eastern Europe. This rose will
survive down to -22°F (-30°C), in Zone 4.

'Ferdinand Pichard' This striped Hybrid Perpetual, raised
by Remi Tanne in Rouen in 1921, is sometimes grouped with
striped Bourbons such as 'Variegata de Bologna' (*see p.113*).
The flowers are rather small, cupped, with little scent.

    Garden notes This rose forms a bushy shrub to 8 ft
(2.5 m), with flowers in clusters in midsummer and autumn.
Hardy to -17°F (-27°C), in Zone 5.

'Hugh Dickson' A Hybrid Perpetual introduced by Dickson
of Newtownards, Northern Ireland in 1905. The very large,
mid-red flowers have an intense scent, and appear continuously
from summer into autumn. The parentage is a cross of the
Hybrid Perpetual 'Lord Bacon' with 'Gruß an Teplitz' (*see p.118*).

    Garden notes This is one of the best Hybrid Perpetuals for
general garden use, with long shoots to 10 ft (3 m), which
respond well to being pegged or tied down. Hardy to -17°F
(-27°C), in Zone 5.

'Ferdinand Pichard at the Rosarium Sangerhausen in Germany

'Erinnerung an Brod' at Mottisfont Abbey, southern England

'Mme Victor Verdier' A Hybrid Perpetual raised by Eugene Verdier in 1863. Rounded, fully double, well-scented flowers of a bright pinkish-red with a pale reverse are arranged in a loose head. This rose is famous as one of the parents of 'La France' (*see p.199*), one of the first Hybrid Teas.
   Garden notes Flowers are produced through the summer on an almost thornless shrub to 5 ft (1.5 m). Hardy to -17°F (-27°C), in Zone 5.

'Triomphe de France' A Hybrid Perpetual introduced by Garçon in 1875. The very large, bright pink, fully double flowers are well-shaped and have a moderate scent. This is rare in cultivation; our example was photographed at the Rosarium Sangerhausen in Germany.
   Garden notes A reliable repeat-flowering rose with stems to 5 ft (1.5 m). Hardy to -17°F (-27°C), in Zone 5.

'Victor Verdier' (also called 'M. Victor Verdier') A rose raised by Lacharme of Lyon in 1859 and classed as a Hybrid Perpetual although by its parentage, 'Jules Margottin' (*see p.124*) crossed with 'Safrano' (*see p.95*), it is a Hybrid Tea. The fully double flowers are clear rose pink, becoming purplish, with little scent.
   Garden notes A good flowerer, forming an upright shrub, and an important parent of early Hybrid Teas such as 'Lady Mary Fitzwilliam' (*see p.199*). Hardy to -10°F (-23°C), Zone 6.

'Triomphe de France'

'Ferdinand Pichard'

'Mme Victor Verdier'

'Alfred Colomb'

'Surpassing Beauty of Woolverstone' in Eccleston Square Garden, London

'Granny Grimmets' at the Rosarium Sangerhausen in Germany

'Prince Camille de Rohan'

'Alfred Colomb' A Hybrid Perpetual introduced by Alfred Lacharme in Lyon, France in 1865; it is a seedling of the Hybrid Perpetual 'Général Jacqueminot'. The strongly scented flowers are fully double, globular to cup-shaped, and dark red with the petals paler on the back. Alfred Colomb was a rose fancier in Lyon.

Garden notes Repeat flowering is good. The stems reach to around 5 ft (1.5 m) in height, with few thorns. Hardy to -17°F (-27°C), in Zone 5.

'Fisher Holmes' (also called 'Fisher and Holmes') A Hybrid Perpetual raised by Eugene Verdier in Paris in 1865. It bears velvety, very dark red flowers, fading purplish, which are fully double, of good shape, repeat-flowering, and with good scent. The parentage is uncertain, but it is possibly a seedling of the Hybrid Perpetual 'Maurice Bernardin'.

Garden notes One of the very best Hybrid Perpetuals, this is strong-growing with cane-like stems to 6 ft (2 m), which respond well to being pegged down to flower along their length. Hardy to -17°F (-27°C), in Zone 5.

'Fisher Holmes'

'Souvenir du Docteur Jamain' at Mottisfont Abbey, southern England

'Granny Grimmets'   A Hybrid Perpetual re-introduced by Hilling in 1955. The flowers are cupped, untidily double with ruffled petals, very dark red to purplish, with an average scent, and repeat flowering well.

Garden notes   This rare rose is found in the collection at the Rosarium Sangerhausen Germany, and is grown by a few nurseries in Texas, California, and Denmark. Hardy to -17°F (-27°C), in Zone 5.

'Prince Camille de Rohan' (also called 'La Rosière') A Hybrid Perpetual introduced by Eugene Verdier in Paris in 1861. The flowers are cupped, a very deep, velvety crimson-maroon, and strongly scented. The parentage is possibly the Hybrid Perpetual 'Général Jacqueminot' crossed with a hybrid of 'Geant des Batailles', itself a Hybrid Perpetual.

Garden notes   Once-flowering only, occasionally with a few autumn flowers, but worth growing for its very large and richly-colored flowers. It may be a climber or large shrub, with stems to 8 ft (2.5 m). Hardy to -17°F (-27°C), in Zone 5.

'Roger Lambelin'   A sport of 'Prince Camille de Rohan', introduced by the widow Schwartz of Lyon in 1890. The petals have crinkled edges, outlined and streaked with white; otherwise the flowers are bright crimson, fading to maroon.

Garden notes   Flowers with a good scent, in loose clusters on stems to 5 ft (1.5 m). Hardy to -17°F (-27°C), in Zone 5.

'Souvenir du Docteur Jamain'   A Hybrid Perpetual raised by Lacharme in Lyon, France in 1865. The flowers open deep crimson and become the color of purple plums; they keep their depth of color better in a cool position. A reliable repeat flowerer with a heavy, sweet scent. One parent is the Hybrid Perpetual 'Charles Lefebvre', the other unknown.

Garden notes   Famous for its very dark color and its scent, though the flowers are below average size. Almost a climber, with stems to 10 ft (3 m). Hardy to -17°F (-27°C), in Zone 5.

'Surpassing Beauty of Woolverstone' also called 'Beauty of Woolverstone', 'Surpassing Beauty', 'The Churchyard Rose', 'Woolverstone Church Rose')   A climbing Hybrid Perpetual introduced by Peter Beales in 1980. This "found" rose was discovered by rosarian Humphrey Brooke in Woolverstone Churchyard, Suffolk, England. It has deep red, double flowers that fade to a dark purple, with a muddled center and excellent old rose perfume.

Garden notes   The stems can reach to 8 ft (2.5 m), so the plent can be grown as a climber or a pillar rose. Subject to a little mildew. Hardy to -17°F (-27°C), in Zone 5.

'Roger Lambelin'

Climbing Roses

'Climbing Ophelia'

THE BREEDING OF CLIMBING roses has always been something of a lottery. Although the first of the Hybrid Tea roses were valued as repeat-flowering low bushes, some of them mutated and produced climbing forms that were similar in growth habit to their climbing Tea rose ancestors. Other Climbing roses have been raised from crosses between roses that were themselves large-flowered climbers.

One of the most significant of the Climbing roses, 'Dr W. Van Fleet' was raised purposely from a cross of a Hybrid Tea with a first-generation hybrid of a wild climber and a Tea rose; it has the large flowers that are associated with Hybrid Teas. 'New Dawn', a repeat-flowering sport of 'Dr W. Van Fleet' that appeared in 1930, is still one of the most popular Climbing roses both in North America and in Europe; when crossed with Hybrid Teas, it became the ancestor of many modern repeat-flowering climbers, much hardier than the old climbing Teas.

Some of the best examples have arisen by chance. They have even appeared when their breeders were aiming for a low shrub: David Austin's beautiful Climber 'Constance Spry' (*see p.138*) was raised from a cross of two low-growing parents, one a

Gallica and the other a Floribunda. Anyone who is interested in the stories of the breeders of Climbing roses should read Charles Quest-Ritson's fascinating account, *Climbing Roses of the World*.

Climbing roses need rich soil and ample water in summer if they are to produce their best flowers. Once-flowering types build up new strong shoots after flowering, so they also need good cultivation to prepare for the following year's flowers. Repeat-flowering climbers need water and feeding for the second flush of flowers: in Mediterranean climates, such as California, this may coincide with the autumn rains, but in the absence of rain, extra water will be needed.

Pruning can be minimal; simply cut back the old flowering side shoots and any stems that are too weak to flower, tying in any strong new shoots that will eventually replace the older wood. If possible, train some of the shoots horizontally, so that they can flower along their length and build up a good framework. The hardiness of these roses varies according to their parentage; tender varieties can be helped to survive winters that would otherwise be too cold by tying their stems close against a wall.

'Climbing Ophelia'

'Dr W. Van Fleet' at The Gardens of the Rose, St Albans, southeastern England

'Climbing Ophelia'   A sport of the Hybrid Tea 'Ophelia', introduced by Dickson in Northern Ireland in 1920. Typical Hybrid Tea flowers with long petals and pointed buds open pale buff or salmon with slightly more yellow tones in the center, and with good scent. 'Ophelia', introduced in 1912 by William Paul and Sons of Waltham Cross, England, is possibly a seedling of the Hybrid Tea 'Antoine Rivoire'. It is the parent of many hybrids and has produced several lovely sports. 'Lady Sylvia' is deeper pink and also has a climbing sport; 'Silver Wedding' is almost white, but no climbing sport has been recorded.

Garden notes   A strong climber reaching 18 ft (6 m) after several years. Hardy to -10°F (-23°C), Zone 6.

'Dr W. Van Fleet'   This once-flowering climber was raised by Dr Walter van Fleet in Ruskin, Tennessee in around 1890, and introduced by Henderson of New York in 1910. The flowers are large, around 4 in (10 cm) across, and fully double. They are pale pink with touches of yellow, and have excellent scent. Its parentage is a cross of the Hybrid Tea 'Souvenir du Président Carnot' and a hybrid of 'Safrano' (*see p. 95*) and *R. wichurana* (*see p. 19*).

Garden notes   Grows to 15 ft (5 m) or more, with disease-resistant, shining leaves. This rose flowers mainly in midsummer, with occasional late flowers, and is now much less common than its repeat-flowering sport 'New Dawn'. Hardy to -22°F (-30°C), in the warmest parts of Zone 4.

'New Dawn'   (also called 'Everblooming Dr W. Van Fleet', 'The New Dawn')   A repeat-flowering sport of 'Dr W. Van Fleet' introduced by Somerset in the United States in 1930. It is almost as vigorous as its parent, and flowers again and again after the first flowering until the start of the winter frosts.

Garden notes   One of the best of all climbers, healthy and free flowering, Eventually reaching 15 ft (5 m) or more. Hardy to -22°F (-30°C), in the warmest parts of Zone 4.

'New Dawn'

CLIMBING ROSES

'Alchymist' in Eccleston Square Garden London

'Alchymist' (also called 'Alchemist') A once-flowering Climbing rose raised by Kordes in Germany in 1956. The fully double flowers are around 4 in (10 cm) across, the outer petals recurving when fully open. They are apricot-orange fading to white on their edge, and the scent is excellent. The parentage is *R. rubiginosa* (*see p.26*) and the Climbing rose 'Golden Glow'.
   Garden notes A smooth-leaved rose perfect for growing into a small tree, such as an apple, or an evergreen, such as a holly, which shows off the richly colored flowers. The hanging shoots are particularly lovely in flower. Hardy to -22°F (-30°C), in warmer parts of Zone 4.

'Easlea's Golden Rambler' (also called Golden Rambler) In spite of its name, this is a large-flowered Climbing rose with shining, dark green leaves, and huge, fully double flowers to 4½ in (11 cm). The buds are tinted red, the open flowers a rich golden yellow. Raised by Walter Easlea near Leigh-on-Sea in Essex, England in 1932; its parentage is not recorded.
   Garden notes Once-flowering only, this throws strong, thick shoots up from the base. If not controlled these can reach 20 ft (6 m) in a season, so the flowers are out of sight at the eaves if it is planted on a house. Hardy to 0°F (-18°C), Zone 7.

'Golden Showers' A climbing Hybrid Tea with loosely double, medium-sized flowers of bright yellow, fading and showing dark stamens when open, with some scent. It was raised by Dr W.E. Lammerts from two Hybrid Teas, the Shrub 'Charlotte Armstrong' and the climbing 'Captain Thomas', and introduced by Germain's of Los Angeles in 1956.
   Garden notes A very good, bushy rose, climbing to 12 ft (4 m) and generally healthy, with dark green leaflets. It repeats well and the flowers stands up to rain; this rose is most suited to cooler, moister climates. Hardy to 0°F (-18°C), Zone 7.

'Lawrence Johnston' A large-flowered Climbing rose, raised by Pernet-Ducher of Lyon, France and introduced in 1922. The semidouble flowers are bright yellow, with yellow stamens.

'Alchymist'

'Easlea's Golden Rambler'

'Mermaid'

It is a hybrid of *R. foetida* 'Persiana' (*see p.30*) and the yellow Tea-Noisette 'Madame Eugene Verdier'. Graham Thomas records that it was rejected by Pernet-Ducher in favour of its sister seedling 'Le Rêve', but bought by Lawrence Johnston, a rich American who, from 1924, made the garden at Serre de la Madone, near Menton on the French Riviera.

Garden notes An attractive, informal Climbing rose, flowering in great profusion in early summer. Hardy to -10°F (-23°C), Zone 6.

'Mermaid' This hybrid of *R. bracteata* (*see p.14*) and a yellow Tea rose was introduced by William Paul of Waltham Cross,

England in 1918. It has shining, healthy, dark green leaves and large, bright yellow, single flowers to 6 in (15 cm) across, with golden stamens, produced over a long season into autumn.

Garden notes This is a wonderful rose when growing well. Its thorny stems tend to shoot up to great height, 20 ft (6 m) or more in a short time; it can die back equally quickly, generally when affected by frost. Hardy to 10°F (-12°C), Zone 8, where it is wonderful growing into a tree. It will survive down to 0°F (-18°C), Zone 7 for short periods if on a wall. Some authorities record it as hardy to -30°F (-34°C), Zone 4, but -8°F (-22°C) with a wind will cut it to the ground, even when grown against a wall.

'Lawrence Johnston'

'Golden Showers'

'Breath of Life'

'Spice So Nice'

'Looping' at the Rosarium Sangerhausen in Germany

'Blairii No. 2'   This Climbing rose, also classed as a Bourbon or a Climbing or Hybrid China, has some of the loveliest flowers among the old roses. They are perfectly round, pale pink, deeper in the center, with a good scent. The stems, to 15 ft (5 m), can be trained on a tree or a pergola. Flowering is

'Blairii No. 2'

mainly in midsummer, but a few later flowers may appear in a good season. Raised in England by a Mr Blair in 1845. 'Blairii No. 1' is similar, but it has paler flowers and is shorter, growing to just 6 ft (2 m).

   Garden notes   I have often admired this rose but never grown it; it is said to suffer from mildew. These once-flowering Climbing roses should be pruned like Ramblers, in autumn or winter. The old shoots that have flowered can be cut away completely, and the long new shoots tied down, as arches or along a low fence. If this seems too drastic, feed the plants well and tidy up the last summer's flowering branches, removing them completely the following year, when strong, new shoots should have been formed. Hardy to -20°F (-29°C), Zone 5.

'Breath of Life' (also called HARquanne)   This Climbing Hybrid Tea was introduced by Harkness of Hitchin, England in 1980. The flowers are large, apricot-orange in color, and sweetly scented. The stems are strong and thorny, growing to 10 ft (3 m). Its parentage is a cross of the Floribunda 'Red Dandy' and 'Alexander' (*see p.214*).

   Garden notes   This rose is both free-flowering through the season and particularly hardy, to -22°F (-30°C), in the warmest parts of Zone 4.

'Compassion' (also called 'Belle de Londres')   A Climbing Hybrid Tea, introduced by Harkness of Hitchin, England in 1972. This has proved to be a very popular Climbing rose, and is widely available just about everywhere that roses are grown. The flowers are large, double, salmon-pink, fading to buff, with excellent scent. It is a hybrid of the Climbing rose 'White Cockade' and the Hybrid Tea 'Prima Ballerina'.

Garden notes The stems grow to around 10 ft (3 m). Hardy to -22°F (-30°C), in the warmest parts of Zone 4.

'Cupid' A single-flowered Climbing Hybrid Tea of unknown parentage, raised by Cants of Colchester in 1915. The upright clusters of large, single flowers open orange-pink, fading to pale pink or white, and are followed by large, orange hips.

Garden notes Free-flowering, but only in early summer, with thorny stems to 15 ft (5 m). Hardy to -20°F (-29°C), Zone 5.

'Lady Waterlow' A Climbing Hybrid Tea introduced by Nabonnand of Golfe Juan, France in 1902. Red buds open to large, loosely double flowers, the petals creamy yellow with a golden base inside, bright pink outside, and delicately scented of apples. The leaves are pale green, with large leaflets, on almost thornless stems. Its parentage is the Hybrid Tea 'La France de '89' and the Noisette hybrid 'Mme Marie Lavalley'.

Garden notes I have not found this as vigorous as most climbers, reaching 10 ft (3 m) in poor soil; it is said to reach 20 ft (6 m) in good conditions. It is seldom without a few flowers in the growing season. Hardy to 0°F (-18°C), Zone 7.

'Looping' (also called MEIrovonex) A climbing Hybrid Tea introduced by Meilland of Marseilles in 1977. Semidouble flowers open orange, turning pink, the petals curling back when fully open to show red stamens; scent is excellent. The Climbing roses 'Royal Gold' and 'Danse des Sylphes', the Shrub rose 'Cocktail', and the Floribunda 'Zambra' are in its parentage.

Garden notes A good grower, to 12 ft (4 m), but liable to blackspot in cold, wet climates. Hardy to -10°F (-23°C), Zone 6.

'Spice So Nice' (also called WEKwesflut) A large-flowered Climbing rose, bred by Tom Carruth and introduced by Weeks Roses in 2002. The blooms, in large clusters, are a warm mixture of apricot-orange with yellow at the base of the petals and on the reverse; the young foliage is mahogany red. An interesting scent, close to juniper with added old rose. It is a hybrid of the Shrub roses 'Westerland' and 'Flutterbye'.

Garden notes Climbs to 12 ft (4 m), and repeats well. Not hardy, probably only down to 10°F (-12°C), Zone 8.

'Compassion'

'Cupid'

'Lady Waterlow' at Mottisfont Abbey, southern England

CLIMBING ROSES

'Mme Grégoire Staechelin'

'Collette' (also called 'Genevieve', 'John Keats', MEIroupis)
A large-flowered Climbing rose or tall shrub with fully double,
bright pink flowers with an excellent scent. It was raised by
Meilland in France in 1996 from a seedling of the Shrub rose
'Fiona' and the Floribunda 'Friesia' (also called 'Sunsprite')
crossed with the Shrub rose 'Prairie Princess'.

   Garden notes This is a low climber, to 12 ft (4 m), useful
for its reliable repeat-flowering. Hardy to -10°F (-23°C), Zone 6.

'Climbing Mme Caroline Testout'   A climbing Hybrid Tea:
the bush form (*see p. 199*) was raised in 1890, and this climbing
sport introduced by J.-B. Chauvry of Bordeaux in 1901.
Branching sprays of sugar-pink flowers open very full double,
large, and blowsy from short, fat buds.

   Garden notes This is a very free-flowering rose. The thorny
stems are upright and stiff; it is better to train this rose on a
pillar, or as in old rose gardens, a pyramid, than to attempt to
make it cover a wall. Hardy to -20°F (-29°C), Zone 5.

'Constance Spry' (AUSfirst, AUStance)   A large-flowered
Climbing rose raised by David Austin in Albrighton, England
in 1961, the first of David Austin's roses to be introduced.

'Constance Spry'

'Climbing Mme Caroline Testout'

'Senateur Lafolette'

The flowers are globular fully double, blush pink, and produced in great quantity in early summer. Their scent has been compared to myrrh, musky but not sweet. This great rose is the ancestor of many of Austin's English Roses, and brought good scent and the old-fashioned flower shape into modern roses. It was raised from 'Belle Isis' (*see p. 40*) crossed with 'Dainty Maid' (*see p. 236*), and commemorates the influential flower arranger.

Garden notes An excellent climber, if only it would flower again in autumn. Stems to 10 ft (3 m) or more. Very hardy, probably surviving -20°F (-29°C), Zone 5.

'Mme Grégoire Staechelin' (also called 'Spanish Beauty') A strong-growing and early-flowering Climbing Hybrid Tea raised by Pedro Dot in Spain in 1927. Large, loosely double, nodding flowers with pointed, crimson buds open pale pink with dark pink veins, becoming paler on the edges. The scent is heavy and sweet. Large, orange hips remain on the plant through the winter. Its parentage is 'Frau Karl Druschki' (*see p. 122*) and the Hybrid Tea 'Chateau de Clos Vougeot.'

Garden notes One of the loveliest of all garden roses, with stems to 7 ft (2.2 m), with few thorns; it flowers once only, but then with a profusion of graceful nodding flowers. 'Frau Karl Druschki' was parent to many good climbers, imparting hardiness, strong growth, thick-petalled flowers and healthy foliage to its offspring. Hardy to -20°F (-29°C), Zone 5.

'Senateur Lafolette' (also called 'La Folette') A giant among Climbing roses, with long, narrow-pointed, bright pink buds opening to large, loose, untidy flowers with muddled petals in the center. The scent is good. The young leaves are also very elegant, with long, limp, reddish leaflets. This unusual

rose was raised by Busby, gardener to Lord Brougham at Chateau Eléonore near Cannes, France and introduced in 1910. The parentage was *R. gigantea* (*see p. 13*), newly introduced from Burma by Sir Henry Collett, crossed with a Hybrid Tea.

Garden notes The stems of this rose can reach 30 ft (9 m) or more, and can climb up and over trees, or along high walls. It is excellent in a warm or Mediterranean climate, such as California or in central London, but needs protection in colder areas. Hardy to 10°F (-12°C), Zone 8.

'Collette'

'Climbing Shot Silk'

'Climbing Shot Silk' A Climbing Hybrid Tea introduced by Knight in 1931; the bush form was raised by Dickson in Northern Ireland in 1924. The flowers are large, shaded with bright pink, with sweet scent. Stems with few thorns.

Garden notes A low climber, to 8 ft (2.5 m). Repeat flowers well in autumn. Hardy to -20°F (-29°C), Zone 5.

'Handel' (also called MACha) A Climbing Hybrid Tea, raised by Sam McGredy IV in Northern Ireland in 1965. The large flowers are strikingly bicolored with each creamy-white petal edged with crimson, which suffuses down towards the base. It is a hybrid of the Floribunda 'Columbine' and the Kordesii rose 'Gruß an Heidelberg' (*see p.141*).

Garden notes Strong-growing, to 20 ft (6 m), and repeat-flowering, but with below average scent. A good Climbing rose for a pillar or a fence: in Eccleston Square, it grows on the netting around a tennis court. Hardy to -20°F (-29°C), Zone 5.

'Kitty Kininmonth' A large-flowered Climbing rose, raised by Alister Clark of Glenara near Melbourne, Australia in 1922. The flowers are very large, semidouble, deep pink, and well scented; the petals do not fade, but are paler beneath. It is a cross of an unnamed seedling and *R. gigantea* (*see p.13*).

Garden notes A tall and fast-growing rose, to 25 ft (7.5m), this is early and free-flowering, and repeats if the developing hips are pruned off regularly. Excellent for a warm climate; all Alister Clark's roses, of which at least 16 are still cultivated, should be ideal for California, the southeastern United States,

'Antike 89' (also called 'Antique', KORdalen) A large-flowered Climbing rose, with the same coloring as 'Handel', introduced by Kordes in Germany in 1988. Flowers large, fully double, pale pink or white with a bright red edge, repeating well through the season. The parentage is a cross of the Climbing rose 'Grand Hotel' and the Hybrid Tea 'Symphonie'.

Garden notes A low climber or pillar rose, to 10 ft (3 m). Hardy to -30°F (-34°C), Zone 4.

'Antike' 89'

and southern Europe, but they are seldom seen in gardens outside Australia. Because of its *R. gigantea* parentage, only hardy to 0°F (-18°C), Zone 7.

'Nancy Hayward' A large-flowered Climbing rose, raised by Alister Clark of Glenara near Melbourne, Australia in 1937. The large, single flowers are deep glowing pink and well scented. This is a seedling of 'Jessie Clark', a *R. gigantea* (*see p.13*) cross. Alister Clark, a rich amateur, raised several lovely roses for Australian gardens using the tender but heat-tolerant *R. gigantea*.

Garden notes The stems grow to 18 ft (6 m) or more. This rose repeat flowers well and is very popular in Australia and New Zealand; surprisingly, it is not yet grown in the southern United States, nor in Europe. Hardy to 0°F (-18°C), Zone 7.

'Sympathie' A Climbing rose introduced in 1964 by Kordes in Germany; a hybrid of the climber 'Don Juan' and the Kordesii rose 'Wilhelm Hansman'. It bears sprays of medium-sized, fully double flowers, of a deep, pure red with a flash or two of white.

Garden notes Stems to 15 ft (5 m), with some later flowers after the first flush, and dark green, very healthy leaves. Hardy to -30°F (-24°C), Zone 4.

'Kitty Kininmonth'

'Handel'

'Nancy Hayward'

'Sympathie'

'Schoener's Nutkana'

'Climbing Alec's Red'   This is a climbing sport of the Hybrid Tea that was originally raised by Cockers of Aberdeen, Scotland in 1973; the climbing form was introduced by Harkness of Hitchin, England in 1975. The large flowers are fully double, with a good Hybrid Tea shape, deep, bright red, and highly scented. The parentage is the Hybrid Tea 'Fragrant Cloud' (*see p.217*) crossed with the Climbing Hybrid Tea 'Dame de Coeur'.
Garden notes   A good all-round red Climbing rose, equally successful in America and in Europe. Stems to 15 ft (5 m). Hardy to -20°F (-29°C), Zone 5.

'Dublin Bay' (also called 'Grandhotel', MACdub)   A popular Climbing Floribunda raised by Sam McGredy IV in 1975. It has a good bright red, loosely double flower, repeating well through the season, though with little scent. Its parentage is a cross of the Climbers 'Bantry Bay' and 'Altissimo' (*see p.142*).
  Garden notes   A Climbing rose widely grown in Europe, particularly for its continuous flowering. The stems grow to 10 ft (3 m). Hardy to -20°F (-29°C), Zone 5.

'Summer Wine'

'Gruß an Heidelberg'

'Eric Tabarly'

'Eric Tabarly' (also called 'Red Eden Rose', MEIdrason)
A large-flowered Climbing rose raised by Meilland in France in 2002. The bright red, fully double flowers repeat well through the season, and have good scent. The parentage has not been recorded.

   Garden notes A new Climbing rose from Europe, good for its continuous flowering; stems to 7 ft (2.2 m). Hardy to -20°F (-29°C), Zone 5.

'Gruß an Heidelberg' (also called 'Heidelberg', KORbe)
A large-flowered Climbing rose raised by Kordes in Germany in 1959. Bright red flowers, the petals paler beneath, are borne in clusters and repeat well through the season. It is a hybrid of the Floribunda roses 'Minna Kordes' (also called 'World's Fair') and 'Floradora'.

   Garden notes Stems to 10 ft (3 m), with dark green, shining foliage. This old variety has been an important parent, for example of 'Handel' (*see p.138*), though it suffers from blackspot in wet climates. Hardy to -20°F (-29°C), Zone 5.

'Schoener's Nutkana' This fine tall shrub or Climbing rose has large flowers around 4 in (10 cm) across, of deep cerise-pink color and good scent, produced in early summer, and was introduced in 1930. Its parentage is 'Paul Neyron' (*see p.125*) crossed with *R. nutkana;* Father Schoener raised several roses in California, crossing wild parents with old garden roses.

   Garden notes This is a large plant with red-brown shoots to 10 ft (3 m), and grayish leaves. The species *R. nutkana* is a wild rose from California and the Rockies to Alaska; this should be very hardy, to -30°F (-34°C), Zone 4.

'Dublin Bay'

'Summer Wine' (also called KORizont) This single-flowered Climbing rose was raised by Kordes in 1985. The flowers are from bright pink buds, opening paler with contrasting red stamens, and well-scented. The petals are dark beneath at first, fading later.

   Garden notes A slender Climbing rose to 12 ft (4 m), with prickly stems and large leaflets. Hardy to -20°F (-29°C), Zone 5.

'Climbing Alec's Red'

'Altissimo'

'Altissimo' (also called 'Altus', DELmur) A tall-growing, single-flowered Climbing rose with large, intense crimson flowers with a small cluster of stamens. The petals overlap, making almost a perfect circle. Raised by Delbard-Chabert in France in 1966, it is a seedling of the Climber 'Ténor'.

Garden notes The plant grows tall and somewhat spindly to 20 ft (6 m), but produces wonderful flowers singly or in clusters throughout the season. Hardy to 0°F (-18°C), Zone 7.

'Calypso' (also called 'Berries 'n' Cream', POULclimb) A Floribunda-like Climbing rose raised by Mogens Olesen and introduced by Poulsen in Denmark in 1997. The flowers are semidouble, striped crimson and pink, and carried in sprays.

Garden notes Good repeat flowering on a tall plant, to 12 ft (4 m), with few thorns. Hardy to -20°F (-29°C), Zone 5.

'Guinée' This is still one of the darkest red of all Climbing roses, a Climbing Hybrid Tea raised by Mallerin in France in 1938. The flowers are medium-sized, densely double, of such a rich crimson as to be almost black, with excellent scent. It is a hybrid of the Hybrid Teas 'Souvenir de Claudius Denoyel' and 'Ami Quinard'.

Garden notes A tall Climbing rose to 15 ft (5 m), flowering mainly in early summer, with later flowers if the plant is kept dead-headed. Hardy to 0°F (-18°C), Zone 7.

'Calypso'

'Climbing Pasadena Tournament' at the Huntington Rose Garden near Los Angeles, California

'Climbing Pasadena Tournament' (also called 'Climbing Red Cécile Brünner') A small-flowered Climbing rose with sprays of flowers like miniature Hybrid Tea flowers, of a bright, velvety crimson, with good scent. It is a sport of 'Pasadena Tournament' (*see p.244*); the original bush form was introduced by Krebs in 1942, the climbing form was introduced by Marsh's Nursery in 1945.

Garden notes A tall grower, with few thorns and bronze-green young growth on long canes to 10 ft (3 m); if it is like its 'Cécile Brünner' parent, it will eventually grow tall enough to cover a small tree. Hardy to 0°F (-18°C), Zone 7.

'Titian' A Climbing Floribunda of unknown parentage raised by Francis L. Riethmuller in Australia in 1950. Deep salmon-pink flowers, shaded with crimson, become paler as they fade.

Garden notes Repeat-flowers well, with stems to 12 ft (4 m). Hardy to 0°F (-18°C), Zone 7.

'Guinée'

'Titian' at Gowan Brae in New South Wales, Australia

143

Ramblers

'Wedding Day'

THE DISTINCTION between Ramblers and Climbers, two terms commonly used for tall-growing roses, is a somewhat hazy one. Both of them can climb up trees or be trained on high walls. We follow the widespread convention of distinguishing Ramblers as once-flowering roses producing masses of small flowers, and Climbing roses as those producing large flowers singly or in smaller groups, often in autumn as well as in midsummer. As in all aspects of nature there are areas of overlap, and some of the roses included here have flowers almost as large as those included in Noisettes and Climbing Roses: which classification a particular rose falls into may vary from country to country, and some rose organizations use quite different terminology.

Most Ramblers originated as crosses between wild roses of the Synstylae group (*see pp. 16–19*), so called because the styles of their white, single flowers are united into a spike-like column. The Synstylae are all rambling roses, putting out long shoots every year, which produce sprays of scented flowers from each leaf bud. Crossed with Teas and Hybrid Teas, they produced the Ramblers; few roses make such a fine show, though most of them are only once-flowering.

In the early 19th century, rose breeders used the Mediterranean musk rose *R. sempervirens* (*see p. 19*) to produce Ramblers such as 'Adélaïde d'Orleans' (*see p. 154*). Next the Chinese musk rose *R. multiflora* (*see p. 17*) was introduced to Europe, and from that another group was raised, of which 'Turner's Crimson Rambler' and 'Goldfinch' (*see p. 148*) are examples. Later still the Japanese roses *R. wichurana* (*see p. 19*) and *R. luciae* were brought to Europe and North America, and these led to another distinct group with very shiny leaves, which includes 'Alberic Barbier' (*see p. 150*) and 'Dorothy Perkins' (*see p. 158*). The American Prairie rose, *R. setigera* (*see p. 19*), produced the enduringly popular 'American Pillar' (*see p. 157*). In each case the crossing of a large-flowered rose with the small-flowered Synstylae gave the typical growth and flowers of the Rambler, combined with greater cold-hardiness than the old Noisettes, although the hardiness of these roses does vary to some degree with the parentage.

Because Ramblers tend to throw up new shoots from the base, those that have flowered should be removed and the new shoots tied in while the plants are dormant.

'Fortuneana' (also called 'Double Cherokee', 'Fortuniana', *Rosa × fortuneana*) This is an old Chinese garden variety, said to be a hybrid between *R. laevigata* (*see p.15*) and *R. banksiae* (*see p.14*). It has a rather untidy, double, white flower, larger than *R. banksiae* var. *banksiae*, and similar shining foliage.

Garden notes A very rampant rose, but not free-flowering in cool areas; it is used as a rootstock in warm climates such as Australia. Probably hardy only down to 23°F (-5°C), in Zone 9.

'La Mortola' (also called *Rosa brunonii* 'La Mortola') A very fine form or hybrid of *R. brunonii* (*see p.16*), introduced by the rosarian Graham Thomas from the garden at La Mortola in northwestern Italy. The leaves are limp and pale green, and the flowers, in generous clusters, are large and creamy-white, with a sweet, musky scent.

Garden notes This is a lovely and rampant rose, the best of the species or near-species climbers. Hardy to 10°F (-12°C), Zone 8, and perhaps into the warmer parts of Zone 7; in borderline areas the shoots should be tied close to a wall in late summer so that they survive the frost.

'Purezza' (also called *Rosa banksiae* 'Purezza', 'The Pearl') One of the few modern hybrids of *R. banksiae* (*see p.14*), raised by Commendatore Mansuiuo at Poggio de San Remo in Italy in 1961 by crossing *R. banksiae* with a Tea rose. Flowers are produced in clusters over a long period through the summer.

Garden notes An attractive rose, slowly becoming popular in Mediterranean climates. Probably hardy only down to 23°F (-5°C), in Zone 9.

Rosa banksiae* var. *banksiae (also called Lady Banks' Rose, *Rosa banksiae* 'Alba Plena', 'White Lady Banks') An evergreen climbing rose. The double flowers are white, around 1¼ in (3 cm) across, and in clusters. Hips are not usually formed. This was the first form of *R. banksiae* (*see p.14*) to be introduced from China; it was brought to Kew by William Kerr from Canton in 1807 and named in honor of Lady Banks, wife of the botanical collector and patron Sir Joseph Banks.

Garden notes This is a very rampant rose, with stems to 50 ft (15 m) or more, with few, hooked thorns. It is one of the earliest of all to flower, and is sweetly scented of violets. It will survive down to 14°F (-10°C), into Zone 8.

'La Mortola'

'Wedding Day' (also called 'English Wedding Day') This originated as a chance seedling at Highdown, Worthing in Sussex, England and was introduced by Sir Frederick Stern in around 1950. It is probably a hybrid of the rampant climbing rose *R. sinowilsonii*, said to be with *R. moyesii* (*see p.20*) although this seems unlikely. The petals have a short, pointed apex and the flowers open pale buff; they are very well scented, but are spoiled by rain, becoming spotted with dull red.

Garden notes A strong climber up to 30 ft (9 m) or more, and free flowering. It is sometimes confused with 'Polyantha Grandiflora' which has fewer, larger flowers with the petals indented at the tip. Hardy to -10°F (-23°C), Zone 6.

Rosa banksiae var. *banksiae*   'Purezza'   'Fortuneana'

'Seagull' in the garden of Richard Rix in Kent, southeastern England

'Seagull'

'Sander's White Rambler' in Eccleston Square Garden, London

'Mountain Snow'

'Bobbie James'   A rampant Rambler introduced by Graham Thomas at Sunningdale Nurseries in England in 1960. It is a hybrid of a wild rose of the Synstylae section, possibly *R. brunonii* (*see p.16*), and originated as a seedling in the garden of rosarian The Hon. Robert James at St Nicholas in Richmond, Yorkshire. The creamy white cupped flowers have two rows of petals and are carried in clusters.

   Garden notes   Ideal for climbing into a tree, with stems to 25 ft (8 m) or more. The sweet scent fills surrounding areas of the garden. Hardy to 0°F (-18°C), Zone 7.

'Mountain Snow' (also called AUSsnow)   A Rambler raised by David Austin in 1985. The white flowers are semidouble, quite large, and in huge clusters producing cascades of white.

   Garden notes   A profusion of flowers on a not very large plant, the stems reaching 15 ft (5 m). Like many David Austin roses, this may grow taller in climates hotter than England. Hardy to -20°F (-29°C), Zone 5.

'Rambling Rector'   A very strong-growing, white-flowered Rambler; the neat, cupped flowers are semidouble, with a good scent, which is carried on the air. The yellow stamens soon become brown, which spoils the close-up appearance of the flowers. It was first recorded in 1912, when it was introduced by Daisy Hill Nurseries in Northern Ireland, and its origin is unknown: it is possibly a hybrid of *R. moschata* (*see p.18*) and *R. multiflora* (*see p.17*).

   Garden notes   A strong-growing rose with very thorny stems, to 40 ft (12 m). Hardy to -20°F (-29°C), Zone 5.

'Sander's White Rambler'   A rather late-flowering Rambler with shining leaves, close to 'Dorothy Perkins' (*see p.158*), introduced in 1912 by Sander, a famous orchid nurseryman in St Albans, England. The small, white flowers are well scented.

   Garden notes   This is not a great climber like most of the roses on this page, but puts up long shoots to 12 ft (4 m) from near the base each year. Hardy to -30°F (-34°C), Zone 4.

'Seagull'   A small-flowered climbing rose, introduced by Pritchard in 1907. Pale pinkish buds in congested heads open to white flowers. The parentage is unknown, but it is probably a hybrid of *R. multiflora* (*see p.17*).

   Garden notes   Grows to 15 ft (5 m), and is free-flowering, with a good scent that is carried on the air. Hardy to -20°F (-29°C), Zone 5.

'Rambling Rector' at The Gardens of the Rose in St Albans, southeastern England

'Bobbie James'

147

'Ghislaine de Féligonde'

'Malvern Hills'

'Ghislaine de Féligonde'   A tall Rambler, raised by E. Turbat of Olivet near Orléans, France and introduced in 1916, said to be a seedling of 'Goldfinch'. The flowers are double, carried in often nodding clusters, and pinkish-yellow. The flowering shoots and stems have bristly red prickles. Unlike most Ramblers, this produces some later flowers after the first flowering.

    Garden notes   An attractive rose, less rampant than many of its relatives, and also suitable for growing as a large shrub. Hardy to -20°F (-29°C), Zone 5.

'Goldfinch'   A Rambler raised by George Paul at Cheshunt in 1907 from a complex cross involving 'Turner's Crimson Rambler' and a Hybrid Tea. The clusters of yellow buds open to cream flowers with a central mass of golden stamens. Their scent is good.

    Garden notes   This rose is a tall grower, with stems to 15 ft (5 m), and free-flowering but only in midsummer. It is tolerant of shade, and good for climbing up an old tree; my parents grew it on an old apple tree, and after the tree collapsed the rose continued for a few years until it succumbed to the honey fungus in the old tree roots. Hardy to -20°F (-29°C), Zone 5.

'Malvern Hills' (also called AUScanary)   A Rambler raised by David Austin in 2000. The small, fully double flowers are a deep, coppery yellow, becoming paler in the sun. It repeat flowers well and has a sweet, delicate scent.

Garden notes   Stems with few thorns reach 10 ft (3 m), so ideal for an arch or trellis. Hardy to -10°F (-23°C), Zone 6.

'Paul's Himalayan Musk'   One of the most robust of all small-flowered climbing roses, introduced by William Paul of Waltham Cross, Hertfordshire in 1899. The flowers are in large sprays of up to 50 and open pale lilac-pink before fading to white; they are small, just over 1 in (2.5 cm) across, fully double, and with a scent that pervades the air. It is possibly a hybrid of *R. filipes* (*see p.16*), which was introduced in 1908.

    Garden notes   Suitable for growing into the tallest tree, with stems to 30 ft (10 m) or more, and particularly good for relieving the dullness of a large evergreen or conifer. Hardy to -10°F (-23°C), Zone 6.

'Treasure Trove' (also called JAClay)   A strong climber that appeared in the garden of clematis grower and nurseryman John Treasure at Tenbury Wells and was introduced in 1977. Large clusters of bright red buds open to double, cupped flowers around 2½ in (6 cm) across, creamy white with pink veins, particularly around the edges. The scent is delicate, like a musk rose. Possibly a hybrid of *R. filipes* (*see p.16*) and a large-flowered climber such as 'Mme Grégoire Staechelin' (*see p.137*).

    Garden notes   Too vigorous for a wall, with stems up to 25 feet (8m), and better planted to climb a large tree or along a hedge. Hardy to -10°F (-23°C), Zone 6.

'Paul's Himalayan Musk'

'Treasure Trove'

'Treasure Trove' in the garden of Richard Rix in Kent, southeastern England

'Goldfinch' at Wilton Cottage, southern England

'Albéric Barbier' by a *chaikana* (teahouse) in Turkey

'Albéric Barbier' This lovely rose, a cross between *R. luciae* and the Tea 'Shirley Hibberd', was raised by René Barbier in Orléans, France in 1900. The flowers are pale yellow in bud, opening white and very double, on reddish stalks; the leaves have shining, widely spaced leaflets.

Garden notes This is one of the most reliable old roses for a range of garden conditions. I have seen it covering an arbor in Turkey, and thriving in a village in the south of France in dry, hot positions, but it does almost as well in the cold and wet of north Devon in England. The Barbier Ramblers are hybrids of Tea roses and the white-flowered, evergreen Japanese climber *R. luciae*, often confused with *R. wichurana* (see p.19). They have shining, evergreen leaves with rather few, small leaflets, and quite large, refined flowers in muted cream, pale yellow, peach, and pale orange-pink, produced over a long period with a few late flowers into autumn. Hardy to 10°F (-12°C), Zone 8, and can be grown in Zone 7, although it will suffer during cold spells.

'Alexandre Girault' Another of the excellent Barbier Ramblers, raised in 1909 by crossing *R. luciae* (see under 'Albéric Barbier') and the Tea rose 'Papa Gontier'. Double flowers, in upright or hanging sprays, are reddish-pink, becoming purplish as they fade, with a delicate scent likened to apples. The leaflets are paler green than most of this group.

Garden notes Good for training on a trellis or pergola, with long and flexible stems eventually reaching 30 ft (10 m).

'Albéric Barbier'

'Auguste Gervais'

'Léontine Gervais'

'Alexander Girault'

It is once-flowering only. There is a famous, huge plant of this on a trellis in the Roseraie de l'Haÿ-les-Roses, near Paris. Hardy to 0°F (-18°C), Zone 7.

'Auguste Gervais'   A Rambler with quite large flowers, raised by René Barbier in Orléans, France in 1918, a cross between *R. luciae* (*see under* 'Albéric Barbier') and 'Le Progrès', a yellow Hybrid Tea. The flowers, produced singly or in small clusters, open apricot-pink from red buds and fade to creamy yellow; they are fully double and cupped with a muddled center.
   Garden notes   The main flowering is in midsummer, but flowers appear intermittently later, on stems that reach 20 ft (6 m). Hardy to 0°F (-18°C), Zone 7.

'François Juranville'   A Rambler with quite large flowers, raised by René Barbier in Orléans, France in 1918, a cross between *R. luciae* (*see under* 'Albéric Barbier') and 'Mme Laurette Messimy', an apricot Tea. Pink buds open to rich peachy pink flowers, which are fully double and flat with a muddled center; the main flowering is in midsummer, the scent is good. The leaves have dark green leaflets with coarse teeth.
   Garden notes   This an unusual and valuable Rambler, suitable for a pergola, trellis, or wall, with long, thin stems to 20 ft (6m). Hardy to 0°F (-18°C), Zone 7.

'Léontine Gervais'   A Rambler with quite small flowers, raised by René Barbier in Orléans, France in 1903, a cross between *R. luciae* (*see under* 'Albéric Barbier') and 'Souvenir de Catherine Guillot', an orange-red China. The flowers are red in bud, opening apricot-pink and fading to creamy yellow, and nearly double, showing red stamens when fully open.
   Garden notes   An excellent rose with some later flowers and very good scent. Deep red stems to 15 ft (5 m). Hardy to 0°F (-18°C), Zone 7.

'Paul Transon'   A Rambler with quite large flowers, raised by René Barbier in Orléans, France in 1900, a cross between *R. luciae* (*see under* 'Albéric Barbier') and the Noisette 'L'Idéal'. The fully double flowers are reddish-apricot, deeper in the center, fading to flesh-pink. Flowering is mainly in midsummer, with some later flowers.
   Garden notes   An excellent Rambler with a delicate scent. It has deep purplish-red stems to 15 ft (5 m) and leaves with small, widely spaced leaflets. Hardy to 0°F (-18°C), Zone 7.

'Paul Transon'

'François Juranville'

'Aviateur Blériot' at the Parc de la Tête d'Or in Lyon, France

'Albertine' A Rambler raised by René Barbier in Orléans in 1921, by crossing *R. luciae* (*see under* 'Albéric Barbier', *p.150*) and 'Mrs Arthur Robert Waddell' a Hybrid Tea. The perfect buds are bright pinkish-orange, opening to shades of pale pink with a yellowish center. The leaves are very glossy, with larger leaflets than most of this group.

Garden notes The stems, to 20 ft (6m), are best trained along a fence or hedge. A very popular rose both for its bright colouring and great freedom of flowering, but it is not very hardy, and is sometimes killed in the coldest winters in east and central England and western Europe. Hardy to 0°F (-18°C), Zone 7.

'Aviateur Blériot' A tall Rambler raised by Fauque et fils of Orleans, France in 1910, by crossing *R. luciae* (*see under* 'Albéric Barbier', *p.150*) with 'William Allen Richardson' (*see p.109*). The flowers are rather small and untidily double, produced in few-flowered clusters. They open creamy white from peach-pink buds, with little scent. The leaves are small and shining dark green.

Garden notes This uncommon rose grew all over an old shed in my parents garden in Kent, southeastern England, although we never knew its name. It is very pretty when growing well, but it does best with hard pruning and rejuvenation every five years or so. Hard winters killed it to the ground; probably hardy to 0°F (-18°C), Zone 7.

'Climbing Cécile Brünner' (also called 'Climbing Mlle Cécile Brünner') This climbing sport of 'Cécile Brünner' (*see p.223*) was introduced in 1894 by F.P. Hosp. The small flowers, like perfect miniature Hybrid Tea roses in shape, are carried in large sprays. They are bright coral-pink in bud, fading as they open. The leaves are smooth, like a small Hybrid Tea.

Garden notes One of the most free-flowering of all the small-flowered roses, repeating through the season, and one of the most vigorous: it can smother a tree and in Eccleston Square, London has brought down a full sized laburnum. It can reach 30 ft (10 m) or even more. Hardy to 10°F (-12°C), Zone 8.

'Climbing Cécile Brunner'

'Gardenia' A large-flowered Rambler, introduced by Manda & Pitcher of South Orange, New Jersey in 1898. The flowers open buff-yellow, soon fading to white, and are around 2 in (5 cm) across, in small clusters.

Garden notes A strong grower with small, dark green shining leaves and red new shoots. Flowering is intermittent throughout the season. Hardy to 0°F (-18°C), Zone 7.

'Penny Lane' (also called HARDwell) A climber with medium-sized flowers, raised by Harkness at Hitchin, Hertfordshire in 1998. The flowers are apricot-yellow, fully double, and quartered, with an excellent scent.

Garden notes A pretty rose, flowering over a long period, but seldom covered with flowers. The stems reach 12 ft (4 m), with lush and healthy leaves. Hardy to -10°F (-23°C), Zone 6.

'Phyllis Bide' This unusual and distinctive rose was raised by Bide in 1923, reportedly by crossing 'Perle d'Or' (*see p.88*) with 'Gloire de Dijon' (*see p.107*). The flowers, which are very freely produced, open gold and become pinkish, and become prettily untidy when open, with curled petals. Their scent is slight. The leaflets are pale green and small, but often look a little too sparse.

Garden notes A repeat-flowering Rambler, dainty rather than particularly striking. Hardy to 0°F (-18°C), Zone 7.

'Phyllis Bide'

'Albertine'

'Gardenia'

'Penny Lane'

'Albertine'

'Baltimore Belle'

'Adélaïde d'Orléans' (also called 'Princesse Adélaïde d'Orléans') A very pretty Rambler raised in 1826 by Antoine Jacques, gardener to the Duc d'Orléans, from *R. sempervirens* (*see p.19*) crossed with 'Parson's Pink China' (*see p.82*). Flowers in early summer only, with pinkish buds opening to creamy white, semidouble flowers. The scent is of primroses.

Garden notes Stems to 20 ft (6 m), with evergreen leaves prone to mildew. Needs a warm site and good soil to do well; should be good in areas with dry summers, such as California. Hardy perhaps to 10°F (-12°C), usually surviving in Zone 8.

'Baltimore Belle' (also called 'Belle de Baltimore') A very pretty hybrid raised by Samuel and John Feast in Baltimore in 1843, using *R. setigera* (*see p.19*) probably crossed with a Noisette to produce a result close to the *sempervirens* Ramblers. The very pale flowers, in large, loose, hanging bunches, are double, with the inner petals curved inwards, but do not open properly in wet weather. They are very well scented. The "Belle" was the first wife of Napoleon's brother; at Napoleon's behest, her husband left her for a political match to a German princess. She remained on good terms with him, living in the castle at Wilhelmshöhe.

Garden notes Useful for flowering late in the rose season, and forming a healthy plant, climbing to 15 ft (5 m). Hardy to -20°F (-29°C), Zone 5, and perhaps into Zone 4.

'Félicité-Perpétue' (also called 'Félicité et Perpétue') Small, neat, fully double flowers in large clusters and a fetching name make this a favorite rose. It has a good musk scent, and is a sister seedling of 'Adélaïde d'Orleans', raised by Antoine Jacques in 1827, and named after his daughters. According to Charles Quest-Ritson the hyphenated spelling is the original one, found in Jacques' 1830 catalog.

Garden notes Late-flowering and good on a north wall, with stems eventually reaching 15 ft (5 m); free-flowering even when neglected. Probably hardy to 0°F (-18°C), Zone 7.

'Lauré Davoust' (also called 'L'Abbandonata', 'Marjorie W. Lester') An interesting hybrid of *R. sempervirens* (*see p.19*) and a Noisette, raised by Jean Laffay of Bellevue-Meudon, France in 1834. The flowers are small, in clusters, and fully double, with petals that are white in the middle and deep pink around

'Adélaïde d'Orléans' in the Bagatelle Rose Garden, Paris

'Félicité-Perpétue'

the edges, later fading to white. Their petals do not drop, and the heads can become a mess towards the end of flowering.

Garden notes In hot climates, this is very strong-growing, reaching more than 25 ft (8 m), as would be expected from a Mediterranean rose crossed with a heat-tolerant one. Hardy to 0°F (-18°C), Zone 7.

***Rosa multiflora* 'Carnea'** Probably an old Chinese cultivar of *R. multiflora* (*see p.17*), perhaps crossed with 'Parson's Pink China' (*see p.82*), introduced to the West in 1804. This would account for the flowers, in rather uncrowded heads, which open pink and fade to white, with curling petals giving a starry effect.

Garden notes An attractive rose with delicate colors, unlike *R. multiflora* 'Platyphylla' (*see p.159*) which has harsh, purplish-pink flowers. Hardy perhaps to -10°F (-23°C), Zone 6.

'Lauré Davoust'

'Adélaïde d'Orléans'

Rosa multiflora 'Carnea'

'Hiawatha' in the Royal Horticultural Society Garden, Wisley, southern England

'Kew Rambler' in Eccleston Square Garden, London

'American Pillar' in the Auckland Botanic Gardens, New Zealand

'Blush Rambler'

thornless canes to 15 ft (5 m). The dense clusters of flowers have a good scent. Hardy perhaps to -20°F (-29°C), Zone 5.

'Hiawatha'   A Rambler raised by Michael Walsh in Woods Hole, Massachussetts in 1904. It is a hybrid of 'Turner's Crimson Rambler', probably with *R. wichurana* (*see p.19*), and is close to 'Dorothy Perkins' (*see p.158*). The flowers open bright red-pink with a white center before fading to pale pink, and are very freely produced in large clusters.

Garden notes   A powerful grower with stems growing to over 15 ft (5 m). Hardy to -20°F (-29°C), Zone 5.

'Kew Rambler'   An attractive, single-flowered Rambler raised at the Royal Botanic Gardens, Kew in 1912 from *R. soulieana* (*see p.17*) crossed with 'Hiawatha'. The flowers, produced in tight clusters, are bright pink with a white center, fading to all white. The scent is good.

Garden notes   Stems reach to 20 ft (6 m), with grayish leaves and small leaflets. Hardy to -20°F (-29°C), Zone 5.

'American Pillar'   A late-flowering Rambler raised by Walter Van Fleet at the USDA Glenn Dale Station in Maryland in 1902, by crossing a hybrid of *R. wichurana* and *R. setigera* (*see p.19 for both*) with a red Hybrid Perpetual. It has no scent, and the glossy leaves are susceptible to mildew, but this is still one of the most popular Ramblers for the reliability of its large clusters of flowers, which are single and intense pink with a white base.

Garden notes   One of the brightest Ramblers, widely grown in Europe as well as the United States. Stems to 20 ft (6 m). The influence of *R. setigera* has made it very hardy, to -20°F (-29°C), Zone 5.

'Apple Blossom'   A small-flowered Rambler raised by Jackson Thornton Dawson, superintendent of the Arnold Arboretum in Boston, Massachussetts around 1890, and introduced by Stark Bros in 1932. The parentage involved 'Dawson', a hybrid of *R. multiflora* (*see p.17*) and the Hybrid Perpetual 'General Jacqueminot', backcrossed to 'General Jacqueminot'. The result is a very hardy rose with dense clusters of semidouble, pink and white flowers.

Garden notes   A strong-growing and very floriferous plant, special for its long-lasting flowers and exceptional hardiness. Hardy to -20°F (-29°C), Zone 5.

'Blush Rambler'   A Rambler raised by B.R. Cant of Colchester, England in 1903, from 'Turner's Crimson Rambler' (an old Chinese garden *multiflora*, *see p.17*) and 'The Garland', an old white Rambler with *R. moschata* (*see p.18*) parentage. The flowers are single, cupped, and pale pink.

Garden notes   The leaves are pale, and can even look yellow on chalky soils, but this is a very vigorous rose with almost

'Apple Blossom'

'Tausendschön'

'Dorothy Perkins'

'Debutante' A Rambler raised by Michael Walsh in Woods Hole, Massachussetts in 1901. It is a hybrid of *R. wichurana* (*see p.19*) and a Hybrid Perpetual, said to be 'Baronne Adolphe de Rothschild' (*see p.124*). Small clusters of double flowers open pink and fade to cameo-pink. The scent is of apples.

Garden notes A graceful grower, with stems to 12 ft (4 m), suitable for training on a fence or pergola. Most of the roses on these two pages are typical of those that owe their habit of growth to their *R. wichurana* parent. Long green stems, seven or nine bright green, rounded, overlapping leaflets, and elongated clusters of flowers are all *wichurana* characteristics; they contrast with the five or seven widely-spaced, narrower, dark green leaflets and the fewer-flowered, flatter sprays of the hybrids derived by Barbier from *R. luciae* (*see under* 'Albéric Barbier', *p.150*). Hardy to -30°F (-34°C), Zone 4.

'Dorothy Perkins' A familiar Rambler in cottage gardens, recognized instantly by its elongated clusters of small, double flowers with mildew on the stalks. They are pink, becoming paler as they fade. It is a hybrid of *R. wichurana* (*see p.19*) with the Hybrid Perpetual 'Mme Gabriel Luizet', introduced in 1901 by Jackson and Perkins, still one of the largest rose breeders in the United States. 'Excelsa', sometimes called 'Red Dorothy Perkins' is very similar, with bright pinkish-red flowers; there are repeat-flowering forms called 'Super Dorothy' and 'Super Excelsa'.

Garden notes Perfect for covering a fence or pergola. Remove old shoots that have flowered as soon as the flowers fade and carefully tie in the new canes, to flower next year. It roots very easily from cuttings and is difficult to remove, as each piece of root can sprout a new plant. Hardy to -30°F (-34°C), Zone 4, and also tolerant of heat.

'May Queen' A Rambler introduced by Conard & Jones in 1898, raised by Walter Van Fleet at the USDA Glenn Dale Station in Maryland by crossing *R. wichurana* (*see p.19*) with a Bourbon. The double flowers are old-fashioned in shape, pale pink with a deeper center, and have a good scent, but only come in summer; May is rather optimistic for England, where it usually flowers in mid-June.

Garden notes Roger and I were most impressed to see this rose covering an old barn at David Austin's nursery in England; it also does well in Australia and North America. The stems can reach 15 ft (5 m). Probably hardy to -10°F (-23°C), Zone 6.

'May Queen'

'Newport Fairy'

'Minnehaha'

Rosa multiflora 'Platyphylla'

'Minnehaha' A Rambler raised by Michael Walsh in Woods Hole, Massachussetts in 1904, by crossing *R. wichurana* (*see p.19*) with a Hybrid Perpetual, said to be 'Paul Neyron' (*see p.125*). In habit it is very similar to 'Dorothy Perkins' but with deeper pink flowers, produced in tighter clusters and a week or two later.

Garden notes A graceful grower, with shoots to 12 ft (4 m), suitable for training on a fence or pergola. Hardy to -30°F (-34°C), Zone 4.

'Newport Fairy' (also called 'Newport Rambler') A Rambler raised by Gardner in 1908, a hybrid of *R. wichurana* (*see p.19*) and 'Turner's Crimson Rambler', an old variety of *R. multiflora* (*see p.17*) from China. The flowers are single and small, in large clusters, and are reported to continue to appear after the first flush. They open deep pink and fade to almost white.

Garden notes A popular and strong climber with stems to 15 ft (5 m). Hardy to -30°F (-34°C), Zone 4.

Rosa multiflora 'Platyphylla' (also called 'Seven Sisters Rose') An old Chinese garden rose, or group of roses, found apparently wild in many parts of China and introduced to the West around 1800. Charles Quest-Ritson suggests that the present European stock originated from seed brought from Japan. The flowers open red and soon fade through pink to light pink, so that seven colors may be seen together by the fanciful, hence the name.

Garden notes This Rambler has shoots to around 10 ft (3 m), and usually forms an arching shrub. Hardy to -20°F (-29°C), Zone 5.

'Tausendschön' (also called 'Thousand Beauties') This hardy Rambler was raised by Hermann Kiese of Vieselbach and introduced in 1906 by J.C. Schmidt's nursery in Erfurt, where Kiese was foreman. The parentage is the Polyantha Rambler 'Daniel Lacombe' crossed with the white-flowered Rambler 'Weisser Herumstreicher'. The fully double flowers open deep crimson-pink and soon fade, giving the clusters an attractive, dappled effect.

Garden notes 'Tausendschön' was an important parent, passing its hardiness and thornlessness to famous Ramblers and to numerous sports as well. The stems of this and related roses are largely thornless, and can extend to 20 ft (6 m); they are hardy to -30°F (-34°C), Zone 4.

'Debutante' in the garden at West Dean, southeastern England

'Veilchenblau'

'Chevy Chase'

'Rose-Marie Viaud'

'Bleu Magenta' A Rambler of unknown origin, but probably an old rose from the early 20th century whose name has been lost; it is grown in the Graham Thomas collection at Mottisfont Abbey in Hampshire, England. The flowers are of medium size, loosely double, opening deep crimson, becoming purplish, in large sprays. The scent is slight. The leaflets are broad, tapering to a sharp point, and have sharp teeth.

    Garden notes A good rose of the *R. multiflora* (*see p.17*) type, stems to 15 ft (5 m); combines well with 'Goldfinch' (*see p.148*) to give an opulent effect. Hardy to -20°F (-29°C), Zone 5.

'Bleu Magenta'

'Chevy Chase' A small-flowered Rambler, raised by Hansen in the United States in 1939; the parentage was *R. soulieana* (*see p.17*) crossed with 'Eboulissant', a red dwarf Polyantha. The flowers are dark crimson, fully double in dense clusters, with only slight scent. The leaves are said to retain some of the grayness of *R. soulieana*.

    Garden notes This is a popular rose in America, with stems to 15 ft (5 m); to acheive its best, the dead flowers should be removed as they fade. Hardy to -20°F (-29°C), Zone 5.

'De la Grifferaie' This is a tall shrub or a low Rambler, raised by Jean-Pierre Vibert of Angers in 1845. The parentage is probably *R. multiflora* 'Platyphylla' (*see p.159*) crossed with a double form of *R. gallica* (*see p.33*). It forms a plant to around 10 ft (3 m), with almost thornless canes: these distinguish it from 'Russelliana', which comes from similar parentage but has very thorny stems. The flowers, which open flat and fully double, are produced in sprays of 10 to 15, and only in midsummer. They are crimson-pink, fading to white, and their scent is good, some say excellent.

    Garden notes This is a tough rose, suckering freely and often found in old gardens because of its use as a rootstock. Hardy perhaps to -30°F (-34°C), Zone 4.

'Rose-Marie Viaud' (also called 'Rosemary Viaud') This Rambler was raised by Igoult and introduced by Viaud-Bruant in France in 1924; like many of the "blue" roses, it is a seedling of 'Veilchenblau'. This has the most tightly double flowers of the purple Ramblers, with lovely pompoms of magenta-crimson

'Russelliana' in the California Gold Country

fading to grayish-pink; the inner petals often have white streaks. Sadly, they have no scent.

Garden notes The almost thornless stems can reach 12 ft (4 m), and the plant is ideal for training over an arch. Hardy to -20°F (-29°C), Zone 5.

'Russelliana' (also called 'Old Spanish Rose', 'Russell's Cottage Rose', 'Souvenir de la Bataille de Marengo') Known since 1826, this is a rose of uncertain origin, possibly a hybrid of a Damask and *R. multiflora* (*see p.17*). Stiff, thorny canes bear clusters of sweetly scented, Damask-type roses. The eye is often green, and the center purplish-red, fading to pink and white on the edge.

   Garden notes Stems to 20 ft (6 m), but usually around 8 ft (2.5 m). A strong climber in good soil, growing and flowering well even in the poorest, this is a tough old rose, often found in hedges or abandoned gardens, and good for planting in an informal setting. Hardy perhaps to -30°F (-34°C), Zone 4.

'Veilchenblau' (also called 'Bleu-Violet') An almost thornless rose, raised by Kiese and introduced by Schmidt in 1908, from a cross of 'Turner's Crimson Rambler' with 'Erinnerung an Brod' (*see p.126*). The semidouble flowers, in elongated sprays, open deep crimson with a pale center, becoming mauve and showing stamens when fully open. The scent is slight.

   Garden notes A robust rose with long, arching stems and the typical feathery stipules of *R. multiflora* (*see p.17*) at the base of the leaf stalks. Perhaps rather coarse compared with other roses in the same color range. Hardy to -20°F (-29°C), Zone 5.

'De la Grifferaie'

Groundcover Roses

'Nozomi'

THESE ARE A RELATIVELY RECENT development in roses; some horticultural organizations do not officially recognize them as a group, classing them instead as Shrub or Miniature roses, but the category has certainly been a marketing success.

Groundcover roses are bred to be low growing, continuous flowering, and if possible, with dense enough leaf cover to suppress weeds that might otherwise grow up between the stems. Many may also be cut back hard with a saw or mechanical mower every few years, to grow up again the following year with renewed vigour.

Two wild parents, both evergreen in their natural ranges, have been important in Groundcover roses: *R. wichurana*, which is a naturally creeping rose from coastal Japan, and a dwarf cushion-forming variety of *R. sempervirens* (usually a climber), found on coastal cliff tops near Nice in southern France.

The European rose breeders Kordes and Meilland have been quick to realise the potential of this type of rose for large-scale landscaping by towns and road-building authorities, with the likelihood that sales would be considerable. These new varieties are sometimes called "landscape roses," to distinguish them from the less rampant ones that are suitable for domestic gardens.

Pruning and other attention should be minimal. The plants can be clipped to keep them tidy, and old stems that have ceased flowering can be removed. The whole plant can be cut to the ground in winter every few years. The name Groundcover roses is slightly misleading: they are not initially successful at supressing weeds, and it is best to mulch beneath them. They are also not limited to this role: many are lovely grown as weeping standards, or make elegantly spreading, arching plants in containers.

GROUNDCOVER ROSES

'Nozomi' in the gardens of Kasteel Hex in Belgium

'Alba Meidiland'

'Alba Meidiland' (also called 'Alba Meillandécor', 'Alba Sunblaze', 'Meidiland Alba', MEIflopan)   A Groundcover or landscape rose introduced by Meilland in France in 1987. The flowers are double, around 2 in (5 cm) across, white, with some scent. Raised from *R. sempervirens* (*see p.19*) and 'Mlle Marthe Carron', a hybrid of *R. wichurana* (*see p.19*).
   Garden notes A strong-growing, repeat-flowering rose, building up into a mound of dense stems with small, pointed leaflets. The arching stems grow to 6 ft (2 m) long in a season, the flowering shoots reaching 4 ft (1.2 m). Hardy to -20°F (-29°C), Zone 5.

'Ferdy' (also called KEItoli)   A small-flowered Groundcover rose introduced by Keisei in Japan in 1984. The flowers are double, around 1½ in (4 cm) across, deep flesh pink, and without scent. It was raised from unnamed seedlings.
   Garden notes A very strong-growing plant, useful both as ground cover and as a climber, with stems creeping to 6 ft (1.8 m), the flowering shoots to 3 ft (1 m), bearing small, matte leaflets. There is some repeat flowering. Hardy to -20°F (-29°C), Zone 5.

'Ferdy'

'Nozomi' (also called 'Heideröslein Nozomi')   A creeping Miniature rose introduced by Onodera in Japan in 1968. The single flowers are around 1 in (3 cm) across and pale pink, with little scent. The parentage is the Climbing Miniature 'Fairy Princess' crossed with the Miniature 'Sweet Fairy'.
   Garden notes This has stems creeping to 5 ft (1.5 m) and very small, glossy leaflets. It is attractive as low groundcover by a path, over rocks, or as a small weeping standard. Hardy to -20°F (-29°C), Zone 5.

'Pheasant'

'Pheasant' (also called 'Heidekönigin', 'Palissade Rose', KORdapt)   A strong-growing Groundcover rose like a trailing rambler, introduced by Kordes in Germany in 1986. The double flowers are around 2 in (5 cm) across, pink, and have good scent. It is a cross of the Miniature 'Zwergkonig 78' and a seedling of *R. wichurana* (*see p.19*).
   Garden notes This is useful both as ground cover or cascading over a low wall, the stems creeping to 10 ft (3 m), the flowering shoots reaching 2 ft (60 cm), with small, round, shiny leaflets. Flowering begins late, with some repeat flowering. Hardy to -20°F (-29°C), Zone 5.

GROUNDCOVER ROSES

'Rosy Cushion'

'Worcestershire'

'White Flower Carpet'

'Baby Blanket' (also called 'Country Lass', 'Oxfordshire', 'Sommermorgen', 'Summer Morning', KORfullwind)
A strong-growing Groundcover rose introduced by Kordes in Germany in 1993. The flowers are fully double, around 2 in (5 cm) across, and bright pink, with little scent. The parentage is a cross of the Groundcover 'Weise Immensee' and the Floribunda 'Goldmarie'.

    Garden notes A repeat-flowering rose with stems creeping to 6 ft (2 m). This is one of a group of Groundcover roses raised by Kordes and introduced in England by Mattocks with English county names. Hardy to -20°F (-29°C), Zone 5.

'Pink Bells' (also called POULbells) A Miniature Groundcover rose introduced by Poulsen in Denmark in 1983. The flowers are in clusters, fully double, around 1 in (2.5 cm) across, and

pale pink, with some scent. The parentage is the Miniature 'Mini-Poul' and the Climbing Miniature 'Temple Bells'.

    Garden notes Flowers for a long period in summer on stems creeping to 4 ft (1.2 m) with small, rounded leaflets. There is a very similar rose, 'White Bells', with creamy flowers. Hardy to -20°F (-29°C), Zone 5.

'Rosy Cushion' (also called 'Rosy Hedge', INTerall) An attractive Shrub or Groundcover rose, a hybrid of 'Yesterday' (*see p.225*) and an unnamed seedling, introduced by Ilsink in the Netherlands in 1979. The single flowers, in dense clusters, are two shades of pink, with some scent, repeat flowering well.

    Garden notes A shrub with arching stems to 4 ft (1.2 m) long and under 30 in (75 cm) high. Use in a mixed border or a dense planting on a bank. Hardy to -10°F (-23°C), Zone 6.

'Silver River'

'Smarty'

'Baby Blanket'

'Swany' covering the tool shed at Meilland Roses in southern France

'Silver River' (also called LENsiver) A Groundcover rose introduced by Louis Lens in Belgium in 1989. The single, blush-pink and white flowers have good scent. The parentage is a seedling of the Hybrid Musk 'Ballerina' (*see p.174*) crossed with the Shrub rose 'Running Maid'.

   Garden notes Flowers continuously through the season. Hardy to -20°F (-29°C), Zone 5.

'Smarty' (also called INTersmart) A Groundcover rose introduced by Ilsink in Holland in 1979. The flowers are small, yellowish-pink shading to white in the centre, and in clusters. It is a seedling of 'Yesterday' (*see p.225*).

   Garden notes Flowers freely throughout the season. Hardy to -30°F (-34°C), Zone 4.

'Swany' (also called MEIburenac) A Groundcover or landscape rose raised by Meilland in France in 1978 from *R. sempervirens* (*see p.19*) and 'Mlle Marthe Carron', a *R. wichurana* (*see p.19*) hybrid. The flowers are around 2 in (5 cm) across, semidouble, white, with some scent.

   Garden notes Strong-growing stems reach 6 ft (2 m) in a season, flowering shoots 3 ft (1 m), forming a dark green mound studded with flowers throughout summer. Hardy to -20°F (-29°C), Zone 5.

'White Flower Carpet' (also called 'Emera Blanc', 'Opalia', 'Schneeflocker', 'Snowflake' NOAschnee) A Groundcover or low Floribunda introduced by Noack in Germany in 1991, this is a cross of the Groundcover rose 'Immensee' and 'Margaret Merrill' (*see p.228*). The clusters of white, semidouble flowers have little scent.

   Garden notes A good low-growing rose with stems to 30 in (75 cm) high. It is free flowering and repeat flowers well. Hardy to -30°F (-34°C), Zone 4.

'Worcestershire' (also called KORlalon) A Groundcover rose introduced by Kordes in Germany in 2000. The single flowers are around 2 in (5 cm) across, yellow, and without scent. The parentage is not recorded.

   Garden notes A strong-growing, repeat-flowering plant with stems arching to 6 ft (2 m) long. This is one of a group of Groundcover roses raised by Kordes and introduced in England by Mattocks Roses with the names of English counties. Hardy to -20°F (-29°C), Zone 5.

'Pink Bells'

'Eye Opener' (also called 'Erica', 'Tapis Rouge', INTerop)
A Groundcover rose raised by Ilsink and introduced
by Interplant in 1979. The flowers are single,
scarlet, and without fragrance. The parentage
involves 'Eyepaint' (*see p.244*) and the Kordesii
rose 'Dortmund'.
    Garden notes Arching stems reach 4 ft
(1.2m), but under 2ft (60cm) high. Flowering
starts a little late, but is then abundant and
continuous. Hardy to -20°F (-29°C), Zone 5.

'Magic Meidiland' (also called
'Magic Meillandécor', MEIbonrib)
A Groundcover or landscape rose
introduced by Meilland in France in
1993. The flowers are semidouble,
around 3 in (7.5 cm) across, bright
pink with a paler centre, and have
some scent. A cross of *R. sempervirens*
(*see p.19*) and a seedling of 'Bonica'
(*see p.192*) and the Floribunda 'Milrose'.
    Garden notes A vigorous, drought-resistant
rose. The arching stems reach 6 ft (2 m) in a
season, the flowering shoots 4 ft (1.2 m), forming a mound
of dense stems, with small, pointed leaflets, well clad with
flowers through the summer. Hardy to -20°F (-29°C), Zone 5.

'Surrey'

'Malverns' (also called 'Heidelinde', KORdehei)
A Groundcover rose or low Floribunda introduced by Kordes
in Germany in 1991. The flowers are fully double, around 2 in
(5 cm) across, and bright pink, with little scent.
    Garden notes A repeat-flowering rose with strong-growing
stems creeping to 4 ft (1.2 m) long. This is one of a group of
Groundcover roses raised by Kordes and introduced in
England by Mattocks Roses with the names of English hills.
Hardy to -20°F (-29°C), Zone 5.

'Pink Meidiland' (also called 'Schloss Heidegg', MEIpoque)
A Groundcover or landscape rose introduced by Meilland in
France in 1982. Unscented, single, bright pink flowers, with
overlapping petals and a white centre, fade to nearly white.
Raised from the Shrub rose 'Anne de Bretagne' and the
Floribunda 'Nirvana'.
    Garden notes Strong-growing stems arch to 6 ft (2 m) in a
season, the flowering shoots reach 4 ft (1.2 m), building up

into a mound of dense stems leaflets small, pointed. It is
repeat-flowering. Hardy to -30°F (-34°C), Zone 4.

'Red Meidiland' (also called 'Rouge Meillandécor', MEIneble)
A Groundcover or landscape rose introduced by Meilland in
France in 1989. The flowers are single, in clusters, and bright
red with a white eye, with little scent. Raised from the Shrub
rose 'Sea Foam' crossed with a seedling of 'Picasso' and
'Eyepaint' (*see p.244 for both*).
    Garden notes Very healthy, hardy, and strong-growing: the
stems arch to 6 ft (2 m) long in a season, and flowering shoots
reach 4 ft (1.2 m), building up into a dense mound with small,
pointed leaflets. The Meidiland series are long-flowering and
drought-resistant roses. Hardy to -30°F (-34°C), Zone 4.

'Malverns'

'Magic Meidiland'

'Wiltshire'

'Eye Opener'

'Surrey' (also called 'Sommerwind', 'Summer Breeze', 'Summerwind', 'Vent d'Été', KORlanum)   A Groundcover rose introduced by Kordes in Germany in 1987. The double flowers are cupped, pink, and without scent. Parentage is not recorded.

Garden notes   Strong-growing, with stems arching to 4 ft (1.2 m) long, and repeat-flowering.This is one of a group of Groundcover roses introduced in England by Mattocks Roses with English county names. Kordes have also produced a large, semidouble flowered Climber that is sometimes called 'Summer Breeze'. Hardy to -20°F (-29°C), Zone 5.

'Warwickshire' (also called KORkandel)   A Groundcover rose introduced by Kordes in Germany in 1991. Single flowers, in clusters, are bright reddish-pink with a white centre. Some scent.

Garden notes   The very free-flowering stems trail, forming dense cover, and the flowerheads reach around 18 in (45 cm) above them. This is one of a group of Groundcover roses introduced in England by Mattocks Roses with English county names. Hardy to -30°F (-34°C), Zone 4.

'Wiltshire' (also called 'Beautiful Carpet', KORmuse)   A repeat-flowering Groundcover rose introduced by Kordes in Germany in 1993, a hybrid of the Groundcover 'Weiße Immensee' and an unnamed seedling. It has semidouble, bright orange-pink flowers without scent.

Garden notes   Vigorous stems arch to 4 ft (1.2 m) long; unfortunately, when flowering begins the new shoots tend to overshadow the flowers. This is one of a group of Groundcover roses introduced in England by Mattocks Roses with English county names. Hardy to -30°F (-34°C), Zone 4.

'Red Meidiland' grown as a standard at Meilland Roses in the south of France

'Warwickshire'

'Pink Meidiland'

167

Hybrid Musk Roses

'Prosperity'

THIS IS A SMALL GROUP, but it includes some of the very best of all garden roses. Hybrid Musks make excellent shrubs with a wonderful show in midsummer, and many of them also flower well a second time. The flowers are produced in large, loose bunches or sprays and are small or medium-sized, usually white, cream, pink, or buff, mostly with excellent scent.

Hybrid Musks have always been associated with the Rev. Joseph Pemberton of Havering-atte-Bower in Essex. He and his sister Florence were successful exhibitors of the large-flowered roses that were in fashion in the late 19th century, such as Hybrid Perpetuals, and he was one of the early members of the National Rose Society of Great Britain. Though taught to bud roses by his father at the age of 12, it was only in around 1913, when he was over 60 and had retired, that he began to breed his own roses at their family home. Pemberton aimed to produce tough garden roses such as he remembered as a child, not the large exhibition types then claiming the attention of professional breeders. By crossing 'Trier', raised in 1904, with various Hybrid Teas, Pemberton produced a new race, eventually called the Hybrid Musks.

'Trier' is a large shrub, very well scented, and repeats through the season, characteristics found in most of Pemberton's roses. Its uncertain parentage contains elements of *R. multiflora* (*see p.17*), which

has given its extra hardiness to the Hybrid Musks, and of Noisettes. After Pemberton's death in 1926, his sister and his gardener J.A. Bentall introduced more of his roses and Bentall later raised and introduced his own Hybrid Musks.

Wilhelm Kordes in Germany introduced some excellent roses of similar appearance; 'Fritz Nobis' has lovely pale pink, nearly double flowers, but in summer only. 'Lavender Lassie' is a pale lavender with good repeat-flowering. 'Wilhelm' is also a good repeat-flowerer in a cheerful red, and had the advantage of being tetraploid and therefore fertile with contemporary Hybrid Teas and Floribundas.

Recently other breeders, and particularly Louis Lens in Belgium, have used dwarf *R. multiflora*, and produced roses many of which have the habit of short-growing, repeat-flowering ramblers, closer to Pemberton's 'Ballerina' (*see p.174*). Lens used other roses such as *R. helenae* crossed with Hybrid Teas to produce climbers with improved flowers; the Lens roses have a somewhat different character and are grouped separately here (*see pp.176–79*).

Hybrid Musks need little pruning, apart from thinning the older wood to make room for the new. Less pruning gives earlier flowers in smaller heads; hard pruning gives later flowers in large heads and is used if the plants are to be moved, or are weak or newly planted. Most Hybrid Musks are hardy to -20°F (-29°C), Zone 5.

'Danaë' This was one of the earliest of Pemberton's Hybrid Musks to be introduced, in 1913. The flowers are yellow, fully double, and well-scented. Its parentage is 'Trier', reputedly crossed with Gloire de Chédane-Guinnoisseau, a Hybrid Perpetual, although this seems an unlikely parent.

Garden notes A shrub to 6 ft (2 m), flowering continually through the season. Hardy to -20°F (-29°C), Zone 5.

'Prosperity' A Hybrid Musk introduced by Pemberton in 1919. The flowers are double and creamy-white, with good scent. The parentage is the Polyantha 'Marie-Jeanne' crossed with 'Perle des Jardins' (*see p.95*).

Garden notes A good, strong-growing garden shrub, reaching 5 ft (1.5 m). Flowers are produced until late in the season, the later flowers in larger clusters than those formed in spring. Hardy to -20°F (-29°C), Zone 5.

'Queen of the Musks' A Hybrid Musk of unrecorded parentage raised by Paul & Son in England in 1913. The blush pink, semidouble flowers have good scent. This rose predates most of Pemberton's Hybrid Musks, but Paul does not seem to have developed this line in his later breeding.

Garden notes A rare but attractive rose, still surviving at the Rosarium Sangerhousen in Germany. It forms a shrub to 5 ft (1.5 m), and has a second flowering after the first flush. Hardy to -20°F (-29°C), Zone 5.

'Trier' A Hybrid Musk, sometimes classed as a Hybrid Multiflora Rambler, raised by Peter Lambert in Trier, Germany in 1904. Numerous pink buds open to small, creamy white flowers with conspicuous golden stamens and good scent. The parentage is uncertain, it is probably a seedling of the Hybrid Multiflora 'Aglaia', whose ancestery included 'Rêve d'Or' (*see p.108*) and the repeat-flowering dwarf *R. multiflora* (*see p.17*).

Garden notes An attractive and informal large shrub that repeat flowers well. Hardy to -20°F (-29°C), Zone 5.

'Queen of the Musks'

'Trier'

'Danaë'

'Prosperity'

'Kathleen' at Kasteel Hex in Belgium

Pemberton's Hybrid Musks are generally large and vigorous in growth, though delicate in flower. The "classic" types, with subtle, pale colours, are shown together here. The red-flowered types have never been as popular, and are with the other reds (*see pp. 174–75*).

'Buff Beauty'

'Buff Beauty'
A Hybrid Musk introduced by Ann Bentall in England in 1939, but said to have been raised by Pemberton some years earlier. The fully double flowers are buff fading to cream, and and well scented. The parentage is the Noisette 'William Allen Richardson' (*see p. 109*) and an unnamed seedling.
   Garden notes   One of the best garden roses, a spreading shrub to 8 ft (2.5 m) with clusters of nodding flowers through the season. Excellent at the back of a border or trained on a fence or low wall. Hardy to -20°F (-29°C), Zone 5.

'Cornelia'   A Hybrid Musk raised by Pemberton in 1925. The fully double flowers are rather flat, with a sweet, heavy scent. They are paler pink in summer and more richly coloured as the weather cools. The parentage is not recorded.
   Garden notes   A spreading shrub with a particularly good late show. Normally this rose is grown as a low shrub to about 4 ft (1.2 m), but in California we have found it growing as a climber or very large shrub up to about 9 ft (2.75 m). Hardy to -30°F (34°C), Zone 4.

'Daybreak'   A Hybrid Musk raised by Pemberton in 1918. The semidouble, creamy yellow flowers have good scent. It is a cross of 'Trier' (*see p. 169*) and 'Liberty', a crimson Hybrid Tea.
   Garden notes   An upright shrub to around 6 ft (2 m), flowering all season. Hardy to -20°F (-29°C), Zone 5.

'Pax' with in the foreground *Alstroemeria* Ligtu Hybrids

'Daybreak'

'Moonlight'

'Penelope'

'Cornelia' in Brompton Cemetery, London

'Felicia' A Hybrid Musk introduced by Pemberton in 1928. It produces clusters of medium-sized, fully double, buff-pink flowers with good scent. The parentage is a cross of 'Trier' (*see p.169*) and 'Ophelia' (*see p.131 for* 'Climbing Ophelia').

   Garden notes A prolific flowerer through the season, which forms a strong-growing shrub to 7 ft (2.2 m). This is a typical Pemberton rose, and one of the best. It is also very hardy, to -30°F (34°C), Zone 4.

'Kathleen' A Hybrid Musk introduced by Pemberton in 1922. The flowers are single, blush pink, in large clusters, and with delicate scent. A cross of Pemberton's first Hybrid Musk 'Daphne' with 'Perle des Jardins' (*see p.95*).

   Garden notes One of the tallest varieties in the group, with stems around 6 ft (2 m), and repeat flowering well. Hardy to -20°F (-29°C), Zone 5.

'Moonlight' A Hybrid Musk raised by Pemberton in 1922, winner of a gold medal. semidouble, white to pale yellow, well scented flowers are produced in loose heads. They are rather small; later flowers are larger than those produced earlier in the season. The parentage is 'Trier' (*see p.169*) crossed with the yellow Tea 'Sulphurea'.

   Garden notes A large, free-flowering shrub, to 7 ft (2.2 m) or more, good for a mixed border. It is particularly valuable for its freedom of flowering late in the season. Pemberton himself recommended its flowers for the house at Christmas, if cut about four days before. It is also very hardy, to -30°F (34°C), Zone 4.

'Pax' A Hybrid Musk rose introduced by Pemberton in 1918 to coincide with the end of the First World War, and winner of a gold medal. The flowers are quite large and fully double, cream fading to white, and have good scent. It is a cross of 'Trier' (*see p.169*) and 'Sunburst', a yellow-orange Hybrid Tea.

   Garden notes A strong-growing shrub to 6 ft (2 m), with flowers produced continuously during the season. Particularly hardy, to -30°F (34°C), Zone 4.

'Penelope' A gold-medal winning Hybrid Musk introduced by Pemberton in 1924, from the same parentage as 'Felicia', 'Trier' (*see p.169*) crossed with the Hybrid Tea 'Ophelia' (*see p.131 for* 'Climbing Ophelia'). Loose heads of pinkish-orange buds open to creamy-yellow, well-scented, semidouble flowers.

   Garden notes One of the most popular of Pemberton's roses, this is a vigorous shrub with stems to 7 ft (2.2 m), and unusually broad leaflets. Hardy to -20°F (-29°C), Zone 5.

'Felicia'

'Francis E. Lester'

'Autumn Delight'   A Hybrid Musk of unrecorded parentage introduced by Bentall in England in 1933. The flowers are soft yellow to white, almost single, with red stamens and little scent.
   Garden notes   A tall shrub to around 5 ft (1.5 m), the stems with few thorns. Repeat flowering is good. Hardy to -20°F (-29°C), Zone 5.

'Bishop Darlington'   A Hybrid Musk rose introduced by Captain Thomas of Beverley Hills in 1926. The flowers are semidouble, cream or pale yellow, large, and sweetly scented of fruit. The parentage is 'Aviateur Blériot' (*see p.152*) crossed with 'Moonlight' (*see p.171*).
   Garden notes   A semiclimber with coppery young leaves and flexible shoots, suited for training on a post or fence, and repeat flowering well. Hardy to -30°F (34°C), Zone 4.

'Erfurt'   A Hybrid Musk aised by Kordes in 1939 from 'Eva' (*see p.174*) crossed with 'Reveil Dijonnais', a climbing Hybrid Tea. The loose, semidouble flowers open pale pink with golden shading before fading to almost white, and have little scent.
   Garden notes   A low shrub to 3 ft (1 m) with coppery red young leaves. The flowers are produced throughout the season. Hardy to -20°F (-29°C), Zone 5.

'Francis E. Lester'   A Hybrid Musk or Rambler introduced by Lester Rose Gardens in the United States in 1946. The single flowers are blush pink fading to white, with average scent. They are borne in large loose sprays and are followed by small, red hips. Though often classed as a Rambler, because of its habit of growth, one of its parents is 'Kathleen' (*see p.171*), so it is more usually grouped with the Hybrid Musks.
   Garden notes   This can form a large shrub or, if supported, a climber to around 12 ft (4 m). It flowers in summer only, but is very striking in full flower. Hardy to -20°F (-29°C), Zone 5.

'Heideröslein'   A Hybrid Musk, sometimes classed as a Climber, introduced by Lambert in Germany in 1932. Red buds open to single, yellowish salmon-pink flowers with slight scent. The parentage is a cross of 'Chamisso', a descendent of 'Trier' (*see p.169*), and 'Amalie de Greiff', a salmon-pink Hybrid Tea.
   Garden notes   This is an attractive single, wild-looking rose to 5 ft (1.5 m), with large clusters of flowers that repeat well. Hardy to -20°F (-29°C), Zone 5.

'Autumn Delight'

'Lichtkönigin Lucia'

'Bishop Darlington'

'Lyda Rose'

'Sally Holmes'

'Heideröslein'

'Erfurt'

'Lichtkönigin Lucia' (also called 'Light Queen Lucia', 'Lucia', 'Queen Lucia', 'Reine Lucia', KORlilub) An award-winning rose of intermediate habit, variously placed in Hybrid Musks, Modern Shrubs, or Climbers, introduced by Kordes in 1966. Bright yellow, fully double flowers with good scent are produced in flattish clusters. It is a cross of the Shrub rose 'Zitronenfalter' and the Floribunda 'Cläre Grammerstorf'.

Garden notes A repeat-flowering rose with glossy, healthy, dark green leaves. Hardy to -20°F (-29°C), Zone 5.

'Lyda Rose' (also called LETlyda) A Hybrid Musk introduced by Kleine Lettunich in California in 1994. The delicate single flowers are blush pink with a deeper edge and with good scent. It is a seedling of 'Francis E. Lester'.

Garden notes A shrub to around 5 ft (1.5 m). It flowers continually, performs well in the shade and is largely disease free, and was rated Best Shrub Rose by the ARS. Hardy to -20°F (-29°C), Zone 5.

'Sally Holmes' A distinctive and excellent, gold-medal winning Hybrid Musk introduced by Holmes in England in 1976. The white or very pale pink flowers are large, single, in often huge, dense heads, with little scent. The parentage is the Floribunda 'Ivory Fashion' crossed with 'Ballerina' (*see p.174*).

Garden notes A shrub to 5 ft (1.5 m), free-flowering well into the season. If pruned hard it grows like a Floribunda, with huge sprays of blooms late in the season; leave these unpruned for a good crop of hips. Hardy to -10°F (-23°C), Zone 6.

'Nymphenburg'

'Robin Hood'

'Eva'

'Ballerina'

'Nur Mahal'

'Ballerina' A pretty Hybrid Musk raised by Pemberton and introduced by Bentall in England in 1937. The parentage is not recorded, but it bears a close resemblance to *R. multiflora* (*see p. 17*). From summer on, masses of deep pink buds open to pale pink, small, single flowers.

Garden notes This is one of the most popular shrub roses of all time, with flowers of cheerful bright pink and white in elongated clusters; it is also very free-flowering. Though called a Hybrid Musk, this bears little resemblance to Pemberton's own introductions, but it is important as the parent of many other roses, especially the Hybrid Musks introduced by Louis Lens (*see pp. 176–79*). It forms a low bush with shoots around 4 ft (1.2 m) tall. It is very hardy, to -30°F (34°C), Zone 4.

'Eva' A Hybrid Musk introduced by Kordes in Germany in 1933. The flowers are semidouble and bright red, with little or no scent. It is a cross of 'Robin Hood' and 'J.C. Thornton', a scarlet Hybrid Tea.

Garden notes A shrub to around 5 ft (1.5 m), flowering continuously during the season. It is also very hardy, to -30°F (34°C), Zone 4.

'Nur Mahal' A Hybrid Musk introduced by Pemberton in England in 1923. The flowers are bright crimson-red, semidouble, in large clusters, with good scent. The parentage is the Hybrid Tea 'Château de Clos Vougeot' crossed with a Hybrid Musk seedling.

Garden notes An upright shrub with stems to 5 ft (1.5 m), with small leaflets, suitable as a pillar rose. Repeat flowers well during the season. Hardy to -20°F (-29°C), Zone 5.

'Nymphenburg' A Hybrid Musk introduced by Kordes in Germany in 1954. Apricot buds open to quite large, fully double, strong salmon-pink flowers, with a good fresh apple scent. Its parentage is the Hybrid Musk 'Sangerhausen' crossed with the Floribunda 'Sunmist'.

Garden notes An upright shrub to around 6 ft (2 m), suitable for a pillar or post. It has lush and shining leaves and flowers continuously during the season. It is also very hardy, to -30°F (34°C), Zone 4.

'Robin Hood' (also called 'Robin des Bois') A Hybrid Musk raised by Pemberton and introduced in England in 1927. The flowers are semidouble and bright red, and have little scent.

HYBRID MUSK ROSES

The parentage is an unnamed seedling crossed with the Polyantha Miss Edith Cavell.

   Garden notes A strong shrub to 5 ft (1.5 m), but repeat-flowering well through the season. Hardy to -20°F (-29°C), Zone 5.

'Vanity' A Hybrid Musk introduced by Pemberton in England in 1920. The large clusters of semidouble flowers are bright reddish-pink, with good scent. The parentage is the Hybrid Tea 'Château de Clos Vougeot' crossed with an unnamed seedling.

   Garden notes A tall shrub to 6 ft (2 m), repeat flowering well during the season. It is very hardy, to -30°F (34°C), Zone 4.

'Will Scarlet' This Hybrid Musk was introduced by Graham Thomas while manager at Hilling's Nursery in 1950. It is a sport of Kordes' Hybrid Musk rose 'Wilhelm' (also called 'Skyrocket'), and is bright scarlet compared with the deep purplish-red of its parent. The flowers are semidouble, with a delicate scent.

   Garden notes The stems can reach 7 ft (2.2 m), and the flowers appear continuously during the season. Very hardy, to -30°F (34°C), Zone 4.

'Will Scarlet'

'Vanity' at Sissinghurst, southern England

175

HYBRID MUSK ROSES

'Guirlande d'Amour'

'Bouquet Parfait'

The Belgian breeder Louis Lens and his successors Rudi and Ann Velle have introduced numerous modern Hybrid Musks. Lens used *R. multiflora* (*see p.17*) and Pemberton's 'Ballerina' (*see p.174*) to produce very hardy, repeat-flowering roses of various heights, with sprays of usually rather small flowers.

'Bouquet Parfait' (also called LENbofa)   A Hybrid Musk introduced by Lens in Belgium in 1989. The flowers are fully double and blush-pink to white, with little scent. The parentage is a seedling of *R. multiflora* var. *adenochaeta* and 'Ballerina' (*see p.174*), crossed with the Miniature 'White Dream'.
   Garden notes   Flowers continuously through the season, and is very hardy, to -30°F (34°C), Zone 4.

'Gravin Michel d'Ursel' (also called LENgravi)   A Hybrid Musk introduced by Lens in Belgium in 1994. The semidouble flowers in loose bunches are blush pink, with pale apricot in the center and a lilac nuance on the edge, with good scent. The parentage is 'Lavender Pinocchio' (*see p.243*) crossed with a seedling of 'Ballerina' (*see p.174*) and the Shrub rose 'Echo'.
   Garden notes   A repeat-flowering shrub with arching stems to 5 ft (1.5 m). It is very hardy, to -30°F (34°C), Zone 4.

'Guirlande d'Amour' (also called LENalbi)   A gold-medal winning climbing Hybrid Musk introduced by Lens in Belgium in 1993. The flowers are semidouble and white, with medium scent. The parentage is 'Seagull' (*see p.147*) crossed with a seedling of *R. multiflora nana* and 'Moonlight' (*see p.171*).
   Garden notes   A climber to 12 ft (4 m) that repeat flowers well. Hardy to -20°F (-29°C), Zone 5.

'Jacqueline Humery' (also called LENtapo)   A Hybrid Musk introduced by Lens in Belgium in 1995. Pink buds open to white, semidouble flowers with wavy petals and excellent scent. It is descended from the Shrub roses 'Poesie' (*see p.207*), 'Tapis Volant', and 'Maria Mathilda'.
   Garden notes   A graceful, arching shrub to 5 ft (1.5 m), exceptionally healthy and flowering continuously during the season. Hardy to -20°F (-29°C), Zone 5.

'Matchball'

'Neige d'Ete'

'Waterloo' at Kasteel Hex in Belgium

'Gravin Michel d'Ursel' at Kasteel Hex in Belgium, the home of the d'Ursel family

'Jacqueline Humery'

'Maaseik'

'Maaseik' (also called 'Maaseik 750', LENclima) A Hybrid Musk introduced by Lens in Belgium in 1994. The single, pale salmon-pink flowers have conspicuous anthers and good musk scent. Its parentage involves *R. multiflora* var. *adenochaeta*, 'Ballerina' (*see p.174*), and 'Kathleen' (*see p.171*).

   Garden notes The shoots have lush, bronzy-green foliage, reach 5 ft (1.5 m) and are well-covered with flowers through the season. Hardy to -20°F (-29°C), Zone 5.

'Matchball' (also called LENadbial) A gold-medal winning Hybrid Musk introduced by Lens in Belgium in 1990. The flowers are single, blush pink and white, and have good scent. Its parentage is a cross of *R. multiflora* var. *adenochaeta* and 'Kathleen' (*see p.171*).

   Garden notes Reaches 5 ft (1.5 m) and flowers continuously through the season. Hardy to -20°F (-29°C), Zone 5.

'Neige d'Eté' (also called LENadne) A rare Hybrid Musk introduced by Lens in Belgium in 1991. It has white to blush, fully double flowers with little scent. Very resistant to rain and wind. Essentially it is a pure white version of the Louis Lens rose 'Bouquet Parfait'. It is a cross of *R. multiflora* var. *adenochaeta* and 'Ballerina' (*see p.174*)

   Garden notes A rose to 5 ft (1.5 m), flowering throughout the season. Hardy to -20°F (-29°C), Zone 5.

'Waterloo' A Hybrid Musk introduced by Lens in Belgium in 1996. It produces large clusters of small, double, white flowers with a hint of cream that are arranged right down each stem in a series of tiers. They have little scent. The parentage is not recorded.

   Garden notes It makes a shrub up to 5 ft (1.5 m), or can be trained as a low climber. Hardy to -20°F (-29°C), Zone 5.

'Walferdange'

'Pink Magic'

'Rosy Purple'

'Françoise Drion'

'Plaisanterie'

'Sibelius'

'Françoise Drion' (also called LENraba)   A Hybrid Musk introduced by Lens in Belgium in 1995. The single, bright pink flowers are in large sprays; they have little scent. It is a cross of the Hybrid Musk 'Ravel' and 'Ballerina' (*see p. 174*).
   Garden notes This rose has robust arching stems with dark, shining leaves, reaching around 5 ft (1.5 m) and can also be grown as a low climber. Flowers continuously during the season. Hardy, to -30°F (34°C), Zone 4.

'Heavenly Pink' (also called LENneei)   A Hybrid Musk introduced by Lens in Belgium in 1997. The strong pink, fully double flowers have an excellent old rose scent. It is a cross of 'Seagull' (*see p. 147*) and an unnamed seedling.
   Garden notes A healthy rose with stems to 3 ft (1 m). The large, pyramidal sprays of flowers, borne continuously during the season, are good for cutting. Hardy to -20°F (-29°C), Zone 5.

'Pink Magic' (also called LENmagika)   A Hybrid Musk introduced by Lens in Belgium in 1990. Deep pink buds open to paler flowers with a white center, single and with little scent.

The parentage is a seedling of *R. multiflora* var. *adenochaeta* and 'Ballerina' (*see p.174*), crossed with 'Kathleen' (*see p.171*).

Garden notes A robust grower with stems to 5 ft (1.5 m), the flowers produced continuously during the season. It is also very hardy, to -30°F (34°C), Zone 4.

'Plaisanterie' (also called LENtrimera) A Hybrid Musk introduced by Lens in Belgium in 1996. Orange buds open to single flowers, at first yellow becoming pink and ending deep pink with purple overtones, with some scent. It is a cross of 'Trier' (*see p.169*) and 'Mutabilis' (*see p.81*).

Garden notes Vigorous and hardy, with reddish young leaves, flowering at around 5 ft (1.5 m). The flowers, produced continuously during the season, are exceptionally long lasting in water when kept cool. Hardy perhaps to -30°F (34°C), Zone 4.

'Rosy Purple' A rare Hybrid Musk of unrecorded parentage introduced by Lens in Belgium in 1995. The small, single flowers in very large pyramidal heads are an old rose purplish-red, with good scent.

Garden notes A once-flowering shrub or low climber, reaching 5 ft (1.5 m), the young leaves reddish. Hardy to -30°F (34°C), Zone 4.

'Sibelius' (also called LENbar) A Hybrid Musk introduced by Lens in Belgium in 1984. Flowers small, fully double, purplish-red, but with little scent, flowering continuously during the season. It is a cross of the Miniature 'Mr. Bluebird' and the Shrub rose 'Violet Hood'.

Garden notes Stems to 3 ft (1 m), arching over; it is also very hardy, to -30°F (34°C), Zone 4.

'Twins' (also called LENtrifel) A Hybrid Musk introduced by Lens in Belgium in 1994. The flowers, in long sprays, are pink and creamy yellow, semidouble, with subtle scent. It is a cross of 'Trier' (*see p.169*) and 'Felicia' (*see p.171*).

Garden notes A very strong grower to 5 ft (1.5 m) that flowers continuously. Hardy to -30°F (34°C), Zone 4.

'Walferdange' (also called LENwal) A Hybrid Musk introduced by Lens in Belgium in 1990. The flowers are fully double and bright carmine pink with shades of yellow, with little scent. The parentage is a seedling of *R. multiflora* var. *adenochaeta* and 'Ballerina' (*see p.174*) crossed with 'Felicia' (*see p.171*). Walferdange is a city in Luxembourg.

Garden notes A strong-growing and healthy rose to around 3 ft (1 m), flowering continuously during the season. Hardy to -30°F (34°C), Zone 4.

'Pink Magic'

'Twins'

'Heavenly Pink'

Rugosa Roses

'Mai Kwa'

THESE ROSES ARE ALL derived from *Rosa rugosa* (*see p. 23*), sometimes called the Japanese Rose. This tough, suckering shrub grows wild along the coasts of eastern Siberia, northeastern China, and northern Japan; it is tolerant of salt spray, and grows well in poor, sandy soils. Its flowering season is longer than that of most roses, starting with the Gallicas in early summer, and continuing for some four months.

The Latin name is derived from the distinctive leaves, which are rugose, or rough with impressed veins. Roses derived from *R. rugosa* resemble the species in both the appearance of the leaves and their health, seldom suffering blackspot or mildew. Their other feature is the large, rounded hips, formed by the single, pure *R. rugosa* roses; most hybrids and double types do not produce hips.

In China, the excellent qualities of *R. rugosa* have been recognized for around a thousand years, in 'Mai Kwa', which is still found in old gardens throughout warm parts of China. We photographed it in southwestern Sichuan. An illustration by a Chinese artist is included in the collection of drawings of Chinese plants made between 1812

and 1817 by John Reeves while working as a tea inspector in Canton. The collection is held at the Royal Horticultural Society Library and the Natural History Museum in London.

When *R. rugosa* was introduced to cultivation in the West in 1845, European breeders, at that time mostly French, were slow to use its good qualities. At the turn of the century, Cochet-Cochet in Coubert introduced 'Blanc Double de Coubert' (*see p. 182*) and 'Roseraie de l'Haÿ' (*see p. 187*); other breeders raised excellent hybrids, such as 'Conrad Ferdinand Meyer' (*see p. 184*), about the same time.

The natural range of *R. rugosa* is a very cold area where the sea may freeze in winter, so it is an exceptionally hardy species, generally hardy down to -40°F (-40°C) Zone 3 or even lower. This is therefore a very cold-tolerant group of roses, with most hybrids hardy to -30°F (-34°C), Zone 4, but they also tolerate heat well, growing successfully in both Texas and Australia. Little pruning is needed. The long shoots can be shortened to keep them to the desired height, and old wood can be removed after flowering if the bush appears crowded.

'Max Graf'

Rosa rugosa 'Alba'

'Pink Surprise'

'Mai Kwa' (also called 'Maikai')   An old Chinese cultivar, grown since the Sung period (960–1279AD) or possibly earlier. The double, slightly nodding, purplish-red flowers have excellent scent. The leaves are *rugosa*-like but paler, with narrower leaflets and shorter, smaller stipules at the base of a crimson leaf stalk. The parentage is unknown, but the absence of large hips suggests that this is a hybrid, possibly with a Damask. In China the half-opened flowers are dried and used to make tea. They are also used medicinally, as were the Damask roses in antiquity.

   Garden notes   An upright shrub, reaching 6 ft (2 m) at most, requiring good, rich soil and ample moisture to flower freely. Probably hardy to -20°F (-29°C), Zone 5.

'Max Graf'   A creeping Hybrid Rugosa rose, sometimes classed as a Groundcover, introduced by James H. Bowditch of Pomfret Center, Connecticut in 1919. The clusters of single flowers are pale pink with a white center and scented of apples. It is a hybrid of *R. rugosa* (*see p.23*) and *R. wichurana* (*see p.19*).

   Garden notes   A rose with a long period of flowering and shoots that trail on the ground, bearing bright green, shining leaves. 'Max Graf' itself is a sterile diploid, but through chromosome doubling produced a fertile, tetraploid seedling, *R. × kordesii*, which led to a new race of hardy climbers. Hardy to -30°F (-34°C), Zone 4.

'Pink Surprise'   A bushy Hybrid Rugosa raised by Lens in Belgium and introduced by David Austin in England in 1987. The flowers are a uniform pale pink with distinct stamens. An unusual hybrid of *R. rugosa* (*see p.23*) and *R. bracteata* (*see p.14*).

   Garden notes   Stems to 5 ft (1.5 m) bear neat, dark, glossy leaves, and flowers are produced throughout summer and until the frosts. Hardy to -10°F (-23°C), Zone 6.

Rosa rugosa 'Alba'
A white-flowered form of *R. rugosa* (*see p.23*), with single flowers around 5 in (13 cm) across, with good scent, followed by large, shiny, orange hips.

   Garden notes   A strong-growing rose, to 6 ft (2 m) in good soil if unpruned, but usually shorter; it can be kept to 5 ft (1.5 m) by shortening the new shoots in early spring. Hardy to -40°F (-40°C), Zone 3, or lower.

'Schneezwerg' (also called 'Snow Dwarf')   A Hybrid Rugosa raised by Lambert in Germany in 1912 from a cross of *R. rugosa* (*see p.23*) and a Polyantha. The flowers are loosely double, pure white with golden stamens, and have excellent scent. They are carried in sprays.

   Garden notes   A good, tough and very healthy rose forming an upright bush around 6 ft (2 m) tall, with smaller leaves than *R. rugosa*. Hardy to -30°F (-34°C), Zone 4.

'Schneezwerg'

'Topaz Jewel'

'Fimbriata'

'Agnes'   A Hybrid Rugosa raised by Dr W. Saunders in Ottawa in 1900. The flowers are fully double, pale yellow with deeper shadows, with a good scent, and produced mainly in late spring, with only a few later flowers. It is a hybrid of *R. rugosa* (*see p.23*) and *R. foetida* 'Persiana' (*see p.30*).

   Garden notes   A lovely rose, forming an upright shrub to 6 ft (2 m) with small, narrow leaflets, the branches arching over under the weight of the flowers. It is susceptible to blackspot, but strong-growing enough not to be weakened by it. Hardy to -30°F (-34°C), Zone 4.

'Blanc Double de Coubert'   A Hybrid Rugosa rose raised by Cochet-Cochet in France in 1892. The flowers are loosely double, the inner petals slightly twisted, showing golden stamens, with an excellent scent. It is probably a sport of *R. rugosa* 'Alba' (*see p.181*), or possibly a cross with 'Sombreuil' (*see p.93*).
   Garden notes   Makes an upright shrub with very prickly shoots to 6 ft (2 m). Hardy to -30°F (-34°C), Zone 4.

'Dr Eckener'   A Hybrid Rugosa raised by Vincinz Berger and introduced by Teschendorff in Germany in 1930. The flowers are semidouble, coppery pink on yellow, fading to soft pink, and have excellent scent. The parentage is 'Golden Emblem', a Hybrid Tea, crossed with a hybrid of *R. rugosa* (*see p.23*).
   Garden notes   A rare rose, and unusual both in color and breeding. It repeat flowers well, with large flowers on a strong, upright, thorny bush, the leaves close to those of *R. rugosa*. Hardy to -30°F (-34°C), Zone 4.

'Rugelda'

'Fimbriata' (also called 'Dianthiflora', 'Phoebe's Frilled Pink') A Hybrid Rugosa raised by Morlet in France in 1891. The flowers are double with a frilled or "pinked" edge, palest pink, and have a good scent. It is said to be a cross of *R. rugosa* (*see p.23*) and 'Mme Alfred Carrière' (*see p.103*).
   Garden notes A strong, upright shrub to 6 ft (2 m), the branches arching under the weight of the flowers throughout the summer. Hardy to -40°F (-40°C), Zone 3.

'Rugelda' (also called KORruga) A Hybrid Rugosa rose raised by Kordes in Germany in 1989. The flowers are loosely double and yellow shaded with orange, with little scent. The parentage is an unnamed seedling crossed with 'Robusta' (*see p.187*)
   Garden notes The stems reach around 5 ft (1.5 m), and repeat flowering is good. Hardy to -40°F (-40°C), Zone 3.

'Topaz Jewel' (also called 'Gelbe Dagmar Hastrup', 'Rustica 91', 'Yellow Dagmar Hastrup', 'Yellow Fru Dagmar Hartopp', MORyelrug) A Hybrid Rugosa raised by Ralph Moore in 1987 and introduced by Wayside Nurseries. The double flowers show some stamens when fully open, and are medium yellow fading to cream, with some scent. It is a cross of the Miniature 'Golden Angel' and the Hybrid Rugosa 'Belle Poitevine'.
   Garden notes The thorny stems reach 5 ft (1.5 m), and the flowers are produced throughout the season. Hardy to -30°F (-34°C), Zone 4.

'Vanguard' A Hybrid Rugosa that can be grown as a shrub or low climber, raised by G. A. Stevens of Harrisberg, Pennsylvania in 1932. The large, double flowers are pale apricot, pink, and orange, with good scent. The parentage is a seedling of *R. rugosa* 'Alba' (*see p.181*) and *R. wichurana* (*see p.19*) crossed with the Hybrid Tea 'Eldorado'.
   Garden notes A rare and unusual rose, strong-growing to 10 ft (3 m), with glossy leaves. Hardy to -30°F (-34°C), Zone 4.

'Agnes'

'Blanc Double de Coubert'

'Dr Eckener'

'Vanguard'

183

'Conrad Ferdinand Meyer'

'Conrad Ferdinand Meyer'

'Conrad Ferdinand Meyer' A Hybrid Rugosa raised by Müller in Germany in 1899. The fully double flowers are pale pink with silvery edges, and excellent scent. The parentage is a seedling of 'Gloire de Dijon' (*see p.107*) and the Hybrid Perpetual 'Duc de Rohan' crossed with the Hybrid Rugosa 'Germanica'.

Garden notes A strong-growing, thorny bush, with stems to around 10 ft (3 m), flowering in early summer and again in autumn. The leaves have little trace of *rugosa* influence, but the plant has been used as a parent by David Austin in some of his English roses. Hardy to -30°F (-34°C), Zone 4.

'Fru Dagmar Hastrup' (also called 'Frau Dagmar Hartopp') A shrub raised by Hastrup in Denmark in 1914. The large, single flowers open silvery pink from a red bud, with a small circle of stamens. It is a seedling of *R. rugosa* (*see p.23*).

Garden notes A lovely rose for hedging or to make a dense bush, with a succession of simple, elegant flowers. Stems reach up to 6 ft (2 m) but they are easily kept shorter. Hardy to -30°F (-34°C), Zone 4.

'Jens Munk' A Hybrid Rugosa raised by Dr Felicitas Svejda in Ontario in 1974, a cross of 'Schneezwerg' (*see p.181*) and 'Fru Dagmar Hastrup'. The semidouble flowers are mid-pink with yellow stamens and an excellent scent. Danish explorer Jens Munk was one of three survivors from a crew of 64 seeking a passage from Hudson's Bay to the Pacific in 1619.

Garden notes Stems to 5 ft (1.5 m); flowers repeat well through the summer. Very hardy, to -40°F (-40°C), Zone 3.

'Martin Frobisher'
A Hybrid Rugosa raised by Dr Felicitas Svejda in Ontario in 1968. The fully double flowers have many similarities to an Alba; they are very pale pink, with excellent scent. It is a cross of 'Schneezwerg' (*see p.181*) and perhaps a *R. pimpinellifolia* (*see p.28*) seedling.

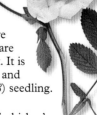

'Martin Frobisher'

'Mrs Doreen Pike'

'Jens Munk'

'Fru Dagmar Hastrup'

'Pink Grootendorst'

This rose is the first of the Explorer series of Hybrid Rugosas: Frobisher was a 16th century English adventurer in Canada.

Garden notes Grows to around 4 ft (1.2 m) with pale yellowish-green leaves and good repeat flowering. Very hardy, probably to -35°F (-37°C), in Zone 3.

'Mrs Doreen Pike' (also called AUSdor) A Hybrid Rugosa raised by David Austin in England in 1993. The fully double flowers open flat and quartered, silvery pink with a yellowish eye in the center, with excellent scent. The parentage is a cross of 'Martin Frobisher' and 'Roseraie de l'Haÿ' (*see p.187*).

Garden notes Bushy and quite low-growing, to 3 ft (1 m) tall and 4 ft (1.2 m) across, repeat flowering well through the summer. Hardy perhaps to -30°F (-34°C), Zone 4.

'Pink Grootendorst' A Hybrid Rugosa introduced by Grootendorst in Holland in 1923. The branched sprays of small, double flowers have pinked edges and excellent scent.

Garden notes This is a pink sport of the red Hybrid Rugosa 'F.J. Grootendorst'; there is also a white sport,

introduced in 1962. An upright shrub to 8 ft (2.5 m), good to stand on its own in grass. Hardy to -30°F (-34°C), Zone 4.

'Sarah Van Fleet' A Hybrid Rugosa raised by Dr Walter van Fleet in Glen Dale, Maryland in 1926. The cupped, loosely double flowers show some stamens when fully open, mid-pink. It is a cross of *R. rugosa* (*see p.23*) and the Hybrid Tea 'My Maryland'.

Garden notes Reaches 10 ft (3 m), but is easily controlled by summer pruning. Flowering is continuous. Hardy to -30°F (-34°C), Zone 4.

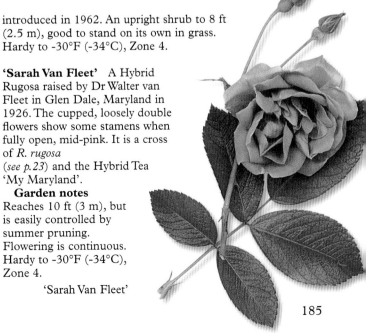

'Sarah Van Fleet'

185

'Moje Hammarberg'

'David Thompson'

'Robusta'

'Hansa' at Descanso Gardens, Los Angeles, California

'Thérèse Bugnet'

'Pierette'

'David Thompson' A Hybrid Rugosa raised by Dr Felicitas J. Svejda in Ontario in 1979, named for the early 19th-century surveyor. The semidouble flowers are red with yellow stamens, with excellent scent, repeat-flowering through the season. Its parentage is a seedling of 'Schneezwerg' (*see p.181*) and 'Fru Dagmar Hastrup' (*see p.184*), crossed with an unnamed seedling.
   Garden notes An upright bush to around 5 ft (1.5 m). Very hardy, perhaps to -40°F (-40°C), Zone 3; certainly close to this.

'Hansa' A Hybrid Rugosa raised by Schaum & Van Tol of the Hansa nursery in Holland in 1905. Large, fully double flowers, deep reddish with purple shades and excellent clove and rose scent, are followed by red hips. Its parentage is unrecorded.
   Garden notes Tall-growing, to 5 ft (1.5 m); the flowers tend to nod under their own weight. The name of Hansa means heron, and is found in Shakespearean English as well as in modern German. Hardy to -40°F (-40°C), Zone 3.

'Moje Hammarberg' A Hybrid Rugosa raised in 1931 by Hammarberg in Stockholm. The double, purplish-crimson

'Robusta' grown as a hedge around the Kordes Rose Garden in Germany

flowers are nodding on weak stems, with excellent scent, and are followed by red hips. The parentage is not recorded.

Garden notes This is a tall grower, with stems reaching 6 ft (2 m), but easily kept shorter by pruning the new shoots; repeat flowering is good. Hardy to -30°F (-34°C), Zone 4.

'Pierette' (also called 'Pierette Pavement', 'Yankee Lady', UHLater) A Hybrid Rugosa raised by Uhl in Germany in 1987, sometimes confused with 'Buffalo Gal'. The flowers are double and deep pink. The parentage is not recorded.

Garden notes This grows to 5 ft (1.5 m) and repeat flowers through the season. Hardy to -30°F (-34°C), Zone 4.

'Robusta' (also called KORgosa) A Hybrid Rugosa raised by Kordes in Germany in 1979. The flowers are single, in tight clusters, bright red with some scent, repeating well. It is a cross of *R. rugosa* (*see p.23*) and an unnamed seedling.

Garden notes A low climber if trained on a pole, which can reach 8 ft (2.5 m). If pruned the plant can be kept shorter, and it can be used to form a very free-flowering hedge with very thorny stems. Hardy to -30°F (-34°C), Zone 4.

'Roseraie de l'Haÿ' A Hybrid Rugosa raised in France by Cochet-Cochet in 1901, from a seedling of *R. rugosa* (*see p.23*). The flowers are very large, loosely double, and purplish-crimson, with excellent scent.

Garden notes A substantial, tough shrub to 7 ft (2.2 m), repeat-flowering well. Hardy to -30°F (-34°C), Zone 4, but also good in warm climates such as Australia.

'Thérèse Bugnet' A Hybrid Rugosa raised by Bugnet in Canada 1950. It bears double flowers, deep pink with white margins, with excellent scent, and the stems turn red in winter. The parentage is complex, and includes two forms of *R. rugosa* (*see p.23*) and *R. acicularis* (*see p.22*).

Garden notes A tall growing bush, to 6 ft (2 m), that flowers throughout the season. Hardy to -40°F (-40°C), Zone 3.

'Roseraie de l'Haÿ'

Shrub Roses

'Raubritter'

SHRUB ROSES ARE OFTEN perceived simply as a "catch all" category of roses that do not fit well in other classes. However, many roses that were once classed as Shrubs are now popularly regarded as separate groups, such as Groundcover Roses or Rugosa Roses, and we have put them in separate sections. Many of the roses in this section were raised from a wild rose crossed with a modern one, aiming to combine the elegance, hardiness, and freedom of flowering of the species with the larger, showier flowers of a Hybrid Tea or Hybrid Perpetual.

There are roses with unusual species in their ancestry: *R. moyesii (see p. 20), R. persica (see p. 31), R. sempervirens (see p. 19), R. multibracteata (see p. 21), R. rubiginosa (see p. 26),* and *R. arkansana* are here, as well as the more familiar *R. rugosa (see p. 23)* and *R. × macrantha.* Some of the roses in this section almost form subgroups of their own, and are sometimes listed as Hybrid Moyesii, Hybrid Persica, and so on. For example, Kordes wonderful 'Frühlings' roses, such as 'Frühlingsgold' and

'Frühlingsmorgen' (*see p. 190 for both*), are often called Pimpinellifolia Hybrids (or Hybrid Spinossisimas, from the old name for the species). However, they show little resemblance to the dwarf, small-flowered *R. pimpinellifolia (see p. 28)* and old varieties of the Scotch rose, because they were based on the much larger *R. pimpinellifolia* var. *altaica;* the tall shrubs with large single or semidouble flowers raised by Kordes have a character of their own.

Most Shrub roses are robust, quite strong enough to stand on their own in a garden setting; if there is any doubt that one plant will produce a good show, three or five can be planted together.

Pruning should aim to cut out the shoots which have flowered and to encourage the new shoots, which will flower the following year, to form a well-shaped shrub. Hardiness varies according to the hardiness of the main parent and the amount of tender Hybrid Tea in the parentage. Most are hardier than Hybrid Teas, and will be hardy to -20°F (-29°C), Zone 5; some are much hardier.

'Euphrates'

'La Belle Distinguée'

'Stanwell Perpetual'

'Euphrates' (also called HARunique)   A cross of *R. persica* (*see p.31*) and an unnamed seedling, raised by Harkness of Hitchin, England in 1986. The flowers are small, single, and flesh-pink with a strong red blotch at the base of each petal. They have little scent.

Garden notes   A low-growing, creeping or spreading shrub to about 20 in (50 cm) tall, 5 ft (1.5 m) across. Hardy to -20°F (-29°C), Zone 5, and should thrive in hot, desert areas.

'La Belle Distinguée' (also called 'La Petite Duchesse', 'Lee's Duchess', 'Scarlet Sweet Brier')   This old Shrub rose is a form or hybrid of *R. rubiginosa* (*see p.26*); its exact date of introduction is unknown, but it is first mentioned around 1820. The flowers are fully double and bright purplish-red, with slight scent.

Garden notes   A spreading shrub to around 5 ft (1.5 m), with small, aromatic leaves, flowering in early summer only. Hardy to -20°F (-29°C), Zone 5.

'Raubritter' (also called *R. macrantha* 'Raubritter')   A Hybrid Macrantha introduced by Kordes in Germany in 1936. A very pretty rose with small but plentiful, cupped, pink flowers with moderate scent. It is a cross of the Hybrid Macrantha Shrub 'Daisy Hill' and 'Solarium', a *R. wichurana* (*see p.19*) Rambler.

Garden notes   A once-flowering rose with spreading shoots to about 5 ft (1.5 m) that make it excellent for training over a low wall; it also makes a lovely weeping standard. Hardy to -20°F (-29°C), Zone 5.

'Stanwell Perpetual'   A Shrub rose introduced by Lee of Hammersmith, London in 1838. The double flowers are blush pink to white, with delicate scent. It is thought to be cross between a Damask and *R. pimpinellifolia* (*see p.28*).

Garden notes   A loose, upright shrub around 5 ft (1.5 m), flowering until late in the season. It is liable to blackspot in wet areas. Hardy to -30°F (-34°C), Zone 4, but also good in warm climates.

'La Belle Distinguée'

'Raubritter' at Mottisfont Abbey, southern England

189

'Prairie Harvest'

'Starry Night'

'Jacqueline du Pré'

'Pearl Drift'

'Frühlingsgold' (also called 'Spring Gold') A Shrub rose, often called a Hybrid Spinossisima, introduced by Kordes in Germany in 1937. Red buds open to large, single, yellow flowers, which have good scent. The parentage is 'Joanna Hill', a yellow Hybrid Tea, crossed with *R. pimpinellifolia* var. *altaica*.

Garden notes An upright, stiff shrub, flowering once only. Hardy to -30°F (-34°C), Zone 4.

'Frühlingsmorgen' (also called 'Spring Morning') A Shrub rose, often called a Hybrid Spinossisima, introduced by Kordes in Germany in 1942. One of the very earliest roses to flower. The large, single flowers are cherry-pink with a soft yellow center. The parentage is a seedling of the Hybrid Teas 'E.G. Hill' and 'Cathrine Kordes', crossed with *R. pimpinellifolia* var. *altaica*.

Garden notes A strong-growing shrub to 6 ft (2 m), repeat flowering a little. Hardy to -30°F (-34°C), Zone 4.

'Jacqueline du Pré' (also called HARwanna) A Shrub rose introduced by Harkness in England in 1988, the year after the celebrated English cellist died of multiple sclerosis at a tragically young age. Tall, pinkish buds open to semidouble, white or slightly blush flowers with a moderate musk scent. The parentage is the Floribunda 'Radox Bouquet' crossed with the Climber 'Maigold'.

Garden notes An average shrub, to 5 ft (1.5 m), with good repeat blooming. Hardy to -20°F (-29°C), Zone 5.

'Nevada' at the edge of a garden in Northamptonshire, England

'Frühlingsgold'

190

'Frühlingsmorgen'

'Marguerite Hilling' in Eccleston Square Garden, London

'Marguerite Hilling' (also called 'Pink Nevada') A Shrub rose introduced by Graham Thomas while working at Hilling's nursery in England in 1959. The bright pink flowers are semidouble, with some scent. It is a sport of 'Nevada'.

Garden notes A large, rounded shrub around 6 ft (2 m) high and wide, flowering mainly in spring. Hardy to -20°F (-29°C), Zone 5.

'Nevada' A Shrub rose introduced by Pedro Dot in Spain in 1927. One of the truly great shrubs in early summer, when it is densely covered in creamy white single flowers with moderate scent; when it repeats later in the year, the flowers tend to be touched with pink. The parentage is uncertain, but it is usually said to be a hybrid of *R. moyesii* (*see p.20*).

Garden notes A large, rounded shrub around 7 ft (2.2 m) high and wide. Hardy to -20°F (-29°C), Zone 5.

'Pearl Drift' (also called 'Pearly Drift', LEGgab) A Shrub rose that also makes a good Groundcover, introduced by LeGrice in 1980 in England. Pink buds open to semidouble, white flowers with a pink flush, which have a slight scent.

The parentage is 'Mermaid' (*see p.133*) crossed with 'New Dawn' (*see p.131*).

Garden notes A robust shrub, repeat flowering well, with glossy foliage. Hardy to -20°F (-29°C), Zone 5.

'Prairie Harvest' A Shrub rose introduced by Buck and Iowa State University in 1985. The flowers are double and mid-yellow, up to 15 in each cluster, and have good scent. The parentage is 'Carefree Beauty' (*see p.192*) crossed with 'Sunsprite' (*see p.231*).

Garden notes A shrub with upright, bushy growth to around 5 ft (1.5 m) and shining, leathery leaves. Repeat blooming is moderate. Hardy to -30°F (-34°C), Zone 4.

'Starry Night' (also called ORAwichkay) A Shrub rose introduced by Orard in France in 2002, winner of the AARS for that year. Single, pure white flowers are produced in large clusters. The parentage is 'Dicky' (*see p.238*) crossed with *R. wichurana* (*see p.19*).

Garden notes A spreading shrub to 5 ft (1.5 m) with very good repeat flowering. Hardy to -30°F (-34°C), Zone 4.

'Marguerite Hilling'

'Nevada'

'Prairie Dawn'

'Country Dancer'

'Bonica' (also called 'Bonica 82', 'Bonica Meidiland', 'Démon', MEIdomonac)   A Shrub, sometimes classed as a Groundcover, introduced by Meilland in France in 1985, awarded the ADR for 1982 and AARS for 1987. The double flowers are mid-pink at the center and lighter toward the edge, with little scent. Its parentage is a cross of *R. sempervirens* (*see p.19*) and the Rambler 'Mlle Marthe Carron', crossed with 'Picasso' (*see p.244*).

   Garden notes   One of the great modern roses, this is ideal for groundcover if planted closely, or for the front of a border or a raised bed, flowering almost continuously. Great rosarian Sharon van Enoo has even planted it by her sidewalk in Los Angeles. Good in heat and hardy to -30°F (-34°C), Zone 4.

'Carefree Beauty' (also called 'Audace', BUCbi)   A Shrub rose introduced by Buck in the United States in 1977, with loosely double flowers of light rose-pink, a true old rose colour, and with moderate scent. The parentage is an unnamed seedling crossed with 'Prairie Princess'.

   Garden notes   A shrub with upright growth and smooth foliage. Very hardy, to -33°F (-36°C), in Zone 3.

'Country Dancer'   A Shrub rose introduced by Buck in the United States in 1973. The flowers are loosely double, rosy-red, and well scented. The parentage is 'Prairie Princess' crossed with 'Johannes Boettner', a Floribunda dating from 1943.

   Garden notes   An upright, bushy shrub to 5 ft (1.5 m) that repeats well. Hardy to -30°F (-34°C), Zone 4.

'First Light' (also called DEVrudi)   A Shrub rose raised by Stanley and Jeanne Marciel and introduced by DeVor Nurseries in the United States in 1998, winner of the AARS for that year. Clusters of pointed, deep pink buds open to single, pink flowers with purple stamens and moderate, spicy scent. It is a cross of 'Bonica' and 'Ballerina' (*see p.174*).

   Garden notes   A charming low shrub with compact growth. Hardy to -30°F (-34°C), Zone 4.

'Fritz Nobis'   A Shrub rose introduced by Kordes in Germany in 1940. Bluish-pink to salmon buds open to lighter, semidouble flowers with strong scent. It is a cross of the Hybrid Tea 'Joanna Hill' and the Rubiginosa Hybrid 'Magnifica'.

   Garden notes   A beautiful shrub of Hybrid Musk habit, with upright stems to 6 ft (2 m), but once-flowering only. Hardy to -20°F (-29°C), Zone 5.

'Prairie Princess'

'First Light'

'Morden Blush'

'Bonica'

'Bonica' growing in southwestern Australia

'Morden Blush' (also called 'Blush')   A Shrub rose introduced by Collicutt and Marshall at Morden Experimental Farm in Canada in 1988. The flowers can be rich pink if grown in shade or very cool weather, but are usually paler. The complex parentage involves the Shrub roses 'Prairie Princess', 'Morden Amorette', and 'Assiniboine', the Floribunda 'White Bouquet', and the very hardy species *R. arkansana.*
   Garden notes   This is one of the Parkland series, which were raised to survive Canadian winters and so are very hardy, to -40°F (-40°C), Zone 3.

'Prairie Dawn'   A Shrub rose introduced by Morden Experimental Farm in Canada in 1959. The double flowers are glowing pink. The complex parentage involves the Shrub rose 'Prairie Youth', 'Ross Rambler', 'Dr W. Van Fleet' (*see p.131*), and *R. pimpinellifolia* var. *altaica.*
   Garden notes   An upright, repeat-blooming rose. Exceptionally hardy, to -40°F (-40°C), Zone 3.

'Prairie Princess'   A Shrub rose introduced by Buck in the United States in 1972. The semidouble flowers are coral-pink, with slight scent. The parentage is the Grandiflora 'Carrousel', crossed with a hybrid of the Shrub roses 'Morning Stars' and 'Suzanne', a hybrid of *R. pimpinellifolia* (*see p.28*).
   Garden notes   This is a strong, upright shrub to around 5 ft (1.5 m) that repeat flowers. Hardy to -30°F (-34°C), Zone 4.

'Carefree Beauty'

'Fritz Nobis'

'Oranges 'n' Lemons'

'Stretch Johnson'

'Distant Drums'

'Kaleidoscope'

'Sparrieshoop'

'Carefree Delight' (also called 'Bingo Meidiland', 'Bingomeillandecor', 'Evermore', MEIpotal)   A very attractive shrub introduced by Meilland in France in 1994. It bears tight clusters of single, bright pink flowers with a white eye and little scent. The parentage is a hybrid of 'Eyepaint' (*see p.244*) and the Floribunda 'Nirvana', crossed with 'Smarty' (*see p.165*).
Garden notes A very healthy, spreading shrub to 5 ft (1.5 m) that flowers freely and continuously during the season. Hardy to -10°F (-23°C), Zone 6.

'Distant Drums'   A Shrub rose introduced by Buck at Iowa State University in 1985. The large, fully double flowers are often borne in clusters, and are rose-purple suffused with orange-brown, with a strong myrrh scent. The parentage is the Grandiflora 'September Song' crossed with the English Rose 'The Yeoman'.
  Garden notes A repeat-flowering shrub to 5 ft (1.5 m). Hardy to -30°F (-34°C), Zone 4.

'Hawkeye Belle'   A Shrub rose introduced by Buck at Iowa State University in 1975. The fully double flowers are white tinted with azalea-pink, with an intense scent. The parentage is a hybrid of the Grandiflora 'Queen Elizabeth' and the Shrub 'Pizzicato', crossed with 'Prairie Princess' (*see p.193*).
  Garden notes A vigorous, upright shrub around 5 ft (1.5 m), with dark green leaves tinged with purple. Hardy to -30°F (-34°C), Zone 4.

'Janet's Pride' (also called 'Clementine')   A Shrub rose introduced in 1892 by Paul in England. The flowers are semidouble, bright pink with a white center, with good old-rose scent. It is a seedling of *R. rubiginosa* (*see p.26*).
  Garden notes A strong-growing shrub with small leaves, flowering only once, in early summer. Hardy to -15°F (-26°C), in Zone 5.

'Kaleidoscope' (also called JACbow)   A Shrub rose raised by John K. Walden and introduced by Bear Creek Gardens in the United States in 1999, winner of the AARS that year. The double flowers, borne in large clusters, are a subtle blend of tan, yellow, reds and mauve, with a delicate, fruity scent. It is a cross of the Shrub 'Pink Polyanna' and the Miniature 'Rainbow's End'.
  Garden notes This makes a low, bushy shrub to 3½ ft (1.1 m), with prickly stems and glossy, dark green leaves.

SHRUB ROSES

Hardy to -10°F (-23°C), Zone 6. There is another 'Kaleidoscope', a yellow and orange Floribunda raised by Fryer's Nursery in England in 1972.

'Oranges 'n' Lemons' (also called 'Papagena', MACoranlem) A Shrub rose introduced by McGredy in New Zealand in 1994. The double flowers, in small clusters, are striped orange and yellow, with a slight, fruity scent. The parentage is the Grandiflora 'New Year' crossed with a seedling of the Hybrid Tea 'Freude' and an unnamed seedling. Typical of the striped and painted roses on which McGredy concentrated in his later years of breeding in New Zealand.

Garden notes A repeat-flowering, spreading, vigorous shrub around 5 ft (1.5 m) tall. Hardy to -10°F (-23°C), Zone 6.

'Rush' (also called 'Rusch', LENmobri) A Shrub rose introduced by Louis Lens in Belgium in 1983. The flowers are single, pink with a white eye, their scent moderate and fruity. It is a cross of 'Ballerina' (see p.174) and *R. multiflora* (see p.17).

Garden notes A tall shrub with arching stems to 5 ft (1.5 m). Hardy to -20°F (-29°C), Zone 5.

'Sparrieshoop' A Shrub rose introduced by Kordes in Germany in 1953. The single, light pink flowers have a strong scent. Its parentage is a hybrid of the Polyantha 'Baby Château' and 'Else Poulsen' (see p.227), crossed with the Rubiginosa Hybrid 'Magnifica'. A stronger pink variety is sometimes referred to as 'Pink Sparrieshoop'.

Garden notes A vigorous shrub to 6 ft (2 m) in height, repeat-flowering well. Hardy to -20°F (-29°C), Zone 5.

'Stretch Johnson' (also called 'Rock 'n' Roll', 'Tango', MACfirwall) A gold-medal winning Shrub rose sometimes classed as a Floribunda, introduced by McGredy in New Zealand in 1988. The flowers are semidouble, orange with a white edge, with moderate scent. The parentage is 'Sexy Rexy' (see p.235) crossed with the Hybrid Tea 'Maestro'.

Garden notes A bushy shrub to around 4 ft (1.2 m), repeat flowering well. Hardy to -20°F (-29°C), Zone 5.

'Janet's Pride'

'Carefree Delight'

'Hawkeye Belle'

'Rush' in the Parc de Bagatelle, Paris

SHRUB ROSES

'Cardinal Hume'

'Cardinal Hume' (also called HARregale)   A Shrub rose introduced by Harkness in England in 1984. The flowers are very well scented of musk, a true old-rose rich violet-purple, and fully double. The complex parentage involves both *R. pimpinellifolia* (*see p.28*) and *R. californica* (*see p.24*).

Garden notes An exceptional rose, repeat flowering well, with stems to 5 ft (1.5 m). Hardy to -20°F (-29°C), Zone 5.

'Carefree Wonder' (also called 'Carefully Wonder', 'Dynastie', MEIpitac)   A Shrub rose introduced by Meilland in France in 1990, the AARS for 1991. The flowers are fully double and mid-pink with a light pink reverse, but they have little or no scent. The parentage is a hybrid of 'Prairie Princess' (*see p.193*)

and the Floribunda 'Nirvana', crossed with a hybrid of 'Eyepaint' (*see p.244*) and 'Rustica', both Floribundas.

Garden notes A bushy shrub suitable for a hedge, reaching around 5 ft (1.5 m). Hardy to -40°F (-40°C), Zone 3.

'Cerise Bouquet'   A Shrub rose raised in Germany in 1937 by Tantau but not introduced until 1958, and then by Kordes. The flowers are fully double, cerise-crimson, and sweetly scented. The parentage is *R. multibracteata* (*see p.21*) crossed with 'Crimson Glory' (*see p.218*).

Garden notes This lovely and distinctive rose makes a very large shrub to about 12 ft (4 m) in both height and width. It flowers only in summer, but the small, rounded leaflets give an attractive effect even when it is not in flower. Hardy to -20°F (-29°C), Zone 5.

'Eddie's Jewel'   A shrub rose introduced by Eddie's Nursery in the United States in 1962. The flowers are medium-sized, semidouble, and bright red. The parentage is the Floribunda 'Donald Prior' crossed with a seedling of *R. moyesii* (*see p.20*).

Garden notes A tall, strong-growing shrub to 9 ft (2.7 m), suitable for a shrubbery or wild planting. It repeats sporadically after the first flowering. Hardy to -20°F (-29°C), Zone 5.

'Elmshorn'   A Shrub rose introduced by Kordes in Germany in 1951, winner of the ADR for 1950. The pompom-like, fully double flowers are deep pinkish-red, with some scent. It is a cross of the Shrub rose 'Hamburg' and the Polyantha 'Verdun'.

Garden notes A shrub to around 6 ft (2 m), repeat flowering well. Hardy to -20°F (-29°C), Zone 5.

'Eddie's Jewel'

'Elmshorn'

'Morden Cardinette'

'Morden Ruby'

'Stars 'n' Stripes Forever'

'Festival Fanfare'

'Carefree Wonder'

'Cerise Bouquet' at Kiftsgate Court, western England

'Festival Fanfare' (also called BLEstogil) This Shrub rose, introduced by W.D. Ogilvie in England in 1982, is a sport of the Shrub rose 'Fred Loads'. The single flowers are bright red striped with pink and white, with slight scent.

Garden notes An excellent large, free-flowering shrub, reaching around 5 ft (1.5 m) and repeat flowering well. Hardy to -30°F (-34°C), Zone 4.

'Fiona' (also called MEIbeluxen) A low-growing Shrub that is sometimes also listed as a Groundcover, introduced by Meilland in France in 1979. The small, double, red flowers are produced continuously through the season. Its parentage is the Shrub rose 'Sea Foam' crossed with 'Picasso' (*see p. 244*).

Garden notes A low shrub with spreading shoots, below 30 in (75 cm). It has a fine display of hips in autumn, which make a wonderful combination with the late flowers. Hardy to -30°F (-34°C), Zone 4.

'Morden Cardinette' A Shrub or Groundcover rose raised by H.H. Marshall at Morden Experimental Farm in Canada and introduced in 1980 as one of their very hardy Parkland roses. The fully double flowers are bright red with little or no scent. This rose is a complex hybrid involving 'Prairie Princess' (*see p. 193*), the Floribundas 'White Bouquet', 'Independence', and 'Donald Prior', the Shrub roses 'Adelaide Hoodless' and 'Assiniboine', and the very hardy species *R. arkansana*.

Garden notes A low shrub, usually less than 30 in (75 cm), repeat flowering well. Will survive to -40°F (-40°C), Zone 3.

'Morden Ruby' A Parkland series Shrub rose, raised by H.H. Marshall at Morden Experimental Farm in Canada and introduced in 1977. The flowers are fully double with little or no scent. This cultivar was developed from a cross between the Floribunda 'Fire King' and a hardy seedling derived from

R. arkansana 'J.W. Fargo' and 'Assiniboine', the latter itself a hybrid of the Floribunda 'Donald Prior' and *R. arkansana*.

Garden notes A shrub to around 5 ft (1.5 m) that repeat flowers well. Probably hardy to -40°F (-40°C), Zone 3.

'Stars 'n' Stripes Forever' (also called CLEhope) A Shrub introduced by John Clements of Heirloom Roses in the United States in 2003. The cupped, semidouble flowers are in sprays, red heavily splashed with white, and well scented. There is also an older Miniature called 'Stars 'n' Stripes'.

Garden notes A shrub to around 4 ft (1.2 m), flowering in profusion through the season. Hardy to -20°F (-29°C), Zone 5.

'Fiona'

Hybrid Tea Roses

'La France'

THIS IS THE MOST POPULAR of all the rose groups and represents the peak of 20th century breeding, with scent, health, and large flowers in all colors but a pure blue. They are called Hybrid Teas because the first were hybrids of Hybrid Perpetuals and Tea roses, combining the tall bud and delicate flowers of the latter with the larger, flatter, coarser blooms of the former. Crosses of Hybrid Teas and Floribundas have resulted in roses with some characteristics of both: in some places these are called Grandifloras or Large-flowered Roses, in others they are still classed as Hybrid Teas, and we have included them here.

The earliest Hybrid Teas roused little interest. 'La France', raised in 1867, was a sterile triploid and it did not lead to a rush of similar crosses. The group was recognized only in 1880, when English breeder Henry Bennett visited French rose breeders. Bennett's 'Lady Mary Fitzwilliam' was among the

earliest deliberate breedings of a rose in the new group. A cross between this and 'La France', 'Mrs W.J. Grant', won a gold medal in 1883. The first Hybrid Teas were of various pale colors and red; the firm of Pernet-Ducher succeeded in introducing bright yellow by crossing with *R. foetida* 'Persiana' (*see p.30*). 'Soleil d'Or', introduced in 1900, was the first of the so-called Pernetianas, which brought bright yellows and orange into Hybrid Teas.

These are generally healthy roses: removing all dead leaves at the end of the season will help control any blackspot. Prune in spring, cutting back to two buds and removing weak or damaged shoots; a trim after flowering will encourage more blooms. In colder areas, it is best to cover the stems with earth or mulch for the winter and uncover them when spring is advanced. Hybrid Teas are almost always repeat-flowering, and so need ample feeding.

'Lady Mary Fitzwilliam'

'Mme Caroline Testout' in a cemetery in California

'La France'   A lovely rose, raised by 1867 by Jean-Baptiste Guillot (fils) of Lyon, and said to be a cross between the yellow Tea 'Mme Falcot' or the white 'Mme Bravy' (*see p.92*) and 'Mme Victor Verdier' (*see p.127*). The petals, which are paler inside, curl back from the high center, and the scent is heavier than that of most Teas. At first this was considered just a hybrid Bourbon, but it was later recognized as the first Hybrid Tea.

Garden notes   The bush form reaches 4 ft (1.2 m), the climbing form 10 ft (3 m). It is reputed to be hardy to -30°F (-34°C), Zone 4.

'Lady Mary Fitzwilliam'   A Hybrid Tea raised by Henry Bennett in Wiltshire, England in 1882. The flowers are light pink, rather flat, and semidouble, the shape taking after its parents 'Devoniensis' (*see p.91*) and 'Victor Verdier' (*see p.127*). Unlike the sterile 'La France', 'Lady Mary Fitzwilliam' was a most important parent of many excellent later Hybrid Teas, such as 'Mme Caroline Testout'. Bennett was originally a cattle farmer, and applied the same scientific breeding methods used in breeding livestock to raising his roses.

Garden notes   Even when first introduced, this rose was said to be a poor grower with wonderful flowers. It is now mainly of historic interest. Hardy to -30°F (-34°C), Zone 4.

'Mme Caroline Testout'   A classic Hybrid Tea raised by Joseph Pernet-Ducher of Lyon, France, and introduced in 1890; there is also a climbing sport (*see p.136*). Large flowers, in branching sprays, open very fully double and blowsy from pointed buds. They are bright pink with a darker center, and the scent is moderate. The parentage is the Tea 'Mme de Tartas' and 'Lady Mary Fitzwilliam'.

Garden notes This is a very free-flowering rose with vigorous, thorny stems, reaching perhaps 8 ft (2.5 m). It suffers slightly from mildew. Hardy to -20°F (-29°C), Zone 5.

'Soleil d'Or'   A chance hybrid of a seedling hybrid between *R. foetida* 'Persiana' (*see p.30*) and the Hybrid Perpetual 'Antoine Ducher', raised by Joseph Pernet-Ducher of Lyon and introduced in 1900. The fully double, pale orange-yellow flowers appear mainly in summer, with a few later. The scent is good. The leaflets are dark green, small, and coarsely-toothed.

Garden notes   This rose does best in warm, dry climates such as California, because the flowers rot before opening in wet weather. In damp climates it is also very prone to blackspot, inherited from *R. foetida*. In the hottest areas it needs some shade, and can make a tall shrub to 6 ft (2 m). Hardy to -20°F (-29°C), Zone 5 perhaps, in a dry climate.

'Soleil d'Or'

199

'Mrs Herbert Stevens'

'Honoré de Balzac' (also called 'Romantic Days', MEIparnin) A Hybrid Tea raised by Meilland Roses in the south of France and introduced in 1988, named for the 19th-century French author. The parentage is a seedling crossed with the Hybrid Tea 'Lancôme'. The flowers are a delicate shade of light pink in the center, fading to white on the outer petals. There is a distinct light peach scent.

   Garden notes This rose grows to about 5 ft (1.5 m) and flowers continuously during the season. The flowers are double and very large and full; in damp weather there is a tendency to ball, so it is best grown in warm, dry climates. Probably hardy to -30°F (-34°C), Zone 4.

'John F. Kennedy' (also called 'JFK', 'President John F. Kennedy') A Hybrid Tea raised by Boerner and introduced by Jackson and Perkins in the United States in 1965. Buds with greenish tints at first open to almost pure white flowers with moderate scent. The parentage is a seedling crossed with the Hybrid Tea 'White Queen'.

   Garden notes A very healthy, tall shrub that repeat flowers well, with long flower stems that are good for cutting. Hardy to -20°F (-29°C), Zone 5.

'Karen Blixen' (also called 'Isis', 'Roy Black', 'Silver Anniversary', 'Susan Blixen', POULari) A Hybrid Tea introduced by Poulsen of Denmark in 1992. Large, round, greenish buds open to large, white, double blooms. It is named for the famous Danish author, who wrote as Isak Dinesen

and whose life formed the basis of the Oscar-winning film 'Out of Africa'. The parentage is not recorded.

   Garden notes Repeat flowers well. This is a useful rose for cold areas, being hardy to -30°F (-34°C), Zone 4.

'Mrs Herbert Stevens' A Hybrid Tea raised in 1910 by Sam McGredy from 'Frau Karl Druschki' (*see p. 122*) crossed with 'Niphetos', a white Tea rose. A climbing sport was introduced by Pernet-Ducher in 1922. The white flowers are well scented and freely produced, and growth is healthy and long lasting.

   Garden notes A vigorous rose, the shrub reaching 5 ft (1.5 m) and the climbing sport 20 ft (6 m). It repeat flowers well, especially in warm climates. Hardy to -20°F (-29°C), Zone 5.

'Pascali' (also called 'Blanche Pasca', LENip) A Hybrid Tea introduced by Louis Lens in Belgium in 1963. The creamy white flowers are well scented. This is a much honored and

'Karen Blixen'

'John F. Kennedy'

'Pascali'

'Renaissance'

recognized rose, winner of two gold medals and the AARS for 1961, and included in the World Federation of Rose Societies' Hall of Fame. The parentage is the Grandiflora 'Queen Elizabeth' crossed with the Hybrid Tea 'White Butterfly'.

Garden notes Combines good disease resistance, vigorous growth to about 3 ft (1 m), and good repeat flowering. Hardy to -20°F (-29°C), Zone 5.

'Renaissance' (also called 'Born Again', 'Cameo Perfume', HARzart)   A Hybrid Tea introduced by Harkness Roses in England in 1994. The large, white flowers have a pale pink center and are highly scented; they have gained this variety two international fragrance awards. There is also a red Hybrid Tea with the same name.

Garden notes A good repeat-flowering rose, growing to an average height about 4 ft (1.2 m). Quite hardy, to -20°F (-29°C), Zone 5.

'Virgo' (also called 'Liberationem')   A classic Hybrid Tea, raised by Mallerin and introduced by Meilland Roses in southern France in 1947. Tall buds open to white flowers, sometimes showing touches of blush pink. The parentage is two Hybrid Teas, 'Blanche Mallerin' and 'Neige Parfum'.

Garden notes A tough plant, growing to just 2 ft (60 cm). It is susceptible to mildew, but the flowers are so perfect that it still deserves a place in the garden.
Hardy to -10°F (-23°C), Zone 6.

'Virgo'

'Honoré de Balzac'

'Marilyn Monroe'

'Frédéric Mistral'

'Gift of Life'

'Jardins de Bagatelle'

'Paul Ricard'

'Pristine'

'Dainty Bess' A Hybrid Tea introduced by Archer in England in 1925. The pale pink, single blooms have very distinct maroon stamens and moderate Tea scent. Its parentage is the Hybrid Teas 'Ophelia' (*see p.131, climbing form*) and 'Kitchener of Khartoum'.
  Garden notes A gold-medal winning rose, with exceptional flowers throughout the season on a vigorous plant to 5 ft (1.5 m) high. Hardy to perhaps -24°F (-31°C), in Zone 4.

'Diamond Jubilee' A great rose raised by Boerner from the Hybrid Tea 'Feu Pernet-Ducher' and 'Marèchal Niel' (*see p.96*), introduced by Jackson and Perkins in 1947. Large, buff-yellow double flowers with a moderate scent are freely produced.
  Garden notes A spreading shrub to 3 ft (1 m) or more, repeat-flowering into autumn. Hardy to 0°F (-18°C), Zone 7.

'Frédéric Mistral' (also called 'The Children's Rose', MEIterbros) A Hybrid Tea introduced by Meilland in France in 1998. The large, fully double flowers are light pink, suffused with rose on the reverse. The scent is intense, and it has won perfume medals all over the world. The parentage is a hybrid of

'Perfume Delight' and 'Prima Ballerina', both Hybrid Teas, crossed with 'The McCartney Rose' (*see p.213*).
  Garden notes An upright plant to about 6 ft (2 m), with good repeat flowering, and much admired by those who choose their plants for their scent. Hardy to -20°F (-29°C), Zone 5.

'Gift of Life' (also called 'Poetry in Motion', HARelan) A gold-medal winning Hybrid Tea introduced by Harkness in England in 1999. The fully double flowers are mid-yellow with a hint of pink on the reverse, and moderate scent; repeat flowering is good. The parentage is the Hybrid Teas 'Dr Darley' and 'Elina'.
  Garden notes This grows to about 3½ ft (1.1 m), with glossy foliage. Hardy to -20°F (-29°C), Zone 5.

'Jardins de Bagatelle' (also called 'Drottning Sylvia', 'Gardin de Bagatelle', 'Karl Neinz Hanisch', 'Queen Sylvia', 'Sarah', MEImafris) A European prize-winning Hybrid Tea raised by Marie-Louise Meilland and introduced in 1986. The large, very double flowers are creamy white, tinted with pale pink in cool weather, and very well scented. The parentage is MEIdragelac, a

'Valencia'

'Dainty Bess'

'Dainty Bess'

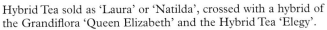

Hybrid Tea sold as 'Laura' or 'Natilda', crossed with a hybrid of the Grandiflora 'Queen Elizabeth' and the Hybrid Tea 'Elegy'.

Garden notes A very healthy rose, growing to about 5 ft (1.5 m), which repeat flowers well and is good in dry conditions. Hardy to -20°F (-29°C), Zone 5.

'Marilyn Monroe' (also called WEKsunspat)   A Hybrid Tea raised by Tom Carruth and introduced by Weeks Roses in California in 2003. Long, pointed buds open to double flowers of apricot-cream with a slight hint of green; the scent is mild. It is a cross of the Tea 'Sunset' and 'St. Patrick' (*see p. 205*).

Garden notes This is a good repeat-flowering rose for hot gardens; its long stems are useful for cut flowers. Hardy to -10°F (-23°C), Zone 6.

'Paul Ricard' (also called 'Moondance', 'Paul Richard', 'Spirit of Peace', 'Summer's Kiss', MEInivoz)   An unusually scented Hybrid Tea introduced by Meilland in France in 1994. The very double flowers are pale amber; their highly distinctive anise scent gave rise to the name, which is an aniseed-flavored French drink. The parentage is a hybrid of 'Hidalgo' and 'Mischief', crossed with 'Ambassador', all Hybrid Teas.

Garden notes An interesting addition to any garden, this maks a strong, bushy plant to about 4 ft (1.2 m) high, with good disease resistance and repeat flowering. Hardy to -20°F (-29°C), Zone 5.

'Pristine' (also called JACpico)   A Hybrid Tea raised by William Warriner and introduced by Jackson and Perkins in

California in 1978. The double flowers are almost pure white, shaded with light pink. It has won an award in the United States for its excellent scent. The parentage is the Hybrid Teas 'White Masterpiece' and 'First Prize'.

Garden notes This is a good repeat-flowering rose with large leaves. Hardy to -10°F (-23°C), Zone 6.

'Valencia' ('New Valencia', 'Valencia 89', KOReklia) A Hybrid Tea raised by Kordes Söhne and introduced in 1989. The large, well-formed yellow flowers are strongly scented. This rose is a winner of many awards, including the Edland Fragrance Medal from the American Rose Society.

Garden notes A compact bush to about 2 ft (60 cm) high, repeat flowering well. Hardy to -30°F (-34°C), Zone 4.

'Diamond Jubilee'

HYBRID TEA ROSES

'Freedom' in the Queen Mary Garden, Regents Park, London

'Helmut Schmidt'

'Midas Touch'

'Grandpa Dickson'

'Freedom' (also called DICjem)   A Hybrid Tea raised by Dickson in Northern Ireland and introduced in 1984. The flowers are chrome yellow with a moderate scent. Winner of an RNRS gold medal. The parentage is a hybrid of the Floribunda 'Eurorose' and the Hybrid Tea 'Typhoon', crossed with the Floribunda 'Bright Smile'.

   Garden notes Recommended as a very healthy plant, to about 4 ft (1.2 m), with exellent repeat flowering. Hardy to -20°F (-29°C), Zone 5.

'Grandpa Dickson' (also called 'Irish Gold')   This popular Hybrid Tea, raised by Dickson in Northern Ireland, won four gold medals when it was introduced by Jackson and Perkins in the United States in 1966. It bears yellow flowers with a moderate scent, which repeat well through the season, on very thorny stems. The parentage is a hybrid of 'Kordes Perfecta' and 'Governador Braga da Cruz', crossed with 'Piccadilly', all three of these roses being Hybrid Teas.

   Garden notes This grows to only about 30 in (75 cm), with good mid-green leaves. Hardy to -20°F (-29°C), Zone 5.

'Helmut Schmidt' (also called 'Goldsmith', 'Simba', KORbelma)   A Hybrid Tea raised by Kordes in 1979, and a winner of two gold medals in Europe. Long, pointed buds develop into clear yellow, double flowers with a sweet, Tea scent. In Britain this rose is sold as 'Goldsmith'. The parentage is the Hybrid Tea 'New Day' crossed with a seedling.

   Garden notes Long-lasting blooms are produced on a plant only about 30 in (75 cm) in height. Hardy to -20°F (-29°C), Zone 5.

'Midas Touch' (also called JACtou)   A Hybrid Tea raised by Jack E. Christensen and introduced by Bear Creek Gardens in 1992, this was the the AARS for 1994. The flowers are a bright, unfading yellow, and double, with a distinct musk scent.

The parentage is a cross of the Hybrid Tea 'Brandy' and the Shrub rose 'Friesensöhne'.

Garden notes A rose with bushy growth to 5 ft (1.5 m) and excellent repeat flowering. Hardy to -20°F (-29°C), Zone 5.

'Philippe Noiret' (also called 'Glowing Peace', MEIZoele) This Hybrid Tea, raised by Meilland and introduced by Conard-Pyle in the United States in 1996, was awarded the AARS for 2001. The double flowers are yellow with pink edges, with moderate scent. The parentage is 'Sun King' crossed with 'Roxane', both Hybrid Teas.

Garden notes Upright, bushy growth to about 4 ft (1.2 m), and good repeat blooming. Hardy to -10°F (-23°C), Zone 6.

'St Patrick' (also called 'Limelight', WEKamanda) A Hybrid Tea raised by Frank A. Strickland in 1991 and introduced by Weeks Roses in 1996. Furled buds open to yellow-gold flowers with fascinating touches of green, especially in hot weather, and slight scent. This rose won the AARS for 1996. The parentage is the Hybrid Tea 'Brandy' and the Grandiflora 'Gold Medal' (*see front cover*).

Garden notes Grows to about 4 ft (1.2 m). Hardy to -10°F (-23°C), Zone 6.

'Sutter's Gold' A well-scented Hybrid Tea raised by Swim in 1950; there is also a climbing form. Orange buds overlaid with Indian red open to rich golden-yellow flowers, the outer petals often red. It is a hybrid of 'Charlotte Armstrong' (*see p.212*) and the Hybrid Tea 'Signora'. Sutter's Creek in California is where gold was found in 1849. This rose won the AARS for 1950 and many gold medals.

Garden notes This will grow to 6 ft (2 m) in good soil. Hardy to -10°F (-23°C), Zone 6.

'Tequila Sunrise' (also called 'Beaulieu', DICobey) This Hybrid Tea, raised by Dickson in 1988, has received many medals and awards. The flowers, a modern blend of strong yellow and red, are often one to a stem but sometimes in clusters. The parentage is the Floribunda 'Bonfire Night' crossed with 'Freedom'.

Garden notes A very successful rose to around 4 ft (1.2 m) with excellent repeat blooming. Hardy to -20°F (-29°C), Zone 5.

'Tequila Sunrise'

'St Patrick'

'Philippe Noiret'

'Sutter's Gold'

HYBRID TEA ROSES

'**Alpine Sunset**' A Hybrid Tea introduced by Cants of Colchester in England in 1973. The flowers are a warm, peachy pink with an apricot reverse, and well scented. The parentage is the Hybrid Tea 'Dr. A.J. Verhage' crossed with 'Grandpa Dickson' (*see p.204*).

Garden notes This grows to around 4 ft (1.2 m), with good repeat flowering after the first main flush. Hardy to -20°F (-29°C), Zone 5.

'**Chicago Peace**' (also called JOHNago) A sport of the great rose 'Peace', introduced by Johnson in 1962. It is very similar to 'Peace,' except that the yellow tones are strongly overlaid with pink and reddish-copper. The fragrance is mild and pleasant, and repeat flowering is good.

Garden notes A strong-growing, disease-resistant plant, this reaches about 4 ft (1.2 m) if pruned, but if allowed to grow up through large shrubs unpruned it may grow to as much as 8 ft (2.5 m). Hardy to -20°F (-29°C), Zone 5.

'**Elle**' (also called MEIbdéros) This Hybrid Tea, introduced by Meilland in France in 1999, has won many awards in Europe and the AARS for 2005. The fragrant flowers are pink with hints of ochre and very freely produced.

Garden notes A very healthy rose that reaches around 3 ft (1 m). Hardy to -10°F (-23°C), Zone 6.

'**Gruß an Coberg**' A Hybrid Tea introduced by Felberg-Leclerc in Germany in 1927, from a cross of the Hybrid Teas 'Alice Kaempff' and 'Souvenir de Claudius Pernet'. The flowers are apricot-yellow with a coppery reverse; the scent is excellent. The leaves, especially on new growth, are an attractive bronze.

Garden notes Reaches an average height about 4 ft (1.2 m), with good repeat flowering. Hardy to -20°F (-29°C), Zone 5.

'**Jean Giono**' (also called 'Romantic Moments' MEIrokoi) A Hybrid Tea raised by Meilland in France and introduced by Conard-Pyle in the United States 1998. The flowers are sunny yellow, veined and edged in orange-apricot, very double, and borne in small clusters. Their scent is moderate. The parentage is a seedling of the Hybrid Teas 'Yakimour' and 'Sunblest', crossed with 'Graham Thomas' (*see p.249*).

Garden notes This rose grows to about 4 ft (1.2 m). Hardy to -10°F (-23°C), Zone 6.

'**Paul Shirville**' (also called 'Heart Throb', 'Saxo', HARqueterwife) A Hybrid Tea raised by Harkness in England in 1981, and recipient of an ARS award in 1982. The flowers

'Tournament of Roses'

are high centered, bright salmon-pink, lighter on the reverse, with a lovely, sweet scent. The foliage is very dark with purple tints when young. It is a hybrid of 'Compassion' (*see p.134*) and the Hybrid Tea 'Mischief'.

Garden notes This rose makes a bush to about 3 ft (1 m), worth growing for the lovely scent. The repeat flowering is generally good, although the later flowers are often a little smaller. It does suffer touches of mildew. Hardy to -20°F (-29°C), Zone 5.

'**Peace**' (also called 'Béke', 'Fredsrosen', 'Gioia', 'Gloria Dei', 'Mme A. Meilland', 'Mme Antoine Meilland') This Hybrid Tea is probably the best-loved rose of all time; it has so many names because it is such a good plant and so important. It was raised by Meilland in France and introduced by Conard-Pyle in the United States in 1945; launched after the Second World War it became a symbol of better times to come. The very large flowers are creamy yellow touched with red; their color is very variable from soil to soil and in different weather, and there are also many color selections. 'Peace' holds many international awards, including the World Federation of Rose Societies' Hall of Fame award 1976. The parentage is uncertain.

Garden notes A strong bush that can easily be allowed to grow to 5 ft high (1.5 m); there is a climbing sport. It repeat flowers well. Hardy to -24°F (-31°C), in Zone 4.

'Jean Giono'

'Elle'

'Alpine Sunset'

'Whisky Mac'

'Gruß an Coberg'

'Tournament of Roses' (also called 'Berkeley', 'Poesie', JACient) A Grandiflora raised by Warriner from an unnamed seedling and the Floribunda 'Impatient', and introduced by Jackson and Perkins in the United States in 1988. It won the AARS for 1989. The flowers are light coral-pink with a deep pink reverse and a light, spicy scent. It is named for the rose parade in Pasadena.

Garden notes A disease-resistant, repeat-flowering rose to 5 ft (1.5 m), especially good in warm gardens. Hardy to -20°F (-29°C), Zone 5.

'Whisky Mac' (also called 'Whisky', TANky) A fine Hybrid Tea raised by Tantau in Germany in 1967. It has bronze to apricot-yellow flowers with a strong scent. The parentage is not recorded; there is also a climbing sport.

Garden notes A fine rose to 4 ft (1.2 m), although it can get a little fungal disease. Hardy to -20°F (-29°C), Zone 5.

'Paul Shirville' in the Queen Mary Garden, Regent's Park, London

'Peace'

'Chicago Peace' in Brompton Cemetery, London

'Blessings'

'Blessings' (also called 'Blesine') A Hybrid Tea raised by Gregory in England in 1967. The coral-salmon flowers have a light, pleasant scent, are often three to a stem, more like a Floribunda, and repeat through the season. The parentage is the Hybrid Tea 'Queen Elizabeth' crossed with a seedling.

Garden notes Well covered in flowers, especially in the first flush. Height to 5 ft (1.5 m). Hardy to -20°F (-29°C), Zone 5.

'Comtesse Vandal' (also called 'Countess Vandal') A Hybrid Tea raised by Leenders in the Netherlands and introduced by Jackson & Perkins in the United States in 1932; it won a gold medal in 1932 and has been grown ever since it was introduced. The flowers are salmon-pink with a coppery pink reverse; their scent is moderate. It has a parentage of three classic Hybrid Teas, all still grown: 'Mrs Aaron Ward', 'Ophelia', (see p.131 for 'Climbing Ophelia'), and 'Souvenir de Claudius Pernet'.

Garden notes This tough rose reaches 3 ft (1 m). Hardy to -20°F (-29°C), Zone 5.

'Julia's Rose' (also called 'Julia') A very popular, gold-medal winning Hybrid Tea introduced by Wisbech in England in 1976. It has semidouble, brownish-copper flowers, the color being even stronger in cold weather. The parentage is 'Blue Moon' (see p.210) crossed with the Hybrid Tea 'Dr. A.J. Verhage'.

Garden notes Although this needs care to keep it in good condition, it is worth it for the unique color. It reaches 3 ft (1 m) and repeat flowers well. Hardy to -20°F (-29°C), Zone 5.

'Just Joey' Raised by Cants in England in 1972, this has won many awards, including the World Federation of Rose Societies Hall of Fame. The flowers are very large, quite loose, and buff-orange with a strong scent. It is a cross of 'Fragrant Cloud' (see p.217) and the Hybrid Tea 'Dr. A.J. Verhage', and probably the most important modern Hybrid Tea after 'Peace' (see p.206).

Garden notes Excellent flowers for cutting are borne on a plant up to about 5 ft (1.5 m). Hardy to -20°F (-29°C), Zone 5.

'L'Oréal Trophy' (also called 'Alexis', HARlexis) A sport of 'Alexander' (see p.214) introduced by Harkness in England in 1981. The unusual, strong buff-orange flowers have a pleasant, slight scent. It has won many prizes, including three gold medals.

Garden notes A healthy, upright plant to 5 ft (1.5 m). The flowers repeat right through the season, and are rather better in cold weather. Hardy to -20°F (-29°C), Zone 5.

'L'Oréal Trophy' at the Royal Horticultural Society Garden, Wisley, Surrey

'Sunset Celebration'

'Just Joey'

'Remember Me'

'Comtesse Vandal'

'Julia's Rose'

'Remember Me' (also called 'Remember', COCdestin)
A Hybrid Tea raised by Cocker in Aberdeen, Scotland in 1984. The double flowers are deep orange, subtly blended with yellow, with some scent. It has received many prizes and medals. This rose is between a Hybrid Tea and a Floribunda, and its parentage includes two Hybrid Teas, 'Anne Letts' and 'Pink Favorite', and the Floribunda 'Dainty Maid' (*see p.236*).
   Garden notes A good bushy plant, to about 4 ft (1.2 m), repeat flowering well. Hardy to -24°F (-31°C), in Zone 4.

'Sunset Celebration' (also called 'Chantoli', 'Exotic', 'Jolie Mome', 'Warm Wishes', FRYxotic) A gold-medal winning Hybrid Tea introduced by Fryer in England in 1999. The large flowers are a blend of creamy apricot and amber, with a pleasant, fruity scent. Its parentage is the Hybrid Tea 'Pot o' Gold' and a seedling.
   Garden notes A bush to about 4 ft (1.2 m) in height, this repeats well up to late autumn and is a good rose for all weather, because it does not show any rain damage. Hardy to -20°F (-29°C), Zone 5.

'Victor Borge' (also called 'Michael Crawford', POULvue) A Hybrid Tea raised by Olesen and introduced by Poulsen in Denmark in 1991. The flowers are a pinky yellow blend and lightly scented. It won an award in 1992.
   Garden notes A disease-resistant rose that reaches 5 ft (1.5 m) and repeat flowers well. It benefits from full sun. Hardy to -20°F (-29°C), Zone 5.

'Victor Borge'

'Savoy Hotel' in the Queen Mary Garden, Regent's Park, London

'Blue Moon'

'Blue Moon' (also called 'Blå Måndag', 'Blue Monday', 'Mainzer Fastnacht', 'Sissi', TANnacht, TANsi) A gold-medal winning Hybrid Tea raised by Tantau in Germany in 1965. The large, double flowers on long stems are pale lilac to lavender, and intensely fragrant. The parentage is a seedling of 'Sterling Silver' and an unnamed seedling.

Garden notes A good rose for cutting that repeat flowers well. It grows to 4 ft (1.2 m), doing best in full sun, and may suffer a little mildew. Hardy to -24°F (-31°C), in Zone 4.

'Sterling Silver' in the garden of Kim Rupert, Los Angeles, California

'Savoy Hotel'

'Blue Skies'

'Charles de Gaulle'

'Blue River' (also called KORsicht)   A Hybrid Tea raised by Kordes in Germany in 1984, winner of a gold medal. The flowers are light lilac in the center with deeper tones on the edges of the outer petals, and well scented. Normally each stem carries three flowers, making it rather close to a Floribunda in style: it is a hybrid of 'Blue Moon' and the Floribunda 'Zorina'.

   Garden notes   This rose flowers to the first frosts on a bush to 4 ft (1.2 m). Hardy to -24°F (-31°C), in Zone 4.

'Blue Skies' (also called BUCblu)   A Hybrid Tea raised by Dr Griffith J. Buck and introduced by J.B. Roses Inc. in the United States in 1983. Long-pointed buds open to large, pink blossoms that fade with age; they are moderately scented. The parentage is a complex cross involving the Hybrid Teas 'Blue Moon', 'Sterling Silver', 'Intermezzo', and 'Simone', the Shrub rose 'Music Maker', and the Floribunda 'Tom Brown'.

   Garden notes   Grows to 4 ft (1.2 m) and repeat flowers to the first frost. Buck roses were raised to withstand the frigid conditions of an Iowa winter, and this is very hardy, surviving down to -35°F (-37°C), in Zone 3.

'Charles de Gaulle' (also called 'Katherine Mansfield', MEIlanein) A Hybrid Tea raised by Marie-Louise Meilland in France and introduced in 1974. The cupped, lilac flowers have an excellent scent. It is a hybrid of a seedling from the Hybrid Teas 'Blue Moon' and 'Prelude' crossed with a seedling from the Floribunda 'Independence' and the Hybrid Tea 'Caprice'.

   Garden notes   A fairly tall rose to about 5 ft (1.5 m), with good repeat flowering; it is at its best in warm, dry areas. Hardy to -20°F (-29°C), Zone 5.

'Savoy Hotel' (also called 'Integrity', 'Vercors', 'Violette Niestlé', HARvintage)   A Hybrid Tea raised by Harkness in England and introduced 1987, winning a gold medal in 1988.

The flowers are light phlox-pink, shaded deeper on the reverse, with a light fragrance. The parentage is a cross of 'Silver Jubilee' (*see p.215*) and 'Amber Queen' (*see p.230*).

   Garden notes   This is an excellent, disease-resistant bedding rose for all temperate regions, growing to 3½ ft (1.1 m) and very free flowering throughout the season. Hardy to -20°F (-29°C), Zone 5.

'Sterling Silver'   A Hybrid Tea raised by Fisher and introduced by Jackson and Perkins in the United States in 1957. The exceptionally tall buds open to flowers of a lovely silvery mauve, becoming lighter, and very well scented. It is a hybrid of an unnamed seedling and 'Peace' (*see p.206*).

   Garden notes   A healthy plant to about 3 ft (1 m); repeat flowering is rather sparse. Hardy to -15°F (-26°C), in Zone 5.

'Blue River'

211

'Kathryn McGredy'

'Miss All-American Beauty'

'Charlotte Armstrong'

'Aloha'

'Aloha' A superb Hybrid Tea that can be grown as a tall bush or a low climber, introduced by Boerner in the United States in 1949. The flowers are rose pink with a deeper colored reverse, and strongly scented. The parentage is the climbing Hybrid Tea 'Mercedes Gallart' crossed with 'New Dawn' (*see p.131*). There are two other Hybrid Teas sold by this name.
  Garden notes Grows to as much as 5 ft (1.5 m), or more if trained as a climber, very healthy and free flowering throughout the season. Hardy to -20°F (-29°C), Zone 5.

'Baronne Edmond de Rothschild' (also called 'Baronne de Rothschild', 'Baronness Edmond de Rothschild', MEIgriso)
A Hybrid Tea introduced by Meilland in France in 1968, from a cross of the Hybrid Teas 'Baccará' and 'Crimson King', crossed with 'Peace' (*see p.206*). The large, double flowers are ruby-red to deep pink with a lighter reverse, and intensely scented.
  Garden notes A repeat-flowering rose to about 5 ft (1.5 m), winner of two gold medals. It prefers warm gardens and may be affected by blackspot. Hardy to -20°F (-29°C), Zone 5.

'Charlotte Armstrong' A Hybrid Tea raised by Lammerts and introduced by Armstrong in the United States in 1940. Long, pointed buds open to tall-centered, double flowers that are blood-red to deep pink, with moderate scent. This is one of the most important parents of modern Hybrid Teas, winner of the AARS for 1941 and] many other prizes. It is a hybrid of the Hybrid Teas 'Soeur Thérèse' and 'Crimson Glory' (*see p.218*).
  Garden notes Vigorous growth to about 4 ft (1.2 m) and repeat flowering. Hardy to -20°F (-29°C), Zone 5.

'Earth Song' A Grandiflora bred by Dr Griffith J. Buck from his Shrub roses 'Music Maker' and 'Prairie Star', introduced by Iowa State University in 1975. The flowers are cupped, and light purplish red to light purplish pink, with moderate scent.
  Garden notes A repeat-flowering rose to 4 ft (1.2 m). The Buck roses were raised to withstand hard winters, and this is hardy to -40°F (-40°C), Zone 3.

'Kathryn McGredy' (also called MACauclad) A Hybrid Tea raised by Sam McGredy IV in New Zealand in 1998. The flowers are medium pink, with a light scent. It is a hybrid of 'City of Auckland' and 'Lady Rose', both Hybrid Teas.
  Garden notes Grows to about 4 ft (1.2 m) and repeat flowers. Hardy to -20°F (-29°C), Zone 5.

'Lovely Lady'

'Earth Song'

'Lovely Lady' (also called 'Dickson's Jubilee', DICjubel) A gold-medal winning Hybrid Tea introduced by Dickson in Ireland in 1986. Large, fully double flowers are coral pink and fragrant. Its parentage is the Hybrid Tea 'Silver Jubilee' crossed with a hybrid of the Floribundas 'Eurorose' and 'Anabell'.

Garden notes Makes a good coverage of very healthy foliage on a plant to 3 ft (1 m), with long-lasting flowers that repeat well over the season. Hardy to -20°F (-29°C), Zone 5.

'Manou Meilland' (also called MEItulimon) Award-winning Hybrid Tea introduced by Meilland in France in 1980. The flowers are delicate mauve-pink with a silvery reverse, cupped, very full, with around 50 petals, and fragrant. Its parentage is a seedling from 'Baronne Edmond de Rothschild' bred onto itself, crossed with a seedling from a cross of 'Ma Fille' and 'Love Song', both Hybrid Teas.

Garden notes This is similar in color to 'Baronne Edmond de Rothschild', but grows to only about 3 ft (1 m). Repeat flowering is good. Hardy to -20°F (-29°C), Zone 5.

'Miss All-American Beauty' (also called 'Maria Callas', MEIdaud) A Hybrid Tea raised by Meilland in France in 1965, winner of a gold medal and the AARS for 1968. The large, deep pink flowers have an intense scent. There is another Hybrid Tea by this name, more red and only lightly scented. The parentage is the Hybrid Tea 'Chrysler Imperial' and 'Karl Herbst' (*see p.217*).

Garden notes This makes a very healthy plant to about 3½ ft (1.1 m). The repeat flowering is especially good late in the season. Hardy to -15°F (-26°C), in Zone 5.

'The McCartney Rose' (also called 'McCartney Rose', 'Paul McCartney', 'Sweet Lady', MEIzeli) A Hybrid Tea raised by Meilland in France in 1995, named for the Beatles member, and winner of four gold medals. The lovely flowers of clear deep pink are very well scented. Its parentage is a cross of the Floribunda 'Nirvana' and 'Papa Meilland' (*see p.217*), crossed with the Hybrid Tea 'First Prize'.

Garden notes Very healthy growth to 5 ft (1.5 m) and good flowering through the season. Hardy to -20°F (-29°C), Zone 5.

'Baronne Edmond de Rothschild'

'The McCartney Rose'

'Manou Meilland'

'**Alexander**' (also called 'Alexandra', HARlex) A Hybrid Tea raised by Jack Harkness and introduced by Harkness Roses 1972. The flowers are bright orange to vermilion, double, and have slight scent. It has received many prizes including the James Mason medal from the RNRS in 1987. The parentage is 'Tropicana' crossed with a seedling from a cross of the Floribundas 'Ann Elizabeth' and 'Allgold'.

Garden notes A rather tall rose, to about 5 ft (1.5 m), and very free flowering throughout the season. Hardy to -20°F (-29°C), Zone 5.

'Alexander'

'**Candelabra**' (also called JACcinqo) A Grandiflora raised by Keith Zary and introduced by Bear Creek Gardens in 1999. Small clusters of long, pointed buds open to coral-orange double flowers with a light Tea scent. Winner of the AARS for 1999. It is a hybrid of 'Tournament of Roses' (*see p.207*) and an unnamed seedling.
Garden notes A tall, repeat-flowering shrub to as much as 5 ft (1.5 m) in height. Hardy to -20°F (-29°C), Zone 5.

'**Catherine Deneuve**' (also called MEIpraserpi) A Hybrid Tea raised by Meilland in France in 1981 and named for the French film actress. The orange-pink flowers are semidouble to fully double and well scented. Its parentage is not recorded.

Garden notes Very healthy, strong-growing, spreading plants to about 4 ft (1.2 m), with excellent repeat flowering. Hardy to -20°F (-29°C), Zone 5.

'**Dolly Parton**' A prize-winning Hybrid Tea raised by Joseph F. Winchel and introduced by Conard-Pyle in 1984, named for the great country singer. The flowers are large, double, and luminous orange, and have an intense fragrance. The parentage is 'Fragrant Cloud' (*see p.217*) and the Hybrid Tea 'Oklahoma'.

Garden notes This grows to 3–4 ft (1–1.2 m) and flowers right through the season. Hardy to -20°F (-29°C), Zone 5.

'Tropicana'

'Solitude' at the Royal Botanical Gardens, Burlington, Ontario

'Catherine Deneuve'

'Candelabra'

'Dolly Parton'

'Perfect Moment' (also called 'Jack Dayson', KORwilma)
A Hybrid Tea raised by Kordes in 1989, winner of the AARS
for 1991. Pointed buds open to double flowers with petals that
are vermilion-red on the outer edge and yellow on the inner
area and the reverse. The scent is light. The parentage is the
Hybrid Tea 'New Day' crossed with an unnamed seedling.

Garden notes A rose to about 4 ft (1.2 m), especially
suited to warm gardens. Hardy to -20°F (-29°C), Zone 5.

'Silver Jubilee' One of the great modern Hybrid Teas,
introduced by Cocker in 1978 and named to commemorate
the 25th jubilee of Queen Elizabeth. It has stood the test of
time and won three gold medals, including one from the
RNRS. It has very large, silvery pink flowers with a darker
reverse and good fragrance. The parentage includes the Shrub
rose 'Color Wonder', the Kordesii rose 'Parkdirektor Riggers',
the Floribunda 'Highlight', and the Hybrid Teas 'Piccadilly'
and 'Mischief'.

Garden notes A very disease-resistant rose that seems to be
always in flower. Height to 3 ft (1 m). Hardy to -20°F (-29°C),
Zone 5.

'Solitude' (also called POULbero) A Grandiflora raised by
Pernille and Mogens Olesen and introduced by Conard-Pyle in
1991. The fully double flowers are orange-yellow shading to
pink and salmon, with a lighter yellowish reverse, and lightly
scented. The parentage is the Hybrid Tea 'Selfridges' and an
unnamed seedling.

Garden notes A healthy plant to 4 ft (1.2 m), with great
freedom of flowering and good repeat bloom; it appears to be
always in flower. Hardy to -24°F (-31°C), in Zone 4.

'Tropicana' (also called 'Super Star', TANorstar) A Hybrid
Tea raised by Tantau in 1960. This was the first of the bright
orange-vermilion roses; its luminous, orange-red flowers are
usually single. Once an extraordinarily popular rose around the
world, it has received the AARS for 1963 and an RNRS award,
among many other accolades. The parentage is a hybrid of an
unnamed seedling and 'Peace' (*see p.206*), crossed with a hybrid
of an unnamed seedling and the Floribunda 'Alpine Glow'.

Garden notes This reaches 4 ft (1.2 m) with strong growth,
if a lanky habit; it may get a little mildew in some areas. The
repeat flowering is excellent. Hardy to -20°F (-29°C), Zone 5.

'Perfect Moment'

'Silver Jubilee'

'Artistry'

'Botero'

'Precious Platinum'

'Fragrant Cloud'

'Karl Herbst'

'Papa Meilland'

'Fame!'

'Deep Secret'

'Isabel de Ortiz'

'Artistry' (also called 'Once Touched', JACirst) A Hybrid Tea raised by Keith Zary, introduced by Bear Creek Gardens in the United States in 1998. The double flowers are creamy coral-orange, less orange on the reverse, and lightly scented. A cross of two unnamed seedlings, it received the AARS for 1997.

Garden notes A rose to 5 ft (1.5 m) that repeats well and does best in warm areas. Hardy to -15°F (-26°C), in Zone 5.

'Botero' (also called 'Duftfestival', 'Winschoten', MEIafone) A Hybrid Tea introduced by Meilland in France, and winner of several awards. The flowers are large and full, strong red, and very fragrant. The parentage is not recorded.

Garden notes A very healthy rose to 4 ft (1.2 m), best in cooler gardens. Hardy to -20°F (-29°C), Zone 5.

'Deep Secret' (also called 'Mildred Scheel') Award-winning Hybrid Tea introduced by Tantau in Germany in 1977. The flowers are crimson, fully double, with about 40 petals, and have a strong fragrance. The parentage is not recorded.

Garden notes Grows to 4 ft (1.2 m) and repeat flowers well throughout the season. Hardy to -20°F (-29°C), Zone 5.

'Fame!' (also called JACzor) A Grandiflora raised by Keith Zary introduced by Bear Creek Gardens in 1998, and winner of the AARS for 1998. The flowers, in small clusters, are deep shocking pink, double, and lightly scented. It is a hybrid of 'Tournament of Roses' (*see p.207*) and the Floribunda 'Zorina'.

Garden notes Grows to a height of 4 ft (1.2 m), with good repeat flowering. Hardy to -15°F (-26°C), in Zone 5.

'Fragrant Cloud' (also called 'Duftwolke', 'Nuage Parfumé', TANellis) A Hybrid Tea raised by Tantau in Germany in 1967, from a seedling crossed with the Hybrid Tea 'Prima Ballerina'. The large, double flowers open coral, turning geranium-red, with a wonderful old-rose scent; they repeat all through the season. Winner of the World Federation of Rose Societies Hall of Fame in 1981 and many other awards.

Garden notes This can reach 5 ft (1.5 m); it may suffer some blackspot. Hardy to -15°F (-26°C), in Zone 5.

'Isabel de Ortiz' A Hybrid Tea introduced by Kordes in Germany in 1962. The flowers are deep pinkish-red with a contrasting light silvery reverse, and very pleasantly scented.

Winner of two gold medals. The parentage is 'Peace' (*see p.206*) crossed with the Hybrid Tea 'Kordes Perfecta'.

Garden notes A good repeat-flowering, low-growing rose, to about 30 in (75 cm). Hardy to -20°F (-29°C), Zone 5.

'Karl Herbst' (also called 'Red Peace') A Hybrid Tea raised by Kordes in Germany in 1950. Very large double flowers with about 60 petals are a dull, dark scarlet, and pleasantly scented. It is a cross of the Floribunda 'Independence' and 'Peace' (*see p.206*); apart from the flower color, it is very similar to 'Peace'.

Garden notes A strong-growing, healthy rose that grows to about 4 ft (1.2 m). The flowers may ball in very wet weather. Hardy to -20°F (-29°C), Zone 5.

'Papa Meilland' (also called MEIsar, MEIcesar) A Hybrid Tea introduced by Meilland in France in 1963. It has lovely velvety, dark crimson flowers with excellent perfume, and received the World Federation of Rose Societies Hall of Fame in 1988 and many other medals, especially for perfume. It is a cross of the Hybrid Teas 'Chrysler Imperial' and 'Charles Mallerin'.

Garden notes A repeat-flowering rose that reaches 4 ft (1.2) or more. Does well in hot dry climates; it can get mildew and some blackspot, but is worthwhile in all conditions for its superb scent. Hardy to -4°F (-20°C), in Zone 6.

'Precious Platinum' (also called 'Opa Pötschke', 'Red Star') A Hybrid Tea introduced by Dickson in Northern Ireland in 1974. The large, cardinal-red flowers hold their color well; their scent is light. It is a cross of the Hybrid Tea 'Red Planet' and the Floribunda 'Franklin Englemann'.

Garden notes A tall rose, growing to 5 ft (1.5 m) or more, with good repeat flowering. Hardy to -20°F (-29°C), Zone 5.

'Ingrid Bergman' in the Queen Mary Garden, Regent's Park, London

'Ink Spots' in the Huntington Rose Garden, California

'Mister Lincoln'

'Big Purple' (also called 'Stephens' Big Purple', 'Nuit d'Orient', STEbigpu)   A Hybrid Tea raised by Pat Stephens in New Zealand in 1985 from a seedling and the Floribunda 'Purple Splendour'. The large flowers are deep, dark purple and have an excellent old rose scent. They do repeat, although not profusely.

Garden notes   The darkest of all the purple shades, and not to be missed for its great perfume. Long stems make this a good rose for cutting. Hardy to -20°F (-29°C), Zone 5.

'Crimson Glory'   An award winning Hybrid Tea raised by Kordes in Germany and introduced by Jackson and Perkins in the United States in 1935. Long, pointed buds open to large, cupped, double flowers of deep velvety crimson with an intense damask scent. It is a cross of 'Cathrine Kordes' and a seedling of 'W. E. Chaplin', both Hybrid Teas.

Garden notes   A vigorous, spreading rose that flowers well right through the season. Hardy to -20°F (-29°C), Zone 5.

'Ernest H. Morse' (also called 'E.H. Morse')   A Hybrid Tea raised by Kordes in Germany and introduced by Morse in England in 1964. The flowers are turkey-red, double, and strongly scented. It won an RNRS gold medal in 1965. The parentage is not recorded.

Garden notes   A good healthy rose that grows to about 3 ft (1 m) in height. It is still popular after 40 years due to its good repeat blooming, excellent perfume, and disease resistance: could one ask for more? Hardy to -20°F (-29°C), Zone 5.

'Ingrid Bergman' (also called POULman)   A Hybrid Tea raised by Olesen and introduced by Poulsen in Denmark in 1984. The flowers are in small clusters and have up to 49 petals. They are a clear, strong, velvety red, with a delicious spicy fragrance. One of the very best red roses, winner of the World Federation of Rose Societies Hall of Fame 2000 and

'Crimson Glory'

'Ernest H. Morse'

'Loving Memory'

'Olympiad'

'Big Purple'

many other distinctions. It is a hybrid of 'Precious Platinum' (*see p.217*) and an unnamed seedling.

Garden notes A disease-resistant, repeat-flowering rose to about 4½ ft (1.4 m). Hardy to -24°F (-31°C), in Zone 4.

'Ink Spots' A Hybrid Tea raised by Weeks Roses in California in 1985. The velvety flowers are exceptionally deep red to almost black, and have a light, old-rose scent. The parentage is not recorded.

Garden notes A good repeat-flowering rose for all kinds of weather, growing to about 3 ft (1 m). Hardy to -15°F (-26°C), in Zone 5.

'Loving Memory' (also called 'Burgund 81', 'Red Cedar', KORgund, KORgund 81) A Hybrid Tea introduced by Kordes in Germany in 1983, a cross of an unnamed seedling and a seedling of the Hybrid Tea 'Red Planet'. It has very good, tall, red flowers with about 40 petals.

Garden notes A very healthy repeat-flowering rose. It is tall, to about 5 ft (1.5 m), and has long flower stems that are good for cutting. Hardy to -20°F (-29°C), Zone 5.

'Mister Lincoln' A Hybrid Tea raised by Swim and Weeks in the United States in 1965. It won the AARS for 1965 and is one of the most popular red roses of all time. The high-centered flowers are strong red and have an intense old rose scent; the foliage is dark and matte. It is a cross of the Hybrid Teas 'Chrysler Imperial' and 'Charles Mallerin'.

Garden notes Excellent for warmer gardens, with vigorous growth to about 4 ft (1.2 m). Hardy to -15°F (-26°C), in Zone 5.

'Olympiad' (also called 'Olympia', 'Olympiade', MACauck) A Hybrid Tea raised by McGredy in New Zealand in 1982; winner of a gold medal and the AARS for 1984. The brilliant mid-red flowers have a light, fruity scent. It is a cross of the Hybrid Teas 'Red Planet' and 'Pharaoh'.

Garden notes Grows to 3½ ft (1.1 m): repeat flowering, and at its best in cooler weather. Hardy to -20°F (-29°C), Zone 5.

'Claude Monet'

'Henri Matisse'

'Cajun Sunrise' A Hybrid Tea raised by Edwards in the United States and introduced in 2001. The flowers are soft pink, mixed with a cream center, with a light scent. It is a cross of the Hybrid Teas 'Crystalline' and 'Elegant Beauty'.

Garden notes A repeat-flowering rose to an average height of about 3 ft (1 m). Hardy to -15°F (-26°C), in Zone 5.

'Candy Stripe' A Hybrid Tea introduced by McCummings in the United States in 1963. The well-scented flowers are very large, with about 60 petals, and a strong, dusty pink streaked and spotted with light pink. It is an unusual sport of the Hybrid Tea 'Pink Peace'.

Garden notes Makes a plant to about 4 ft (1.2 m) and repeat flowers well. Hardy to -24°F (-31°C), in Zone 4.

'Claude Monet' (also called JACdesa) A Hybrid Tea of unknown parentage introduced by Jackson and Perkins in the United States in 1992. Carmine buds open to cupped petals of striped red, white, orange, and pink. The scent is light and fruity.

Garden notes Vigorous growth to about 4 ft (1.2 m), and strong repeat flowering. Hardy to -15°F (-26°C), in Zone 5.

'Diana Princess of Wales' (also called 'The Work Continues' JACshaq) A Hybrid Tea raised by Keith Zary, introduced by Bear Creek Gardens in the United States in 1998. The flowers are a blend of luminous pink and creamy ivory, lightly scented. It is a cross of the Hybrid Teas 'Anne Morrow Lindbergh' and 'Sheer Elegance'.

Garden notes A good repeat-flowering rose to an average height of about 3 ft (1 m). Hardy to -15°F (-26°C), in Zone 5.

'Double Delight' (also called ANDeli) A highly popular Hybrid Tea raised by Swim and Ellis in the United States in 1977 from the Hybrid Teas 'Granada' and 'Garden Party'. The flowers are creamy white in the center, strawberry-red at the edge, a combination that has been much copied. They have a strong, spicy scent. It has received many awards, including the AARS for 1977 and the World Federation of Rose Societies Hall of Fame.

Garden notes A very eye-catching rose, to 5 ft (1.5 m). Hardy to -20°F (-29°C), Zone 5.

'Henri Matisse' (also called DELstrobla) A Hybrid Tea raised by Delbard in France in 1995, one of a series commemorating French painters. The very large, double flowers are a mixture of red, pink, and white stripes; the complex fragrance is a blend of old rose and fruit. The parents are a cross of 'Lara' and 'Candia' and a cross of 'Aromaepi' and 'KORpek', all Hybrid Teas.

Garden notes Grows to 3 ft (1 m), strong and vigorous, flowering freeling and with good repeat blooming. Hardy to -10°F (-23°C), Zone 6, or below.

'Jubilé du Prince de Monaco' (also called 'Cherry Parfait', 'Prince de Monaco', MEIsponge) A Grandiflora introduced by Meilland in France in 2001. The flowers are well formed, with a high center, each petal white edged in deep magenta. The scent is good. Its parentage is 'Jacqueline Nebout' (*see p.237*) and a hybrid of 'Tamango' and 'Matangi' (*see p.239*), all Floribundas.

Garden notes A healthy rose to around 3 ft (1 m), with good repeat flowering. Hardy to -15°F (-26°C), in Zone 5.

'Love and Peace' (also called BAIpeace) A Hybrid Tea raised by Lim and Twomey, introduced in the United States in 2002. The tall, firm-centered flowers are yellow with cerise-red on the edges and outer petals and continue throughout the season;

'Nostalgie'

the scent is mild. A cross of 'Peace' (*see p.206*) and an unnamed seedling, this won the AARS for 2002.

Garden notes A shapely, healthy bush to 3 ft (1 m), very good in humid areas. Hardy to -15°F (-26°C), in Zone 5.

'Nostalgie' (also called TANeiglat) A Hybrid tea introduced by Tantau in Germany in 1996. The flowers are very large and open flat, in the style of an old rose; they are creamy white in the center, edged pink and red. It has very good perfume, for which it has received an award. The parentage is not recorded.

Garden notes A plant to 3 ft (1 m) or less, with very dark foliage. Good repeat flowering. Hardy to -20°F (-29°C), Zone 5.

'Rose Gaujard' (also called GAUmo) Award-winning Hybrid Tea raised by Gaujard, introduced by Armstrong in the United States in 1957. Tall, very double flowers with 80 petals are silvery pink edged in bright shocking pink, with a silvery white reverse; the scent is light. It is a cross of 'Peace' (*see p.206*) and a seedling of the Hybrid Tea 'Opera', and a great addition to any collection.

Garden notes A very healthy plant to 4 ft (1.2 m), with excellent repeat flowering. Hardy to -20°F (-29°C), Zone 5.

'Double Delight'

'Rose Gaujard'

'Jubilé du Prince de Monaco'

'Candy Stripe'

'Cajun Sunrise'

'Love and Peace'

'Diana Princess of Wales'

Polyantha Roses

'Ellen Poulsen'

POLYANTHA ROSES ARE RECOGNIZED by their many small flowers on a dwarf plant. Both the flowers and the name come from *Rosa multiflora*, which was sometimes called *R. polyantha*. Polyanthas had a brief period of popularity in the first half of the 20th century, soon after their introduction, but then they were pushed aside by their progeny the Floribundas, to which they gave both clustered flowers and extreme freedom of flowering.

The first recognized Polyantha was raised in France by Guillot fils in Lyon; this was named 'Paquerette', and was introduced in 1875. This was a hybrid of *R. multiflora*, probably the dwarf, repeat-flowering form 'Nana', and probably a China; the result has semidouble white flowers and repeats well. 'Mignonette', probably of similar parentage but with some pink in the flower, was introduced in 1880, and Guillot also raised the bright pink 'Gloire des Polyanthas' in 1887. Soon Polyanthas were appearing in a variety of colours, even, in the case of 'Baby Faurax' (*see p.224*) a purple that fades to near blue.

It was D. T. Poulsen in Denmark who in 1911 raised 'Ellen Poulsen' a bright pink double dwarf Polyantha; in 1924, using 'Orléans Rose' crossed with a Hybrid Tea, his son Sven produced the first

of the so-called Poulsen roses, 'Else Poulsen' and 'Kirsten Poulsen'(*see p.227*) which later came to be known as Floribundas.

Two other groups are close to the Polyanthas. The Hybrid Musks, which were raised by Pemberton, are mostly much larger in habit and flower, but 'Ballerina' (*see p.174*) is certainly closer to the Polyanthas, and is often classified as one; it has all the characters of the dwarf *R. multiflora*.

Other hybrid Polyanthas are closer to miniature Teas, with perfect tall buds and flowers that have quilled petals when fully open. The influence of *R. multiflora* is greatly weakened, and shows mainly in the sprays of flowers; this group is sometimes called Polypom or dwarf China. 'Perle d'Or' also called 'Yellow Cecile Brunner' is a member of this group, as is 'Marie Pavie' (*see p.224*).

It is not quite true to say that the Polyanthas as a group are a relic from the past. In 1974, Harkness in England introduced 'Yesterday' (*see p.225*), an excellent rose that has won several awards.

Polyanthas need little attention, other than good soil and the removal of shoots that have flowered down to a good leaf. Many of them are susceptible to mildew, so should be well fed and watered, particularly in dry weather or crowded conditions.

POLYANTHA ROSES

'Gloire des Polyanthas'

'Orléans Rose'

'Paquerette'

'Cécile Brünner' (also called 'Mlle Cécile Brünner', 'Mignon', 'Sweetheart Rose')   A classic Polyantha, introduced by Pernet-Ducher in Lyon, France in 1881, now in the World Federation of Rose Societies Old Rose Hall of Fame. Long, pointed, Tea-shaped buds open to small, delicate flowers, light pink on a creamy ground. The parentage is said to be a double-flowered *R. multiflora* (*see p.17*) crossed with either 'Souvenir d'un Ami' or a seedling of 'Mme de Tartas', both Teas.
   Garden notes   This is a charming and long-lived rose, with almost thornless stems that reach 3 ft (1 m) and end in loose sprays of flowers, repeat flowering well through the season. There is also a climbing sport (*see p.152*), a rampant, leafy climber that occurred in California and was introduced in 1894. This is probably reliably hardy to -10°F (-23°C), Zone 6, although some authorities do rate it as hardy down to -30°F (-34°C), Zone 4.

'Ellen Poulsen'   A Hybrid Polyantha introduced by Poulsen in Denmark in 1911. The cherry-pink, medium-sized flowers are double and in clusters, and have a moderate scent. The parentage is the Polyantha 'Mme Norbert Levavaseur' and 'Dorothy Perkins' (*see p.158*).
   Garden notes   An interesting historic rose that influenced Floribundas (*see p.227*), with good repeat flowering and some resistance to mildew. The upright stems grow to 5 ft (1.5 m) or more, large for a Polyantha. Hardy to -30°F (-34°C), Zone 4.

'Gloire des Polyanthas'   A seedling of the Polyantha 'Mignonette', sister to 'Paquerette', introduced by Guillot in France in 1887, when the bright pink of its flowers was a new colour. The flowers are small, fully double, and often have a red stripe on one of the inner petals.
   Garden notes   Grows to around 2 ft (60 cm); it is susceptible to mildew. Hardy to -30°F (-34°C), Zone 4.

'Orléans Rose'   A Polyantha raised by Levavasseur et fils in France in 1909. The flowers are bright pinkish-red, small, and loosely double, produced in stiff, upright sprays. The parentage is uncertain, but it is thought to be a seedling of the Polyantha 'Mme Norbert Levavasseur', a red rose that fades to purple. This was significant as a parent of the first Poulsen roses.
   Garden notes   Easily grown, with stems around 18 in (45 cm) tall. Hardy to -30°F (-34°C), Zone 4.

'Paquerette'   This is one of the first Polyantha roses, raised by Guillot fils in Lyon, France in 1875. It has loosely double, small, white flowers about 1 in (2.5 cm) across, produced in clusters, and repeats well through the season. Its parentage is not recorded but is assumed to have been *R. multiflora* (*see p.17*), probably the 'Nana' variety, crossed with a China.
   Garden notes   Easily grown, with stems around 1 ft (30 cm) tall. Hardy to -30°F (-34°C), Zone 4.

Rosa multiflora 'Nana'   This is probably an old Chinese garden rose (*see p.17 for the species*), though it was first reported in cultivation in Europe in the late 19th century. It is attractive in itself, but most important as a parent, reinforcing the repeat-flowering of Teas, Chinas, and Hybrid Perpetuals. The flowers are single, white or very pale pink, with little scent.
   Garden notes   An easily grown dwarf, with stems around 1 ft (30 cm) tall. It is repeat flowering, but susceptible to mildew. Hardy to -30°F (-34°C), Zone 4.

'White Cécile Brünner'   A white sport of 'Cécile Brünner' introduced by Fraque in France in 1909. It is a free-flowering dwarf with creamy white flowers.
   Garden notes   Like its parent, but said to be more delicate and susceptible to disease if neglected. Hardy to -10°F (-23°C), Zone 6.

'White Cécile Brünner'

'Cécile Brünner'

Rosa multiflora 'Nana'

POLYANTHA ROSES

'Baby Faurax' A Polyantha rose introduced by Leonard Lille in France in 1924. The small, double flowers open purplish-red and fade almost to blue; they are produced in large clusters but have only moderate scent. The parentage is not recorded.

Garden notes This is a dwarf shrub, with stems growing to around 18 in (45 cm). Hardy to -30°F (-34°C), Zone 4.

'Clotilde Soupert' A Polyantha rose introduced by Soupert et Notting in Luxembourg in 1890. The very attractive flowers are fully double, pearly white with a soft pink center, and have a good scent. The parentage is said to be a cross of the Polyantha 'Mignonette' and the Tea rose 'Mme Damaizin'.

Garden notes This makes a bushy shrub not more than to 20 in (50 cm) tall, and is reasonably healthy. Hardy to -30°F (-34°C), Zone 4.

'Heinrich Karsch' A Polyantha rose introduced by Leenders in Tegelen in the Netherlands in 1927. The medium-sized flowers are purplish with white streaks, and faintly scented.

'Baby Faurax'

The parentage is a cross of 'Orléans Rose' (*see p.223*) and the Hybrid Musk 'Joan'.

Garden notes A dwarf with stems around 16 in (40 cm). Hardy to -30°F (-34°C), Zone 4.

'Jean Mermoz' A Polyantha rose introduced by Chenault in 1937. The fully double, pink flowers are neatly shaped and carried in long clusters. It is a cross of *R. wichurana* (*see p.19*) and a Hybrid Tea.

Garden notes A vigorous grower, around 30 in (75 cm) tall, but susceptible to mildew. It flowers well again towards the end of the season. Hardy to -20°F (-29°C), Zone 5.

'La Marne' A Polyantha rose introduced by Barbier in 1915. The single flowers are blush to white, edged with vivid pink. It is a cross of the Polyantha 'Mme Norbert Levavasseur' and the China 'Comtesse du Caÿla' (*see p.86*).

Garden notes A low-growing rose, to around 16 in (40 cm), repeat flowering well. Hardy to -30°F (-34°C), Zone 4.

'Leonie Lamesch' A Polyantha introduced by Lambert in Germany in 1899. Very bright, deep crimson-red buds open to coppery red and finally orange flowers, fully double but loose, produced singly or in large clusters throughout the season. It is a cross of the Shrub 'Aglaia' and the Polyantha 'Kleiner Alfred'.

Garden notes An upright, relatively tall Polyantha, to around 3 ft (1 m). Hardy to -20°F (-29°C), Zone 5.

'Marie Pavié' (also called 'Marie Pavic') A Polyantha rose introduced by Allégatière in 1888; a climbing sport was recorded in 1904. Perfect, scrolled, Tea-shaped buds open to

'Clotilde Soupert'

'Marie Pavié'

'White Pet'

'Heinrich Karsch'

'Mevrouw Nathalie Nypels'

'Yesterday'

'La Marne' in Cypress Hill Cemetery, California

'Jean Mermoz'

'Yvonne Rabier'

double pale pink flowers with a deeper, flesh-coloured center; their scent is good. The parentage is not recorded.

Garden notes The growth is low and bushy, to around 18 in (45cm), with almost no prickles. Flowers are produced repeatedly through the season. Hardy to -30°F (-34°C), Zone 4.

'Mevrouw Nathalie Nypels' (also called 'Nathalie Nypels') A Polyantha hybrid introduced by Leenders in the Netherlands in 1919. The flowers are semidouble, cup-shaped, and pale pink with a deeper center. They have good scent. The parentage is 'Orléans Rose' (*see p.223*) crossed with a seedling of the China 'Comtesse du Caÿla' (*see p.86*) and *R. foetida* 'Bicolor' (*see p.30*).

Garden notes An excellent rose with stems to around 2 ft (60 cm) and exceptional repeat flowering. Hardy to -20°F (-29°C), Zone 5.

'The Fairy' (also called 'Fairy', 'Féerie') A Polyantha that can be grown as a Groundcover, introduced by Bentall in England in 1932. The flowers, in long sprays, are very small, tightly double, and light pink. It is a cross of the Polyantha 'Paul Crampel' and the Rambler 'Lady Gay'.

Garden notes Rather late flowering, this is generally at its best in mid- or late summer, but then repeats well. The stems reach around 30 in (75 cm); it is often grown as a standard. Hardy to -30°F (-34°C), Zone 4.

'White Pet' (also called 'Little White Pet') A Polyantha rose introduced by Peter Henderson & Co of New York in 1879. Large clusters of small, bright pink buds open to densely double white flowers; this is a dwarf sport of 'Félicité-Perpétue' (*see p.154*).

Garden notes A dwarf grower, usually around 12 in (30 cm), this makes an excellent standard. Repeat flowers well. Hardy to -20°F (-29°C), Zone 5.

'Yesterday' (also called 'Tapis d'Orient') A Polyantha rose raised by Harkness in England in 1974.

'Leonie Lamesch'

'The Fairy'

The lilac-pink flowers are almost single, with long golden stamens, in clusters, repeat flowering well. The parentage is a seedling of 'Phyllis Bide' (*see p.153*) and the Floribunda 'Shepherd's Delight' crossed with 'Ballerina' (*see p.174*).

Garden notes A good garden rose, forming a rounded bush covered with flowers, and the recipient of many awards and gold medals, including the ADR 1978. Hardy to -30°F (-34°C), Zone 4.

'Yvonne Rabier' A Polyantha rose introduced by E. Turbat et Cie of Orléans in France in 1910. Clusters of long, pointed buds open to semidouble, pure white flowers with yellow stamens, with good scent. It is a cross of *R. wichurana* (*see p.19*) and a Polyantha.

Garden notes A vigorous plant with many stems to 4 ft (1.2 m), the leaves glossy and generally healthy. Repeat flowers well in late summer. Hardy to -20°F (-29°C), Zone 5.

Floribundas

'Else Poulsen'

THE DOMINANT ROSE GROUPS of the 20th century were the Floribundas and the Hybrid Teas. While Hybrid Teas were prized for the perfection of their large, individual flowers, Floribundas were bred for their masses of smaller flowers; these combine with their freedom of flowering to give a show of color throughout the season.

Floribundas owe their existence to Dines Poulsen in southern Denmark, who crossed a Polyantha rose with a Hybrid Tea to produce the hardy and free-flowering 'Rödhätte' in 1907. At the time this was called a Hybrid Polyantha, or Poulsen rose. Further crosses of the same type followed with bright pink 'Ellen Poulsen' appearing in 1911 and 'Kirsten Poulsen' and 'Else Poulsen' in 1924.

Other breeders produced similar roses by chance, such as 'Gruß an Aachen' in 1909, produced by crossing the large, white 'Frau Karl Druschki' (*see p.122*) with the yellow Hybrid Tea 'Franz Deegen'.

Further crosses with Hybrid Teas have produced sprays of larger flowers, more perfectly Hybrid Tea in type, until the distinction between the two groups has become blurred. A new group, the Grandifloras, has been recognized in some countries; here these have been included in the Hybrid Tea section.

Single-flowered Floribundas were very popular in the 1930s, and several of these still hold their own for health and freedom of flowering. 'Betty Prior' is still an excellent pink, and 'Dainty Maid' (*see p.236*), 'Dusky Maiden' (*see p.240*), and 'Lilac Charm', all raised by Edward Le Grice, are still grown in both North America and Europe. 'Dainty Maid' is also significant as one of the parents of 'Constance Spry' (*see p.136*) the first of David Austin's English Roses.

Because they are generally low growing and very floriferous, Floribundas are ideal for the front of mixed border. Old stems can be pruned well back before growth starts in spring.

FLORIBUNDAS

'Betty Prior' A Floribunda introduced by Prior in England in 1935, from 'Kirsten Poulsen' and an unnamed seedling. It bears large heads of bright pink, single flowers, with good scent.

Garden notes An excellent rose for bedding or for a mixed border, with stems to around 4 ft (1.2 m). This is still very popular in North America, holding its own against modern varieties. Hardy to -30°F (-34°C), Zone 4.

'Ellen Poulsen' The appearance of this Hybrid Polyantha (*see p.223*) influenced the early Floribundas. It was introduced by Poulsen in Denmark in 1911. The clusters of bright pink, double flowers have moderate scent. It is a cross of the Polyantha 'Mme Norbert Levavaseur' and 'Dorothy Perkins' (*see p.158*).

Garden notes A good repeat-flowering upright plant to 5 ft (1.5 m) or more. Hardy to -30°F (-34°C), Zone 4.

'Else Poulsen' (also called 'Joan Anderson') A Floribunda introduced in 1924 by Poulsen in Denmark. It bears large sprays of semidouble, bright pink flowers with little scent, and is a cross of 'Orléans Rose' (*see p.223*) and a Hybrid Tea 'Red Star'.

Garden notes Flowers of intense color are freely produced. The leaves are tinted bronze. Hardy to -30°F (-34°C), Zone 4.

'Gruß an Aachen' (also called 'Salut d'Aix la Chapelle') A Floribunda rose introduced by Geduldig in Germany in 1909. The flowers are blush-pink in the center, almost white on the edges, cupped, and very double, with delicate scent. The parentage is 'Frau Karl Druschki' (*see p.122*) and the Hybrid Tea 'Franz Deegen'.

Garden notes A lovely rose, with beautifully formed flowers in small clusters, in form a very refined Floribunda, though

with Hybrid Tea parentage. Good as bedding or in a mixed planting, it grows to 5 ft (1.5 m) and is slightly spreading; repeat flowers well. Hardy to -20°F (-29°C), Zone 5.

'Kirsten Poulsen' A Floribunda introduced by Poulsen in Denmark in 1924. The flowers are single and bright pink, produced in sprays, and have some scent. The parentage is the 'Orléans Rose' (*see p.223*) and a Hybrid Tea 'Red Star'.

Garden notes This is a more graceful sister seedling to 'Else Poulsen'. Hardy to -30°F (-34°C), Zone 4.

'Kirsten Poulsen'

'Betty Prior'

'Ellen Poulsen'

'Gruß an Aachen' at Hidcote, western England

'Cream Abundance'

'Love Letter'

'Margaret Merril'

'White Simplicity'

'Cream Abundance' (also called 'Crème Abundance', HARflax)   A Floribunda introduced by Harkness in England in 1999. It bears copious, creamy colored flowers, which are moderately scented. The parentage is not recorded.
   Garden notes This makes a low, mound-forming bush around 2 ft (60 cm) in height, and repeat flowers throughout the season. Hardy to -20°F (-29°C), Zone 5.

'French Lace' (also called JAClace)   A Floribunda raised by Warriner and introduced by Jackson and Perkins in the United States in 1981, winner of the AARS for 1982. The well-formed flowers are pale ivory-white with a hint of apricot. The parentage is the Hybrid Tea 'Dr A.J. Verhage' crossed with the Floribunda 'Bridal Pink'.
   Garden notes This grows to 4 ft (1.2 m) in height and repeat flowers well throughout the season. Hardy to -20°F (-29°C), Zone 5.

'Iceberg' (also called 'Feé des Neiges', 'Schneewittchen', KORbin)   This Floribunda is one of the most important roses raised in the last 50 years, introduced by Kordes in Germany in 1958. It has won many prizes including the WFRS Hall of Fame in 1983. The wonderful, fresh white flowers are borne in abundance and have a light scent. Its parentage is 'Robin Hood' (*see p.174*) crossed with 'Virgo' (*see p.201*). There is also a Kordes a Hybrid Tea by the name 'Iceberg'.
   Garden notes This is a a very healthy plant, growing to about 4 ft (1.2 m) in height, with good repeat flowering. It is a valuable addition to a mixed border, and makes a superb standard. There is also an excellent climbing sport. Hardy to -20°F (-29°C), Zone 5.

'Love Letter'   A Floribunda introduced by Lens in Belgium in 1977. The flowers are creamy white, double, cupped, and very well scented. The parentage is the Grandiflora or Floribunda 'Pink Parfait' crossed with the Floribunda 'Rosenelfe'.
   Garden notes A vigorous, bushy, healthy plant to about 4 ft (1.2 m) in height. Hardy to -20°F (-29°C), Zone 5.

'Margaret Merril' (also called HARkuly)   A Floribunda introduced by Harkness in 1977. The large flowers are white with a pale blush center, the prominent stamens yellow to red.

FLORIBUNDAS

They have excellent scent, for which this rose has won prizes all over the world. The parentage is a seedling of 'Rudolph Timm' and 'Dedication', both Floribundas, crossed with 'Pascali' (*see p.200*).

Garden notes A very healthy rose that grows to about 3 ft (1 m). It flowers continuously and is at its best in cooler areas. Hardy to -20°F (-29°C), Zone 5.

'Royden' A Floribunda introduced by R.F. Cattermole in New Zealand in 1989. The bright gold flowers fade quickly to white, and are strongly scented. It is a cross of the Floribundas 'Liverpool Echo' and 'Arthur Bell'.

Garden notes An upright plant to about 4 ft (1.2 m), with good repeat flowering. Hardy to -10°F (-23°C), Zone 6.

'White Simplicity' (also called JACsnow) A white sport of the pink Floribunda 'Simplicity', introduced by Jackson and Perkins in the United States in 1991. The flowers are semidouble with a moderate scent.

Garden notes A useful hedging rose with lax, loose growth to as much as 5 ft (1.5 m), and good repeat flowering. Hardy to -20°F (-29°C), Zone 5.

'Iceberg'

'French Lace' in the garden of Kleine Lettunich, Aptos, California

'Royden'

'**Amber Queen**' (also called 'Prinz Eugen von Savoyen', HARroony) A lovely Floribunda introduced by Harkness in 1983, which has won prizes all over the world. The double, cupped flowers are a warm apricot-gold color, with a moderate, spicy scent, and the foliage opens copper-red. The parentage is 'Southampton' (*see p.233*) crossed with the Hybrid Tea 'Typhoon'.

Garden notes A very disease-resistant plant, to just over 2 ft (60 cm), flowering continuously during the season. Hardy to -10°F (-23°C), Zone 6, perhaps lower.

'**Apricot Nectar**' A Floribunda introduced by Boerner at Jackson and Perkins in 1965, one of the best apricot-colored hybrids ever raised and winner of the AARS for 1966. The cupped, double flowers are a wonderful pinkish-apricot, with an intense, fruity scent. It is a cross of an unnamed seedling and the Floribunda 'Spartan'.

Garden notes At its best in a warm climate, this makes bushy growth with very freely produced flowers, repeat flowering well. Hardy to -20°F (-29°C), Zone 5.

'**Chinatown**' (also called 'Ville de Chine') One of the best of the older Floribundas, introduced by Poulsen in Denmark in 1963. It has won many awards, especially in Britain. The large flowers are yellow with a pink flush at the edge as they age, with a delicate, fruity scent. The parentage is the Floribundas 'Columbine' and 'Cläre Grammerstorf'.

Garden notes A very healthy rose that can be allowed to reach 6 ft (2 m) and flowers through the season. Hardy to -20°F (-29°C), Zone 5, perhaps lower.

'**Glenfiddich**' A Floribunda named very appropriately for the malt whisky, introduced by Cocker in Aberdeen in 1976. The loosely double flowers are a rich amber-yellow color with some fragrance. The parentage is the Floribunda 'Arthur Bell' and a cross of the Hybrid Tea 'Sabine' and the Floribunda 'Circus'.

Garden notes Grows to around 3 ft (1 m) with good repeat blooming. Hardy to -20°F (-29°C), Zone 5, perhaps lower.

'**Gold Bunny**' (also called 'Gold Badge', 'Rimosa 79', MEIgronuri) An excellent Floribunda raised by Paulino and introduced by Meilland in France in 1978. It has very double,

'Golden Holstein'

yellow flowers with a mild, pleasant scent. The parentage is 'Poppy Flash' and a seedling of 'Charlston' crossed with 'Allgold', all Floribundas.

Garden notes A healthy rose to about 2–3 ft (60–90 cm), flowering abundantly throughout the season. It is especially successful in warm areas. Hardy to -20°F (-29°C), Zone 5.

'**Golden Holstein**' (also called 'Goldyla', 'Surprise', KORtikel) A Floribunda of unrecorded parentage, introduced by Kordes in Germany in 1989. It bears lovely strong yellow, almost single blooms that are lightly scented.

Garden notes A good repeat-flowering addition to a border, to 3 ft (1 m) or more. It may suffer mildew, and is at its best in cooler climates. Probably hardy to -30°F (-34°C), Zone 4.

'Amber Queen' grown as a standard at the Parc de Bagatelle, Paris

'Gold Bunny'

'Apricot Nectar'

'Chinatown'

'Glenfiddich'

'Norwich Union'

'Sunsprite'

'Victoria Gold'

'Mountbatten' (also called 'Lord Louie', 'Lord Mountbatten', HARmantelle) This Floribunda, introduced by Harkness in 1982, has won many medals and is popular in Europe, but not as well known as it should be elsewhere. The flowers are a good, clear yellow with some scent; the very distinctive foliage is mid-green and somewhat leathery. The parentage includes 'Anne Cocker', 'Arthur Bell', and 'Southampton' (*see p. 233*), all Floribundas, and the Hybrid Tea 'Peer Gynt',

Garden notes Depending on how hard you prune it this rose can be 3 ft (1 m) to 6 ft (2 m). It is very healthy and repeat flowers well. Hardy to -20°F (-29°C), Zone 5.

'Norwich Union' A Floribunda introduced by Peter Beales in 1975. The cupped flowers are deep yellow fading to lemon yellow, with a very good scent. The parentage is the Floribunda 'Arthur Bell' crossed with the offspring of an unnamed seedling and the Floribunda 'Allgold'.

Garden notes A good, healthy, repeat-flowering rose raised by the man responsible for keeping so many old roses available for rose lovers. Hardy to -20°F (-29°C), Zone 5.

'Sunsprite' (also called 'Friesia', 'Korresia', KOResia) This Floribunda, introduced by Kordes in Germany in 1977, has won prizes all over the world. It has deep-yellow flowers with a strong scent. The parentage is seedling crossed with the Floribunda 'Spanish Sun'.

Garden notes A healthy, medium to low-growing rose that repeat flowers extremely well. Hardy to -20°F (-29°C), Zone 5.

'Victoria Gold' (also called WELgold) This Floribunda was introduced by Welsh in New South Wales in 1999 for the centenary of the Rose Society of Victoria in Australia. The large clusters of flowers are fully double and yellow-gold, the petals edged with the in cooler weather. One parent is 'Gold Bunny'.

Garden notes Grows to about 1m (3ft), with good repeat flowering. Hardy to -10°F (-23°C), Zone 6.

'Mountbatten'

FLORIBUNDAS

'Brass Band'

'Atlantic Star'

'Jacob van Ruysdael'

'English Sonnet'

'Wandering Minstrel'

'Atlantic Star' (also called FRYworld)   A Floribunda of unrecorded parentage, introduced by Fryer in England in 1993. The cupped flowers are soft salmon-pinky orange and well scented, and repeat right through the season.

   Garden notes   Grows to as much as 3 ft (1 m), with good disease resistance. Hardy to -20°F (-29°C), Zone 5.

'Brass Band' (also called JACcofl)   This Floribunda, raised by Jack E. Christensen and introduced by Jackson and Perkins in the United States in 1993, won the AARS for 1995. The flowers open yellow-orange darkening towards a deeper orange; they are well scented, with a fruity fragrance. This is a cross of 'Gold Bunny' (*see p.230*) and an unnamed seedling.

   Garden notes   A good repeat-flowering rose to 3 ft (1 m). Hardy to -10°F (-23°C), Zone 6, or lower.

'English Sonnet' (also called 'Fragrant Surprise', 'Lawrence of Arabia', 'Samaritan', HARVerag)   A Floribunda introduced by Harkness in England in 1999. The flowers are very double and apricot to pinkish-orange, with lighter, more pinkish petals toward the outside, intensely scented. It is a cross of the Hybrid Teas 'Silver Jubilee' (*see p.217*) and 'Dr A.J. Verhage'.

   Garden notes   A disease-resistant rose to 3 ft (1 m) with strong, dark green foliage. The repeat flowering is good. Hardy to -20°F (-29°C), Zone 5.

'Jacob van Ruysdael'
A Floribunda introduced by J.B. Williams in the United States in 1997. The peachy orange flowers are lightly scented. Their form is single with a few semiformed petals (petaloids) in the center, making them very distinctive.

   Garden notes   Grows to 3 ft (1 m), with good repeat flowering. Hardy to -30°F (-34°C), Zone 4.

'Sheila's Perfume'

232

'Southampton' in the Queen Mary Garden, Regent's Park, London

'Livin' Easy' (also called 'Fellowship', HARwelcome) This Floribunda, introduced by Harkness in England in 1992, holds the AARS for 1996 and many other prizes. The frilly, apricot-orange flowers have a moderate, sweet citrus scent. It is a cross of 'Southampton' and 'Remember Me' (*see p.209*).

    Garden notes Very free flowering throughout the season, on healthy growth to 3 ft (1 m). Hardy to -20°F (-29°C), Zone 5.

'Sheila's Perfume' (also called HARsherry) A Floribunda raised by John Sheridan and introduced by Harkness in England in 1982. It has has received international awards for its excellent perfume. The flowers have pale yellow petals attractively edged with crimson tones, which strengthen with maturity. The parentage includes the Hybrid Teas 'Peer Gynt' and 'Prima Ballerina', and the Floribundas 'Daily Sketch' and 'Paddy McGredy'.

    Garden notes A rose to 3 ft (1 m) or more, with good disease resistance. Hardy to -20°F (-29°C), Zone 5.

'Southampton' (also called 'Susan Ann') A Floribunda introduced in 1971 by Harkness in England. It is much sought after in Europe, where it has won many awards, but not as well known elsewhere. The apricot-blend flowers have moderate scent. The parentage is a seedling of 'Ann Elizabeth' and 'Allgold', crossed with 'Yellow Cushion', all Floribundas.

    Garden notes Flowers, which tend to be lighter in warm gardens, are borne freely throughout the season on a very healthy plant to 4 ft (1.2 m). Hardy to -20°F (-29°C), Zone 5.

'Wandering Minstrel' (also called 'Daniel Gelin', 'The Quest' HARquince) A Floribunda introduced by Harkness in England in 1986. The flowers are golden, suffused with strong orange shades, and lightly scented. It is a cross of the Floribunda 'Dame of Sark' and 'Silver Jubilee' (*see p.215*).

    Garden notes A disease-resistant plant to 3 ft (1 m) or more, repeat flowering well. Hardy to -20°F (-29°C), Zone 5.

'Livin' Easy'

'Ma Perkins'

'Great Expectations'

'City of London' (also called HARukfore)   A gold-medal winning Floribunda introduced in England by Harkness in 1986. The light pink flowers fade to blush pink, and have an intense perfume. The parentage is the Floribunda 'Radox Bouquet' crossed with 'Margaret Merril' (*see p.228*).

Garden notes   A healthy plant to 3 ft (1 m) that can also be trained as a low climber. Repeat flowering is very good. Hardy to -20°F (-29°C), Zone 5.

'English Miss'   One of the best older Floribundas, introduced in England by Cants of Colchester in 1977. The very double flowers are pale blush pink, with a strong scent. It is a cross of 'Dearest' and 'Sweet Repose', both Floribundas.

Garden notes   A very healthy, low-growing shrub with purplish to dark green leaves. Hardy to -20°F (-29°C), Zone 5.

'Great Expectations' (also called MACkalves)   A Floribunda of unrecorded parentage introduced by McGredy in New Zealand in 2001. The flowers are fully double with orangey-pink tones in the center, and well scented. Named Rose of the Year in the United Kingdom for 2001. There is also a yellow Hybrid Tea by this name.

Garden notes   A healthy, low-growing shrub with good repeat flowering. Hardy to -20°F (-29°C), Zone 5.

'Ma Perkins'   One of the older Floribundas, raised by Boerner and introduced by Jackson and Perkins in the United States in 1952. It won the AARS for 1953 and has stood the test of time. The large flowers are salmon- to shell-pink, with a moderate scent. The parentage is the Hybrid Tea 'Red Radiance' and the Floribunda 'Fashion'.

Garden notes   Grows to about 3 ft (1 m) in height and repeat flowers well. Hardy to -10°F (-23°C), Zone 6, perhaps lower.

'Pink Iceberg' (also called 'Blushing Pink Iceberg', PROberg) This Floribunda, raised by Lilia Weatherly and introduced in 1997 by Swanes in Australia, is the first of a family of sports that are derived

from 'Iceberg' (*see p.228*). Others are 'Brilliant Pink Iceberg' (*see p.236*) and 'Burgundy Iceberg' (*see p.242*). The double flowers are shaded with pink, with a light scent.

Garden notes   Like the parent this is a very healthy, free-flowering rose, growing to as much as 3 ft (1 m). Hardy to -20°F (-29°C), Zone 5.

'Queen Mother' (also called 'Queen Mum', KORquemu) A Floribunda introduced by Kordes in Germany in 1991. The light pink flowers are very freely produced, and are semidouble and lightly scented.

Garden notes   Repeat flowers right through the season on slightly weeping growth to about 3 ft (1 m). Hardy to -20°F (-29°C), Zone 5.

'City of London'

234

Floribundas

'Seduction' (also called 'Charles Aznavour', 'Matilda', 'Pearl of Bedfordview', MEIbeausai) A Floribunda introduced by Meilland in France in 1988, winner of several gold medals. The flowers are semidouble, white very prettily edged with pink, and lightly scented. 'Matilda' is officially the main name but this is most popular in Australia, under the name 'Seduction', and hard to find elsewhere. It is a cross of MEIgurami and 'Nirvana', both Floribundas. Meilland also introduced a Grandiflora by the name 'Matilda' in 1994.

Garden notes A rose with very healthy growth to about 4 ft (1.2 m); it makes an excellent standard. Repeat flowering is good. Hardy to -20°F (-29°C), Zone 5.

'Sexy Rexy' (also called 'Heckenzauber', MACrexy) This Floribunda, introduced by Sam McGredy in New Zealand in 1984, has won a great many awards all over the world. The fragrant, very double pink flowers open flat. The parentage is 'Seaspray' crossed with 'Dreaming', both Floribundas.

Garden notes A healthy rose to to 3 ft (1 m) that repeats well throughout the season. Hardy to -20°F (-29°C), Zone 5.

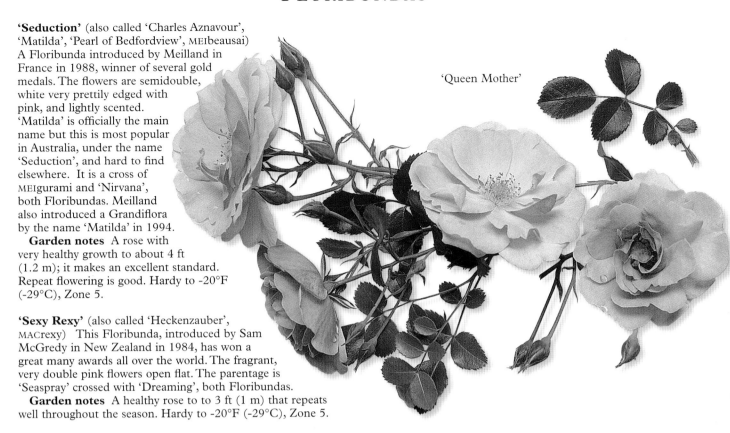

'Queen Mother'

'English Miss'

'Pink Iceberg'

'Sexy Rexy'

'Seduction' photographed in south Australia

Floribundas

'Bad Birnbach'

'Angel Face'   A Floribunda introduced by Swim and Weeks in the United States in 1968. The lovely lavender-mauve flowers are well scented. It is a hybrid of a seedling of the Floribundas 'Circus' and 'Lavender Pinocchio' (*see p. 243*) crossed with 'Sterling Silver' (*see p. 211*).
  Garden notes   Grows to 3 ft (1 m). Repeats throughout the season and is a great favourite in warm climates. Hardy to -10°F (-23°C), Zone 6, or a little lower.

'Bad Birnbach' (also called 'Busy Bee', 'Electric Blanket', KORpancom)
A Floribunda of unrecorded parentage introduced by Kordes in Germany in 1999. The strong pink flowers are displayed well above the leaves.
  Garden notes   A very healthy rose, to 2 ft (60 cm), and suitable for use as groundcover. It flowers continuously throughout the season. Hardy to -20°F (-29°C), Zone 5.

'Brilliant Pink Iceberg' (also called PRObril)   A Floribunda introduced by Swanes in Australia in 1999; it is a sport of 'Pink Iceberg' (*see p. 234*) raised by Lilia Weatherly. The bright pink flowers have a light scent and repeat well. 'Burgundy Iceberg' (*see p. 242*) is another sport in this family.
  Garden notes   A very healthy plant to 3 ft (1 m) or more. These sports all are worth growing should gain popularity beyond Australia. Hardy to -20°F (-29°C), Zone 5, or lower.

'Centenaire de Lourdes' (also called 'Mrs Jones', DELge)
A Floribunda introduced by Delbard-Chabert in France in 1958. It bears masses of semidouble, cupped, mid-pink flowers. A descendant of 'Frau Karl Druschki' (*see p. 122*) crossed with unnamed seedlings, this is popular in Europe and should be grown more in America.

  Garden notes   Makes a very healthy, tall plant, growing to at least 4 ft (1.2 m). It is very free flowering and repeat flowers continuously. Hardy to -10°F (-23°C), Zone 6.

'Dainty Maid'   A favourite Floribunda for lovers of single roses ever since it was introduced by LeGrice in England in 1940. The flowers are almost single, creamy-cerise pink with deeper red tones on the reverse, and lightly scented. It is a cross of the Floribunda 'D. T. Poulsen' and an unnamed seedling.
  Garden notes   A healthy rose to 3 ft (1 m), which flowers freely and repeat flowers well. Hardy to -20°F (-29°C), Zone 5.

'Escapade' at the Rosarium Sangerhausen, Germany

'Jacqueline Nebout'

'Angel Face'

'Brilliant Pink Iceberg'

'Dainty Maid'

'Escapade' (also called HARpade)   An award-winning Floribunda introduced by Harkness in England in 1967. The pinky-violet, semidouble blooms are lightly scented and change color very prettily as they age. Its parentage is the Floribunda 'Pink Parfait' crossed with 'Baby Faurax' (*see p.224*).
   Garden notes Makes healthy, bushy growth to 3 ft (1 m), with excellent continuous flowering throughout the season. Hardy to -30°F (-34°C), Zone 4.

'Jacqueline Nebout' (also called 'City of Adelaide', 'Sanlam-Roos', MEIchoiju)   A Floribunda introduced by Meilland in 1989. The flowers are mid-pink, with a light scent.
   Garden notes Healthy growth to 3 ft (1 m), flowering very freely all season. Hardy to -10°F (-23°C), Zone 6, or below.

'Nearly Wild'   A Floribunda introduced by Brownell in the United States in 1941, and still as popular today. It is a cross of 'Dr. W. Van Fleet' (*see p.131*) and the Hybrid Multiflora 'Leuchstern'. The single flowers have a sweet scent.
   Garden notes Makes healthy growth to 3 ft (1 m) and repeat flowers very freely. Hardy to -10°F (-23°C), Zone 6.

'Centenaire de Lourdes'

'Nearly Wild' in the garden of David Austin's Nursery in central England

237

'Betty Harkness'

'Dicky'

'Rose 2000'

'Betty Harkness' (also called HARette)   A Floribunda of unrecorded parentage introduced by Harkness in England in 1998. An exceptional tangerine pink, it has an excellent scent, which is unusual in this sort of color.

Garden notes A very healthy rose to 3 ft (1 m), with good repeat flowering. Hardy to -20°F (-29°C), Zone 5.

'Brown Velvet' (also called 'Colorbreak', MACultra) A Floribunda introduced by McGredy in New Zealand in 1982, a cross of the Floribundas 'Mary Sumner' and 'Kapai'. The lightly scented flowers have orange and brown tints, the brown being more dominant in cooler climates.

Garden notes Grows to about 3 ft (1 m), with good repeat flowering. Hardy to -20°F (-29°C), Zone 5.

'Dicky' (also called, 'Ainsley Dickson', 'Münchner Kindl', DICkimono)   A Floribunda introduced by Dickson in Northern Ireland in 1983. The flowers are reddish-salmon pink with a lighter reverse, and lightly scented.

Garden notes An ideal, healthy bedding rose to 3 ft (1 m) that repeat flowers well. Hardy to -20°F (-29°C), Zone 5.

'Elizabeth of Glamis' (also called 'Irish Beauty', 'Elisabeth', MACel) A Floribunda introduced by Sam McGredy in Northern Ireland in 1964. Named for the Queen Mother, a great rose lover who had a rose garden at her family home, Glamis Castle in Scotland. A very good bedding rose with an intense

scent. The parentage is 'Spartan' crossed with 'Highlight', both Floribundas.

Garden notes A healthy rose to 3 ft (1 m) that repeats throughout the season. Hardy to -20°F (-29°C), Zone 5.

'Fragrant Delight'   This Floribunda, introduced by the Wisbech Plant Co. in 1978, has won many awards for its exceptional fragrance. The flowers are light orange-salmon with a deeper reverse and colors may fade in a very hot climate; the young foliage is reddish-purple. The parentage is the

'Fragrant Delight'

Floribunda 'Chanelle' crossed with 'Whisky Mac' (*see p.207*).

Garden notes A good repeat-flowering, healthy rose, to 3 ft (1 m) in height. Hardy to -20°F (-29°C), Zone 5.

'Matangi' (also called MACman) One of McGredy's Hand Painted Floribundas, introduced in New Zealand in 1974 and winner of many prizes all over the world. The silvery petals are smudged with strong areas of orange, the reverse is silver. It is a cross of an unnamed seedling and 'Picasso' (*see p.244*).

Garden notes A very healthy, repeat-flowering rose to just over 2 ft (60 cm). Hardy to -20°F (-29°C), Zone 5.

'Rose 2000' (also called 'Rose Two Thousand', COCquetrum) A Floribunda introduced by Cockers of Aberdeen in 1998. The semidouble flowers are coral-vermilion with a lighter reverse and moderate scent. It is a cross of the Floribundas 'Trumpeter' (*see p.241*) and 'Clydebank Centenary'.

Garden notes A bedding rose to 2 ft (60 cm), with good repeat flowering. Hardy to -20°F (-29°C), Zone 5.

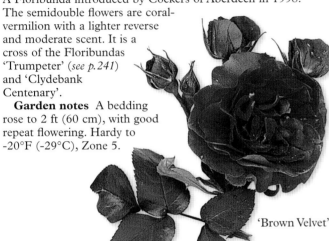

'Brown Velvet'

'Matangi'

'Elizabeth of Glamis' at the Parc de Bagatelle, Paris

'Black Ice'

'Lafayette'

'Lilli Marleen'

'Satchmo'

'Showbiz'

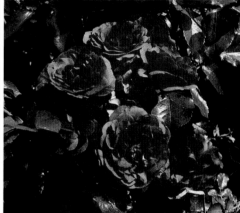

'Trumpeter'

'Black Ice' A Floribunda introduced by Douglas L. Gandy in 1971. Dark flower buds open to good strong red flowers with a moderate scent. Its parentage is a seedling of 'Iceberg' (*see p. 228*) and 'Europeana', crossed with 'Megiddo', all Floribundas.

  Garden notes A healthy rose to 2 ft (60 cm), with good repeat flowering. Hardy to -20°F (-29°C), Zone 5.

'Disco Dancer' (also called DICinfra) A lightly scented Floribunda introduced by Dickson in Northern Ireland in 1984. Orange-scarlet, semidouble flowers are borne in large trusses. It is a cross of the Floribundas 'Cathedral' and 'Memento'.

  Garden notes A very free flowering rose to 3 ft (1 m) or more, repeat flowering well. Hardy to -20°F (-29°C), Zone 5.

'Dusky Maiden' An exceptional Floribunda introduced by Le Grice in England in 1947. The single flowers are a deep, velvety red and well scented. Its parentage is a seedling of the Hybrid Teas 'Daily Mail Scented Rose' and 'Etoile de Hollande', crossed with 'Else Poulsen' (*see p. 227*).

  Garden notes A good repeat-flowering rose to 2 ft (60 cm). Hardy to -20°F (-29°C), Zone 5.

'Gartenzauber' (also called 'Gartenzauber 84', KORnacho) A large, double-flowered Floribunda introduced by Kordes in Germany in 1984. The intense red flowers are lightly scented. Its parentage is a cross of an unnamed seedling and 'Tornado', crossed with 'Chorus', both Floribundas.

  Garden notes A plant to 3 ft (1 m), with dark green, healthy foliage. Hardy to -20°F (-29°C), Zone 5, or lower.

'Lafayette' (also called 'August Kordes', 'Joseph Guy') One of the earliest of the Floribundas, introduced by Nonin in France in 1924. The strong pink flowers are borne in clusters of up to 40. It is a cross of the Floribunda 'Rödhätte' and the Hybrid Tea 'Richmond'.

  Garden notes A vigorous and bushy rose to 3 ft (1 m), this can be difficult to get hold of, but is worth growing for historic interest. Hardy to -20°F (-29°C), Zone 5.

'La Sevillana' (also called MEIgekanu) A Floribunda introduced by Meilland in France in 1978. Very large clusters of conical buds open to semidouble flowers of deep vermilion. They are lightly scented. The complex parentage involves crosses of MEIbrim, the Hybrid Teas 'Jolie Madame' and 'Tropicana' (*see p. 215*), and the Floribundas 'Zambra', 'Rusticana' and 'Poppy Flash'.

  Garden notes Makes dense, bushy growth to 4 ft (1.2 m), with good repeat blooming. A good rose for hot, dry areas. Hardy to -20°F (-29°C), Zone 5.

'Lilli Marleen' (also called 'Lilli Marlene', KORlima) One of the most successful of the deep velvety-red-flowered Floribundas, introduced by Kordes in Germany in 1958. It has won many prizes all over the world. The flowers are very fragrant. The parentage is a seedling of 'Our Princess' and 'Rudolph Timm', crossed with 'Ama', all Floribundas.

  Garden notes This is a rather low-growing rose, to about 2 ft (60 cm) in height. It is healthy, with good repeat flowering Hardy to -20°F (-29°C), Zone 5, or lower.

FLORIBUNDAS

'Satchmo' A gold-medal winning Floribunda introduced by McGredy in Northern Ireland in 1970, named for Louis 'Satchmo' Armstrong. The bright scarlet flowers have a light scent. It is a cross of the Floribundas 'Evelyn Fison' and 'Diamant'.
    Garden notes Healthy, bushy plants to 3 ft (1 m), with good repeat flowering. Hardy to -20°F (-29°C), Zone 5.

'Showbiz' (also called 'Bernhard Daneke Rose', 'Ingrid Weibull', TANweieke) A very popular Floribunda of unrecorded parentage introduced by Tantau in Germany in 1983. The bright medium-red flowers have little scent. Winner of the AARS for 1985.
    Garden notes A very healthy rose to 3 ft (1 m), with good repeat flowering. Hardy to -20°F (-29°C), Zone 5.

'Trumpeter' (also called MACtrum) An excellent red Floribunda introduced by McGredy in New Zealand in 1977, winner of many medals and prizes. The flowers are lightly scented. It is a cross of 'Satchmo' and an unnamed seedling.
    Garden notes Healthy growth to 3 ft (1 m), with purplish young foliage and long-lasting flowers that repeat well. Hardy to -20°F (-29°C), Zone 5.

'Gartenzauber'

'Disco Dancer'

'La Sevillana' in the Meilland rose fields, southern France

'Dusky Maiden' in the San Jose Heritage Rose Garden, California

241

'Singin' in the Rain'

'Burgundy Iceberg'

'Shocking Blue'

'Lavender Pinocchio' at the San Jose Heritage Rose Garden, California

'Rhapsody in Blue'

'Burgundy Iceberg' (also called PROse)   This gold-medal winning sport of 'Brilliant Pink Iceberg' (*see p.236*) is owned by Swanes Nurseries, where it occured, and Prophyl, Lilia Weatherly's company; it was introduced in Australia in 2003. The flowers have a unique, true burgundy colour with a light reverse, and delicate scent. A most exciting color break that should be available all over the world very rapidly. The original sport is 'Pink Iceberg' (*see p.234*).

Garden notes   A healthy, sprawling shrub to 4 ft (1.2 m) that repeat flowers well. Probably hardy to -20°F (-29°C), Zone 5.

'Blue Bajou' (also called 'Blue Bayou', 'Blue-Bijou', KORkultop) A Floribunda of unrecorded parentage introduced by Kordes in Germany in 1993. It is not blue, as the name implies, but an interesting blue-gray tone that will appeal to collectors of gray and brown roses. The excellent scent is reminiscent of apples.

Garden notes   Grows to 3 ft (1 m) at most, repeat flowering well until the frosts. Hardy to -20°F (-29°C), Zone 5.

'Blueberry Hill' (also called WEKcryplag)   A Floribunda raised by Tom Carruth in the United States 1999. The flowers are semidouble, pale pinkish-violet, and very well scented of apples; nearly all violet-blue roses are well scented. It is a cross of 'Crystaline' and 'Playgirl', both Floribundas.

Garden notes   A healthy plant to 4 ft (1.2 m), flowering through the season. Hardy to -20°F (-29°C), Zone 5.

'Harry Edland'   A lilac-pink Floribunda introduced by Harkness in England in 1975; it has won many prizes for its superbly scented flowers. The parentage includes the Floribunda 'Lilac Charm', 'Sterling Silver' (*see p.211*), 'Blue Moon' (*see p.210*), and the Hybrid Tea 'Africa Star'.

Garden notes   One of the best roses for a shady area. Just under 3 ft (80 cm), it repeats well. Hardy to -20°F (-29°C), Zone 5.

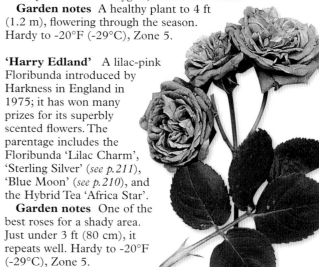

'Magenta'

'Harry Edland'

'Lavender Princess'

'Blueberry Hill'

'Lavender Pinocchio'   A Floribunda introduced by Boerner in the United States in 1948 and still in demand. Well-scented, pale, milky chocolate-brown flowers age pinky lavender. A cross of the Floribunda 'Pinocchio' and the Hybrid Tea 'Grey Pearl'.

Garden notes   A lovely healthy, low-growing rose to about 2 ft (60 cm) or a little more. Hardy to -20°F (-29°C), Zone 5.

'Lavender Princess'   A Floribunda introduced by Boerner at Jackson and Perkins in the United States in 1959. The flowers are lavender to purplish-lavender, with a delicate, fruity scent. It is a cross of a seedling of the Floribunda 'World's Fair' and a seedling of 'Lavender Pinocchio' (*see p.243*).

Garden notes   Grows to 3 ft (1 m) at most. Hardy to -20°F (-29°C), Zone 5.

'Magenta' (also called 'Kordes' Magenta')   A Floribunda sometimes listed as a Modern Shrub, introduced by Kordes in Germany in 1954. The large trusses of light purply-mauve flowers are very well scented. It is a cross of an unnamed yellow Floribunda seedling and 'Lavender Pinocchio' (*see p.243*).

Garden notes   A superb, healthy rose to as much as 5 ft (1.5 m), which can be used for a hedge. It repeat flowers throughout the season. Hardy to -20°F (-29°C), Zone 5.

'Rhapsody in Blue' (also called FRANtasia)   A Floribunda raised by amateur Frank Cowlishaw in England, introduced in 2000 by Warners Roses and Rose of the Year for 2003. The masses of strongly scented, semidouble flowers are dark purplish-blue with a lighter reverse, the most distinctive coloring yet in the purplish-blue range; many of the best blue roses, including 'Violacea' and 'Blue Moon' (*see p.210*), were used in its breeding.

Garden notes   This is a low-growing rose, reaching about 2 ft (60 cm); it is very healthy and repeat flowers well. Hardy to -20°F (-29°C), Zone 5.

'Shocking Blue' (also called KORblue)   A Floribunda introduced by Kordes in Germany in 1974. The lilac-mauve double flowers have an intense fragrance. The parentage is an unnamed seedling crossed with the Hybrid Tea 'Silver Star'.

Garden notes   A healthy plant to 3 ft (1 m), with good repeat flowering. Hardy to -20°F (-29°C), Zone 5.

'Singin' in the Rain' (also called 'Love's Spring', 'Spek's Centennial', MACivy)   A Floribunda introduced by McGredy in New Zealand in 1994, winner of the AARS for 1995. The large clusters of very double flowers are apricot-copper, with a moderate, sweet scent. The parentage is 'Sexy Rexy' (*see p.235*) crossed with the Hybrid Tea 'Pot O' Gold'.

Garden notes   This is a healthy rose, growing to as much as 4 ft (1.2 m) in height, with good repeat flowering. Hardy to -10°F (-23°C), Zone 6, or possibly lower.

'Blue Bajou'

FLORIBUNDAS

'Blastoff' (also called MORflash) A Floribunda raised by Ralph Moore in the United States in 1995. Bright orange flowers with a white reverse and a light spice scent. It is a cross of the Floribunda 'Orangeade' and the Miniature 'Little Artist'.
    Garden notes Very good repeat flowering on a healthy plant to 3 ft (1 m). Hardy to -10°F (-23°C), Zone 6, perhaps lower.

'Eyepaint' (also called 'Eye Paint', 'Tapis Persan', MACeye) A Hand Painted Floribunda, introduced by McGredy in New Zealand in 1975 and winner of two gold medals. The lightly scented, single flowers are bright red with a white eye and white reverse, and golden stamens. The parentage is an unnamed seedling crossed with 'Picasso'.
    Garden notes A very healthy rose to 3 ft (1 m) that repeats well through the season. Hardy to -20°F (-29°C), Zone 5.

'Intrigue' (also called JACum) This Floribunda, raised by William A. Warriner and introduced by Jackson and Perkins in the United States in 1982, won the the AARS for 1984. The large, double, reddish-purple flowers have excellent scent. It is a cross of the Hybrid Teas 'White Masterpiece' and 'Heirloom'.
    Garden notes Makes healthy growth to about 2 ft (60 cm). Hardy to -20°F (-29°C), Zone 5.

'Laughter Lines' (also called DICkerry) A medal-winning Hand Painted Floribunda introduced in 1986 by Dickson in Northern Ireland. It has lightly scented, semidouble flowers, pale pink marked and veined with red, with a light reverse. The parentage is a seedling from a cross of 'Pyecolour' and 'Sunday Times', crossed with 'Eyepaint', all Floribundas.
    Garden notes Healthy growth to 3 ft (1 m) or less. Hardy to -20°F (-29°C), Zone 5.

'Old Master' (also called MACesp) A Hand Painted Floribunda introduced by McGredy in New Zealand in 1974. The semidouble, lightly scented flowers have silvery-white petals with carmine patches on the inside. The parentage is a seedling of the Floribundas 'Maxi' and 'Evelyn Fison', crossed with a seedling of the Floribunda 'Orange Sweetheart' and 'Frühlingsmorgen' (*see p.190*).
    Garden notes Healthy growth to around 2 ft (60 cm), with good repeat flowering. Hardy to -20°F (-29°C), Zone 5.

'Pasadena Tournament' (also called 'Red Cécile Brünner') A Floribunda introduced by Krebs in the United States in 1942. Long, pointed buds open to medium-sized, velvety red flowers with a moderate scent. The parentage is 'Cécile Brünner' (*see p.223*) crossed with an unnamed seedling; there is also a climbing sport (*see p.143*).
    Garden notes Grows to as much as 4 ft (1.2 m) in height. The young foliage is bronze and repeat flowering is good. Hardy to 0°F (-18°C), Zone 7.

'Picasso' (also called MACpic) The first of McGredy's Hand Painted Floribundas, introduced in Northern Ireland in 1971. The semidouble flowers have basically white to pale pink petals, marked on the inside with deep pink areas that look hand painted; the edges, the reverse, and the central eye show the base color. Their scent is light. The parentage involves 'Frühlingsmorgen' (*see p.190*) and the Floribundas 'Marlena', 'Evelyn Fison', and 'Orange Sweetheart'.
    Garden notes Reaches a maximum of 3 ft (1 m), and flowers continuously through the season. Hardy to -20°F (-29°C), Zone 5.

'Eyepaint'

'Blastoff'

'Picasso'

'Sarabande'

'Intrigue'

'Old Master' at the San Jose Heritage Rose Garden, California

'Regensberg' (also called 'Buffalo Bill', 'Young Mistress', MACyou, MACyoumis)   A gold-medal winning Hand Painted Floribunda introduced by McGredy in New Zealand in 1979. The flowers have white petals with deep cerise-pink markings, and yellow stamens; they are moderately scented. Its parentage is the Floribunda 'Geoff Boycott' crossed with 'Old Master'.
   Garden notes   A low-growing rose, to 2 ft (60 cm), that repeat flowers well. Hardy to -20°F (-29°C), Zone 5.

'Sarabande' (also called MEIhand, MEIrabande)   This Floribunda, introduced by Meilland in 1957, has won several awards including the AARS for 1960. The large trusses of semidouble flowers are bright orange with yellow stamens, and lightly scented. The parentage is 'Cocorico' crossed with 'Moulin Rouge', both Floribundas.
   Garden notes   A very healthy rose, to 3 ft (1 m), with good repeat flowering. Hardy to -20°F (-29°C), Zone 5.

'Laughter Lines'

'Regensberg'

'Pasadena Tournament'

'Christopher Columbus'

'Orange Splash'

'Scentimental'

'Peppermint Twist'

'Purple Tiger'

'Betty Boop' (also called 'Centenary of Federation', WEKplapic) A Floribunda raised by Carruth and introduced by Weeks Roses in the United States in 1999. The semidouble flowers are white to pale yellow with a strong cerise-pink picotee marking. It is a cross of the Floribundas 'Playboy' and 'Picasso' (*see p. 244*).

Garden notes A wonderful rose, to 2 ft (60 cm) or a little more, with a fruity scent. Repeat flowers consistently, and drops the old petals. Hardy to -20°F (-29°C), Zone 5.

'Camille Pissarro' (also called 'Rainbow Nation', DELstricol) A Floribunda of unrecorded parentage introduced by Delbard in France in 1996, one of the excellent Impressionist series. The flowers have red and pink stripes over yellow aging to white.

Garden notes A healthy rose, to 4 ft (1.2 m), lightly scented, with good repeat flowering. Hardy to -20°F (-29°C), Zone 5.

'Christopher Columbus' (also called 'Candy Cover', 'Dipper', 'Flamboyance', POUlbico, POUlstripe) A Floribunda introduced by Poulsen in Denmark in 1992. It bears delicately scented flowers of white layered with pink and striped with red. It is a cross of the Floribunda 'Coppélia '76' and a seedling of the Hybrid Tea 'Ambassador' and 'Romantica '76'. There is also an unstriped, orange Hybrid Tea of the same name.

Garden notes A healthy rose to 3 ft (1 m) that repeats well. Hardy to -30°F (-34°C), Zone 4.

'Hannah Gordon' (also called 'Nicole', 'Raspberry Ice', KORweiso) A Floribunda introduced by Kordes in Germany in 1983. It has double white flowers with a strong magenta-pink picotee and a light scent. It is a cross of an unnamed seedling and the Floribunda 'Bordure'.

Garden notes A healthy rose to 2 ft (60 cm) that repeats through the season. Hardy to -30°F (-34°C), Zone 4.

'Hannah Gordon'

'Scentimental' in the San Jose Heritage Rose Garden, California

'Orange Splash' (also called JACseraw)   A Floribunda raised from unnamed seedlings by Jack E. Christensen, introduced by Bear Creek Gardens in the United States in 1991. The flowers are white splashed with pink, orange, and red; the scent is mild.

Garden notes   A healthy rose, reaching around 2 ft (60 cm), with good repeat flowering. Hardy to -20°F (-29°C), Zone 5.

'Peppermint Twist' (also called 'Red & White Delight', JACraw) A Floribunda raised by Jack E. Christensen, introduced by Bear Creek Gardens in the United States in 1992. The cupped flowers are white striped and splashed with red and pink, and lightly scented. It is a cross of 'Pinstripe' (*see p. 265*) and the Hybrid Tea 'Maestro'; at the time of breeding, the intended name for the latter was 'King Juan', and this name is still sometimes given in notes on the parentage of 'Peppermint Twist'.

Garden notes   A healthy rose to 3 ft (1 m) or a little more that repeats well. Hardy to -20°F (-29°C), Zone 5.

'Purple Tiger' (also called 'Impressionist', JACpurr)   A much sought-after Floribunda raised by Jack E. Christensen and introduced by Bear Creek Gardens in the United States in 1991. The flowers are white almost entirely covered by pinkish-purple tones and deep wine-purple flecks and stripes; they have a moderate Damask scent. It is a cross of 'Intrigue' (*see p. 244*) and 'Pinstripe' (*see p. 265*).

Garden notes   A healthy rose, reaching 3 ft (1 m) or a little less, with good repeat flowering throughout the season. Hardy to -20°F (-29°C), Zone 5.

'Scentimental' (also called WEKplapep)   A Floribunda raised by Carruth and introduced by Weeks Roses in the United States in 1999, winner of the AARS for 1997. The double, cupped flowers are swirled with red and white or cream, with an intense fragrance. The parentage is the Floribunda 'Playboy' crossed with 'Peppermint Twist'.

Garden notes   A healthy rose that reaches 3 ft (1 m), with good repeat flowering. Hardy to -20°F (-29°C), Zone 5.

'Camille Pissarro'

'Betty Boop'

English Roses

'Abraham Darby'

DAVID AUSTIN'S ENGLISH ROSES combine the shapes, scents, and subtle colors of the old roses with the repeat flowering and disease resistance of the modern roses. Unlike the previous groups featured, English Roses are a brand, bred only by David Austin, originally a Shropshire farmer, whose love of old roses made him want to breed his own varieties. Encouraged by Graham Thomas, who was then making a collection of old French roses at Sunningdale Nurseries in Surrey, his first successful crosses, between the Gallica 'Belle Isis' (*see p.40*) and the Floribunda 'Dainty Maid' (*see p.236*), produced the wonderful climber 'Constance Spry' (*see p.136*). It is typical of the uncertainty of rose breeding that this early seedling of two low shrubs was a climber, but the offspring did combine the shape of the old rose with the thicker petals of the modern one. This was the beginning of his pink breeding line. At the same time, he crossed the deep purple-red Gallica 'Tuscany Superb' (*see 'Tuscany', p.35*) with another Floribunda, 'Dusky Maiden' (*see p.240*), and the resulting cross, the once-flowering 'Chianti' was crossed with the old

Hybrid Tea 'Château de Clos Vougeot', producing a series of dark reds with elegant, nodding flowers, but rather weak growth, needing the input of more robust genes. Other modern varieties were used to introduce yellow and white into the color range, and more recently the blackspot resistance of *Rosa rugosa* (*see p.23*) has been brought into the gene pool, resulting in very healthy new varieties such as 'The Mayflower' (*see p.253*).

Many big rose breeders who concentrated on Hybrid Teas and Floribundas decried Austin's early efforts, but his roses have been very popular with rose lovers, in Europe as well as in North America, where they grow better than they do in their native England. Their success has been such that other growers are now copying the English Rose style, producing new roses that hark back to the romantic roses grown in the early 19th century.

English Roses need little pruning other than tidying up after the first flush of flowers, removal of old wood in winter, and shortening of particularly long shoots. As with all roses they do best when very well fed with a generous mulch of manure.

'Graham Thomas' in Eccleston Square Garden, London

'Wife of Bath' growing with peonies

'Abraham Darby' (also called 'Abraham', 'Country Darby', AUScot) A strong-growing English Rose raised by David Austin in 1985. The large, shallow-cupped, fully double flowers are shades of pink and apricot, yellow outside and fading at the edges as the flowers age, with a sharp, fruity scent. It is a cross of the Floribunda 'Yellow Cushion' and 'Aloha' (*see p.212*).

Garden notes With its large, heavy flowers this makes an excellent standard rose, but it can also be grown as a large shrub, reaching 5 ft (1.5 m) or more; good repeat flowering and disease resistance. Hardy to -30°F (-34°C), Zone 4.

'Gertrude Jekyll' (also called AUSbord) An English Rose raised by David Austin in 1986, commemorating the great garden designer, who worked with the architect Sir Edwin Lutyens on English country houses in the Arts and Crafts style. The leaves are lush and the flowers are large, loosely double, opening flat, and bright pink with deeper shadows; the scent is typical old rose, in fact, this rose was selected for its scent to produce rose essence in England. It is a cross of 'Wife of Bath' and 'Comte de Chambord' (*see p.78*).

Garden notes This is an excellent strong-growing, upright rose to use as an accent in a border, and has stems to around 5 ft (1.5 m). The flowers appear at head height, ideal for smelling, and are produced continuously during the season. Hardy to -30°F (-34°C), Zone 4.

'Graham Thomas' (also called 'English Yellow', 'Graham Stuart Thomas', AUSmas) An English Rose raised by David Austin in 1983. The medium-sized, cup-shaped, fully double flowers are yellow, slightly deeper in the center, with a scent of Tea rose with hints of violets. It is a cross of the English Rose 'Charles Austin' and an unnamed seedling. Graham Thomas, who died in 2003, was one of the most influential plantsmen of the 20th century, and an important influence in the renewal of interest in old roses in the latter half of the century.

Garden notes This makes an excellent low climber or an elegant tall shrub, with arching stems to 6 ft (2 m), or up to 10 ft (3 m) and more on a wall. It has oval, pale green, shining and well-spaced leaflets, and flowers all along the branches when they are bent over. It may get blackspot after its first flowering, but it soon recovers to flower well a second time late in the season. Hardy to -20°F (-29°C), Zone 5.

'Wife of Bath' (also called AUSbath) One of David Austin's earliest English Roses, raised in 1969, this is still widely grown. The stems have small, scattered thorns; the leaflets are mid-green and rounded. The medium-sized flowers, held in small sprays, are pale rose-pink, fully double, opening cup-shaped with pale edges, and with a strong myrrh scent. The parentage is 'Mme Caroline Testout' (*see p.137*) crossed with a seedling of 'Ma Perkins' (*see p.234*) and 'Constance Spry' (*see p.136*).

Garden notes A tough, bushy, spreading shrub growing to around 4 ft (1.2 m) high. The flowers are delicate, unlike the eponymous character in Chaucer's *Canterbury Tales*. Hardy to -20°F (-29°C), Zone 5.

'Gertrude Jekyll'

'Mistress Quickly'

'Windrush'

'Cottage Rose'

'Scepter'd Isle' at Wilton Cottage

'Alnwick Castle' (also called AUSgrab)   An English Rose raised by David Austin in 2001. Deep pink buds open to rich pink flowers with paler edges, cupped with a dense, muddled center and good scent, said to have a hint of raspberry. Alnwick Castle (pronounced Annick) in northern England is the seat of the Dukes of Northumberland. The present Duchess is making a magnificent garden at Alnwick, including a large rose garden with many English Roses, for which this rose has been named. The parentage is not available.

Garden notes   A spreading shrub with stems reaching 4 ft (1.2 m), flowering continuously through the season. Hardy to -20°F (-29°C), Zone 5.

'Cottage Rose' (also called AUSglisten)   An English Rose raised by David Austin in 1991. The pink flowers are fully double, medium-sized, cupped when they first open and rather frilly later. The scent is very good, especially in warm weather, with hints of almond and lilac. The parentage is not available.

Garden notes   A low shrub with much-branched stems to 3½ ft (1.1 m). The side branches appear immediately after the first flowers have faded, to give it a particularly free-flowering habit through the season. Hardy to -30°F (-34°C), Zone 4.

'Emily' (also called AUSburton)   An English Rose raised by David Austin in 1992. It has pale pinkish-blush, fully double flowers with excellent scent. It is a cross of the English Roses 'The Prioress' and 'Mary Rose' (*see p.252*).

Garden notes   A low-growing shrub to 3 ft (1 m). This is one of the less robust roses, and requires extra feeding to do well. Hardy to -30°F (-34°C), Zone 4.

'Emily'

'Winchester Cathedral'

'Alnwick Castle'

'The Generous Gardener'

'Mistress Quickly' (also called AUSky)   An English Rose raised by David Austin in 1995. The small flowers are soft lilac-pink with little scent, of old rose shape, and borne in sprays like a Noisette. It is a cross of 'Blush Noisette' (*see p.103*) and 'Martin Frobisher' (*see p.184*), a quite different line of breeding from most of David Austin's earlier roses. Mistress Quickly is a Shakespearian character, hostess of a tavern in Eastcheap in the City of London.

Garden notes   A particularly tough and healthy rose, suitable for a mixed border, with stems to 5 ft (1.5 m). Hardy to -30°F (-34°C), Zone 4.

'Redouté' (also called 'Margaret Roberts', AUSpale)   This English Rose, introduced by David Austin in 1992, is a pale-flowered sport of 'Mary Rose' (*see p.252*). The flowers are solitary or in small clusters, palest pink, loosely double, with a delicate, sweet, old-rose scent. Pierre Joseph Redouté is the most famous painter of flowers, and his work *Les Roses* is a wonderful record of the roses that were grown in France in the early 19th century.

Garden notes   A low, bushy shrub, flowering regularly throughout the summer, with thorny stems around 4 ft (1.2 m) high and matt green leaflets. Hardy to -30°F (-34°C), Zone 4.

'Scepter'd Isle' (also called AUSland)   An English Rose raised by David Austin in 1992. The flowers, in small clusters, are pink, medium-sized, semidouble, and deeply cupped, with about eight rows of overlapping petals around a good head of stamens, with strong myrrh scent. The name is taken from John of Gaunt's speech describing England, "This royal throne of kings, this scepter'd isle … This precious stone set in the silver sea" from Shakespeare's *Richard II*. The parentage is not available.

Garden notes   A low shrub with upright stems around 3 ft (1 m) high, the flowers produced continuously throughout the summer and held well above the leaves. Hardy to -30°F (-34°C), Zone 4.

'The Generous Gardener' (also called AUSdrawn)   An English Rose raised by David Austin in 2002, commemorating and supporting the National Gardens Scheme in England. The flowers are soft pink in the center shading to pale pink at the edge, semidouble, with numerous stamens. Excellently scented of old rose, musk, and myrrh. The parentage is not available.

Garden notes   A very healthy rose, this makes a large shrub or a climber to 8 ft (2.5 m). Hardy to -30°F (-34°C), Zone 4.

'Winchester Cathedral' (also called AUScat)   This English Rose, introduced by David Austin in 1998, is a sport of 'Mary Rose' (*see p.252*), named on behalf of the Winchester Cathedral Trust to support restoration of the cathedral. The parentage is 'Wife of Bath' (*see p.249*) crossed with another English Rose, 'The Miller'. Crimson buds in small sprays open to white, medium-sized, fully but loosely double flowers, rather flat with the outer petals curled back, and with a delicate scent.

Garden notes   A strong, bushy shrub with almost thornless stems to around 4 ft (1.2 m) high. A very good rose, repeating well and free from disease. Hardy to -20°F (-29°C), Zone 5.

'Windrush' (also called AUSrush)   An English Rose raised by David Austin in 1984. The flowers are large, almost single to semidouble, and pale lemon yellow with yellow stamens, fading as they age. Their scent is slight and spicy. Its parentage is a seedling crossed with a hybrid of the English Rose 'Canterbury' and the Shrub 'Golden Wings'.

Garden notes   A vigorous, bushy shrub around 7 ft (2.2 m) high and more across with pale green, rather narrow leaflets. It is similar to 'Golden Wings', but more free-flowering and repeating well if the first crop of hips is removed. Hardy to -30°F (-34°C), Zone 4.

'Redouté'

'Hyde Hall'

'The Ingenious Mr. Fairchild'

'Spirit of Freedom'

'Charles Rennie Mackintosh' (also called AUSren)   An English Rose raised by David Austin in 1988, commemorating the Scottish architect, designer, and painter. The flowers are fully double, medium-sized, globular, and incurved, the outermost petals sometimes reflexed in hot weather. They are lilac to lilac-pink according to temperature, with a strong old-rose scent. The parentage is a seedling of the English Rose 'Chaucer' and 'Conrad Ferdinand Meyer' (*see p.184*), crossed with 'Mary Rose'.

    Garden notes A tough, bushy, low shrub with *R. rugosa* genes through 'Conrad Ferdinand Meyer'. Stems to 3 ft (1 m), or 5 ft (1.5 m) in warm areas, the twigs with many thorns and round, light green leaflets. Repeat flowers particularly well, even in late-summer heat. Hardy to -30°F (-34°C), Zone 4.

'Hyde Hall' (also called AUSbosky)   An English Rose raised by David Austin in 2004. The cupped, loosely double, pink flowers have a light, warm, fruity scent, almost like cooked jam. The parentage is not available.

    Garden notes This is a tall and very bushy rose, reaching 5–6 ft (1.5–2 m) in height, and 4–5 ft (1.2–1.5 m) across. Hardy to -20°F (-29°C), Zone 5, and possibly lower.

'John Clare' (also called AUScent)   An English Rose raised by David Austin in 1994. The medium-sized, loosely double and cupped flowers, in clusters, are deep pink; the scent is light. John Clare was a 19th century poet of rural England. In the early poem 'The Rose' he desires to be transformed into a rose:

> My wish for the change is to win Chloe's bosom
> Those two swelling mountains of snow
> Where so nice in the Valley – each side to repose on!
> I could see them both heave to and fro.

David Austin regards this as the "most prolific" English Rose. It is a cross of 'Wife of Bath' (*see p.249*) and an unnamed seedling.

    Garden notes A spreading shrub with stems to around 3 ft (1 m), and broad, bright green leaflets. Flowers particularly freely to the end of the season. Hardy to -30°F (-34°C), Zone 4.

'Mary Rose' (also called 'Country Marilou', 'Marie Rose' AUSmary)   One of the most popular English Roses, introduced by David Austin in 1983, the year after Henry VIII's flagship Mary Rose, which sank in 1536, was raised from the sea bed. The loosely double flowers are solitary or in small clusters, rose-pink with deeper shadows, with a delicate scent. It is a cross of two English Roses, 'Wife of Bath' (*see p.249*) and 'The Miller'.

    Garden notes A bushy shrub with thorny stems around 4 ft (1.2 m) high and matt green leaflets, flowering regularly throughout the summer. Hardy to -30°F (-34°C), Zone 4.

'Mortimer Sackler' (also called AUSorts)   An English Rose raised by David Austin in 2002. The flowers are medium-sized, of delicate and unusual shape, shallow-cupped when first open, the rather narrow and pointed outer petals becoming spreading and reflexed, looking like a waterlily, with a central tuft of stamens. The color is pale shell pink with a deeper center, the scent sweet with a hint of fruit. The parentage is not available. The right to name this rose was auctioned for the National Trust in England, and won by Theresa Sackler, wife of the international philanthropist.

    Garden notes A tall, graceful shrub or climber to 8 ft (2.5 m), with few thorns and narrow, widely spaced foliage. The leaflets are healthy and dull green, reddish when young. Hardy to -20°F (-29°C), Zone 5.

'Wisley 2004'

'John Clare'

'The Ingenious Mr. Fairchild' (also called AUStijus)
An English Rose raised by David Austin in 2003. The large flowers have an unusual shape like a double peony, deeply cupped with a mass of untidy, upright petals, bluish-pink with deeper pink, crinkled edges. The scent is complex, with elements of peach, raspberry, and mint. Thomas Fairchild, a London nurseryman and fellow of the Royal Society, was one of the earliest plant breeders, producing in 1720 a cross between a Sweet William and a carnation, known as 'Fairchild's Mule'. The parentage is not available.

Garden notes Spreading and arching branches eventually form a rounded shrub, with very healthy foliage. Hardy to -20°F (-29°C), Zone 5.

'The Mayflower' (also called AUStilly) An English Rose raised by David Austin in 2001. The flowers, in small clusters, are fully double and often quartered, opening flat, and deep purplish-pink, with strong, old-rose scent, especially in cool weather. The name of the boat that carried the Pilgrim Fathers to America was chosen to commemorate the opening of the David Austin rose garden at Matterhorn Nurseries, north of New York city. The parentage is not available.

Garden notes An upright, twiggy shrub to around 4 ft (1.2 m) high, or perhaps more; the narrow, widely spaced, olive-green leaflets appear to be particularly resistant to rust, blackspot, and mildew. Hardy to -20°F (-29°C), Zone 5.

'Spirit of Freedom' (also called AUSbite) An English Rose raised by David Austin in 2002. The flowers are of perfect old-rose character, pale pink, becoming bluer as they age, with a paler edge, cupped and fully double with masses of petals. The scent is good. The parentage is not available.

Garden notes This can be grown as a robust shrub or as a low climber reaching around 8 ft (2.5 m), but flowering from top to near ground level. The foliage is disease resistant. Hardy to -20°F (-29°C), Zone 5.

'Wisley' (also called AUSintense) An English Rose raised by David Austin in 2004. The flowers are deep pink and the scent is very strong and fruity, with elements of citrus and old rose. The parentage is not available.

Garden notes Makes a bush 5 ft (1.5 m) tall and 3 ft (1 m) wide, and probably a climber to 8 ft (2.5 m) in warmer areas. Hardy to -20°F (-29°C), Zone 5.

'The Mayflower'

'Charles Rennie Mackintosh' in the garden of David Austin's Nursery at Albrighton in the English midlands

'Mary Rose'

'Mortimer Sackler'

'Blythe Spirit'

'Crown Princess Margareta'

'Grace'

'Jude the Obscure'

'Molineaux'

'Pat Austin'

'Blythe Spirit' (also called AUSchool)   An English Rose raised by David Austin in 1999. The flowers are quite small, in loose sprays, and slightly nodding. They are double, bright yellow on opening, becoming flat and paler on the edges, delicately scented of musk and myrrh. The parentage is not available.

Garden notes   Rather like a Hybrid Musk, forming a well-shaped bush around 4 ft (1.2 m) high and wide, with quite narrow, widely spaced leaflets. Hardy to -20°F (-29°C), Zone 5. There is also a Hybrid Tea called 'Blithe Spirit'.

'Crown Princess Margareta' (also called AUSwinter)   An English Rose raised by David Austin in 1999. The large, cupped flowers are apricot-orange with a paler edge, and a scent of Tea Rose. The parentage is not available. Crown Princess Margareta was an accomplished landscape gardener who laid out the garden at Sofiero, the Swedish summer palace in Helsingborg.

Garden notes   A tall shrub with arching stems to around 5 ft (1.5 m) and large, dark green, shining leaflets. Very hardy, to -33°F (-36°C), in Zone 3.

'Golden Celebration' (Also called AUSgold)   An English Rose raised by David Austin in 1992. The rich yellow flowers are of typical Austin shape, large, fully double, at first cupped opening full and rather flat, solitary and facing to the side. The scent is initially of Tea Rose, later of sweet wine and strawberries. It is a cross of 'Charles Austin' and 'Abraham Darby' (*see p.294*).

Garden notes   A robust, medium-sized shrub. Hardy to -30°F (-34°C), Zone 4.

'Grace' (also called AUSkeppy)   An English Rose raised by David Austin in 2001. The flowers are apricot, deeper in the center, pale pinkish at the edges, fully double with pointed petals, opening flat with the outer petals reflexed. They have a good rich scent. It is a cross of the English Rose 'Sweet Juliet' and an unnamed seedling.

Garden notes   A much-branched shrub with stems to 4 ft (1.2 m), and as wide, with narrow, grayish-green leaflets. Hardy to -30°F (-34°C), Zone 4.

'Jubilee Celebration'

'Jubilee Celebration' (also called AUShunter)   An English Rose raised by David Austin in 2002, commemorating the Queen's Golden Jubilee. The flowers are large, opening rather flat with an indented center, salmon pink with gold on the reverse of the petals. The scent is rich and fruity with overtones of lemon and raspberry. The parentage is not available.

Garden notes   A strong-growing shrub with stems to 4 ft (1.2 m), and as wide, and very healthy foliage. Hardy to -30°F (-34°C), Zone 4.

'Jude the Obscure' (also called AUSjo)   An English Rose raised by David Austin in 1995. The exceptionally beautiful flowers are very large, loosely double, incurved and cupped, and medium yellow inside, paler outside. The scent is strong, of exotic fruit and wine. It is a cross of 'Abraham Darby' (*see p.249*) and 'Windrush' (*see p.251*). *Jude the Obscure* is the last novel by Thomas Hardy: it is said that the horrors of his own creation in this novel turned Hardy away from novels, to poetry.

Garden notes   A spreading, bushy shrub with stems around 3½ ft (1.1 m) high. The flowers sometimes fail to open in wet summers in England, though they are good in warmer climates. Hardy to -20°F (-29°C), Zone 5.

'Molineux' (also called AUSmol)   An English Rose raised by David Austin in 1994. The rich yellow flowers, in small sprays, are upright, medium sized, fully double, and opening flat. The scent is Tea rose with hints of Musk; this rose won the Henry Edland Medal for scent and was first of David Austin's roses to win the RNRS President's International Trophy for the best new seedling of the year. The parentage is 'Graham Thomas' (*see p.249*) crossed with 'Golden Showers' (*see p.132*).

Garden notes   A bushy, vigorous shrub, one of the shorter-growing of Austin's yellows, with stems around 3 ft (1 m) high. A tough and healthy rose, particularly free-flowering. Hardy to -20°F (-29°C), Zone 5.

'Pat Austin' (also called AUSmum)   An English Rose raised by David Austin in 1995 and named after his wife. The large, fully double flowers open cupped. They are an unusual color, deep coppery orange on the inside of the petals, paler on the back, and Tea-scented. It is a cross of 'Graham Thomas' and 'Abraham Darby' (*see p.249 for both*)

Garden notes   A strong, upright shrub with stems around 4 ft (1.2 m) high. Hardy to -20°F (-29°C), Zone 5.

'Yellow Charles Austin' (also called AUSling) An English Rose raised by David Austin in 1981. The flowers, in small sprays, are large, fully double, opening flat, and pale yellow, with a strongly fruity scent. It is a sport of the English Rose 'Charles Austin', which is a cross of the English Rose 'Chaucer' and 'Aloha' (*see p.212*).

Garden notes   A tall shrub with shining, mid-green leaflets, not overlapping, smooth twigs, and stems to 5 ft (1.5 m), or 10 ft (3 m) in a warm climate. The plant is a strong grower, and the long shoots should be pegged down or trained horizontally so that they flower along their length; they can be reduced in length by half to encourage repeat flowering. Hardy to -30°F (-34°C), Zone 4.

'Yellow Charles Austin'

'Golden Celebration'

'Benjamin Britten'

'Falstaff'

'Noble Antony'

'Benjamin Britten' (also called AUSencart)   An English Rose raised by David Austin in 2001, commemorating the English composer. The flowers are medium-sized, cup-shaped, and fully double, opening to a rosette, with toothed petals, bright red with hints of orange. The scent is good, of wine and fruit. It is a cross of the English Rose 'Charles Austin' and an unnamed seedling.

   Garden notes   A dense shrub to 4 ft (1.2 m), with medium green, well-spaced leaflets. Hardy to -10°F (-23°C), Zone 6.

'Falstaff' (also called AUSverse)   An English Rose raised by David Austin in 1999. The large, fully double, cupped flowers, in loose sprays, are dark crimson-red. They have a strong, old-rose scent. The parentage is not available. Falstaff is one of Shakespeare's most robust and finally most pathetic characters, proverbial for his love of "sack", a dry, sherry-like wine.

   Garden notes   A strong, bushy, wide-spreading shrub to 5 ft (1.5 m), or 10 ft (3 m) in the climbing form, with few, large, well-spaced, dark green leaflets and very sparse thorns. Hardy to -20°F (-29°C), Zone 5.

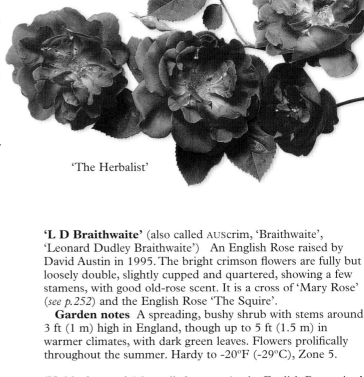

'The Herbalist'

'Sir Edward Elgar'

'L D Braithwaite' (also called AUScrim, 'Braithwaite', 'Leonard Dudley Braithwaite')   An English Rose raised by David Austin in 1995. The bright crimson flowers are fully but loosely double, slightly cupped and quartered, showing a few stamens, with good old-rose scent. It is a cross of 'Mary Rose' (*see p.252*) and the English Rose 'The Squire'.

   Garden notes   A spreading, bushy shrub with stems around 3 ft (1 m) high in England, though up to 5 ft (1.5 m) in warmer climates, with dark green leaves. Flowers prolifically throughout the summer. Hardy to -20°F (-29°C), Zone 5.

'Noble Antony' (also called AUSway)   An English Rose raised by David Austin in 1995. The deep purplish-crimson flowers are large, fully double, and opening with the outer petals recurved; they have a very strong, old-rose scent. Its parentage is not available. The description 'noble Antony' is from the "Friends, Romans, countrymen" scene in *Julius Caesar*.

   Garden notes   A low, bushy shrub with stems around 3 ft (1 m) high and dark green leaves, slightly prone to blackspot. Hardy to -20°F (-29°C), Zone 5.

'**Sir Edward Elgar**' (also called AUSprima)   An English Rose raised by David Austin in 1992, named for the composer. The solitary, cerise-crimson flowers are double, opening flat, with strong scent. It is a cross of 'Mary Rose' (*see p.252*) and the English Rose 'The Squire'.

   Garden notes   An upright shrub with stems to around 4 ft (1.2 m) high, and flowering continuously throughout the summer. Hardy to -20°F (-29°C), Zone 5.

'**The Dark Lady**' (also called AUSbloom) An English Rose raised by David Austin in 1991. The name is that given to the mysterious beauty to whom many of Shakespeare's later sonnets are written, because of the many references to darkness, such as this in Sonnet 132:
   "Then will I swear beauty herself is black,
   And all they foul who thy complexion lack"
The flowers are dark crimson, loosely double and opening wide. They have a delicate scent. The parentage is 'Mary Rose' (*see p.252*) crossed with the English Rose 'Prospero'.

   Garden notes   A spreading shrub around 3 ft (1 m) high and slightly more across. Hardy to -20°F (-29°C), Zone 5.

'**The Herbalist**' (also called AUSsemi)   An English Rose raised by David Austin in 1991, named because of its similarity to the Apothecary's rose, *R. gallica* 'Officinalis' (*see p.33*). The flowers, in clusters, are semidouble and deep pink or light crimson. The parentage is an unnamed seedling crossed with 'Louise Odier' (*see p.114*).

   Garden notes   An upright and bushy shrub to around 3 ft (1 m), repeat flowering well. Hardy to -20°F (-29°C), Zone 5.

'**Tradescant**' (also called AUSdir)   An English Rose raised by David Austin in 1994. The medium-sized, slightly nodding flowers are fully double, quartered, and open flat, with a few stamens showing in the fully open flower. They are of deepest velvety maroon with excellent old-rose scent. It is a cross of the English Rose 'Prospero' and a seedling of the English Rose 'Charles Austin' and the Hybrid Perpetual 'Gloire de Ducher'. The John Tradescants, father and son, were important 17th-century gardeners, and introduced many plants to Europe.

   Garden notes   An arching shrub with sparsely thorny stems to around 3 ft (1 m) high in England, 5 ft (1.5 m) in warmer

'Tradescant'

climates, and smallish, broad, dark green leaflets. It needs good cultivation and rich feeding to give its best. In warm areas the long shoots can be trained horizontally to flower along their length. Hardy to -30°F (-34°C), Zone 4.

'**William Shakespeare 2000**' (also called AUSromeo) An English Rose raised by David Austin in 2000. The flowers are in sprays, large, fully double, opening flat and quartered, and dark velvety crimson, becoming purplish. The scent is strong, of the old-rose type. The parentage is not available.

   Garden notes   An upright shrub with stems to 3 ft (1 m), or more in a warm climate, and bluish-green leaflets. It is a good grower and healthy, the newest and best of David Austin's dark reds. It supercedes Austin's earlier 'William Shakespeare' from 1987, which has excellent deep crimson flowers, but suffers from blackspot. Hardy to -30°F (-34°C), Zone 4.

'L D Braithwaite'

'The Dark Lady'

'William Shakespeare 2000'

Romantica Roses

'Pierre de Ronsard'

ROMANTICAS PROMISE HEALTHY, modern rose plants with wonderfully scented, very double old-fashioned flowers. They are a brand raised by Meilland, and may be found listed as Hybrid Teas, Climbers, and Floribundas. The Meilland family in southern France have been at the forefront of rose breeding for over a century. At the end of the Second World War, Francis Meilland launched perhaps the most famous rose ever bred, 'Peace' (see p.206). The firm has since been successful with Landscape and Groundcover roses, but more recently they have been developing the Romantica roses. This group really started with 'Pierre de Ronsard', raised by Marie-Louis Meilland. It has been followed by many excellent roses, perhaps the most outstanding being Alain Meilland's 'Leonardo de Vinci'. Romanticas are best grown as shrubs and pruned back by about one third each year. Sustain their growth with plenty of feeding.

'Auguste Renoir'

'Guy de Maupassant'

'Leonardo da Vinci'

'Yves Piaget'

'Michelangelo'

'André Le Nôtre'

'André Le Nôtre' (also called 'Miriam Makeba', MEIceppus) A Romantica Hybrid Tea introduced by Meilland in 2001. The pale pink flowers have a wonderful traditional old-rose form with more than 60 petals. It has received two gold medals and also many fragrance awards for its excellent scent. The parentage is not available.

Garden notes A very healthy modern shrub, growing to about 5 ft (1.5 m). Hardy to -10°F (-23°C), Zone 6.

'Auguste Renoir' (also called MEItoifar) A Romantica Hybrid Tea introduced by Meilland in 1995. Its deep pink, almost red flowers are very large and blowsy like a Renoir lady, often quartered with about 60 petals, and very fragrant. The parentage is a seedling of the Hybrid Tea 'Versailles' and 'Pierre de Ronsard' crossed with the Floribunda 'Kimono'.

Garden notes Grows to 4 ft (1.2 m) or a little more, with healthy, dark foliage, and repeat flowers well. Hardy to -15°F (-26°C), in Zone 5.

'Guy de Maupassant' (also called 'Romantic Fragrance', MEIsocrat) A Romantica Floribunda introduced by Meilland in 1996. The cupped, very double flowers are flesh-pink with a slightly paler reverse, and delicious delicate perfume. The parentage is a seedling of the Shrub MEIturaphar and 'Mrs John Laing' (*see p.125*), crossed with the Floribunda 'Egeskov'.

Garden notes Grows to as much as 5 ft (1.5 m) in height. Hardy to -10°F (-23°C), Zone 6.

'Leonardo da Vinci' (also called MEIdeauri) A Romantica Floribunda introduced by Meilland in 1994. The rich pink flowers have a delicate, sweet perfume. The parentage is 'Surrey' (*see p.167*) crossed with a seedling from the Floribundas 'Milrose' and 'Rosamunde'.

Garden notes An excellent free-standing shrub, healthy and continuous-flowering, growing to as much as 4 ft (1.2 m). Hardy to -10°F (-23°C), Zone 6, or lower.

'Michelangelo' (also called MEItelov) A Romantica Hybrid Tea, raised by Meilland and introduced in 1996. The yellow flowers are large and double, with 55 petals, and have a distinct lemony fragrance. There is a red-and-white striped Floribunda with the same name. The parentage is not available.

Garden notes A good repeat-flowering, disease-resistant rose to about 4 ft (1.2 m). Hardy to -10°F (-23°C), Zone 6.

'Pierre de Ronsard' (also called 'Eden Rose 88', MEIviolin) This exceptional low Climbing rose, raised by Marie-Louise Meilland in 1985, commemorates an important medieval French poet and was the first Romantica to be introduced.

The flowers are lightly scented, very large, and very double, with an old-rose appearance. Green buds open flat, like a Centifolia, the outer petals creamy white grading to delicate pink in the center. It is a cross of the Climbing Floribunda 'Kalinka' and a seedling of the Climbing roses 'Danse des Sylphes' and 'Handel' (*see p.138*).

Garden notes This is one of the loveliest modern roses, particularly in a warm, dry climate. Usually less than 10 ft (3 m) high, with thick, tough, healthy leaves and good repeat flowering, it can be trained on a low wall or the trunk of a small tree. Hardy to -20°F (-29°C), Zone 5.

'Polka' (also called 'Lord Byron', 'Scented Dawn', MEItosier) A Romantica Climber introduced by Meilland in 1991. The flowers are ivory yellow with a deeper, more peachy colour in the center, with a strong old-rose perfume. The parentage is a seedling of MEIpalsar and 'Golden Showers' (*see p.132*) crossed with 'Lichtkönigin Lucia' (*see p.173*).

Garden notes Grows to as much as 12 ft (4 m) and shows good disease resistance. Hardy to -20°F (-29°C), Zone 5.

'Yves Piaget' (also called 'Queen Adelaide', 'The Royal Brompton Rose', MEIvildo) An award-winning Romantica Hybrid Tea introduced by Meilland in 1985. The very double, cupped flowers have around 80 petals. They are deep mauvish-pink, and intensely scented. The parentage is a seedling from crosses of 'Chrysler Imperial', 'Charles Mallerin', 'Pharaoh', and 'Peace' (*see p.206*), all Hybrid Teas, crossed with the Floribunda 'Tamango'.

Garden notes Reaches about 3 ft (1 m) and flowers through the season. Hardy to -20°F (-29°C), Zone 5, or possibly below.

'Polka'

Genererosa Roses

GENEROSA ROSES ARE RAISED by Guillot in France, and officially listed as Floribundas or Shrub roses. They are bred to combine the rich colors, strong scents, and full-flowered form that distinguished the old Guillot roses with the reliability, repeat flowering, and health found in modern roses.

For five generations, since 1829, the Guillot family has been growing and breeding roses near Lyon in France, and it was Jean-Baptiste Guillot fils who introduced the first Hybrid Tea 'La France'.

He was also the first to introduce budding as a method of rose propagation, a method soon adopted all over the world to produce strong, healthy plants in larger numbers than was possible from rooted cuttings. Today, Jean-Pierre Guillot and his cousin Dominique Massad have developed a whole new line in roses for the modern garden, and Guillot are producing many new forms of Generosa each year. They thrive best on fertile soil with plenty of well-rotted manure; cut back by about a third annually.

'La France'

'Marquise Spinola'

'Martine Guillot'

'William Christie'

'Jardin de Viels Maisons'

'Sonia Rykiel'

GENEROSA ROSES

'Claudia Cardinale' (also called MAScatna)   A Generosa
Shrub rose introduced by Guillot-Massad in 1997, named for
the Italian actress. The large, well-scented flowers open flat and
quartered like an old Damask rose. They are yellow-amber with
light yellow outer petals, and deeper centers that age to a
coppery-red. The parentage is not available.
   Garden notes   Strong, arching growth reaches 5 ft (1.5 m)
in height and 6 ft (2 m) in width, flowering freely all along the
stems. Hardy to -20°F (-29°C), Zone 5.

'Jardin de Viels Maisons' (also called MASframb)
A Generosa Shrub rose introduced by Guillot-Massad in 1998.
The flowers are deeply cupped and raspberry pink, with a
fruity fragrance. The parentage is not available.
   Garden notes   A healthy plant to 4 ft (1.2 m) in height,
with good repeat flowering. Hardy to -20°F (-29°C), Zone 5.

'La France'   The first Hybrid Tea (*see p.199 for full entry*), this
Guillot rose was a breakthough; today, with the Generosa roses,
the Guillot family is still at the forefront of rose breeding.
   Garden notes   The bush form reaches 4 ft (1.2 m). Reputed
to be hardy to -30°F (-34°C), Zone 4.

'Marquise Spinola' (also called MASmarti)   A Generosa
Shrub rose raised by Guillot-Massad and introduced in 1998.
The flowers are deeply cupped and quartered, light pink
towards the outer petals with a deeper flush in the center, and
sweetly scented. The parentage is not available.
   Garden notes   A healthy, repeat-flowering rose that reaches
to 4 ft (1.2 m) in height. Hardy to -20°F (-29°C), Zone 5.

'Martine Guillot' (also called MASmabay)   A Generosa Shrub
rose raised by Guillot-Massad in 1997. The large, very double,
blush-pink flowers have an intense scent reminiscent of gardenia,
especially in cool weather. The parentage is not available.
   Garden notes   Growth to 4 ft (1.2 m) tall and more across,
healthy and repeating well. Hardy to -20°F (-29°C), Zone 5.

'Paul Bocuse' (also called MASpaujeu)   A Generosa Shrub rose
introduced by Guillot-Massad in 1997. The very large, cupped,
orange-pink flowers have a fruity scent. The parentage is not
available. Celebrated chef Paul Bocuse is a native of Lyon.
   Garden notes   A good repeat-flowering rose to 4 ft (1.2 m),
though it may get some blackspot in warm, humid areas.
Hardy to -20°F (-29°C), Zone 5.

'Sonia Rykiel' (also called MASdogul)   A Generosa Shrub rose
introduced by Guillot-Massad in 1995. The very double flowers
open to a flat, shallow cup with quartered petals, and tend to
nod, like an old Tea rose. They are coral pink and have an
excellent, strong and fruity scent. The parentage is not available.
   Garden notes   Grows to a height of 4 ft (1.2 m) with good
repeat flowering. Hardy to -20°F (-29°C), Zone 5.

'Versigny' (also called MASversi)   A Generosa Shrub rose
raised by Guillot-Massad and introduced in 1998. The very
large flowers are salmon-pink with a deeper, more orange
center, and have a strong scent. The parentage is not available.
   Garden notes   Reaches about 4 ft (1.2 m) in height and
repeat flowers well. Hardy to -20°F (-29°C), Zone 5.

'William Christie' (also called MASsad)   A Shrub rose raised
by Guillot-Massad and introduced in 1998. The flowers are
very large and cupped, with a multitude of pink petals, and
have a strong scent. The parentage is not available. William
Christie is a renowned musician and musicologist.
   Garden notes   Grows to about 5 ft (1.5 m) in height with
good repeat flowering. Hardy to -20°F (-29°C), Zone 5.

'Versigny'

'Claudia Cardinale'

'Paul Bocuse'

Miniature Roses

'Imperial Palace'

ALTHOUGH THEY ARE an ancient group, Miniature Roses only became really important in the mid-20th century. The genius of breeder Ralph Moore in Visalia, California led to a surge in their popularity, and other breeders saw the potential of these dwarfs as flowering pot plants. The first miniature, perpetual-flowering roses were certainly bred in China, and they appear both in 18th-century Chinese paintings and in illustrated books such as Mary Lawrance's *A Collection of Roses* in 1796, and, as *Rosa chinensis* 'Minima' (a single), in Redoute's *Les Roses* in 1821. Once-flowering miniatures had long been grown in Europe, but they were dwarf cultivated mutants of Gallicas and Centifolias, which were known in the 17th century.

The first flowering pot rose to be grown on a large scale was the dwarf China 'Pompom de Paris' (*see p. 88*), popular in Paris in the mid-19th century, but the modern miniatures owe their perpetual flowering to 'Roulettii' (*see p. 89*), a really low-growing, continuous-flowering dwarf, said to have been found growing in a pot on a windowsill in Switzerland and brought to M. Correvon in Geneva. It is not known whether this was a survival of an early importat from China or a new mutation, but it soon became the start of a new race.

Ralph Moore began his program in the late 1930's with a 'Roulettii' hybrid, 'Peon', raised by Jan de Vink in Holland in 1936, and 'Oakington Ruby', which was said to have been found by an old lady in the garden of Ely Cathedral in England.

'Golden Moss' (*see p. 69*) introduced in 1932 and 'Baby Gold Star' in 1940, both raised in Spain by Pedro Dot, were other early crosses that showed the potential of these miniatures, and Dot produced several more that proved popular. These miniatures are close to Hybrid Teas or Floribundas in both habit and shape of flower, but the whole plant is no more than 12 in (30 cm) high at the most. In the varieties that are bred for sale in pots, the plants are rooted from cuttings and sold as soon as they begin to flower; the ideal pot rose has the flowers that open between half and three-quarters and remain without opening further or fading for several weeks. Ralph Moore broke away from this utilitarian product. He found that genes from other groups of roses, such as Mosses, were more easily introduced into Miniature breeding lines than into full-sized roses, so among his roses (*see pp. 264–265*) have been mossy dwarf ramblers, crested climbers, and varieties with petals that are wavy, folded, or even oak-leaf shaped.

The name Patio roses describes slightly larger miniatures of the Floribunda type, generally between 18 in (45 cm) and 3 ft (1 m) tall, at which height they merge into the lower Floribunda roses. Patio roses are particularly suited to small gardens and yards, where full-sized roses would take up too much space. The pruning of Miniature and Patio roses is similar to that of Hybrid Teas, designed to promote as much new growth as possible through the flowering season.

'Peon'

'Snow Ruby'

'Halo Rainbow'

'Halo Rainbow' (also called MORrainbow)   A Miniature introduced by Moore in California in 1994. The flowers are single and pinky-red with a creamy white center. It is a cross of an unnamed seedling and the Miniature 'Make Believe'.

    Garden notes   A spreading dwarf with shining leaves and no prickles; repeat flowers well. Hardy to -20°F (-29°C), Zone 5.

'Imperial Palace' (also called POULchris)   A Miniature Floribunda introduced by Poulsen in Denmark in 1996. The buds are ovoid and pointed, the deep red, double flowers are cupped, opening to a lovely old rose shape. The parentage is not available.

    Garden notes   A free-flowering plant with very dark green leaves. Hardy to -20°F (-29°C), Zone 5.

'Joey's Palace' (also called POULjoey)   A Mini Floribunda introduced by Poulsen in 1997. The flowers are tinted apricot. The parentage is not available.

    Garden notes   A repeat–flowering rose, hardy to -20°F (-29°C), Zone 5.

'Lady Sunblaze' (also called 'Lady Meillandina', 'Peace Meillandina', 'Peace Sunblaze', MEIlarco)   A Miniature raised by Marie-Louise Meilland in France in 1986. Pointed buds

open to a very double, pale pink flower with a darker center. The parentage is a seedling of the Floribundas 'Fashion' and 'Zambra', crossed with the Miniature 'Belle Meillandina'.

    Garden notes   Flowers almost continuously throughout the season, and grows well in pots both indoors and out. Hardy to -20°F (-29°C), Zone 5.

'Peon' (also called 'Tom Thumb')   A most important early Miniature, introduced by Jan de Vink in Holland in 1936 and widely used by later breeders including Ralph Moore. The semidouble flowers are deep crimson with a white center, and have little or no scent. It is a cross of 'Rouletii' (*see p. 89*) and 'Gloria Mundi', an early Polyantha. 'Peon' was the original name in Europe; it was later called 'Tom Thumb' in America.

    Garden notes   The growth is very dwarf, reaching 4–6 in (10–15 cm) in height, and repeat flowering is good. Hardy to -10°F (-23°C), Zone 6.

'Snow Ruby' (also called CLEsruby)   A Miniature Floribunda rose introduced by Heirloom Roses in 1996. Tall buds open to double, bright velvety orange-red flowers with a white reverse, but with little or no scent.

    Garden notes   This reaches 14–22 in (35–55 cm) and repeat flowers well. Hardy to -20°F (-29°C), Zone 5.

'Lady Sunblaze'

'Joey's Palace'

'Crazy Quilt'

'Candy Cane'

'Pinstripe'

'Café Olé'

'Baby Darling'

'Orange Honey'

Ralph Moore began breeding miniatures with 'Peon' (*see p. 263*) and 'Oakington Ruby', a miniature found in England. Over several decades he has introduced Miniature roses with unique flower shapes and petal configurations, as well as other more novel characteristics.

'Baby Darling' A Miniature introduced by Moore in 1964. Pointed buds open to semidouble, apricot-orange flowers. The scent is moderate. It is a cross of the Floribunda 'Little Darling' and the climbing Miniature 'Magic Wand'. There is also a climbing sport.
   Garden notes Growth remains low, reaching about 12 in (30 cm). Hardy to -20°F (-29°C), Zone 5.

'Café Olé' (also called MORolé) A Miniature introduced by Moore in 1990. The medium to large, very double, cupped flowers have a moderate spicy scent. It is a sport of the Miniature 'Winter Magic'.
   Garden notes The growth reaches 2 ft (60 cm) or a little more, and the repeat flowering is good. Hardy to -20°F (-29°C), Zone 5.

'Candy Cane' A climbing Miniature raised by Moore in 1958. The semidouble flowers are deep pink with white stripes, and up to 1½ in (3.5 cm) across; their scent is slight. It is a cross of an unnamed seedling and the climbing Miniature 'Zee', an important rose in Moore's breeding lines.
   Garden notes This rose reaches a height of 4 ft (1.2 m) and is repeat flowering. Hardy to -10°F (-23°C), Zone 6.

'Crazy Quilt' (also called MORpari, MORtrip) A Miniature introduced by Moore in 1980. Pointed buds open to double flowers that are striped red and white. It is a cross of the Floribunda 'Little Darling' and an unnamed seedling.
   Garden notes The growth is compact and bushy to about 2 ft (60 cm) in height. Hardy to -20°F (-29°C), Zone 5.

'Dresden Doll' A Miniature introduced by Moore in 1975, one of a series of Moss rose Miniatures. The mossy buds open to small, cupped, semidouble flowers of soft pink, with a moderate scent. It is a cross of the Miniature 'Fairy Moss' and a Moss rose seedling.
   Garden notes Makes bushy, compact growth to 18–24 in (45–60 cm). Hardy to -20°F (-29°C), Zone 5.

'Golden Angel' A Miniature introduced by Moore in 1975. The very double, deep orange-yellow flowers are 1 in (2.5 cm) across, with a moderate scent. The parentage is the Climber 'Golden Glow', crossed with a seedling of the Floribunda 'Little Darling' and an unnamed seedling.
   Garden notes A compact and bushy rose to about 2 ft (60 cm) in height. Hardy to -20°F (-29°C), Zone 5.

'Green Ice' A Miniature raised by Moore in 1971. Pointed buds open to small, double flowers, white with delicate soft green tones. The scent is light. The parentage is a cross of *R. wichurana* (*see p. 19*) and the Floribunda 'Floradora'.
   Garden notes A bushy rose to about 2 ft (60 cm). Hardy to -10°F (-23°C), Zone 6.

'Hi Ho' in the San Jose Heritage Rose Garden, California

'Rise 'n' Shine'

'Hi Ho' A Climbing Miniature introduced by Moore in 1964. The small, double, deep pink flowers are borne in clusters. Their scent is slight. It is a cross of the Floribunda 'Little Darling' and climbing Miniature 'Magic Wand'.

Garden notes Makes vigorous, climbing growth to around 4 ft (1.2 m). Hardy to -10°F (-23°C), Zone 6.

'Magic Carousel' (also called MOORcar, MORrousel) This is one of the all-time great Miniatures, introduced by Moore in 1972. It has won many awards, including the ARS Miniature Hall of Fame 1999. The small, double flowers are white edged with red. It is a cross of the Floribunda 'Little Darling' and the Miniature 'Westmont'.

Garden notes A vigorous, bushy rose to around 2 ft (60 cm). Hardy to -20°F (-29°C), Zone 5.

'Orange Honey' A Miniature introduced by Moore in 1979. The double flowers are orange-yellow and have a moderate, fruity scent. It is a cross of the Floribunda 'Rumba' and the Miniature 'Over the Rainbow'.

Garden notes Bushy spreading growth to about 2 ft (60 cm); repeat flowering. Hardy to -10°F (-23°C), Zone 6.

'Pinstripe' (also called MORpints) A Miniature raised by Moore and introduced by Armstrong in 1985. The fully double red flowers have white stripes with a light fragrance. It is a cross of the Floribunda 'Pinocchio' and an unnamed seedling.

Garden notes Low, mounded growth to about 18 in (45 cm). Hardy to -20°F (-29°C), Zone 5.

'Rise 'n' Shine' (also called 'Golden Meillandina', 'Golden Sunblaze') A Miniature introduced by Moore in 1977, winner of many prizes including the ARS Miniature Hall of Fame 1999. Long, pointed buds open to double flowers 1½ in (4 cm) across, rich medium yellow with moderate scent. It is a cross of Floribunda 'Little Darling' and the Miniature 'Yellow Magic'.

Garden notes Makes bushy growth to 30 in (75 cm) in height. Hardy to -20°F (-29°C), Zone 5.

'Golden Angel'

'Green Ice'

'Magic Carousel'

'Dresden Doll'

'Baby Betsy McCall'

'Angela Rippon'

'Anna Ford'

'Hula Girl'

'Angela Rippon' (also called 'Ocarina', OCAru)   A Miniature or Patio rose raised by deRuiter and introduced by Fryer's in 1978. The small salmon-pink flowers have a moderate scent. It is a cross of the Miniature 'Rosy Jewel' and Floribunda 'Zorina'.
   Garden notes   A compact rose to around 2 ft (60 cm). Hardy to -20°F (-29°C), Zone 5.

'Anna Ford' (also called 'Anne Ford', HARpiccolo)
A miniature or Patio rose raised by Harkness in 1980, winner of many awards including three gold medals. The semidouble flowers are deep salmon-orange with a yellow eye, and lightly scented. It is a cross of 'Southampton' (*see p.233*) and the Miniature 'Darling Flame'.
   Garden notes   Grows to about 30 in (75 cm) in height. Hardy to -20°F (-29°C), Zone 5.

'Baby Betsy McCall'   A Miniature raised by Dr Dennison Morey and introduced by Jackson and Perkins in 1960. The double, pale pink flowers are 1 in (2.5 cm) across, and moderately scented. It is a cross of 'Cécile Brünner' (*see p.223*) and the Miniature 'Rosy Jewel'.
   Garden notes   A repeat-flowering, very low-growing rose to 8 in (20 cm). Hardy to -10°F (-23°C), Zone 6, perhaps lower.

'Gentle Touch' (also called DIClulu)   A Miniature or Patio rose raised by Dickson in 1986. The loosely double, light pink flowers have a light scent. The parentage is a hybrid of the

Floribunda 'Liverpool Echo' and the Miniature 'Woman's Own', crossed with the Floribunda 'Memento'.
   Garden notes   A rose with bushy growth to 30 in (75 cm), very free flowering with good repeat flowering. Hardy to -20°F (-29°C), Zone 5.

'Glowing Amber' (also called MANglow)   A Miniature raised by George Mander and introduced by Select Roses in 1996. The double flowers are scarlet red, with a deep yellow eye and reverse, and lightly scented. It is a cross of the Miniatures 'June Laver' and 'Rubies 'n' Pearls'.
   Garden notes   Makes bushy growth to about 18 in (45 cm). Hardy to -20°F (-29°C), Zone 5, or lower.

'Gourmet Popcorn' (also called 'Summer Snow', WEOpop)
A Miniature raised by Luis Desamiro and introduced by Wee Ones Miniature Roses in 1986. The medium-sized, semidouble flowers are pure white with a good rose scent. It is a sport of the Miniature 'Popcorn'.
   Garden notes   Makes upright, bushy, slightly weeping growth to 2 ft (60 cm), and shows great disease resistance. An excellent rose that has been growing in popularity since its introduction. Hardy to -20°F (-29°C), Zone 5.

'Hula Girl'   A Miniature raised by Ernest D. Williams and introduced by Sequoia Nursery in 1975. It has long, elegant buds that open to double, bright orange flowers about 1 in

'Gentle Touch'

'Gourmet Popcorn'

'Jeanne Lajoie'

'Glowing Amber'

'Neon Cowboy'

'What a Peach'

(2.5 cm) in width. The scent is moderate and fruity. It is a cross of the Hybrid Tea 'Miss Hillcrest' and the Miniature 'Mabel Dot'.

Garden notes A bushy, repeat-flowering plant to 2 ft (60 cm). Hardy to -10°F (-23°C), Zone 6.

'Jeanne Lajoie' A Climbing Miniature introduced by Sima Mini-Roses in 1975. This is placed as a Miniature because of the small, mid-pink flowers, about 1 in (2.5 cm) across, which open from pointed buds. The parentage is a hybrid of the Climber 'Casa Blanca' and the Floribunda 'Independence', crossed with the Miniature 'Midget'.

Garden notes A repeat-flowering large shrub or low climber, to as much as 8 ft (2.5 m) when supported. Hardy to -10°F (-23°C), Zone 6.

'Mandarin' (also called KORcelin) A Miniature introduced by Kordes in 1987. The flowers open very flat, with orange petals in the center and pink petals around the edge. The parentage is not available.

Garden notes Well worth growing, this reaches 30 in (75 cm). Hardy to -20°F (-29°C), Zone 5.

'Neon Cowboy' (also called WEKemilcho) A Miniature raised by Tom Carruth and introduced by Weeks Roses in 2003. The single to semidouble flowers are scarlet with a yellow eye. It is a cross of the Miniature 'Emily Louise' and a seedling of the Floribunda 'Playboy' and the Miniature 'Little Artist'.

Garden notes Reaches 12–16 inches (30–40cm); the flowers are good in all climates. Hardy to -10°F (-23°C), Zone 6.

'Space Odyssey' (also called WEKsnacare) A Miniature raised by Tom Carruth and introduced by Weeks Roses in 2001. The semidouble flowers are velvet red with a white eye, and have a mild scent. It is a cross of the Miniature 'Santa Claus' and the Shrub 'Times Square'.

Garden notes A very disease-resistant rose, 12–16 in (30–40cm) tall. Hardy to -10°F (-23°C), Zone 6.

'What a Peach' (also called CHEWpeachdell) A Miniature raised by Warner in 2001. The pure yellowy-peach flowers are double, with moderate, fruity scent. It is a cross of the climbing Miniature 'Laura Ford' and the Miniature 'Sweet Magic'.

Garden notes Bushy and upright, to about 2 ft (60 cm), with red young foliage. Hardy to -10°F (-23°C), Zone 6.

'Space Odyssey'

'Mandarin'

Roses in
the Garden

The Floribunda 'Inner Wheel' is combined with lavender and silver-leaved *Santolina chamaecyparissus* in a mixed but still formal planting at Arley Hall, England.

THE CLASSIC ROSE GARDEN can be both beautiful and valuable; the success of the Rosarium at Sangerhausen in Germany, just celebrating its centenary, is a credit to both skill of cultivation and careful maintenance by generations of gardeners and curators. Numerous roses, lost elsewhere in the world, have survived here through two world wars and fifty years of isolation under communism. Other special rose gardens are to be found near Paris at L'Hay-les-Roses and at Bagatelle, classic collections that were set up at the beginning of the 20th century and have continued to be maintained to a very high standard. In Italy, a lovely garden has been set up by Professor Fineschi at Roseto di Cavriglia in Arezzo, among the olive orchards of the Tuscan hills. Most roses do very well here, and the plantings are grouped botanically and by breeder, an interesting arrangement.

However, we believe that the old practice of planting roses in beds by themselves, or even beds of one variety, has led to their relative decline in popularity. Pests and diseases thrive in these monocultures, necessitating repeated spraying, and the soil accumulates pathogens and becomes 'rose sick', making successful replanting difficult. Roses look better and are happier growing with other flowers, and planted in situations that suit them: the climbers up trees or on walls, the shrub roses associated with herbaceous plants or other shrubs of similar size and cultural needs. One of the most beautiful examples of this is the Graham Thomas collection of heritage roses in the walled garden at Mottisfont Abbey in Hampshire, England; here the roses are planted in a decorative parterre, accompanied by perennials with shapes and colours that provide emphasis and contrast. The walls of this ancient walled kitchen garden are covered with climbers.

However many roses are grown in a garden, there is no excuse to plant them in a boring way. The following pages give examples of mixed plantings that we have seen while studying roses around the world, and show roses growing in different climates and in varied garden styles.

The Gallica hybrid 'Complicata' (*on the left*) and Hybrid Musks in the garden of La Bonne Maison, above Lyon, France. The raised bank behind a wall produces a good depth of fertile soil combined with good drainage, particularly favorable soil conditions for the Musks, while Gallica roses are good for heavier, damper soil, and blue catmint provides useful groundcover.

A concrete waterlily tank set against weeping standard ramblers in the Westfalenpark Dortmund, Germany.

The lovely 'Sally Holmes' growing in the long grass at Wilton Cottage in England.

WILD ROSES ARE FOUND in many situations, but the climbers are usually found in hedges or growing up trees, and the smaller shrubs on open hills, among rocks or rough grass.

Increasingly, many rose lovers are trying to plant roses in a natural setting. It is generally the wild species or their hybrids that do best when subjected to competition from other plants such as grasses or tree roots, and produce a good show without regular manuring. The larger Gallicas, such as 'Complicata', whose natural habitat is rough grassland, will thrive particularly when not budded, but grown on their own roots; they will then sucker through the turf to form large thickets. Albas and Damasks are also probably ideal roses for planting in grass, and in cooler areas forms of *R. moyesii* do well; all these can make billowing shrubs, and may need discreet supports. These large single or informal double roses look good in a natural setting and can be used to link the garden with the surrounding landscape if planted along a fence or as an informal hedge.

The quality and fertility of the natural soil into which the roses are planted will have a large bearing on their success. Most roses will thrive on deep rich clays, but few will do well on poor, acid, sandy soils; the exceptions are the rugosas and the pimpinellifolias and their hybrids. If you have difficulty establishing roses in grassland, begin by killing or removing the old turf where the roses are to go; the grass can be allowed to grow back once the roses are established. It is beneficial to keep some area round the roots clear of grass, because then fertilizer can be applied if the rose needs help. Roger has planted a number of English Roses and other modern roses in

his orchard in England, and many have thrived in the long grass. Any roses that prove too strong-growing for a cultivated, fertile bed will be more restrained when planted out in grass; 'Sally Holmes', shown here, is a good example of a rose strong enough to thrive with some competition; 'Sceptred Isle' has also flowered well.

A position close to water suits roses. In an informal setting, climbing roses are lovely cascading through trees into the edge of a pool or, in a grander setting, a lake. However, the informal approach is not for all gardens nor for all gardeners. Formal plantings have their roots in the Moghul gardens of India and Persia, and can also be seen in the restored gardens of the Alhambra in Spain. Water is also an integral part of these gardens, bringing coolness to any garden; in hot, dry climates water is essential to a garden, and running water brings life and movement and preserves its own purity. No scene is more restful than a line of roses reflected in the still surface of a garden canal or a small pool.

Roses grafted as weeping standards work well in a formal setting; ramblers such as 'Dorothy Perkins' and 'Sander's White Rambler' are particularly suitable for this treatment; 'Felicite et Perpetue' is excellent too and forms neater, less weeping stems. Formal settings and trained rose forms may be regarded by some as appropriate only for older buildings and a historical style, but this is not always the case. In the Westfalenpark Dortmund, standard roses are associated with a modern concrete pool, the upright reeds emphasising the cascading roses, with a background of dark trees; the effect would more striking if the tank was brim full.

ROSES IN THE GARDEN

This sunlit rose garden, enjoyed from a bench in the cool shade of pines around a fountain, is in the Westfalenpark Dortmund, Germany.

The Huntington gardens in Pasadena, near Los Angeles, have particularly large and interesting collection of roses of all types, and it would be hard to beat the abundance of the rose beds here.

Growing on an old brick wall at Sissinghurst Castle in southeast England are the climber 'Galway Bay', its color echoed by the pale orange irises, and a dark red *kordesii* hybrid.

'Alchymist' growing over a tree in Eccleston Square Garden, London.

ROSES IN THE GARDEN

MOST WILD ROSES ARE CLIMBERS, and the ancestors of the main cultivated roses were large-flowered climbers growing in the wilds of western China. Their descendants, the modern Hybrid Teas and Floribundas, have a natural tendency to produce climbing sports or seedlings, and these are the large-flowered Climbers that are commonly grown; small-flowered Climbers and Ramblers are generally once-flowering hybrids with one of the small-flowered climbing species. Large-flowered Climbers generally form more permanent woody shoots, while Ramblers produce new flexible shoots yearly from the base, and can be twined around their support.

Climbers are used in three main ways in gardens: fanned out on walls, trained on pergolas, or tied to poles. All of these need retraining every year, preferably during autumn or winter, or in spring in very cold climates where the long shoots must be protected on the ground to survive frost. In the garden at Sangerhausen, hundreds of different ramblers are grown on larch or pine poles over 12 ft (4 m) high, making a fine sight and giving height to the plantings. Expensive smooth poles are not necessary for this approach; the bark and short stumps of the side branches are left on to help support the rose shoots. A variation on poles is used at the Royal Horticultural Society's garden at Wisley, where lines of cut and squared oak poles are joined by thick, loose ropes onto which the rose shoots are tied.

Trellis is also a popular support for climbers; it can be simple and two dimensional, like a fence, or built up into an arch, tunnel, or even a trellis temple with roses and other climbers tied all over the outside. Sally Allison, a great rosarian and collector of roses in New Zealand, has built a large garden dome on which to train climbing roses, and particularly elaborate examples of treillage work can be seen near Paris at the garden at L'Haÿ-les-Roses. The Barbier hybrids, such as 'Alberic Barbier', are particularly suitable for this type of planting, and 'Alexandre Girault' is grown on white-painted trellis at the Huntington gardens near Los Angeles.

The woody, large-flowered Climbers are more suited to walls, and a good example is shown here, growing in the garden at Sissinghurst castle in England, home of the great

An arched pergola with a red-flowered *kordesii* hybrid frames weeping standards in the Westfalenpark Dortmund, Germany.

garden writer and rose lover, Vita Sackville-West. House walls also have the advantage of protecting tender roses in winter, and the greater warmth ripens the wood even in cool summers.

Small- and large-flowered roses can be planted to flower together, and Roger and I found a good example of this in China, where we saw *Rosa banksiae* (*see p.14*) entwined with a large-flowered, double, pink *Rosa gigantea* (*see p.13*).

Climbers however, are not only suitable for large gardens. They are ideal roses for the small town garden, as they can be used to cover the perimeters, whether walls or fences, and trained through shrubs with a different flowering period to give extra flowers. Where ground space is at a premium, climbers use the vertical dimension of a garden. A fine example is the garden of rose enthusiast Sharon Van Enoo, in Torrence, California, who has made great use of climbers in her garden planting them closely up the walls, over the roof of the garage, and along the roadside fence.

Ramblers on a pergola, the strong lines of the framework contrasting with the drifts of perennials.

Roses are grown over a multitude of supports in Sharon Van Enoo's rose garden in California.

ROSES IN THE GARDEN

THROUGH MOST OF THE LATE 19th and 20th centuries, it was the custom to plant roses in rose beds or special rose gardens, areas where a collection of rose bushes were planted in otherwise empty beds, possibly surrounded with box edging and with height provided by standard roses, or by climbers trained on a pergola. Examples of this type of rose garden can be seen still in many countries, but it is now more usual to plant roses among other flowers in mixed beds, or at least to plant other flowers in rose beds. In the next few pages we give some examples of plants suitable for growing with roses, starting with shrubs and climbers, to relieve the monotony of rose beds, especially when the roses are not flowering.

Combining roses with other shrubs will provide contrast and can extend the flowering season if well planned. The most appropriate genera are those that naturally grow with roses and appreciate the same soils, shrubs such as lilac (*Syringa*), *Philadelphus*, *Deutzia*, *Indigofera*, and many viburnums. Evergreens can be used to give structure and interest in the winter months when the roses are dormant. Good choices here include *Ceanothus* in mild climates, and hollies in colder areas.

Climbing roses can also be planted with other climbers. The best climbers for this are those that do not have too much foliage. *Clematis* are particularly suitable, as they are not likely to smother roses on which they are climbing. Large-flowered clematis and *C. viticella* hybrids are superb with large-flowered roses; the smaller-flowered, early *C. alpina* and *C. sibirica* are excellent with *R. moyesii*, enjoying the same cool, moist climate and flowering just as the rose is coming into leaf. Pale yellow *R. banksiae* 'Lutea' and blue *Wisteria sinensis* are a particularly lovely combination, commonly seen in Mediterranean countries; both flower rather earlier than most roses. Jasmines, such as *Jasminum officinale*, and climbing *Solanum* species are also suitable in warmer climates. The decorative leaves of vines, such as *Vitis tomentosa* and *V. vinifera* 'Brant', set off rose flowers beautifully; the orangey flowers of a climbing 'Lady Hillingdon' are perfectly complemented by *V. vinifera* 'Purpurea'.

In Mary Glasson's garden in New South Wales, Australia, the eucalyptus provide welcome shade, but the roses need ample water and protection from the tree roots to flower well.

Dawn at Rose Acres in Diamond Springs, California; a beautiful group of Hybrid Teas and Floribundas quite at home in the rugged landscape.

The very long-flowering Tea 'Général Schablikine' coincides with *Camellia × williamsii* 'Donation' in Eccleston Square.

A classic combination of the Climber 'Blairii no. 2' with a white Clematis, possibly 'Sylvia Denny', in the garden at la Bonne Maison near Lyon, France.

Roses with silver shrubs in a Californian coastal garden.

The late-flowering Noisette 'Aimee Vibert' growing with *Solanum crispum*.

'Bella Rosa', sometimes called 'Toynbee Hall', a modern German Floribunda with the look of an old rose, underplanted with the annual love-in-a-mist, *Nigella damascena*.

OLD SHRUB ROSES, Hybrid Teas, and David Austin's English Roses are grown for the beauty and scent of their individual flowers, as much as for their beauty as whole plants. In this they contrast with Floribundas, Ramblers, and Groundcover roses, grown mainly for their colour impact in mass plantings. These beautiful and sweetly scented flowers deserve close admiration, and so should be planted in rather narrow beds or near a path where they can be appreciated easily.

In these situations roses look better when combined with herbaceous plants, either between the rose bushes to give contrasting shapes and added interest to the planting, or as groundcover beneath the roses. In either situation, choose herbaceous plants that will thrive on the heavy fertilizing that roses appreciate. Examples of suitable low perennials are violas, *Alchemilla mollis*, various geraniums, catmint (*Nepeta*), peonies, heucheras, and hostas. Plants like pinks, which are lovely with dwarf roses, need extra care if they are not to become too lush.

Tall, upright herbaceous plants with a spiky form will provide valuable contrast in shape with the rounded outlines of rose bushes. Good examples are foxgloves, lupins, delphiniums, upright linarias, white-woolly *Stachys*, grey *Lysimachia ephemerum*, campanulas with spires of flowers, and tall grey *Artemisia*. The white form of the common foxglove, *Digitalis purpurea*, is widely used among the roses at Mottisfont. Japanese anemones, in shades of pink and white, are particularly valuable for late flowering, tolerating heavy soil, sun or deep shade.

Annuals are also very useful in this situation, as they can be changed so easily and will produce lovely effects very quickly; most also thrive in rich soil. Poppies, love-in-a-mist (*Nigella*), larkspur, mignonette (*Reseda*), and the Californian *Nemophila*, are all suitable, and easy to combine in different colour schemes. Tall cosmos and tobaccos are valuable for their late flowering periods.

In this classic white planting of the kind popularised by Vita Sackville-West, the Floribunda 'Iceberg' is growing with Delphiniums, *Lychnis coronaria* 'Alba', the striped grass *Phalaris arundinacea* 'Picta' and, in the foreground, the starry flowers of the white form of *Viola cornuta*.

'Autumn Sunset' a modern Shrub with *Hosta sieboldiana* and *Salvia officinalis*.

The Rugosa hybrid 'Delicata' with *Alchemilla mollis*, a very tough and hardy perennial from eastern Europe and the Caucasus.

The Damask 'La Ville de Bruxelles' in a dense perennial border with *Linaria* 'Canon Went' and silver *Artemisia*.

'Rush', a Shrub raised by Louis Lens in Belgium, with spikes of purple loosetrife, *Lythrum salicaria*, a plant of shallow water and boggy fields that is a noxious weed in parts of North America, but no trouble in its native Britain.

On the thin, chalky soil at Mottisfont Abbey, pinks form a suitable ground cover for the dwarf *Rosa chinensis* 'Sanguinea'.

The lovely modern hybrid 'Bonica' with annual Shirley poppies, selected from the wild red field poppy by the Rev. William Wilkes.

The pretty, old-rose-like double geranium *G. pratense* 'Plenum Violaceum' combines well with the rose 'Queen of the Musks'.

The lovely 'Pierre de Ronsard' planted with *Yucca recurvifolia* and *Campanula lactiflora* at the Westfalenpark Dortmund, Germany.

Exuberance is the key feature of the planting in Monet's garden at Giverny in France, where wide iron rose arches line the paths between beds densely planted with peonies, opium poppies, and other annuals and perennials.

A background of delphiniums and foreground of lavender frame a group of English Roses in the Duchess of Northumberland's new garden at Alnwick Castle in northern England.

Glossary

AARS All-American Rose Selections, a nonprofit association of rose growers and breeders. They select new rose varieties that they consider outstanding after two years of trials.

ADR Anerkannte Deutsche Rose, an award given after three or four year trials by The Association of German Nurserymen. The health of the rose is the most important criterion.

allotetraploid A hybrid plant with twice the normal number of *chromosomes*, half from each parent species, as a result of *chromosome doubling* after hybridization. Allotetraploids usually behave as new fertile species.

apomixis A process by which some plants can produce viable seeds without fertilization. It is found particularly in dog roses, but also in many other plants.

ARS American Rose Society, a nonprofit organization that runs workshops, seminars, and rose shows, and publishes standards and guidelines for competitions.

attar of roses A scent distilled from rose petals.

balling Flowers failing to open and rotting in wet weather.

bipinnate A *pinnate* leaf in which the leaflets are themselves pinnately divided.

chromosome Part of the nucleus of every living cell, containing the DNA. The number of chromosomes differs according to the organism.

chromosome doubling This can happen as a result of a fault occuring in normal cell division as a plant grows, yielding a branch or even an entire plant with double the *chromosome number* of its parent. It is very rare in nature, but it can be induced artificially by treating the cells with chemicals such as colchicine.

chromosome number The normal number of *chromosomes* in a particular species.

clone A plant genetically identical to its parent, usually grown from a bud or cutting of the parent. See also *apomixis*.

connective (n) The part of the stamen that connects the pollen-bearing anther to the filament that carries it.

code names These are used to register for "plant breeders rights", like a copyright on a plant. The first three letters (properly written in capitals) indicate the nursery, thus MEI for Meilland, AUS for Austin, WEK for Weeks. They are often awkward "nonsense" words, but remain the same worldwide and give certainty where two roses share the same catchy selling name, which may also vary from country to country.

cyme A roughly flat-topped cluster of flowers, the central flower opening first.

diploid Having the basic number of *chromosomes*, a multiple of two (see *tetraploid*).

DNA Deoxyribonucleic acid, a molecule that carries the genes that determines an organism's characteristics. When cells divide or fuse, the DNA groups itself into sausage-like *chromosomes*, which can be seen through a microscope.

egg-shaped An oval with the end towards the stem broader than the apex, a shape also called ovate.

elliptic A symmetrical shape longer than it is broad, widest at the middle. See also *lance-shaped*.

glands Strictly any cell secreting a substance, such as the scent glands in rose petals. On roses, visible glands exuding a scented, resinous substance are sometimes found on the leaves and stems; these are the "moss" on Moss roses.

grafting Joining together two separate plants so that they grow as one, generally joining a cutting from one plant (the scion) onto the roots of another (the rootstock). The type of grafting used in roses is "budding". It is used to reproduce sterile roses, to control the size of the plant by using a more or less vigorous rootstock, to control roses whose own roots have a tendency to produce suckers, and commercially to raise large numbers of roses for sale.

hybrid A plant produced from a cross of two genetically dissimilar parents. The more distantly related the parents are, the more likely it is that their offspring will be sterile.

imbricated Overlapping, with each ring of petals slightly smaller than the one outside it; the effect is like roof tiles.

inversely egg-shaped An oval with the apex broader than the base or stem end, also called obovate.

lance-shaped or lanceolate A shape longer than it is broad, with the widest point below the middle and tapering to a point. See also *elliptic*.

microspecies Populations derived from *apomixis* that are barely distinguishable from one another but rarely interbreed.

mutation A change in *DNA* resulting in new characteristics.

nursery codes See *code name*.

pinnate A leaf made up of leaflets of two rows along a central axis. Nearly all rose leaves are pinnate.

pinnatifid A leaf indented, but not divided, in a *pinnate* form.

RNRS The Royal National Rose Society in England runs lectures and shows, carries out research, and arranges trials roses over two or three years before issuing awards. It has run the Gardens of the Rose in St Albans for many years.

scion See *grafting*.

section A group of species within a genus, sharing enough characteristics to be differentiated from other sections, but not distinct enough to be a separate *subgenus* or genus. There are several sections in the genus *Rosa*.

sepals The green modified leaves that enclose a flower bud.

stipules Pointed or leafy appendages at the base of a leaf stalk.

styles A filament that receives pollen and takes it to the ovary.

subgenus A group of species within a genus, sharing enough characteristics to be differentiated from other subgenera, but not distinct enough to be a separate genus. Differences are greater than those which differentiate *sections*.

tetraploid Having four sets of *chromosomes*, rather than the normal *diploid* arrangement of two sets. This can occur as a result of *chromsome doubling*. See also *allotetraploid*, *triploid*.

triploid Having three sets of *chromosomes*, rather than the normal *diploid* arrangement of two sets. This usually results in a plant that is sterile or has reduced fertility, but may be more vigorous. See also *tetraploid*.

Zone A hardiness indication devised by the United States Department of Agriculture. See *Rose websites* opposite.

Rose care

Planting Bare-rooted roses should be planted while dormant in winter. Order from a nursery in summer, and they will be sent out at a suitable time according to local conditions. When they arrive, open at once and store in a cold place; plant as soon as possible, shortening the roots to around 12 in (30 cm) with a clean cut, and making sure that the soil is good and well-drained. If it is at all poor or heavy, add compost or sand to encourage good root growth. A container-grown rose in flower can be kept in its pot until winter or planted at once without disturbing the roots; keep it well watered and fertilized. If the roots are coiled round the pot, it may be better to lift the rose in winter and replant it, straightening and shortening any coiled roots. However, I have seen large, healthy roses with a small pot still attached to the bottom, the roots having split the pot.

Pruning There is much unnecessary fuss about rose pruning; put simply, hard pruning produces fewer, larger flowers. Repeat-flowering roses flower well if they are pruned hard in spring and dead flowers are cut off with the top two leaves. Once-flowering roses can be pruned after flowering, in autumn or spring, removing the stems that have flowered, thereby encouraging the new growth to flower next year.

Mildew on leaves

Mosaic virus

Blackspot on 'Zéphirine Drouhin'

Caterpillar damage

Diseases Most rose diseases weaken rather than kill the plant. Spraying may control some; it is best to visit a local garden store and find what is recommended against any local pest or disease. The healthier and better fed a rose is, the less likely it is to be harmed by disease, so keep plants watered, fed, and mulched. There are three common leaf diseases. Blackspot attacks mainly old leaves, and particularly yellow roses with *R. foetida* in their ancestry. It is worst in wet climates, where some roses may not be worth growing. Remove affected leaves, and do not compost them. Mildew is unsightly but not too damaging, and most common in cool, humid air combined with dry soil, so improve watering and ventilation. Rust usually attacks late in the season, but does not reappear in spring. Viral diseases are rare on new roses.

Pests Common pests such as aphids and small caterpillars can be combatted by spraying with soap or other pesticides that are recommended or allowed locally. Beetles, such as Japanese beetles in North America or nectar scarab beetles in Australia, can attack flowers and strip leaves: pick the adults off as soon as they appear, or obtain pheromone traps; most chemical controls are deadly to other insects.

Bibliography

Reference books on roses

Climbing Roses of the World by Charles Quest-Ritson (Timber Press 2003).
Roses by Jack Harkness (J.M. Dent & Son 1978).
Roses by Wilhelm Kordes, translated and edited by N.P. Harvey (Studio Vista 1964).
Botanica's Roses, The Encyclopedia of Roses (Grange Books 1998).
Roses of Great Britain and Ireland by G.G. Graham and A.L. Primavesi (BSBI handbook no. 7 1993).
The Quest for the Rose by Roger Phillips and Martyn Rix (BBC Books 1993).
Traditional Old Roses and how to grow them by Roger Phillips and Martyn Rix (Pan Books 1998).

The Heritage of the Rose by David Austin (Antique Collector's Club 1990).
The Old Rose Advisor by Brent C. Dickerson (Timber Press 1992).
The Old Rose Adventurer by Brent C. Dickerson (Timber Press 1999).
Modern Roses 11 (American Rose Society 2000).
Combined Rose List compiled and edited by Beverly R. Dobson and Peter Schneider (Peter Schneider, updated annually).
The Graham Stuart Thomas Rose Book by G.S. Thomas (Timber Press 1994).
100 English Roses for the American Garden by Clair G. Martin (Workman Publishing 1999).

General reference books

The European Garden Flora I–VI (Cambridge University Press 1986–2001), scientific account of cultivated plants.
The RHS Plant Finder (Dorling Kindersley, updated annually), a good source of modern plant names and a list of nurseries in Great Britain and Ireland.
Manual of Cultivated Broad-leaved Trees and Shrubs by Gerd Krüssmann (Batsford 1986).

Floras of regions where roses are found

Flora Europaea by V.H. Heywood et al. (Cambridge University Press 1964–80).
Flora of Turkey by P.H. Davis et al. (Edinburgh University Press 1965–87).
Flowers of the Himalaya by Oleg Polunin and Adam Stainton (Oxford University Press 1984) and *Supplement*, by Adam Stainton (Oxford University Press, Delhi 1988).
Flora of Bhutan by A.J.C. Grierson and D.G. Long (Royal Botanic Garden, Edinburgh 1983–94).
Plantae Wilsonianae by J.S. Sargent 1913 (reprinted by Dioscorides Press 1988).
Travels in China by Roy Lancaster (Antique Collectors Club 1989).
Flora of China online at http://flora.huh.harvard.edu
Flora of Japan by J. Ohwi (Smithsonian Institution 1965).
Flora of North America north of Mexico ed. Flora of North America editorial committee vols. 1–3 (Oxford University Press 1993 and continuing).

Rose websites

www.everyrose.com A large database aimed at giving information on availability of cultivars.
www.helpmefind.com An alternative database for locating roses in cultivation.
www.rogersroses.com Worldwide website concentrating on high quality photographic images and text. Over 6000 images.
www.usna.usda.gov/Hardzone/ Gives details of the USDA Plant Hardiness Zone system, including a map.

Rust on *Rosa × alba*

Nectar scarab beetle in Australia

Index

The entries in bold are for the the correct names of the roses, under which their profiles appear. The entries in lighter text are alternative, old, or incorrect names, which are also listed in the profiles.

Acknowledgments

Most of the specimens came from the following gardens, and we would like to acknowledge the generous help we had from them and their staff:

In England: Alnwick Castle Rose Garden; The David Austin Rose Garden; The Garden of the Rose; Hidcote Manor; Kiftsgate Court; Longleat House; Mattocks Roses; Mottisfont Abbey; Queen Mary's Garden, Regent's Park; The Royal Botanic Gardens, Kew; The Royal Horticultural Society Garden Wisley; The Sir Harold Hillier Gardens; Sissinghurst Castle; Symnel Cottage garden, Kent; West Dean Gardens

In mainland Europe: Jardin Botanique Exotique Val Rahmeh, France; Kasteel Hex, Belgium; W. Kordes' Söhne, Germany; La Bonne Maison, France; Meilland Roses, France; Monet's garden at Giverny, France; Parc de Bagatelle, Paris; Parc de la Tête d'Or, Lyon, France; Rosarium Sangerhausen, Germany; Roseraie de l'Haÿ-les-Roses, Paris; Roseto di Cavriglia, Italy; Westfalenpark Dortmund, Germany

In North America: Descanso Gardens, California; The Huntington Botanical Gardens, California; Kleine Lettunich's garden in Corralitos, California; Rose Acres, California; The Royal Botanical Gardens, Burlington, Ontario; The San Jose Heritage Rose Garden, California; The University of California Botanical Garden

In Australia and New Zealand: Gowan Brae, New South Wales, Australia; The Auckland Regional Botanic Gardens, New Zealand

We would also like to thank the following individuals, gardens, and organizations for their help, encouragement, or for providing roses: Sally Allison; Arley Hall; David Austin; Peter Beales; Fred Boutin; Helga Brichet and The World Federation of Rose Societies; Tom Carruth at Weeks Roses; John and Louise Clements at Heirloom Roses; Alex Cocker; Ghislain and Stephanie d'Ursel at Kasteel Hex in Belgium; Gianfranco Fineschi; Ethel Freeman; Mary Glasson; Anne Graber; Jean-Pierre and Jean-Marc Guillot; Phillip and Robert Harkness; Kevin Hughes; François Joyaux; Ruth Knopf; W. Kordes' Söhne; Kleine Lettunich; Gregg Lowery at Vintage Roses; Clair Martin; Michael Marriot at David Austin Roses; Kathryn Maule Eccleston Square Garden; Odile Masquelier; Alain Meilland and Jacques Mouchotte at Meilland Roses; Laura Mercer; Kathie Mills; Laurie Newman; Trevor Nottle; Sam Phillips at Glide Technologies; Helene Pizzi; Richard Rix; Mike Shoup at The Antique Rose Emporium; Sharon van Enoo; David Vanrip; Rudy and Ann Velle at Lens Roses; Lilia Weatherly; Miriam Wilkins of the Heritage Rose Group; Paul F. Zimmerman

Photo credits

We would like to thank the following for allowing us to use their photographs: **David Austin Roses** 'Mistress Quickly' *p.250*, 'Falstaff' and 'Noble Antony' *p.256* **Louise Clements** 'Stars 'n' Stripes Forever' *p.196* **Roseraie Guillot** 'Jardin de Viels Maisons' 'Marquise Spinola' 'Sonia Rykiel' and 'William Christie' *p.260*, 'Versigny' *p.261* **Bill Grant** 'Alba Foliacea' *p.52*, 'Royal Blush', 'Summer Blush', and 'Tender Blush' *p.56*, 'Lord Scarman' *p.37*, 'Mousseaux du Japon' *p.70*, 'Crimson Globe' *p.75*, 'Souvenir de Thérèse Levet' *p.101*, *Rosa multiflora* 'Platyphylla' *p.159*, 'Nur Mahal' and 'Nymphenburg' *p.174*, 'Lyda Rose' *p.173*, 'Rosy Purple' *p.178*, 'David Thompson' *p.186*, 'Starry Night' *p.190*, 'Kaleidoscope' *p.194*, 'Pascali' *p.201*, 'Jean Giono' *p.206*, 'Julia's Rose' *p.209*, 'Blue Skies' *p.211*, 'Tropicana' *p.214*, 'Candelabra' *p.215*, 'Artistry' *p.216*, 'Claude Monet' *p.220*, 'Cajun Sunrise' and 'Love and Peace' *p.221*, 'La Marne' *p.225*, 'Lafayette' *p.240*, 'Michelangelo' *p.259* **Heirloom Roses** 'Snow Ruby' *p.263* **Richard Rix** 'Lemon Blush' and 'Princesse Lamballe' *p.56* **Meilland Roses** 'Eric Tabarly' *p.140*, 'Philippe Noiret' *p.205*, 'Elle' *p.206*, 'Botero' *p.216*, 'Jubilé du Prince de Monaco' *p.221*, 'André Le Nôtre' *p.259* **Ralph Moore** 'Halo Rainbow' *p.263*, 'Pinstripe' *p.264* **Lilia Weatherly** 'Pink Iceberg', *p.235*, 'Brilliant Pink Iceberg' *p.237* **Weeks Roses** 'Marilyn Monroe' *p.202*, 'Neon Cowboy' 'Space Odyssey', and 'What a Peach' *p.267*.

See more roses at: www.rogersroses.com
See more Firefly titles at: www.fireflybooks.com